CRITICAL REFLECTIONS ON TRANSNATIONAL ORGANIZED CRIME, MONEY LAUNDERING, AND CORRUPTION

Edited by Margaret E. Beare

Transnational crime, organized crime, money laundering, and corruption are topics that have gained considerable attention in recent years. But is the information given to the public concerning these activities realistic or is it distorted by the vested interests of some politicians, media, police, and international organizations whose existence or enhanced resources depend on the perception that there is an ever-growing threat? In responding to organized crime and corruption, countries are expected to comply with various international agreements, conventions, and accords. But at what cost are these enforcement measures applied, and do they in fact effectively address specific criminal activities?

In this volume, internationally renowned contributors challenge commonly held views on transnational crime. The collection offers a wide range of critical perspectives, including a historical analysis of current accepted interpretations of organized crime, a discussion of the failure of the war on money laundering, an evaluation of white-collar and corporate crimes, and an examination of the impact of foreign policy on the war on drugs. Theoretical essays are balanced with empirical studies that look at organized crime in terms of structure, commitment to specific crime, and accumulated wealth. At present, transnational crime, organized crime, money laundering, and corruption are often no longer seen as separate entities but as a 'package' believed to be connected to and supported by terrorism. Provocative and insightful, the volume argues that enforcement and policy efforts must be directed towards appropriate targets, and perceived threats must be more closely evaluated to prevent an escalating rhetoric of fear and wasted resources.

MARGARET E. BEARE is an associate professor of sociology and law at York University, and is the director of the Nathanson Centre for the Study of Organized Crime and Corruption.

EDITED BY MARGARET E. BEARE

Critical Reflections on Transnational Organized Crime, Money Laundering, and Corruption

UNIVERSITY OF TORONTO PRESS
Toronto Buffalo London

© University of Toronto Press Incorporated 2003
Toronto Buffalo London
Printed in Canada

ISBN 0-8020-4375-5 (cloth)
ISBN 0-8020-8190-8 (paper)

Printed on acid-free paper

National Library of Canada Cataloguing in Publication Data

Beare, Margaret E.
  Critical reflections on transnational organized crime, money
  laundering, and corruption / edited by Margaret E. Beare.

  ISBN 0-8020-4375-5 (bound)   ISBN 0-8020-8190-8 (pbk.)

  1. Organized crime.   2. Transnational crime.   3. Money
  laundering.   4. Criminal justice, Administration of – International
  cooperation.   I. Title.

  HV6252.C75 2003   364.1′06   C2002-904575-4

This book has been published with the help of a grant from the Humanities
and Social Sciences Federation of Canada, using funds provided by the
Social Sciences and Humanities Research Council of Canada.

University of Toronto Press acknowledges the financial assistance to
its publishing program of the Canada Council for the Arts and the
Ontario Arts Council.

University of Toronto Press acknowledges the financial support for its
publishing activities of the Government of Canada through the Book
Publishing Industry Development Program (BPIDP).

We dedicate this book to the memory of Rosa del Olmo,
a leading Latin American criminologist and a friend.

Contents

Acknowledgments

I would first like to thank the contributors to this book for their timely submissions and good-natured responses to my queries. While swearing never to edit another collection, I am grateful to these authors for making the task as pleasant as possible. I wish to acknowledge all of the critical thinkers and writers who over the years have helped us to question, and in some cases reject, taken-for-granted 'truths' and the policy decisions that flow from them. The contributors to this volume are certainly dominant among that group, but of course there are many others and I shall not attempt to identify them. William Chambliss is only one such scholar, but an extremely significant one, who continues to encourage us to challenge the motives and the activities of the state, corporations, politicians, and police.

The Nathanson Centre for the Study of Organized Crime and Corruption, Osgoode Hall Law School, York University, provided the research environment that assisted with this publication. The SSHRC provided funds through a strategic grant to study money laundering that gave support to graduate students. Some of their research found its way into this manuscript. I wish to thank the editors of *Crime, Law and Social Change* for allowing us to include two updated versions of papers that appeared previously in their journal.

Four specific individuals were critically important to getting the manuscript transformed into a publishable text: Virgil Duff, executive editor at University of Toronto Press, who supported the project; Margaret Allen, who served as the copy-editor; Mary Newberry, who completed the index and did a final check for errors and omissions; and Peter Kiatipis, who was always thorough, always reliable, and always patient in assisting me with the minutiae of publication.

Introduction

Margaret E. Beare

Transnational crime, organized crime, money laundering, and corruption are four concepts with an international and domestic profile of growing magnitude. In the case of all four of these concepts, countries are under pressure to respond in a uniform manner in accordance with numerous international agreements, conventions, and guidelines. In none of these cases does the issue involve a fretting over 'definitions'; rather, more fundamentally, it involves a debate over the nature of the entities that are subsumed under the concepts. Likewise, this book is not about denying the significance of transnational crimes or organized criminal activity. Neither do we underestimate the size or the impact of illicit proceeds upon specific markets, or the worldwide legitimate concern with diverse forms of corruption. The articles in this book do, however, challenge some of our current narrow preoccupations with these concepts and attempt to examine the rhetoric in the light of empirical realities.

Perhaps most plainly, we ask the reader to judge 'at what cost' the various enforcement strategies are being applied. The contributors to this book argue that what is required is a critical look at the concepts and an appreciation of the consequences – direct or indirect, intended or unanticipated, domestic or international – of current and future law enforcement strategies. One essential aspect of understanding the entwined issues must be an appreciation of the 'politics' of transnational organized crime and corruption and all of the issues that touch upon these forms of activity.

Specific to *organized transnational crime*, countries are bringing into force legislation that authorizes extra police investigative powers and longer sentences. In the case of *money laundering*, seizing the proceeds of crime, both criminally and civilly, has become a main enforcement strategy. Countries with forfeiture powers want more legislation to facilitate seizure of the proceeds of crime. Countries without these powers look covetously upon the much-publicized seized 'wealth' of their neighbours. Likewise, countries without sufficiently robust seizure powers can be deemed to be in violation of various international agreements and task forces[1] and to risk various negative sanctions for being out of step with the thinking of the current international community. And finally, under the rhetoric of *corruption,* a Western financial machinery appears to be uniting around one dimension of the term – the dimension that is seen to hamper foreign global investment and commerce. This apparently 'narrow' concern with corruption runs alongside evidence of massive governmental and corporate complicity in large-scale financial frauds and schemes.

The fiscal restraint of the 1980s and 1990s that encouraged makeshift partnerships across enforcement agencies ended abruptly one morning in September 2001. What did not end, and in fact increased, was the direction and momentum of pressures towards the 'harmonization' of policies. Talk of a near-global 'alliance' and variously vigorous commitments to uniformity in policies, legislation, and actions followed. Post 11 September 2001, money laundering is seen to be closely linked to terrorism. Likewise, organized crime and drug trafficking are linked to terrorism. Also since 11 September, terrorism has become another major 'umbrella' concept that now subsumes a wide array of real threats, ordinary crimes, and societal annoyances.

What we are experiencing is a hijacking of criminal justice, as well as of wider governmental and financial institutions, to meet political and strategic ends. Aid, foreign trade, immigration, the operation of financial institutions, criminal laws and policies, policing agreements and policies, privacy and civil rights, traditional notions of due process, and sovereignty rights – all have been affected and significantly altered by the responses from governments to the attacks on the United States. There may be nothing new about imperialism and the self-interest of powerful states; but what is new is the 'alliance' that has been demanded around this anti-terrorism response.

I have made the argument elsewhere that the international community has actually been more interested in tax evasion and capital flight than in the laundering of criminal proceeds (see Beare, 2002). The powerful rhetoric around drug trafficking, and 'organized crime' more generally, has helped to 'sell' a concern over the movement of these proceeds. That was 'then.' Drug trafficking, presented as a societal threat, pales in comparison to 'terrorism,' introduced into the formula with the vision of horror captured by coverage of the destruction of the World Trade Center towers. Terrorism has ratcheted up the rhetoric *and the compliance* tenfold!

One of the immediate casualties after the attacks was open debate on the issues. All critics were silenced or severely sanctioned. In early October, the White House informed the U.S. television networks that they should think long and hard before beaming another pre-recording from Osama bin Laden (MacDonald, 2001: A9). Television networks ABC, CBS, CNN, Fox, and NBC issued statements promising not to air al-Qaeda statements live without a review. Critics in the media and outside it saw this as coming close to 'a war on press freedom.' Later it was reported that there was a meeting between the heads of all of the major studios in Hollywood and Karl Rove, the top political adviser to U.S. President Bush. Rove outlined twenty ideas for how Hollywood could help the war by communicating 'internationally our solid American values' (Walker, 2001: B1). On 20 February 2002, newspapers reported on the Pentagon's plans to use their Office of Strategic Influence (established after 11 September) to plant deliberately false news stories with foreign media.[2]

A study of the media coverage of the 11 September attacks was carried out by the Project for Excellence in Journalism. The researchers analysed stories from four newspapers, *Time*, *Newsweek*, and a variety of television programs, categorizing the stories according to whether they were 'fact,' analysis that could be attributed to a source, or unattributed opinion or speculation. They found that immediately following the attack, the media took care to stick to 'factual' reporting. However, as time went on, the amount of factual reporting dropped to 63 per cent. Printed stories were found to be more often fact-based than television coverage. The explanation for the decline in factual reporting included the restrictions imposed on journalists by government, cutbacks to newsrooms, and the pressures of twenty-four-hour journalism. They also found that half of all relevant stories contained only viewpoints in agreement with American or Bush Administration policy and, again, television news was less likely to include criticism of the administration.[3]

Perhaps the developments since the 11 September attacks serve better than other examples to highlight the various agendas that can be advanced by using the fear generated by specific forms of criminal

conduct. In the aftermath, many groups are benefiting from the terrorist attacks. Few spoke in a more forthnight manner about this 'opportunity' than the European Commission. According to media accounts,
Romano Prodi, the commission's president, told all of his commission-
ers to 'step on the policy accelerator,' declaring that: 'the current crisis
favours integration by highlighting the need for more intense action'
('Belgium: A Beneficial Crisis,' 2001). EU officials spoke of the 'beneficial crisis.' In the United Kingdom, Peter Hain (described as Blair's
'cheerleader' on the Euro) exclaimed that the European Union was
being taken much more seriously now by the United States and that
therefore 'the horror of the terrorist attacks may turn out to be both an
imperative and an opportunity for Europe.' For example, the EU arrest
warrant, which gained Italian consent only on 11 December, is seen as a
giant leap towards judicial union. In addition, Europol has gained an
intelligence-gathering function and Britain has agreed to the establishment of 'Eurojust,' under which national prosecutors are to coordinate
their investigations.

Seizing an 'opportunity' is perhaps wise. 'Opportunism' is merely
cynical. Requests for the much-desired helicopter for the Metropolitan
Toronto Police was just one indication of the range of requests that
would follow from the 'windows of opportunity' created by the planes
through the World Trade Center towers.

Compliance with 'money-laundering' laws has moved forward with
incredible speed – but with what consequences we do not know. A
search in the media reveals a flurry of activity regarding a commitment
to enhanced concern over money laundering to help in the 'terrorism
war.' If the Financial Action Task Force (FATF) was at all concerned
about obtaining a renewed lease on its mandate, it now has it. On
31 October 2001, the FATF issued new international standards to combat terrorist financing. Basically, these recommendations reiterate the
previous U.N. instruments, but also include a mention of 'alternative
remittance systems' and a focus on non-government organizations that
might be used to finance terrorist groups.

In a press release, the FATF confirmed that it would 'intensify' its
cooperation with groups such as the Egmont Group of Financial Intelligence Units. This cooperation must feel very natural given the close
clutch of key men who are involved in the various management positions: Ronald Noble, secretary general of Interpol, had been head of
FATF and had previously worked with Stan Morris when the two of
them were at Financial Crimes Enforcement Network (FinCEN). Morris

is now Noble's director of cabinet at Interpol and was a co-founder of the Egmont Group. As Noble states, 'we want to build bridges to the Egmont group. With the Egmont group's 56 nations and Interpol's 179 member States working on operational matters, we can provide the FATF with valuable and current data on the financing of terrorist activity within our member States.'[4] More so than in the recent past, organized crime, money laundering, and corruption have ceased to be seen as separate entities. Popular rhetoric treats them as part of a major threat 'package' that is now more often than not perceived to be motivated by terrorist objectives – and advanced by a widening array of groups that are now defined as terrorists.

Organized Crime/Transnational Crime Control as 'Industry'

Comparisons have long been made between the operation of business and the operation of organized crime. That is as true today as in the past – but possibly not more so. What is 'new' is the growth of industries involved in combating organized crime, and therefore in a sense 'feeding off' organized crime. Of greater significance, these groups and individuals become dependent on the priority that societies continue to give to the control of this form of criminal activity. This reminds us of the research that spoke of the predatory, parasitic, and symbiotic links between different forms of organized crime and the larger 'legitimate' society. Looked at from the perspective of the organized criminals, one might use the same typology to describe the relationship between those who build their careers around writing about, studying, policing, or legislatively controlling organized crime and the criminal activity.

There is the array of innumerable 'experts,' representing a range of countries, who work internationally to draft highly compromised agreements, conventions, treaties, or guidelines. These processes are prolonged and, in the case of groups such as the FATF, can provide full-time employment for regional representatives for years. Any municipal, state, provincial, or federal police department of any size will have specialized enforcement units – joint-force or other forms of integrated units that target organized crime and on occasion seize and confiscate the illicit proceeds. Political careers get built on get-tough platforms and 'wars' on organized crime activities.

Government departments whose research departments have been gutted turn to contract employees to spend their annual organized crime budgets. Academics who specialize in organized crime research and who wish to enjoy repeat contracts must attempt to meet the needs of government and the police while maintaining professional honesty. In addition to writing, 'experts' (academics or professionals) are tempted with invitations to travel the circuit speaking on one organized crime issue after another, to various types of audience. Given the nature of the subject matter, the talks can be 'made to fit' different audiences with little requirement to document or defend sweeping statements of the pending 'threats.' Likewise, organized crime specialists are increasingly in demand to serve (and be paid) as 'expert' witnesses in court.

What is often missing is empirical information. Police keep their organized crime 'intelligence' guarded from public debate, with the justification that this secrecy is necessary in order to advance their investigations. Governments hold *in camera* fact-finding meetings on organized crime and disclose neither the content of discussions nor the names of witnesses, with the justification that this secrecy is necessary in order to protect participants from retaliation by the criminals. The result is that the information that is generally shared among policy makers is seldom exposed to wider debate.

In an extremely revealing Canadian 'biker' court case, Judge Fradsham in the Alberta Provincial Court (18 August 2000)[5] stated that

> The opinions of the police experts are often founded, in whole or in part, on information they receive at events such as the National Outlaw Motorcycle Gang Seminar. One has to worry about the quality of the material provided to them. It can become a vicious circle: if inaccurate information is spread at a conference held by the police for the police, that information is then repeated by the audience members when they speak to other police officers. The inaccurate information tends to take on a life of its own. It become [sic] the stuff of legends: it supports a particular view, but may not be at all reliable. (paragraph 212)

A note following this section emphasizes that 'unreliable conclusions reached, do not become more reliable because they are repeated over and over again' (ibid., n238). This profound declaration can be applied to much organized crime discourse.

A number of different factors culminate in a frenzy of anti-organized crime rhetoric and, in some cases, action. The public police now have competition from the private policing sector in an array of policing functions – for example, in the area of sophisticated international financial frauds. The public police must illustrate their 'worth' through ongoing strategies to achieve high-profile organized crime drug busts. After almost ten years of frozen budgets, police in some countries are once again able to secure resources. Recently we are seeing an even greater commodification of the concept of organized crime – by governments and by the police – delivered to the public largely by the media. The fight against organized crime is seen politically as a worthy activity to fund. Hence, each budget process sees the build-up of threat rhetoric and resource demands.

In Canada, an RCMP officer was fired for 'leaking' to an investigative journalist a confidential document outlining the 'National Strategy to Combat Outlaw Motorcycle Gangs.'[6] The discussions, by senior police from the major police departments across Canada, consisted largely of a campaign to publicize police actions and continually reinforce the idea of the danger of the outlaw motorcycle gangs (OMGs). The objective was to secure support in the form of resources to sustain the OMG initiatives. The fired officer felt that too much emphasis was being placed on the 'propaganda strategy' and too little on an adequate 'enforcement strategy.'

We either welcome or are concerned about what might be seen as a gradual 'Americanization' of international policing practices and powers (Beare and Martens, 1998) – including giving increased priority to seizing the proceeds of crime and uncovering money laundering activities. The proceeds of crime are up for grabs as police begin to mimic the policing policies and enforcement strategies of the United States. Some of these policies, we would argue, make the police increasingly amenable to forms of corruption and less amenable to supervision or traditional accountability mechanisms. Deep undercover and reverse-sting operations, increasing numbers of cross-jurisdictional (both domestic and international) operations, widening immunity for violations by police of certain 'approved' categories of laws, combined with the increasing militancy of police unions, may be seen to be creating a policing environment in which it is becoming harder to hold police accountable.

An additional change is the blurring of policing and military functions and the increasing overlap between national security intelligence and criminal intelligence. This may mean a threat to traditional accountability mechanisms that rely to some extent on a degree of transparency in police conduct and on an environment where citizen complaints are treated as legitimate. Police find themselves in peacekeeping operations that are in fact military exercises. The military are brought in to police what are actually domestic forms of civil disobedience. Even street policing can become militaristic. As an extreme example, Joseph McNamara[7] argues that the police in the United States feel that they are under such pressure to make drug arrests that a militaristic form of policing develops where the holy anti-drug war means literally that – a war where there are no rules. The Bill of Rights means nothing because the goal is to kill the enemy. Illegal searches, perjured testimony, and violence become the norm in order to 'defeat' the enemy (Saunders, 2000).

In matters of crime control one can speak about being influenced by foreign jurisdictions. However, with regard to anti-terrorism enforcement, there is even stronger pressure to conform to a uniform, near-global response. Under an anti-terrorism slogan, amid a rhetoric of 'evil,' large populations are deemed dangerous and are seen to pose threats grave enough to override civil, due process, and Charter protections. Lack of specified charges, enhanced police investigatory powers, and altered (or undermined) lawyer/client privileges open the door to discrimination and excess. The police assure us that these broad anti-terrorism powers will be very selectively used. 'Trust' may be our only recourse, given our limited ability to oversee policing effectively.

I recite this list only as a cautionary exercise. There may be nothing wrong with any separate activity that is mentioned. Together, however, the various elements are evidence of an increasingly large population of professionals and organizational infrastructures whose livelihood, status, and reputation depend on the public's perception of a growing threat of transnational crime and corruption. There is also, however, a risk, for those who market anti-organized crime activity, that open debate about and greater scrutiny of current enforcement responses will show that the 'real threats' are of a different nature than current expertise *or current political will* can address.

The Structure of This Book

A number of common themes run through the eleven chapters in this volume: the exploitable nature of the concepts that we are discussing; the non-empirical basis for many of the media, police, and political responses; and the unintended consequences that can result from well-intentioned enforcement initiatives. Of additional interest are the industries that have grown up to 'combat' organized crime and corruption – and whose livelihood therefore depends on our assigning a high priority to combating these forms of criminality.

Development of the Concepts

These concepts share the advantage of being easily exploited. Each can imply whatever the speaker wants: a massive threat; a theatrical legacy; or petty criminals and hoodlum bikers. The police, politicians, public, and media tend to use the terms as an undifferentiated blanket under which most 'serious' crimes can be shoved – *as long as the criminals are of a certain type.*

As overly broad as the organized crime category is, socially powerful, white-collar professionals are still excluded. Given the wide definitions of organized crime, there is nothing in the allegations that surround the Enron bankruptcy case (December 2001) that should exclude it from being discussed as an 'organized crime' case. It follows, therefore, that the key figures and the facilitating accountancy firm, *if guilty* of the allegations, should be classified as 'organized criminals.' Typical characteristics of organized crime – such as the number of conspirators, the duration of the operation, the seriousness of the economic ruin that followed, and the corruption or influence that may have facilitated the operation – were all present. However, that is not the rhetoric that is being used as the responsible officials are 'invited' to participate in the various investigatory processes. The social impact of the Enron collapse and the long list of firms 'in trouble,' including WorldCom, Global Crossing, Tyco, etcetera, is arguably greater than that of most organized crime operations, and the personal gain reaped by those engaged in the fraudulent conduct far exceeds the wealth of even 'king-pin' organized criminals.[8] Analysis of these cases will provide criminologists in the future with a vivid description of justice and the law at work. If criminal charges are not brought, it will be in part because the law does not cover this sort of 'business' behaviour – regardless of the harm done.[9]

In chapter 1 of this book, Michael Woodiwiss provides a historical map of the U.S. roots of our current understanding, documenting the bias of what has come to be labelled 'organized crime.' Woodiwiss questions the 'newness' of the concepts and not only illustrates the antiquity of concern over organized crime but also traces ways in which our current focus distorts the original understanding of the concept. He acknowledges the overwhelming impact that the U.S. definitions have had – and continue to have – within the present international community.

Chapter 2, by Tom Naylor, at a more micro-level, asks the reader to re-examine the claims that are typically made about profit-driven crimes and to question just how clear (or blurred) the line is between profit-driven crime and 'normal' economic activity. He differentiates among three classes of profit-driven crimes: predatory crimes for profit involving involuntary transfers; market-based exchanges that involve illegal goods or services that are sold for profit; and, finally, commercial exchanges involving the illegal production or illegal distribution of otherwise legal goods or services. Each of these categories has a different impact on society, and that impact is not always negative. Hence, society might be wise to differentiate among the categories rather than to shove all profit-driven criminal activity under the heading 'organized crime.' Each type of behaviour requires a distinct response.

In chapter 3, Valsamis Mitsilegas provides us with the current European interpretation as represented in the legislation of Italy, Germany, the United Kingdom, the European Union, and the United Nations. He documents the degree to which country and organizational responses to organized crime are vague and ill-defined. This analysis outlines the emergence of the campaign against organized crime at the global level and inquires how compatible anti-organized crime initiatives are with fundamental legal principles. Mitsilegas discusses the emergence of a 'global' definition of organized crime under the various international conventions and reveals for us the negotiations and compromises that go into obtaining such multi-jurisdictional agreements. Whether or not anything of value remains at the end of the negotiations is open to debate.

Themes on Transparency

Discussions related to organized crime and transnational crime – about the factors leading to the creation of illegal markets, about the size of the 'threat,' and about the passing of extraordinary legislation to attack the problem – are steeped in politics. For constructive debate, an informed public is essential; yet with news increasingly being packaged as entertainment, accurate information about transnational crime may be hard to obtain.

Discussions about organized crime must be opened up to include researchers and interested and informed members of the public, in addition to law enforcement practitioners, so that the official rhetoric of the anti-organized crime forces can be 'tested' or at least debated. There are, of course, various types of information that must be kept confidential in order to protect informants or for other clear investigative reasons.[10] However, there is considerable variance among countries as to how strictly they limit access to information. Many countries severely restrict access even to *publicly funded information*.[11] While official explanations of such restrictive policies may specify security reasons, in some cases it may simply be that this information would not stand up to public scrutiny. It is easier to speak freely about the 'threats' to our democratic institutions in a closed, *in camera* session where there is no need to substantiate the claims.

We often link our current *borderlessness* with respect to financial transactions and the movement of commodities, and in some cases also people, to an increase in transnational crime, as if there were no local base to the criminal operations. In focusing on the cross-border transnational aspects, we remove the serious crime activity from the *originating* political, economic, and social context within which the criminal activity might be better understood or explained and dealt with by law enforcement. For example, take three of the 'big' transnational crime commodities today – drugs, fraud, and counterfeiting. Each of these activities has both a local and a global aspect (see Hobbs, 1998). As Hobbs notes (quoting Strathern 1995),[12]

'Networks are the media through which individuals and groups move between the local and the global, but this does not indicate the kind of structural determinism suggested by many writers on organized crime. Networks here refer to metaphors for relationality ... relations between individuals vary according to differentiation in demographic dispersion, familial composition, ethnic distribution and integration, commercial practice, trading patterns, the economic backcloth of the legitimate culture and the particular use of space. Organized crime is not experienced globally or transnationally, for these are abstract fields devoid of relations.' (Hobbs, 1998: 419)

If our focus is dominated by the 'transnational' aspect, we may be ignoring not only the local aspect as outlined above but also what might be seen to be the lower-level crimes that are part of the transnational crime processes. Empirical research reveals a complex mix of criminals ranging from sophisticated 'specialists' to 'opportunists' – all operating within the same crime field. Empirical research, such as ethnographic studies of serious crime networks directed at individual criminal markets, reveals that the dialectic between the local and the global determines both the legitimate and the illegitimate markets.

Chapter 4, by James Williams and Margaret Beare, takes on the transparency theme. This chapter examines the role of the World Bank, the International Monetary Fund (IMF), and other international organizations such as Transparency International in packaging the current focus on one specific form of corruption – that which hinders the economies of the more developed countries. The chapter traces the growth, not in corruption, but in the response of the international community to corruption, and argues that globalization has created new political and economic spaces that are being largely filled by initiatives that conform to an economic logic that is primarily defined by the Western or developed countries. International organizations that may appear to have separate voices can actually be seen to be all reading from the same script – a script that supports global business and finance.

James Sheptycki and Kyle Grayson both examine the rhetoric used in discussions of transnational crime and the powerful impact it can have. The 'war' rhetoric that is applied specifically to drug trafficking is a common focus. In chapter 5, James Sheptycki examines the language that has built up around the activities subsumed under 'transnational organized crime.' He describes the veil that is being drawn over police work as policing becomes increasingly international. The police apparatus that is being geared to address this 'out-there' form of criminality includes security forces and élite squads operating according to diverse international standards. Traditional accountability mechanisms are no longer appropriate. Hard-won gains in the fight for increased openness in the workings of the domestic police are being eroded by pressures for an all-out war against transnational organized crime.

In chapter 6, Kyle Grayson analyses U.S. foreign policies against drug trafficking from a Foucauldian perspective. He examines how the 'war on drugs' and the 'security-threat' rhetoric have succeeded in merging, in the public mind, drugs, transnational crime, traditional conceptions of security, and all of the images and symbols associated with each of these discourses. His objective is to understand both the reasons why the United States has chosen to link drug-trafficking issues with security issues and the methods by which this linkage has been made.

Globalization of Markets

Both the word 'globalization' and the term 'organized crime' are overused, with the concept of globalization comprising everything and anything, and all crimes within the international arena becoming 'transnational crimes.' Labelling every crime that has the remotest 'transnational' aspect a 'transnational crime' sullies the concept. However, no matter how narrowly or broadly defined, transnational crime has been affected by changes in the way business and finance are being conducted. Changes in technology, commodity routing, and labour markets have altered both the forms of transnational crimes and the forms of sanctions that are being applied against them.

Understanding transnational crime within the global context requires a market-by-market analysis. Yet this is not typically how the phenomenon is dealt with by governments. There is pressure to pass special laws or grant the police extra powers in order to combat transnational crime/organized crime, based on a working assumption that this covers a range of fairly uniform activities. In reality, the various types of transnational/organized crime may have little in common beyond the desire for profit. Sophisticated frauds, schemes, and thefts may involve both illicit and legitimate commodities, all operating according to market principles that ensure a profit to the players. The players range from the totally legitimate to the totally criminal, with a fascinating middle ground occupied by 'business persons' knowledgable enough, or criminal enough, to exploit the gaps in legislation and regulatory or enforcement mechanisms.

In chapter 7, Vincenzo Ruggiero presents case materials that illustrate the essential role of professionals in facilitating many 'transnational' crimes. He argues that the lines between white-collar crime and organized crime are increasingly blurred within the international cross-jurisdictional criminal environment. Ruggiero emphasizes the close links between legitimate business and illegitimate operations and argues that forms of social control help to determine the forms that crime will take. 'Globalization' is seen to have changed social control mechanisms, in turn causing changes in criminal activity – with one result being an increasingly blurred relationship between the concepts of white-collar crime and organized crime. Cases are presented that illustrate the role of corporations and other 'legitimate' segments of society in supporting or facilitating criminal activity. This chapter questions whether the stigma that has been attached to 'organized crime' will decrease as transnational crimes increasingly take on the appearance of white-collar criminality.

After these somewhat theoretical, conceptual papers, the remaining four chapters look at distinct enforcement issues. In chapter 8, Margaret Beare discusses the case of the tobacco companies and their immunity from prosecution until the anti-tobacco health groups began to gain publicity that exposed some of the industry's previously ignored criminal transactions. This chapter looks in depth at one example of white-collar organized crime. The tobacco industry is used as the example of an international corporation that has been proven to have used means identical to those thought to belong to traditional organized crime: smuggling, fraud, money laundering, and violence. The revelations regarding the practices of these powerful corporations prompts questions about why they so long enjoyed immunity from the label 'criminal.' While some of this immunity relates to the general difficulty of proving white-collar crime, equally relevant reasons relate to the power of the corporations and stereotyped ideas about the categories of people who engage in 'organized crime.'

Challenging Assumptions and Responses

Ironically, while certain types of harmful behaviour are excluded from criminal sanction, the definition of the concept 'organized crime' is excessively broad. In fact, the accepted definition includes virtually all economically motivated serious crime that is committed by more than one person. Obviously, the wider the definition, the more 'organized crime' there can be claimed to exist. This breadth reached a new all-inclusiveness when the Canadian government accepted a definition offered by Sam Porteous in a report to the federal Ministry of the Solicitor General. Organized crime was defined as being 'economically motivated illicit activity undertaken by any group, association or other body consisting of two or more individuals, whether formally or informally organized, where the negative impact of said activity could be considered significant from an economic, social, violence generation, health, and safety and/or environmental perspective' (Porteous, 1998: 2). Not much 'tighter' is the more recent United Nations definition. The United Nations Convention against Transnational Organized Crime, signed in Palermo in December 2000, defined organized crime as a 'structured group of three or more persons, existing for a period of time and acting in concert with the aim of committing one or more serious crimes or offences in order to obtain, directly or indirectly, financial or other material benefit.' Key officials involved in the negotiations for this U.N. convention emphasized the importance of this 'flexible' broad definition.[13]

The concept of organized crime has become stretched and mythologized to the point of total distortion, rendering it useless for anything but political mileage and the bargaining for resources by law enforcement bodies, leading some critics to suspect that those results might have been the objective. The international literature reveals sparse and/ or unreliable evaluative information on the impact of transnational crime and the impact of law enforcement efforts against these crimes. These evaluations require estimations, which in many instances are only guesses – and often exaggerated ones. Aside from anecdotal accounts of successes, police make little attempt to link their strategies to an empirical measurement of danger or risk, and it may be that this would be impossible to do accurately in any case.

Market-by-market analysis would make us acknowledge that, aside from the profit motive, the separate markets are very different from one another. For example, the issues involved in smuggling humans are vastly different from the issues involved in smuggling drugs. And, in fact, even the activity of smuggling humans is not a uniform one – different methods are used, involving different degrees of exploitation and violence and different motivations and goals. In its protocols, the U.N. convention recognizes the distinction between trafficking in humans and smuggling humans, and this distinction is a significant step towards understanding these forms of illegal migration. What may need more in-depth examination is the complicity of states in these forms of criminal activity.

Chapters 9, 10, and 11 challenge the responses that have been taken to address transnational organized crimes. Governments have come to accept the rhetoric regarding not only the nature of the criminal activity but also the appropriateness of currently popular law enforcement strategies.

In chapter 9, Juan Gabriel Ronderos challenges the rhetoric of the 'war on drugs' and the law enforcement responses that result from the foreign policies that support the rhetoric. Specifically, he examines the impact of these policies on Colombia, with an emphasis on the unintended consequences of either misdirected enforcement strategies or misguided priorities.

In chapter 10, Fred Desroches illustrates empirically that the popular rhetoric about 'high-level drug traffickers' is largely false. Based on research done in 1999, this study is part of a growing body of empirical research that indicates that even 'high-level drug traffickers' come in many different varieties – and with many different working arrangements among the members of the network. The key finding was that the majority of traffickers were individual entrepreneurs who could quit, aspire to move up in the illicit occupational chain, or change and work with the competition. The respondents in Desroches's study spoke of *dealing networks*, loosely coupled with links to the importing source. From 'a distance' this is a 'transnational crime' with all of the enforcement difficulties inherent in cross-jurisdictional policing. Seen from another perspective, it is a chain of 'local' criminal transactions that impact most directly on local communities.

The 'traffickers' often combined selling drugs with legitimate employment. Desroches's study, based on interviews with 'high-level drug traffickers' in prisons across Canada, dispels some of the myths regarding who these criminals are and what their relationship is to some larger entity that we collectively term 'organized crime.' If ever there was a group that 'ought' to represent organized crime, it should be this group of criminals. If these criminals are different from the common stereotype, we ought to question other unverified assumptions we might hold regarding organized crime groups.

Desroches's findings are supported by empirical research based on other types of criminal activity. Mike Levi's analysis of credit-card fraud, another major 'transnational crime,' revealed a diverse array of criminal involvement in terms of sophistication, of the tightness of the networks, and of the local versus international dimension. As Levi states:

> Interviews both with fraudsters and with the police confirm the portrait of socially and culturally distinct fraudster networks in the Montreal research of Mativat and Tremblay (1997), though the smaller size and the greater population density of England and Wales than Canada means that it is easier and quicker for British criminal groups to operate in different regions of the country. But none of the above indicates that plastic fraud is disorganized; *what it means is that different forms of crime require different levels of organization and that there is no one optimal size of firm for plastic fraud overall.* (Levi, 1998: 382)

These empirical research projects reveal a population of mainly low-level entrepreneurs who can move up or down or even exit from all involvement in the criminal organization in question.

The final chapter is a second essay by R.T. Naylor, written specifically for the Nathanson Centre, about fallacies in the enforcement strategies related to money laundering and the targeting of proceeds of crime.

Naylor examines forfeiture laws and the international acceptance of 'going after the illicit money' as a number-one policing strategy. He challenges the assumptions upon which the prioritizing of anti–money-laundering initiatives are based. He offers us alternative approaches that he maintains are based on more appropriate justifications with fewer of the unintended consequences.

Dissecting the Activity

In a presentation given in Toronto, Jonathan Winer, a former U.S. deputy assistant secretary of state,[14] characterized the Canadian view of global security issues as being 'soft security,' and criticized Canada as a country where 'the rights of people trump the rights of "states."'[15] A dominant theme in Winer's talk was that Canada's 'soft' approach was no match for what he termed 'Global Security and Concrete Mega-Threats.' But what should one do in the face of 'global security mega-threats'? If the threats from transnational crimes are everywhere, and are massive, and are out of the control of any one nation or any group of nations, then societies might as well throw up their hands and retreat. Retreat where? The obvious direction would be to retreat into gated communities and/or to hand over privacy rights, Charter protections, or considerations of due process to the state in exchange for 'more' protection against this ill-defined enemy. The essays in this book suggest that these responses might be inappropriate and may contribute nothing to the security of communities at home or abroad. Instead, we need to dissect the threats and try to understand who is threatening whom and what can be done to reduce the threat.

Unfortunately, the typical international response tends not to be an empirical approach but a rhetorical one. The threats must seem to escalate with each report or they are not 'news.' In reality, organized crime activity or corruption is serious enough to require more than rhetoric. In fact, we need action to help identify and understand what are and what are not the real threats. The argument would then be to cut out the rhetoric that blankets everything and target what is both 'fixable' and 'serious.' The absence of either of these two characteristics renders the use of limited resources, possibly the risking of lives, and the creation of varying states of panic or despair a pointless and stupid exercise.

The multiple agendas and hidden constituencies in this area of study complicate the process of formulating and enforcing crime-fighting policies and assessing their success. Equally important, the proliferation of sometimes incompatible agendas makes it difficult or impossible to *reverse* an ineffective policy. Some policies, of course, may make a situation worse, rather than being merely ineffective. Hence the need to consider the issues raised by John Braithwaite (1993) and others regarding the 'cost' of enforcement and enforcement policies – in terms of dollars versus gain and also in terms of the unanticipated or unaddressed consequences stemming from the enforcement strategies.

Leadership changes in the international organizations, national governments, or local police services will mean that new priorities are identified to allow each wave of officials to leave its mark. The public is reduced to waiting passively for pronouncements about the latest threat. A critical perspective is needed to evaluate these threats aggressively and prevent further unnecessary fear and waste of resources.

Notes

1 Financial Action Task Force, for example, and the 2000 *United Nations Convention against Transnational Organized Crime.*
2 See, for example, Ibbitson, 2002.
3 See 'Study: Fewer Facts in Media Coverage,' *Project for Excellence in Journalism (http://www.journalism.org)*, reported by Jennifer Loven, Associated Press, 28 January 2002.
4 Special session of the Financial Action Task Force, Washington, DC, 29 October 2001.
5 *R. v. McCurrach*, [2000] A.J. No. 966, 2000 ABPC 127.
6 Staff Sgt Bob Stenhouse was fired from the RCMP for leaking the document to Yves Lavigne for inclusion in *Hells Angels at War* (1999: 283).
7 Former police chief of Kansas City and San Jose and currently a research fellow at Stanford University.
8 Weeks of media coverage that will develop into years of litigation will follow from the sequence that began with the announced bankruptcy of Enron. See Jim Yardley, David Barboza, and Don Van Natta, Jr, 'Influence Lost, Ex-Enron Chief Faces Congress,' *New York Times*, 3 February 2002; Alex Berenson, 'The Biggest Casualty of Enron's Collapse: Confidence,' *New York Times*, 10 February 2002; 'Week in Review': 1; Barrie McKenna, 'Enron Auditor Stonewalls' *Globe and Mail*, 6 February 2002; 1; Barrie McKenna, 'Lay "Troubled" Pleading the Fifth,' *Globe and Mail*, 13 February 2002: B1; Peter Morton, 'Anger, Anguish at Enron Hearings,' *Financial Post*,

6 February 2002: FP1; Kevin Drawbaugh, 'Ex-Enron Boss Ordered to Appear before Congress,' *Toronto Star*, 6 February 2002: C1.

9 See Glasbeek (2002). *Wealth by Stealth* dissects the legal machinery that supports corporations and their 'offending' deeds.

10 In Canada there is the tendency to wrap all organized crime discussions in unnecessary and counterproductive secrecy. The *in camera* House Justice Committee hearings on organized crime during fall 2000 are one example.

11 A look at the websites from immigration and policing agencies in Australia reveals real information that can allow for and, in fact, encourage genuinely open debate.

12 See 'Afterword: Relocations' in Strathern (1995).

13 Discussions from the 22–3 February 2002 UNICRI and ILO Symposium 'The United Nations Convention against Transnational Organized Crime: Requirements for Its Effective Implementation.' Symposium held in Turin, Italy.

14 22 February 2000 at the University Club.

15 A section of his paper that he did not present stated that Canadian banks were attractive to Russian organized crime because of our lack of laws against money laundering. This must have been written prior to the Bank of New York/Russia money-laundering fiasco! He appeared to be using 'soft security' as a synonym to refer to the 'human security' policies of our Department of Foreign Affairs and International Trade that have been advanced within the past two years – and that appear to be much hated and/or misunderstood by some U.S. officials.

CRITICAL REFLECTIONS ON TRANSNATIONAL
ORGANIZED CRIME, MONEY LAUNDERING,
AND CORRUPTION

1 Transnational Organized Crime: The Strange Career of an American Concept

Michael Woodiwiss

Defined literally, 'organized crime' is systematic illegal activity for power or profit. As such, organized crime is as old as government and law and as international as trade. Smuggling, piracy, fraud, extortion, and trading in illegal goods and services all have ancient antecedents and modern manifestations. A history of organized crime in a literal sense would have to acknowledge the participation of all levels of society in systematic criminal activity and, in particular, the persistent and active participation of the powerful in society throughout ancient and modern civilizations. Organized crime, understood in a literal sense, is a problem to which there is no simple solution; combating it would require governments to effect major legislative and administrative changes at local, state/provincial, and international levels.

However, largely as a result of the process outlined in this chapter, most people today understand 'organized crime' in a way that is much more acceptable to governmental and commercial interests in virtually every country. Most policy makers, commentators, and media outlets around the world now use 'organized crime' as a term that is virtually synonymous with gangsters in general, or the Mafia (or Mafia-type organizations) in particular. Histories of organized crime in this limited sense tend to rely on assertion, speculation, and exaggeration about groups of career criminals. It is also usually implied or stated by those using the term that gangster organizations have gained an unacceptable level of power in many countries today through violence and the ability to corrupt weak, greedy, and therefore passive public officials, private professionals, and business interests. Organized crime has thus become a threat to, rather than part of, society. The implied or stated answer to the problem of organized crime understood in this second sense is much simpler than the first. It involves increasing the law enforcement power of every individual nation state and, because these crime organizations are now known to operate globally, increasing the collective law enforcement power of the international community. The threat posed by organized crime as it is currently understood therefore requires nations to commit more resources towards increasing the effectiveness of policing efforts at home and of collaborative transnational policing efforts between nations. Essentially, this is the line taken by the United Nations, which, at the time of writing, is in the process of encouraging governments to complete the ratification process of its Convention against Transnational Organized Crime.

This chapter presents an outline of American and international efforts to conceptualize and combat organized crime. My intention is to use the American experience to illuminate the quagmire in which many countries now find themselves when faced with a poorly understood phenomenon. I argue that making the term 'organized crime' synonymous with gangster or Mafia-type organizations will not help in efforts to combat a problem that is increasingly damaging and destructive but is rarely so structured and never so separate from legitimate institutions as the common use of the term now implies.

Organized Crime as an American Problem

When people first used 'organized crime' as a phrase in late-nineteenth-century America, it had no fixed meaning and could be understood only in context. Depending on their political inclination, contemporaries could have applied it to the schemes of the rich or the poor. They might have read about combinations of business interests or politicians or police officers or lawyers or professional thieves in terms that suggest their crimes were organized. Only a few would have associated organized crime almost exclusively with conspiratorial groups among foreign career criminals.

Even when some anti-crime groups began to give the phrase a more specific meaning at the end of the nineteenth century and beginning of the twentieth, they made organized crime almost synonymous with local political corruption rather than associating it solely with career criminals. In 1895, for example, the Reverend Charles Parkhurst described a police captain in New York who tolerated illegal gambling operations as one factor in 'a colossal organization of crime.' He contended that the police represented 'organized municipal criminality,' the machine, 'the organization of crime' (Gilfoyle, 1992: 251–69). Parkhurst was by then president of the New York Society for the Prevention of Crime, which described itself in its 1896 annual report as a body 'completely organized for offensive operations and thoroughly committed to a policy of exposing and breaking down official misconduct and organized crime.'[1] This was perhaps the first time reformers had used the phrase 'organized crime,' and they were referring to gambling and prostitution operations that were protected by public officials.

Parkhurst had rescued the New York anti-crime group from obscurity, largely by getting the support of wealthy business interests. It was therefore probably not a coincidence that he also dropped the society's earlier hostility to the criminal methods of big business.[2] Instead, as Parkhurst made plain in his most famous sermon, his main targets were local machine politicians associated with the Democratic party's Tammany Hall organization: 'There is not a form under which the devil disguises himself that so perplexes us in our efforts ... as the polluted harpies that, under the pretense of governing the city, are feeding day and night on its quivering vitals. They are a lying, perjured, rum-soaked and heinous lot.'[3]

Moral campaigners such as Parkhurst wasted no time trying to communicate or compromise with their opponents; instead they used 'sets of stereotypes' to confront their opponents or, to borrow another phrase from the historian Robert Wiebe (1967: 96), 'frozen images that were specifically intended to exclude discussion.' These techniques were particularly effective in the campaigns against prostitution, gambling, and liquor, and they anticipate the 'sets of stereotypes' and 'frozen images' used in more recent campaigns against drugs and organized crime.

Those who wished to prohibit alcohol, for example, illuminate the use of 'frozen images' to exclude rational discussion of alcohol control. They tended, for example, to lump the many thousands of breweries, distilleries, and saloons together and refer to them all as the 'Liquor Power.' This, according to the Reverend Mark Matthews, the nation's most prominent Presbyterian, was 'the most fiendish, corrupt and hell-soaked institution that ever crawled out of the slime of the eternal pit' (N.H. Clark, 1976: 4). Josiah Strong's verdict after detailing cases of bribery and corruption in *Our Country* (1885) was that the cities were already under the heel of the Liquor Power. He warned that the Liquor Power would get even more opportunities to paralyse and corrupt government when the cities with their rapidly expanding populations came to dominate the whole nation politically. He drew an unjustified distinction between the methods of the Liquor Power and other businesses, and then claimed that 'Such a powerful organization, resorting to such unscrupulous methods in the interests of legitimate business – mining, railroading – would be exceedingly dangerous in a republic; and the whole outcome of this traffic, pushed by such wealth, such organized energy and such means, is the corrupting of the citizen and the embruting of the man' (Strong, 1963: 132).

In the same vein, during the first congressional debate on a national prohibition amendment in 1914, Representative Clyde Kelly of Pennsylvania claimed that Congress should pass the prohibition resolution because of the very forces against it, 'the allied powers that prey, the vultures of vice, the corrupt combinations of politics, the grafters and gangsters, the parasites that clothe themselves in the proceeds of a woman's shame, the inhuman ones that bathe themselves in the tears of little children, the wastrels who wreck and ruin material things while they contaminate childhood, debauch youth, and crush manhood; the plunder-laden ones who fatten themselves upon the misery and want and woe that their own greed has created, the Hessians in the black-bannered troop whose line of march is over wrecked homes and broken hearts and ruined lives' (Sinclair, 1962: 173–4).

Kelly's emotive language was not untypical, and the arguments of those who opposed the amendment seemed weak by comparison!

By 1918, the Eighteenth Amendment, prohibiting the manufacture, transportation, sale, or importation of intoxicating liquor within the United States, had received the necessary support to be added to the Constitution. The following year, the Volstead Act was passed, providing for the enforcement of Prohibition and putting in place the final link in the legislative chain of America's moral reform program. There were now prohibition laws, at the local, state, and federal levels, covering prostitution, gambling, and the use of certain kinds of drugs as well as liquor. A host of entrepreneurial opportunities in the illegal economy thus became available.

America's early-twentieth-century moral reformers were successful in getting the laws they wanted on the statute books and, eventually, as the Reverend Parkhurst had hoped, in ensuring that city police forces were professionalized and insulated from direct local political control. But the problem with America's moral crusade from the beginning was that Americans continued to buy liquor, gamble, take drugs, and fornicate, whether or not they were breaking laws and no matter what system of policing was used in the attempt to stop them. As E.R. Hawkings and Willard Waller observed in 1936, 'It happens that society has put these goods and services under the ban, but people go on producing them and people go on consuming them, and an act of legislation does not make them any less part of the economic system' (Hawkings and Waller, 1936: 684–5).

New forms of organized crime emerged as corrupt networks, often including police in the new reformed police departments, ensured that prohibited activities continued as part of America's economic system.

Commentators and academics began to make serious efforts to define and discuss organized crime as a distinct American phenomenon in the 1920s and 1930s. The phrase 'organized crime' was used in several different senses, though still only rarely in the limited sense signifying separate associations of gangsters. To most academics and professionals concerned with the subject, organized crime usually referred to certain types of criminal activity and was virtually synonymous with racketeering. The word 'racket' was by then well established as meaning an illegal business or fraudulent scheme, and it followed that racketeering was understood to refer to such activities as dealing in stolen property, insurance frauds, fraudulent bankruptcies, securities frauds, credit frauds, forgery, counterfeiting, illegal gambling, trafficking in drugs or liquor, or various forms of extortion. Many writers made it clear that criminal networks often included the active involvement of police, politicians, judges, lawyers, and seemingly legitimate businessmen.

All efforts to understand organized crime in the 1920s and early 1930s were constrained by limits to knowledge and understanding shared by most white Americans at this time. Systematic and profitable crimes against Native Americans and African Americans, and, since the end of early-twentieth-century 'muckraking' journalism, crimes committed by big business were not thought to be aspects of the problem. Most early efforts to describe and analyse organized crime were also constrained by the class bias of liberal reformers and the widely held assumption that it was a problem mainly confined to city slums. Despite these limits, many early efforts to analyse or portray organized crime did have the important merit of asking questions about American laws and institutions.

No serious commentator writing about the problem of organized crime before the 1940s suggested that conspirators among Italians, Jews, or any other group actually controlled or dominated urban crime. To explain immigrant involvement, as opposed to domination of rack-eteering and other types of crime, some academics pointed to the process of assimilation. 'The overwhelming mass' of foreigners accord-ing to James Thurlow Adams, were 'law-abiding in their own lands. If they become lawless here it must be largely due to the American atmos-phere and conditions' (quoted in Tyler, 1967: 110). Moreover, immi-grants, like others of the 'socially inferior,' to use the words of sociologist Harry Barnes, 'tend to ape the socially superior.' Barnes testified before a senate committee in 1933 that the businessmen and financiers of the previous generation had

> capitulated pretty thoroughly to the prevailing 'something-for-nothing psychology' of the era ... Freebooting in railroads, banks, utilities, receiverships – and other high-toned racketeering – becomes shockingly frequent.
>
> It was inevitable that, sooner or later, we would succeed in 'Americaniz-ing' the 'small fry.' Their ancestors, if they lived in this country, had usually made an honest living conducting shoe-shining parlors, clothes-cleaning establishments, fruit stands, restaurants, and the like or at hard labor on roads, streets, and railroads. The younger generation looked with envy, not at the bowed backs and wrinkled brows of their parents, but rather at the achievements of the American financial buccaneers who had made away with their millions, with little or no service to society. If our usurers of high estate could get theirs, why should anybody drown him-self in perspiration? That was the question they asked themselves. (Barnes, 1967: 178–9)

Most serious commentators saw organized crime as much less static and hierarchical than do current orthodox thinkers on the problem. In a 1926 article, for example, Professor Raymond Moley (1926: 78–84) sug-gested that the 'conception of organized crime as a vast underworld organization, led by a "master mind" with workers, lieutenants, cap-tains, was melodramatic nonsense.' Frederic Thrasher (1960: 416), in the first fully developed study of the problem, made it clear that 'orga-nized crime must not be visualized as a vast edifice of hard and fast structures.' Frank Tannenbaum in *Crime and the Community* (1936: 115) noted that 'while crime is organized, it is not unified.' Edwin Suther-land, in *The Professional Thief* (1937: 209), stated that organized crime was 'not organized in the journalistic sense, for no dictator or central office directs the work of the members of the profession.'

Instead of a hierarchical organization, Moley suggested that organized crime should best be seen in terms of a division of labour involving 'shop-keepers who dispose of loot, lawyers who have more than a professional relationship to defendants, and others who grow rich on the proceeds of vice and bootlegging and who because of this wealth become masters of many criminals who actively perform the work of crime.'

This 'semi-integrated underworld,' he continued, had its indirect relations with political organizations and could thus influence 'officials who dwell in the very citadels of "respectability"' (Moley, 1926: 83). Thrasher noted the importance of 'certain specialized persons or groups, who perform certain indispensable functions' for professional criminals. These included doctors, political manipulators, professional or obligated bondsmen, criminal lawyers, and corrupt officials.

Even when he was focusing on the community of career criminals itself, Thrasher emphasized its fluidity:

> While there is considerable definite organization, largely of the feudal type, there is no hard and fast structure of a permanent character. The ease of new alliances and alignments is surprising. Certain persons of certain groups may combine for some criminal exploit or business, but shortly they may be bitter enemies and killing each other. One gang may stick closely together for a long period under favorable conditions; yet if cause for real dissension arises, it may readily split into two or more bitter factions, each of which may eventually become a separate gang. Members may desert to the enemy on occasion. Leaders come and go easily; sometimes with more or less violence, but without much disturbance to the usual activities of the gangs. There is always a new crop coming on – of younger fellows from whom emerge men to fill the shoes of the old 'barons' when they are slain or 'put away ...' (Thrasher, 1960: 414–17)

Moley, Thrasher, and other commentators also followed in the progressive urban reform tradition and emphasized that certain political conditions were essential for successful organized crime. Moley's experience in organizing the major Cleveland and Missouri crime surveys had brought him to a conclusion that was similar to that of the Reverend Parkhurst – machine politics was in effect a form of organized crime: 'The political machine is a group of men, usually without legal standing as a group, possessed of power to help or to injure others, and the possession of this power is the real reason it receives substantial support. This is a racket in every sense in which the word is commonly used' (Moley, 1930: 2).

Thrasher's study emphasized the use politicians made of gangsters at election times and argued that in these and other ways, crime and politics in Chicago were joined in 'an intimate unity' that tied the hands of the police and secured virtual immunity for many types of illegal activity (Thrasher, 1960: 458–62).

Other commentators pointed to the active complicity of lawyers in the organization of crime. 'In every racket is a lawyer,' according to Henry Barrett Chamberlin (1931–2: 668) of the Chicago Crime Commission: 'This lawyer has studied in a law school; he is an associate of most of the lawyers of the community; he has a decent appearing home; ... he is a member of his bar association; he is invariably a lawyer who is in politics; he is so strong in all sorts of activities that he can't be disbarred.'

Towards the end of the 1920s, more commentators began to see Prohibition and other aspects of America's moral reform program as exacerbating the problem of organized crime. According to E.W. Burgess in the Illinois Crime Survey of 1929, there was 'no blinking the fact that liquor prohibition has introduced the most difficult problems of law enforcement in the field of organized crime.' 'The enormous revenues derived from bootlegging,' he continued, 'have purchased protection for all forms of criminal activities and have demoralized law enforcing agencies' (quoted in Friedman, 1993: 340). And, as Harry Barnes (1967: 179) added, 'Prohibition promoted other rackets – the hijacking racket among the wet outlaws, rackets in foods, milk, transportation, building construction, and the like.'

Some extended the point to cover other prohibitions such as the anti-gambling, drugs, and prostitution laws. Tannenbaum (1936: 46), for example, argued: 'The number of unenforceable laws increased the field of criminal activity and nurtured the criminals who profited by these laws to the point of creating a system definitely outside of the law and beyond the police power ... The profit-making aspect made such organization possible, and played an important role in paralyzing law-enforcing agencies through political manipulation and direct corruption.'

Providing illegal but popular goods and services, according to Walter Lippmann in 1931, requires 'law-breaking, bribery and coercion,' and enlists 'men and women who have little or no stake in the social conventions, in honest government, or in the even-handed, effective administration of the law.' 'The high level of lawlessness,' he argued, 'is maintained by the fact that Americans desire to do so many things which they also desire to prohibit.' The underworld, according to Lippmann, was a servant that would exist as long as it continued to serve consumers and business interests (Lippmann, 1967: 59–69).

Chamberlin made the connection between unworkable laws and successful organized crime explicit. He wrote in 1931 that 'Organized crime is today a great, unmanageable threatening fact in the lives of our communities. It is not enough to ask whether the machinery of law enforcement is good, we must go further, call in question the wisdom of the laws themselves and discover whether or not some of our experiments are not as menacing in their effect as criminal activities. It may be found that some of the very best intentions of our idealists have supplied the pavement for the hell of organized crime' (Chamberlin, 1931–2: 669).

August Vollmer was another who suggested that the problem of organized crime was in the laws and the system, and he was better informed than most about the problems of policing 'vice' of all kinds. As the foremost police reformer of the day, Vollmer had drastically improved the efficiency and organization of several police forces and then used this experience as the basis of a book called *The Police and Modern Society*, published in 1936. Vollmer argued that the duty of the police was to protect society from criminals and not to try to control morality. Any other approach was dangerously counterproductive, distracting the police and fostering crime and corruption. He considered that regular policing could not solve the problems of prostitution, gambling, and drug addiction. On the drug traffic he wrote, 'Stringent laws, spectacular police drives, vigorous prosecution, and imprisonment of addicts and peddlers have proved not only useless and enormously expensive as a means of correcting this evil, but they are also unjustifiably and unbelievably cruel in their application to the unfortunate drug victims. Repression has driven this vice underground and produced the narcotics smugglers and supply agents, who have grown wealthy out of this evil practice and who by devious methods have stimulated traffic in drugs' (Vollmer, 1936: 99–118).

No expert suggested that prison was the answer to organized crime, and some made it very clear that prison was part of the problem of crime in general. Tannenbaum, for example, argued strongly that imprisonment ensures that the criminal continues his career 'by providing him with an intensified stimulus and heightened experience' and elaborated:

> It would be difficult to invent a more effective method for conditioning the criminal in his career than imprisoning him with some hundreds of other prisoners, each of whom has a tale of adventure, of pride, of success and of failure, of ends and plans, all in terms of the past career as a criminal and in terms of a future career in the same field ... The way to confirm the criminal in his career is to throw him with other criminals for a long enough time for him to become thoroughly saturated with all their emotional and ethical insights into the ways of the world, and long enough for him to share, vicariously at least, in the criminal experiences of all his new found friends in prison. (Tannenbaum, 1936: 476)

Or, as the sociologist Fred Haynes put it more succinctly, 'Our prisons probably train more criminals than they deter or reform' (quoted in Calder, 1993: 69).

The first federal government attempt to study organized crime was conducted under the auspices of the National Commission on Law Observance and Enforcement under the chairmanship of George W. Wickersham between 1929 and 1931. Two of the commission's consultants, Goldthwaite H. Dorr and Sidney Simpson, can be credited with making a genuine effort to come to an objective understanding of the nature and extent of organized crime in the United States.

In their report to the commission on the costs of crime, Dorr and Simpson found that organized crime consisted of two main types of activity. The first was criminal fraud, and they included insurance frauds, fraudulent bankruptcies, securities frauds, credit frauds, confidence games, forgery, counterfeiting, and the use of the mails to defraud. 'It must be emphasized,' they elaborated, 'that the criminal frauds which cause the largest losses are organized schemes, carried on as a regular business, and, in many of the most serious cases, masquerading as legitimate business enterprises. Such criminal schemes shade off by imperceptible degrees into enterprises which are so conducted as to avoid criminal liability although employing unethical or even illegal methods of doing business; and the line between criminal and non-criminal activity is thus frequently a rather arbitrary one. Commercialized fraud is more often business run amuck than an offshoot of ordinary crimes against property, and the typical criminal of this class is not the bandit or the recidivist, but the business man gone wrong' (quoted in D.C. Smith, 1991: 139).

The second type of organized crime activity for Dorr and Simpson was extortion or racketeering, or 'the forcing of persons to pay voluntary tribute to the perpetrators of the crime as a result of fear for life, liberty, bodily safety, reputation, or property.' According to the consultants,

> Both of these forms of crime, in their more important manifestations, are examples of organized crime as a business. Both are modern in development and methods, and constitute, it is believed, by far the most serious with which criminal justice in present-day America must deal. It is strongly recommended that some responsible organization or organizations undertake detailed and comprehensive scientific studies, carried out by competent and properly directed staffs furnished with adequate financial resources, of (a) commercialized frauds, including methods employed, losses resulting, and all other important phases; and (b) the extent, character, causes and economic effects of racketeering. Such studies are urgently needed, and should be organized immediately. (quoted in D.C. Smith, 1991: 139–40)[4]

The commission accepted Dorr and Simpson's understanding of the meaning of organized crime and the need for more study and wrote the following to the President and Congress: 'The importance of dealing effectively with organized crime, whether commercialized fraud or extortion, can not be over-emphasized. Intelligent action requires knowledge – not, as in too many cases, a mere redoubling of effort in the absence of adequate information and a definite plan. The carrying out of our recommendation for immediate, comprehensive, and scientific nation-wide inquiry into organized crime should make possible the development of an intelligent plan for its control' (D.C. Smith, 1991: 140).

As Dwight Smith has shown in his analysis of the development of an 'official' definition for organized crime, the commission's consultants 'organized their data around categories based on criminal law, not categories based on criminals. What was more important than Who.' 'Once Dorr and Simpson focused on events not people,' Smith continued, 'the logic by which the businessman was linked to the gangster was simple. Given that business men and gangsters behaved like each other what was the sense in having two categories that, by definition, were not mutually exclusive?' Researchers, according to Smith, could have used Dorr and Simpson's statements 'as the basis of testable propositions by which a body of theory about organized crime could have been assembled' (ibid.: 142).

The Wickersham Commission published, in all, fourteen reports on U.S. law enforcement, criminal justice, and penal systems, and these exposed numerous patterns of brutality, corruption, and inefficiency. The conclusion was inescapable that, as one report put it, something was fundamentally wrong in 'the very heart of ... government and social policy in America' (Friedman, 1993: 274).

Edwin Sutherland, one of the nation's foremost criminologists, found that there was also something fundamentally wrong in the heart of the American business system. His work went beyond the class bias of most early criminologists and the pro-business attitudes of crime commissions and located the most significant organized criminal activity among the respectable and powerful in society. In *White Collar Crime* (1949), he documented cases of bribery, fraud, embezzlement, antitrust violations, false advertising, and theft of trade secrets by such major corporations as Armour and Company, Swift and Company, General Motors, Sears Roebuck, and Westinghouse. In the steel and automobile industries, he found evidence that corporations were often ready, willing, and able to use violence to win industrial disputes or break unions. He also suggested that there were forms of corporate violence other than strike-breaking, using the New Kanawha Power Company, a subsidiary of Union Carbide, and the Gauley Bridge disaster as his main example. Between two hundred and five hundred workers died as a result of the company's non-observance of state and federal laws concerning silica during a tunnel construction project at Gauley Bridge, West Virginia. Finally, Sutherland showed that the American 'free enterprise' system was a misnomer, since practically all large corporations engaged in illegal restraint of trade (*White Cellar Crime*, 1983: 79–152).

Sutherland found that the criminality of the corporations, like that of professional thieves, was persistent, extensive, usually unpunished, most often deliberate, and involved the connivance of government officials or legislators. It was, in sum, organized (Sutherland, 1983: 227–339).

Although they looked at different aspects of the problem, Sutherland, Dorr, Simpson, and every other serious commentator between the 1920s and 1940s would have agreed on one thing: American organized crime had developed from distinctively American conditions. They shared a sense that organized crime was an unfortunate and avoidable part of the nation's political, economic, social, and legal structures rather than a threat to these structures. Politicians, public officials, professionals, and other representatives of the 'respectable' classes were clearly part of the problem of organized crime, not passive victims or tools of distinct gangster-dominated entities.

Organized Crime as an Outside Threat

Unfortunately for Americans, the Wickersham Commission's call for a comprehensive and scientific nation-wide inquiry into organized crime was ignored, and no intelligent plan for its control was formed. Most of its other recommendations to address the many flaws in American crime control were similarly ignored. In the decades that followed, the phrase 'organized crime' acquired a meaning that was much more acceptable to people of power. Reversing Dorr and Simpson's approach, evidence related to organized crime was organized around categories of criminals rather than around categories of criminal law. 'Who' would increasingly become more important than 'What.' From the late 1940s, conceptualizations of the problem now focused on career criminals and began to exclude or at least de-emphasize the part played by representatives of officialdom and the 'respectable' classes in the problem. A useful by-product of this process was that discussion of the problem tended to be directed towards devising ways to lock up these career criminals and away from reconsidering America's remaining prohibition laws, notably those involving gambling and drug control. The body of professional theory about organized crime would become locked in an analysis that whitewashed a flawed system and justified endless recommendations for more misdirected effort at local, national, and eventually, in the case of drugs in particular, international levels. As we shall see, the American approach to organized crime, based as it was on a limited understanding of the problem, failed to address many problems associated with systematic criminal activity and actually succeeded in perpetuating many others.

The perception of organized crime as systematic illegal activity and part of the social, economic, and political systems began to be supplanted in the post-Prohibition era by one that involved unsubtle shifts of grammar and image. Among other things, this new understanding of the problem of organized crime shifted attention away from defects in the system and in the laws, and towards the perception that organized crime was a separate association of gangsters and thereby constituted a threat to the nation's institutions. Journalists gave the illusion of historical and contemporary substance to the newly redefined problem, and filmmakers provided its imagery. The consensus of opinion that emerged among politicians, law enforcement officials, and the press changed the perception of organized crime from one that questioned the workability of certain laws and demanded honest and effective local law enforcement to one that demanded much more nationally coordinated action to enforce existing laws.

This consensus of opinion effectively defined important groups in American society out of the problem of organized crime. As has already been made clear, the police, for example, had been considered to be very much part of the problem of organized crime in early conceptualizations. However, from the 1930s, local police forces began to change their images, if not their behaviour. Corruption was as endemic as it ever had been, but public relations units had become more effective in concealing its extent and pervasiveness. These units set out to cultivate the goodwill of newspaper and magazine publishers as well as radio and movie producers. They gave out handouts to reporters and editors, supplied brochures and pamphlets to citizens' groups, and otherwise put the police point of view. This view tended to stress the idea of the police as a thin blue line standing between society and hordes of criminals.

Given the pro-police line that prevailed in all forms of mass media from the 1930s, it is not surprising that some police officers felt confident enough to use semantics to define themselves out of the problem of organized crime. In November 1947, California police officers from all over the state met in Sacramento in one of the law enforcement community's earliest efforts to define organized crime. Their intention was 'to secure a consensus of opinion from the agencies and officers represented as to the principal fields in which organized crime is to be found and their relative importance from the point of view of size, degree of organization, and menace to the public welfare.' The definition they arrived at was as follows: 'the operations of two or more persons who combine to obtain financial advantages or special privileges by such unlawful means as terrorism, fraud, corruption of public officers or by a combination of such methods.'

The officers also agreed that 'the largest and most serious organizations of criminal character are to be found in connection with gambling of a commercialized nature, prostitution, narcotics, and theft and fraud schemes ...' (California Board of Corrections, 1948: 31–2). Departing radically from earlier conceptualizations, this was an understanding of organized crime that was appropriate to the bureaucratic needs of the newly professionalized big-city police departments. Organized crime was now better seen as something that terrorized, defrauded, or corrupted the police rather than, as before, something in which the police were directly involved.

There was, however, still a long way to go before mainstream opinion was totally reconciled to such an interest-serving understanding. Indeed some of those who worked on the definition might have been embarrassed by a series of revelations beginning soon after the conference that showed that California police officers were as actively involved in the organization of illegal enterprises as any of their colleagues nationwide.[5]

While the police were still struggling to dissociate themselves from the problem of organized crime, corporate interests had long since succeeded. Given their control over the media, business organizations were able to keep much systematic and damaging illegal activity effectively hidden from public view. And as Edwin Sutherland pointed out, newspapers would anyway have been unlikely to highlight violations of regulatory laws and thus risk an investigation into their own illegal working practices (Sutherland, 1983: x).

Just before the publication of *White Collar Crime*, Sutherland was made even more aware of the difficulties of 'whistle blowing' on the crimes of the powerful in America by his publisher's reluctance to allow the naming of the guilty corporations in case they took court action. The publisher, Dryden Press, had been advised by its counsel that it would be liable for damages because the book called certain corporations 'criminal' although they had not been dealt with under criminal statutes. Sutherland had insisted that the white-collar behaviours he detailed were criminal rather than civil offences and that the persons who committed them ought to be punished as severely as persons who committed personal or property crimes. However, Sutherland finally agreed to drop the corporate names, after more pressure from his university's administrators. The book appeared in a form that would not offend the corporate criminals involved (ibid.: x–xi). Although *White Collar Crime* has now been read by generations of criminology students, its impact was thus massively reduced by what amounted to a form of censorship.

Until the 1960s and 1970s, few criminologists chose to risk their careers by stepping outside the prevailing pro-business consensus and exposing pervasive organized crime in business. Two exceptions were Frank Hartung and Marshall Clinard. In 1950, Hartung reported on patterns of fraud in the wholesale meat industry in Detroit during the Second World War. Clinard studied wartime violations of the rules of the Office of Price Administration. In *The Black Market* (1952), he demonstrated that the assumption that the black market was caused primarily by the entrance of shady or gangster elements into U.S. business was a misconception. The big manufacturers and suppliers gained most from wartime violations, and any racketeers involved simply engaged in the wholesale black marketing of U.S. wartime business in general (Hartung, 1950; Clinard, 1952).

Sutherland, Hartung, and Clinard might have demonstrated that organized crime permeated the higher reaches of the American economic structure at least as much as the lower, but the point would have been lost on most people by the late 1940s. It was considered almost unpatriotic to challenge the integrity of the American political and economic system during the first two decades of the Cold War against Communism at home and abroad. Anything nasty such as organized crime had to have come from foreign parts, and changing people's understanding of organized crime required the establishment of a strong image of all-encompassing evil emanating from abroad.

Between the 1950s and 1960s, the idea of the Mafia as controlling or dominating organized crime came to pervade public and professional perceptions of the problem. The Kefauver Senate Investigating Committee was an important part of this process when it highlighted organized crime in 1950 and 1951 and gave undeserved substance and respectability to Mafia mythology.

The committee's *Third Interim Report* traced the history of the Sicilian Mafia and its 'implantation' into America, and then made the following much-quoted assertions:

> There is a nationwide crime syndicate known as the Mafia, whose tentacles are found in many large cities. It has international ramifications which appear most clearly in connection with the narcotics traffic.
>
> Its leaders are usually found in control of the most lucrative rackets of their cities.
>
> There are indications of a centralized direction and control of these rackets, but leadership appears to be in a group rather than in a single individual.

> The Mafia is the cement that helps bind the Costello-Adonis-Lanksy syndicate of New York and the Accardo-Guzik-Fischetti syndicate of Chicago as well as smaller criminal gangs and individual criminals throughout the country ...
>
> The domination of the Mafia is based fundamentally on 'muscle' and 'murder.' The Mafia is a secret conspiracy against law and order which will ruthlessly eliminate anyone who betrays its secrets. It will use any means available – political influence, bribery, intimidation, etc. – to defeat any attempts on the part of law enforcement to touch its top figures or to interfere with its operations. (U.S. Congress, Senate Special Committee to Investigate Crime in Interstate Commerce, 1951: 147–50)[6]

Despite a great deal of hopeful effort, however, no evidence was produced at the hearings to support the view of a centralized Sicilian or Italian organization dominating organized crime in the United States. The committee expressed incredulity during its open hearings when Italian-American racketeers denied they were in an organization called the Mafia. These, if they testified at all, were constantly prodded, probed, and encouraged by committee members and counsel to admit that they were in the Mafia, but none did so. This effort became farcical when the committee's counsel, Rudolph Halley, asked New Jersey racketeer Willie Moretti whether he was a member of the Mafia. Moretti answered with another question: 'What do you mean by a member, carry a card with Mafia on it?'[7]

The only evidence the report offered for its Mafia conclusions were a number of drug-trafficking stories supplied by the Federal Bureau of Narcotics involving Italian-American gangsters. Neither these stories nor any testimony at the hearings were at all convincing about the idea of a centralized organization that dominated or controlled organized crime. In fact, virtually all of the hard evidence produced by the committee contradicted its Mafia conclusions. The committee found men with different ethnic origins at the head of criminal syndicates around the nation, and there was frequent contact and cooperation between criminals of different ethnic groups. All significant gangsters had been born or at least nurtured in America. The networks of illegal activities that the committee described cut across ethnic designations and always depended on the compliance of local officials. The evidence the committee uncovered showed that gambling operators in different parts of the country had sometimes combined in joint ventures, in the same way as businessmen everywhere, and had made a lot of money for themselves and for public officials (Moore, 1974: 113).[8]

The Kefauver report did not attempt to substantiate the crudely inadequate historical and contemporary analysis contained in the quoted excerpts. Once the report had been issued, however, it became a significant historical source, adding the illusion of weight and coherence to the idea of organized crime in America as an alien implant.

Although acknowledging that federal agencies could not be a substitute for state and local enforcement in dealing with organized crime, the Kefauver Committee recommended a large step in the direction of a federalization of American law enforcement. The federal government must, it argued, provide leadership and guidance, establish additional techniques for maximum coordination of law enforcement agencies, take a positive approach in using its power to fight organized crime, and seek legislation when its power was insufficient. Given that organized crime was by then mainly associated with gambling operators and drug traffickers, the committee was effectively arguing the case for increased federal involvement in the enforcement of the gambling and drug laws. Kefauver and his colleagues had thus set an important process in motion. The federal government was more and more committed to the policing of illegal markets – a task that had proved to be beyond the capacity of local administrations.

The committee's lack of evidence for its Mafia conspiracy theory did not matter since its conclusions had been decided upon before the hearings began. In effect, the committee's goal was to reduce the complexities of organized crime to a simple 'good-versus-evil' equation. The committee had accepted the arguments against gambling and drugs, and no serious consideration was given to the possibility of government regulation and control of these activities. The public had to be convinced that prohibitions were the only options, and prohibitions had to be made effective. Enforcement had to be seen as the only answer. The committee thus chose to put the weight of its opinion behind a bizarre and unsubstantiated interpretation of America's organized crime problems. Organized crime was, according to this interpretation, a centralized conspiracy. Alternative ways of regulating and controlling gambling and drugs were out of the question; that would be a capitulation to powerful and alien criminal interests. The only solution, according to the committee and a growing consensus of opinion in the law enforcement community and among opinion makers, was increased federal commitment. This involved the enactment of more laws and the establishment of a federal law enforcement capacity that was capable of succeeding where local authorities had failed. By some means, according to the new line, people had to be prevented from indulging in activities that filled the coffers of the Mafia.

President Lyndon Johnson's Commission on Law Enforcement and the Administration of Justice articulated what had become the conventional wisdom about organized crime in 1967: 'the core of organized crime in the United States consists of 24 groups operating criminal cartels in large cities across the nation. Their membership is exclusively Italian, they are in frequent communication with each other, and their smooth functioning is insured by a national body of overseers.'

The commission's report emphasized that gambling was the greatest source of revenue for organized crime, followed by loan sharking, narcotics, 'and other forms of vice.' But, the report added, 'organized crime is also extensively and deeply involved in legitimate business and in labor unions.'

The commission's definition still serves as a template for more recent attempts. It reads as follows: 'Organized crime is a society that seeks to operate outside the control of the American people and their governments. It involves thousands of criminals, working within structures as complex as those of any large corporation, subject to laws more rigidly enforced than those of legitimate governments. Its actions are not impulsive but rather the result of intricate conspiracies, carried on over many years and aimed at gaining control over whole fields of activity in order to amass huge profits ...'

The commission recommended a complete package of laws to combat the Cosa Nostra's subversion of 'the very decency and integrity that are the most cherished attributes of a free society' (President's Commission on Law Enforcement and the Administration of Justice, 1967: 187–209).

By the 1960s, the phrase 'organized crime' had thus become a term signifying a hierarchically organized criminal conspiracy with a meaning far removed from its early use. It now threatened the integrity of local government. It corrupted police officers and lawyers. It infiltrated legitimate business. It subverted the decency and integrity of a free society. Essentially, every organized group in mainstream American society had been defined out of the problem by a shift of grammar. Organized crime was now seen as a criminal army, far away from earlier perspectives that emphasized the involvement and responsibility of 'respectable' society for the pervasive problem of organized crime activity in the United States.

A definition had finally been found that most important groups in

American society could accept. Local politicians and officials found the new understanding of organized crime a convenient way of explaining their failure to check vice-related or industry-related racketeering in their cities. Nationally ambitious politicians found organized crime a useful vehicle to raise their profiles. National agency officials, including J. Edgar Hoover from the 1960s, found it a useful vehicle to raise their budgets and increase their powers. Legal experts and bar associations used references to organized crime to help explain away the 'few unworthy members' of the bar who were 'of the criminal type' (quoted in Ploscowe, 1952: 242). And American business could assert its basic integrity by claiming that it was threatened by organized crime. Some academics and commentators continued to point to evidence that showed that 'respectable' interests and poorly thought-out laws remained part of the problem of organized crime, but they were voices without political influence.

Instead, a consensus of opinion had been established suggesting that the Mafia had poisoned an otherwise satisfactory system - the Mafia was a threat to America's political, economic, and legal systems and needed to be countered by any means necessary. The Mafia, according to this line, dominated gambling and drug trafficking in the United States - it lurked behind every neighbourhood bookie and drug pusher and therefore weakened the 'vitality and strength of the nation.' And, as Robert Kennedy put it in a book called *The Enemy Within*, 'If we do not on a national scale attack organized criminals with weapons and techniques as effective as their own, they will destroy us' (Kennedy, 1960: 253).

In 1969, President Nixon added his weight to this line of analysis to support new legislation that increased federal jurisdiction over criminal activity to unprecedented levels. He warned that the Mafia's influence had 'deeply penetrated broad segments of American life' and announced a series of measures designed 'to relentlessly pursue the criminal syndicate.' In 1970 Congress supported this line and passed the Organized Crime Control Act. This and other legislation gave federal law enforcement and intelligence agencies an unprecedented array of powers - they could now more easily use wiretapping and eavesdropping devices, cultivate informants, secure convictions that would result in long sentences, and seize the financial assets of their targets. This amounted to a major alteration in constitutional guarantees – it was compared to a grenade attack on the Bill of Rights – and it was all justified by the belief that organized crime was a massive, well-integrated, international conspiracy. The balance in America was tipped towards a much stronger, far richer, and far less accountable policing presence.[9]

Since 1970, the FBI's concentration on the twenty-plus Italian-American crime syndicates that undoubtedly existed has found evidence showing that many Italian-American gangsters swore blood oaths of allegiance, made interstate or regional alliances to try and regulate competition, and used murder and intimidation to protect territory, markets, and operations. But the evidence also showed the limits of Mafia power and the non-existence of a centralized national underworld power structure. The trials of 'Fat Tony' Salerno and 'Tony Ducks' Corallo in the mid-1980s, for example, proved that aging gangsters met in dingy New York social clubs and tried to resolve some of the conflicts among their associates. At the same time, the evidence also indicated that they could not direct or control criminal activity in New York, let alone nationally. They were certainly powerful gangsters but definitely not part of a tightly knit, all-powerful, national syndicate.[10]

Thanks to wiretaps, bugs, and informants, American 'Mafiosi' have been talking to the federal authorities for the past three decades, and the evidence suggests that no single organization or cartel was or is capable of exercising effective control over illegal markets, notably the illegal markets that concerned Americans most: gambling and drugs. However, the federal government still based its organized crime control strategy on the 'Mafia conspiracy' interpretation of organized crime. Out of a mass of contradictory evidence came an organized crime control strategy that has not controlled organized crime activity. No neat and tidy hierarchy of capos, *consiglieri*, and soldiers could explain the tidal wave of crime, corruption, and violence associated with gangsterism and other forms of systematic illegal activity.

By the 1980s, it was clear that gangsters from every racial and ethnic origin were involved in systematic criminal activity and that making organized crime synonymous with the Mafia was no longer viable. In 1983, President Ronald Reagan appointed Judge Irving Kaufman to chair a commission to investigate organized crime. The commission's stated intention was to investigate the power and activities of 'traditional organized crime' and 'emerging organized crime groups.'[11]

After three years' investigation of its identified problem areas of drugs, labour racketeering, money laundering, and gambling, the commission adapted Mafia mythology to a new age. It did so by repeated claims that although the Mafia had once been the dominant force in U.S. organized crime, it was now being challenged by several crime 'cartels' that were 'emerging' among Asian, Latin American, and other groups. As Gary Potter argues in *Criminal Organizations* (1994), this was an adaptation of the alien-conspiracy interpretation rather than an overhaul in official thinking about organized crime. The argument remained the same: forces outside of mainstream American culture threaten otherwise morally sound American institutions. Potter describes the new official consensus as the 'Pluralist' revision of the alien-conspiracy interpretation (Potter, 1994: 7).

Despite the evidence of continuing failure, the commission did not challenge the essential correctness of the law enforcement approach to organized crime control – based, as it was, on long-term investigation, undercover operations, informants, wiretaps, and asset forfeiture. It's a strategy best described as a 'rat-trap' strategy – criminal justice becomes like those 1930s experiments where psychologists built labyrinthine traps for rats, to learn whether or how soon they can get out of them (Strolberg, 1940: 140–7).

Throughout the hearings, successes against the Mafia and the need to 'stay in front' of the emerging 'cartels' were emphasized. In sum, the commission concluded that the government's basic approach to the problem was sound but needed a harder line on all fronts: more wiretaps, informants, and undercover agents in order to get more convictions, which, in turn, would require more prisons. And, more assets had to be forfeited to help pay for at least some of this. Witnesses who might have pointed out the deficiencies of this approach were not consulted.

By the 1980s, however, Americans saw organized crime as groups of separate and distinct gangsters rather than organized crime as the more fluid, varied, and integrated phenomenon portrayed by the earlier commentators. The commission therefore did not consider corruption within the business or criminal justice systems or unworkable laws as part of the problem of organized crime, and by the 1980s they did not have to – people had been conditioned to ask the wrong questions.

Shortly after the Kaufman Commission issued its final report, the first of a long series of scandals involving massive fraud in a large number of newly deregulated savings and loan institutions began to attract some attention. By the end of the 1980s, many of these institutions had collapsed, and it cost the American taxpayer an estimated $153 billion to bail out insolvent thrifts. Only a few commentators made the point that it all could have been avoided by rigorous regulation; many more were claiming that business regulation was burdensome and should be avoided at all costs. The extent of the fraud amounted to organized crime on a heroic scale among mainly respectable American business people, yet it was not recognized as such. This was partly because that would have suggested that deregulation was wrong, and by then deregulation had been elevated to the status of an almost incontestable truth (Calavita and Pontell, 1993; Calavita and Pontell, 1991: 94; Galbraith, 1992: 61, 179–80; Slapper and Tombs, 1999: 189).

By highlighting the Mafia and other supercriminal organizations, American opinion makers ensured that people's perception of organized crime was as limited as their own. The constant speculation, hyperbole, preaching, and mythmaking had served to confuse and distract attention away from failed policies, institutional corruption, and much systematic criminal activity that was more costly, damaging, and destructive than 'Mafia' crimes. The mistake that has always dogged U.S. organized crime control efforts was the misperception that organized crime was composed of conspiratorial entities that were alien to and distinct from American life.

Organized Crime and the Dumbing of Global Discourse

While the United States was constructing an organized crime control framework that did not control systematic illegal activity, U.S. influence was helping to ensure that most countries fell into step with an international prohibition-based drug control regime built around the framework established by U.N. conventions. The 1961 Single Convention on Narcotic Drugs, the 1971 Convention on Psychotropic Substances and the 1988 Convention against Illicit Traffic in Narcotic Drugs and Psychotropic Substances were all established as a result of intense and long-term U.S. pressure. The United Nations itself, as David Bewley-Taylor (1999: 7) has concluded, now 'promotes and perpetuates the American prohibitive approach to drug control, while simultaneously legitimizing unilateral skirmishes in the United States's overseas fight against drugs.'

But the war on drugs, by the United Nations' own admission, has failed. According to recent U.N. estimates, coca cultivation has doubled since 1985, and drug prices generally have fallen sharply.[12] And, as several money-laundering scandals have shown, the massive profits available from the distribution as well as production of illegal drugs have encouraged the development of significant international criminal associations and networks among professionals such as lawyers and accountants, corrupt officials, career criminals, and simple opportunists.

The violence and corruption that have accompanied the global prolif-eration of networks involved in the drug trade since the 1961 U.N. convention brings to mind Chamberlin's 1931 warning that the inten-tions of American idealists may have supplied 'the pavement for the hell of organized crime' (Chamberlin, 1931–1932: 669). By the post–Cold War era, however, American idealists were setting the interna-tional agenda and could not countenance conceptualizations of organized crime that implied a critique of American laws and institu-tions. On the contrary, they needed the international community to accept a conceptualization of organized crime that both excused the failure of national and international efforts against drugs and justified the expansion of these efforts. American politicians, government offi-cials, journalists, and academics thus sought ways to reduce the world's complexities to the same type of good-versus-evil propositions that had served so well during the Cold War. The menace of transnational or global organized crime not only helped explain away the failure in the drug war but was as easy to communicate as the Cold War policy of containing the worldwide spread of Communism.

At a Washington, D.C., conference in September 1994, high-level American law enforcement and intelligence community personnel led the way in internationalizing America's pluralist revision of the Mafia conspiracy theory. They began to propagate a very simple idea. Because forces outside of mainstream national cultures now threatened national institutions everywhere, American organized crime control techniques should be employed everywhere. These techniques were necessary to combat what the conference title referred to as 'Global Organized Crime: The New Empire of Evil.'

According to the executive summary of the conference, 'The dimen-sions of global organized crime present a greater international security challenge than anything Western democracies had to cope with during the cold war. Worldwide alliances are being forged in every criminal field from money laundering and currency counterfeiting to trafficking in drugs and nuclear materials. Global organized crime is the world's fastest growing business, with profits estimated at $1 trillion.'

The keynote speaker at the conference, FBI director Louis Freeh, stressed that 'the ravages of transnational crime' were the greatest long-term threat to the security of the United States' and warned that the very fabric of democratic society was at risk everywhere. CIA director R. James Woolsey followed up this line by noting that 'the threats from organized crime transcend traditional law enforcement concerns. They affect critical national security interests ... some governments find their authority besieged at home and their foreign policy interests imperiled abroad.'[13] This new global threat of organized crime required a tougher and more collaborative international response. More specifically, it required more thorough information sharing between police and intelligence officials in different countries and improved methods of transcending jurisdictional frontiers in pursuing and prosecuting criminals (Naylor, 1995: 38).

Two months after the Washington conference, the United Nations held the World Ministerial Conference on Organized Transnational Crime and provided an international forum for the global pluralist theory of organized crime. The conference was held in Naples and attended by high-level governmental representatives from 142 countries. The rhetoric and analysis were essentially the same as those employed by Freeh and Woolsey. According to the U.N. press release, participants at the conference recognized the growing threat of organized crime, with its 'highly destablizing and corrupting influence on fundamental social, economic and political institutions.' This represented a challenge demanding increased and more effective international cooperation. 'The challenge posed by transnational organized crime,' the document continued, 'can only be met if law enforcement authorities are able to display the same ingenuity and innovation, organizational flexibility and cooperation that characterize the criminal organizations themselves.'[14] Essentially, this was the same line that had been articulated by American politicians from the 1950s onwards.

All the speakers, including U.N. secretary general Boutros Boutros-Ghali, echoed the same themes: the threat posed by organized crime to societies and governmental institutions around the globe and the need for more international cooperation to meet this threat. The seriousness of the perceived threat was emphasized in the language of many of the speeches. For example, Elias Jassan, secretary of justice in Argentina, described organized crime as 'a new monster ... the Anti-State,' and Silvio Berlusconi, Italy's prime minister, described crime organizations as 'armies of evil' that could be defeated 'only by international collaboration.'[15]

U.S.-approved organized crime control strategies were emphasized by most speakers, and this deferential consensus was most clearly reflected in another background document for this conference that singled out 'the 1970 Racketeer Influenced and Corrupt Organizations' (RICO) statute as an example of 'dynamic' legislation able to 'adapt itself to ... developments.' The document then elaborated as follows: 'In the United States, the RICO statute is generally considered to be the starting point of a new process of awareness of organized crime by the United States Government and its criminal justice system. Its effectiveness has been demonstrated in the many indictments and convictions of members of organized crime groups that have resulted since the legislation was passed' (United Nations Economic and Social Council, 1994).

Western governments had been clearly moving towards the American organized crime control model even before the conference. To those others that were lagging behind, President Bill Clinton issued this warning in October 1995: 'Nations should work together to bring their banks and financial systems into conformity with the international money laundering standards. We will work to help them do so. And, if they refuse, we will consider appropriate sanctions.'

He called for a joint declaration on international crime, including a 'no sanctuary' clause to facilitate extradition, 'so that we could say together to organized criminals, terrorists, drug-traffickers and smugglers: You have nowhere to run and nowhere to hide.'[16] Clinton was clearly demanding that the global organized crime control model come into line with the American organized crime model as soon as possible.

Such ambitions will undoubtedly become more of a reality if and when the United Nations Convention against Transnational Organized Crime is ratified, and it is hoped that this will happen in 2003.[17] The purpose of this convention, according to Article 1, its statement of purpose, is 'to promote cooperation to prevent and combat transnational organized crime more effectively.' The convention defined an 'organized crime group,' as 'a structured group of three or more persons existing for a period of time and having the aim of committing one or more serious crimes or offences established in accordance with this Convention in order to obtain, directly or indirectly, a financial or other material benefit ...'[18]

At the top of the list of serious crimes, according to an attachment to a draft of the convention, were the illicit traffic in narcotic drugs or psychotropic substances and money laundering, as defined in the United Nations Convention against Illicit Traffic in Narcotic Drugs and Psychotropic Substances of 1988 (United Nations, General Assembly, 1999: 52). When U.S. assistant secretary of state Rand Beers announced that the convention would go to the Senate for review and ratification in February 2001, he also made it clear that the new convention was a 'follow-on' to the 1988 drug convention. Thus, among other things, it was hoped that the convention would finally make global drug prohibition effective.

The Naples speeches and the language used in the making of the transnational organized crime convention demonstrate that the American understanding of organized crime is now shared globally.

As in the case of the Mafia conspiracy theory and its American pluralist offspring, some evidence does support the global pluralist theory articulated at the Washington and Naples conferences. No one disputes the existence of gangster groups all over the world, some of which are powerful and durable. Enough serious research has been conducted in the United States and elsewhere to reveal at least some of the ways various Triads, Mafiosi, Camorrista, and other groups have survived and adapted to enforcement efforts and more frequent periods of competitive bloodletting. More recent groupings of Colombian and Mexican drug traffickers and outlaw bikers have proved just as likely to use violence and intimidation in the pursuit of business activities that are often in themselves damaging and destructive.[19]

There are, however, problems with the global pluralist theory of organized crime that render it practically useless as an analytical tool in any serious effort to understand and combat the problem. To begin with, Mafia-type groups only participate in illegal markets; they rarely, if ever, control them, despite countless claims to the contrary. Instead, as most conscientious researchers have noted, fragmentation and competition characterize drug and other illegal markets, not monopolization.[20] Looking at the European situation, Vincenzo Ruggiero and Nigel South found, for example, that flux is the norm in illegal markets, which 'seem populated by small firms, some of which are peripheral and ephemeral, in a highly mobile and active scenario' (Ruggiero and South, 1995: 86). Peter H. Smith's recent study of the situation in Mexico found larger operations but more rivalry than coordination among drug-trafficking syndicates. Leaders in these syndicates 'have little connection with (or respect for) counterparts in other organizations – they are ruthless and relentless, and they readily resort to violence' (P.H. Smith, 1999: 199).

While those who advocate variations of the global pluralist theory of organized crime emphasize ethnicity, hierarchical organization, centralized control, and expansionist tendencies as characteristics of criminal organizations, more thoughtful scholars emphasize opportunity. Groups in Italy, Colombia, and Mexico became significant participants in transnational organized crime only in response to an upsurge in demand for prohibited drugs in the United States and other Western countries from the late 1970s. Some of these have made attempts to set up operations in other countries, but this does not amount to the gigantic global conspiracy identified by writers such as Jeffrey Robinson in *The Merger: The Conglomeration of International Organized Crime*, published in 2000. Anthony P. Maingot's study of Caribbean criminal enterprises is more convincing on the issue of criminal group expansion. He notes that Colombian traffickers did make an attempt to set up subsidiaries in the Dominican Republic in the 1990s, but stresses that local criminals soon became independent of the Colombians and set up their own smuggling, transporting, and wholesaling enterprises. The situation in the Dominican Republic, he writes, is one 'of decentralized and localized gangs without hierarchy or enduring central control, opportunistically engaging in whatever conspiracies are necessary to carry on the lucrative business' (Maingot, 1999: 164).[21]

Governments, whether individually or jointly, would have few problems combating organized crime if it really were dominated by a relatively small number of supercriminal organizations. They would eliminate the leadership of these organizations, and that would be the end of the problem. However, as the Americans have found, orchestrating the downfalls of Al Capone, Lucky Luciano, Tony Salerno, John Gotti, and the rest did not see the end of the messy reality of American gangsterism, let alone the much more pervasive and multifaceted problem of organized crime.

Another problem with the global pluralist theory is that, like the Mafia conspiracy theory, it uses semantics to camouflage the involvement of respectable institutions in organized criminal activity. Throughout Boutros-Ghali's speech in Naples, for example, the implication was always that respectable institutions were threatened by organized crime. Organized crime, he said, 'poisons the business climate'; it 'corrupts political leaders'; it 'infiltrates the State apparatus.' Understood in this way, the only response to the organized crime 'forces of darkness' is a harmonized international effort on behalf of 'legitimate society.'[22] However, as a great deal of historical and contemporary research shows, key 'legitimate' institutions, such as corporations, have frequently gained from and sometimes helped to sustain organized crime.[23]

The history of U.S. organized crime itself demonstrates the inadequacy of global pluralist analysis, as doubtless could the history of organized crime in any of the hundred-plus countries whose representatives have signed the U.N. convention. Organized criminal activity was never a serious threat to established or evolving economic and political power structures in the United States but more often a fluid, variable, and open-ended phenomenon that complemented rather than conflicted with those structures.

A final problem with the global pluralist theory is the oft-repeated implied or stated assumption of its adherents that American organized crime control methods are the answer to transnational organized crime. In a recent overview essay on transnational organized crime, Rensselaer W. Lee, III, reflected the conventional wisdom on the success of U.S. organized crime control when he wrote that 'The United States has largely contained or marginalized its organized crime problem' (Lee, III, 1999: 11). Bruce Swartz, deputy assistant attorney general in the administration of George W. Bush, similarly implied U.S. superiority in the field in an article entitled 'Helping the World Combat International Crime.' He noted the deficiencies of police and judicial systems in other countries, their 'vulnerability to criminal groups,' and U.S. efforts 'to improve the criminal justice capacities of other governments ... helping their police forces, prosecutors, and judges become more effective crime fighters' (Swartz, 2001). However, there is a great deal of evidence that contradicts such judgments. Rackets of every variety continue to proliferate at every level of American society. Countless scandals have indicated that the bribe and the fix are still features of the American criminal justice system. The problem of police corruption is as acute as ever, as evidenced by the recent scandal in the Los Angeles Police Department, where officers in the Ramparts division were using prostitutes to sell drugs. Even inside the prisons, gangs compete for commercial dominance in systems based on corruption and brutality. In sum, after decades of intense effort against gangsters, U.S. organized crime control measures have done little to control organized crime activity in either legal or illegal markets. Since the 1970s, undercover policing operations, witness-protection programs, and asset forfeitures have made U.S. organized crime problems more complex, but they have not come close to solving or 'marginalizing' them.

At the Naples conference, every speaker represented a nation with a great deal of dirty linen to conceal. The American concept of organized crime as a threat to legitimate society gave all of them a way of formulating organized crime control policy without examining past and current evidence of government, corporate, or professional involvement in systematic criminal activity. And so they were happy to go along with the construction of a giant labyrinthine trap for rats to learn whether or how soon they can get out of it.

The U.S. 'rat-trap' organized crime control strategy of targeting and immobilizing specific criminals or criminal networks has already been successfully exported to many parts of the world and will continue to provide successes for diligent policing and prosecuting agencies. This will certainly ensure sensational arrests and convictions of major international crime figures. The 'rat-trap' strategy will, however, be as inadequate in addressing the problems of international organized crime in the twenty-first century as it has been in the United States during the twentieth century.

Rather than reduce organized crime analysis to the sets of stereotypes and frozen images that have clouded American perceptions of serious criminal activity throughout the twentieth century, the international community might learn more from the American experience of the 1930s. During this decade, government action not only ensured the conviction of large numbers of gangsters and at least some of their political protectors, but, more significantly, it also reduced the opportunities for successful organized criminal activity. In 1933, the repeal of the Prohibition amendment almost immediately ended the exploitation of the liquor industry by gangsters, and there was no sudden upsurge in alcohol-related problems. In the same year, the administration of President Franklin D. Roosevelt announced a New Deal for the American people and began an intense period of legislative and executive activity. Roosevelt's reforms saw a decline in the corporate employment of gangsters in labour–management disputes and made large-scale fraud, tax evasion, and embezzlement more difficult and risky. Unfortunately for Americans, there has been little similar government wisdom since the 1930s. On the contrary, counterproductive wars on gambling and drugs have been pursued, and, particularly since the 1980s, business activity, including criminal business activity, has been set free from the burdens of government regulation. The large-scale larceny that characterized savings and loan institutions during the Reagan era, for example, was made possible by the Garn–St Germain Depository Institutions Decontrol Act of 1982 (Hagen and Benekos, 1992: 24). More recently, the deregulation of the telecommunications industry has been accompanied by fraud on a similarly epic scale (Hutton, 2001).

The international community's understanding of the problem of organized crime is based on an analytical framework that only serves to justify unworkable laws governing personal behaviour, and avoids facing the consequences of an overenthusiastic approach to the deregulation of business. There are ways of limiting illegal markets, and controlling illegal behaviour in legal markets, but these do not gel with an American ideology that dominates current global discourse. The United Nations Convention against Transnational Organized Crime is therefore unlikely to reduce significantly the costly and destructive impact of organized crime in all its many and varied forms.

Notes

1 New York Society for the Prevention of Crime, *Annual Report*, 1896, quoted in Paul W. Rishell and Albert E. Roraback (n.d.: 29).

2 Howard Crosby, the first director of the Society for the Prevention of Crime, for example, wrote an article for the *North American Review* in 1883 called, 'The Dangerous Classes.' Crosby concluded that 'the rich and powerful classes in the community' had made and maintained 'a system of plunder and oppression of the poorer classes and of the public generally' (348).

3 Quoted in Rishell and Roraback (n.d.: 21).

4 Quoted in D.C. Smith (1991: 138–42).

5 For details of these scandals see Woodiwiss (1988: 90–4).

6 Hereafter called the Kefauver Committee.

7 Kefauver Committee, *Hearings*, Moretti Testimony, Part 7, 334, 348.

8 Moore's book is indispensable to all students of the Kefauver Committee.

9 For a full discussion of the background to the Organized Crime Control Act, see Block and Chambliss (1981: 193–217). Levy quoted in Pizzigati (1976).

10 For edited versions of wiretap transcripts from the Salerno and Corrallo trials see Goode (1988).

11 See President's Commission on Organized Crime, *Hearing 1, Organized Crime: Federal Law Enforcement Perspective* (1983).

12 Recent estimates quoted in Mark Tran (1998: 19). See also Paul B. Stares (1996).

13 Quotations taken from Raine and Cilluffo (1994: ix). FBI Director Freeh has

elsewhere defined organized crime as 'a continuing criminal conspiracy having a firm organizational structure, a conspiracy fed by fear and corruption.' Quoted in Stephens (1996).

14 See United Nations (1994a).

15 All quotations taken from United Nations (1994b).

16 President Bill Clinton, speech at the United Nations, 22 October 1995, quoted in *International Crime Control Strategy – June 1998*, available at *http://www.fas.irg/irp/offdocs/iccs/iccsv.html*.

17 A prediction that the convention would be ratified by 2002 was made in a speech by Pino Arlacci, the executive director of the United Nations Office of Drug Control and Drug Prevention in a speech to the International Conference on Strategies of the European Union and the United States in Combating Transnational Organized Crime, on 24 January 2001. Circulated by the United Nations Office of Drug Control and Drug Prevention. Retrieved from *http://www.undcp.org/speech_2001.01-24_l.html*.

18 The U.N. Convention against Transnational Organized Crime (Document A/55/383) is available on *http://www.odccp.org/palermo/theconvention.html*.

19 See, for example, Paoli (1998); Scott and Marshall (1998); Beare (1996).

20 See, for example, Adler (1985, 1993: 191); Reuter and Haaga (1989).

21 See also Federico Varese's perceptive review essay, 'Why the Mafia Must Have Home Cooking,' in the *Times Literary Supplement* (23 February 2001: 3–4).

22 See note 14.

23 See, for example, Pearce (1976); Ruggiero (1996); Rawlinson (1998).

2 Predators, Parasites, or Free-Market Pioneers: Reflections on the Nature and Analysis of Profit-Driven Crime

R.T. Naylor

There is a perception, widely held among police, public, and politicians alike, that the world is being swept by an epidemic of profit-driven crimes.[1] Some are the work of traditional 'organized crime' groups; some are the work of emerging 'organized crime' groups; and some are the work of previously legitimate business people gone (temporarily?) astray. Some of these crimes are supposedly new; others are old but perpetrated with greater frequency and more lucrative results than previously. At the same time, profit-driven crimes, both new and old, whether committed by career criminals or bent entrepreneurs, supposedly have been rendered easier to perpetrate and more difficult to detect by modern technology and 'globalization.'[2]

The traditional criminal justice system seems quite unprepared to face these challenges. As a result, there are frequent calls for dramatic new investigatory and prosecutorial powers. These take the form, among others, of increased freedom for police to use illegal means in conducting undercover operations, measures to trace and seize the proceeds of crime, and laws to make membership in a criminal 'organization' a crime per se.

However, before rushing to the legislative barricades to grant such emergency powers for the war on crime, it might be appropriate to ask a few basic questions. For example, just what is the impact of this supposed epidemic of profit-driven crime? How clear is the frontier between profit-driven crime and normal economic activity? Is it really a matter of black and white or a continuum of varying shades of grey? To the extent that the line of demarcation is blurry, how should responsibility for detecting, deterring, and dealing with profit-driven crime be shared between the criminal justice system and the regulatory apparatus? And what other options are available?

To date, the answers have relied much too heavily on hysteria and hyperbole, myth and misinformation. The usual picture is one of the thin blue line forming a frail but steadfast defensive barrier to protect the innocence of civil society against the barbarian hordes. But the reality is a little more complex in terms of both the nature of the 'enemy' and the appropriate solutions.

Understanding Profit-Driven Crime

Much of the failure to comprehend the true impact of profit-driven crime, and therefore much of the danger of an inappropriate legislative and law-enforcement response, results from the fact that there has, to date, been little attention paid to what profit-driven offenders actually do and to the economic effects their actions actually have. Although all offences deemed criminal are treated under a uniform criminal code, this actually obscures major distinctions between them, and therefore also glosses over major complications in assessing impact and pin-pointing responsibility. It may also lead to excessive reliance on traditional criminal justice methods when, in fact, administrative or regulatory responses may be more apt. Indeed, it may also foster knee-jerk criminalization, even of matters that might best be left to civil courts to arbitrate.

The key lies in the fact that, although they are all treated just as criminal code offences, differentiated only by degree of 'seriousness' (which, by a remarkable circularity of logic, usually translates into how long the prescribed sentences are), there is a fundamental difference between three distinct forms of profit-driven crime. Some are predatory in that they cause involuntary transfers of wealth through force or guile; some are market-based, involving free-market exchanges of illegal goods and services for money between suppliers and willing customers; and some are commercial, in so far as they involve illegal production or distribution of legal goods and services. The traditional justice system, and in fact most criminological investigations, are premised on crimes that fall into the first, predatory, category in which there exists there are clearly defined victims and on which a broad social consensus that the underlying act is unacceptable. Today, however, more and more crimes fall into the second and third categories where the issues are far more complex, the morality is fuzzier, the victims are harder to define, and the anti-social consequences are much more subject to debate.[3]

Pioneers or Profiteers?

For one thing, social norms against certain types of behaviour should never be assumed to be invariable. Indeed, one of the main things plaguing the criminal justice system today is society's collective lack of historical memory. Opium trafficking, slave trading, and privateering (piracy under a national flag against ships of designated enemies) were, until quite recent times, much more likely to secure for their perpetrator a knighthood than a noose.[4] In medieval Europe, usury (simply lending at interest, regardless of the rate) was, much like drug trafficking today, more than a crime: it was a sin. Indeed, it still is in countries where Islamic law prevails. In the old Soviet Union, two of the most serious economic crimes were 'exploitation' and 'speculation' – that is, hiring labour outside the household and buying with intent to resell at a profit, things that are the essence of a capitalist economy.[5]

Today, prominent in the list of 'economic' crimes are violations of intellectual property laws. The United States pushes particularly hard for serious action by host countries to curb piracy of patents, trademarks, and industrial designs – apparently forgetting the degree to which its own industrial supremacy was built in the nineteenth and early twentieth centuries on deliberate copying of other countries' technology without accreditation or compensation.

Thus, it is misleading to assume that economic activities currently seen as criminal will always be so regarded. Someone viewed as a profiteering criminal by one set of people at one point in time might be viewed by others, or even by the original set at another point in time, as a pioneering entrepreneur. After all, many, if not most, of the business people who are leading the drive to a market economy in the former East Bloc were trained not in (then non-existent) business schools but in the black market. Suffice it to say that if, in the 1920s, U.S. Treasury agents manning the front lines in the booze war had been told that McGill University's Faculty of Management would someday operate out of the Bronfman Building, they would not have been amused.

So What's Wrong?

Clearly, once beyond the realm of simple predatory crimes involving involuntary (forced or duplicitous) redistribution of wealth, rights and wrongs become fuzzy. With market-based offences, that position is rendered especially awkward by the apparently willing participation of so many members of legitimate society, and by the fact that so much police activity involves interfering in decisions about personal moral choices.

This, in fact, can be gauged from the internal logic of the offences. With a predatory crime, both the act and the method are illegal, and the public has a clear understanding of the nature of the offence and the harm done. With market-based crimes, the act is illegal, though whether it should be is subject to debate, while the method is not, making the morality doubly debatable. With commercial crimes, involving the provision of legitimate goods and services in illegal ways, while they are always to be deplored in principle, they are often hard to define in practice. Except in the most blatant cases (the rare ones), it is very difficult to determine where sharp business practice ends and fraud begins. (All advertising involves a con job – if people really needed or wanted the stuff, it would not be necessary to pour so much time, effort and money into coaxing them into acquiring it.) And there is the additional complication that sometimes the general public, not to mention juries and perhaps some law enforcement officers and judges, do not understand just what the offence really is.

Granted, surveys have shown that the public seems to view some market-based offences such as heroin trafficking as high up on the 'seriousness' scale (though considerably below most crimes of violence), with sellers ranked as much more reprehensible than buyers.[6] However, not only should criminal justice not be a function of public-opinion polls, but also it can be argued that much of the public ranking is due to a misunderstanding of the nature of the offence. The public view, fed by the mass media and by police stereotypes, is that heroin traffickers, for example, are members of great crime cartels dripping filthy lucre, while heroin users are sorry victims. In fact, the supply side is characterized by loose networks of opportunistic dealers, few of whom make serious money. On the demand side, while heroin is certainly addictive, it is not inevitably and automatically so – there are considerably more casual than habitual users. To the extent that heroin use flourishes among the socially marginalized, it is not clear of whom they are victims – the dealer or the society. Then, too, there is the morass of attempting to explain to a detached observer just why certain drugs are legal while others are banned – it often seems to come down to whether or not someone has managed to get a trademark for them. But even in that case, it should never be forgotten that 'heroin' is actually a brand name for a cough medicine, widely endorsed by the medical profession and mass marketed by Bayer before the opiate bans early in the twentieth century.[7]

Moreover, with a predatory offence, the victim takes the initiative in counteraction, and the victim, along with most other citizens, can be expected to cooperate fully with the police. In a market-based offence, the police take the initiative, and the public response might be indifferent or even hostile. Even worse, there is an expectation (even if in practice it turns out to be impossible to fulfil) that each and every predatory offence will be investigated. In market-based crimes, since those who buy are really as guilty as those who sell, there are so many 'guilty' parties that the police are necessarily selective about whom to target. The choice can often be arbitrary and capricious, further debasing police actions in the minds of the general public. Not least, police actions are often ineffective, since they go after only the most visible and vulnerable, who are also the most easily replaced components of the trafficking networks, leaving the illicit market operating largely unscathed.

Whose Business Is It?

Even within North America, the creation of modern market-based offences was scarcely free from controversy. During the nineteenth century, most governments accepted the sensible notion that personal vice was the business only of the person with the vice, thereby excluding from the criminal code a whole host of offences that would later be incubators of modern 'organized' crime. Not only was personal vice a matter left to individual consciences, but the business of satisfying it, although regarded as on the shady side of the enterprise spectrum, was mainly legal. Even when laws proscribing such behaviour existed, they were rarely enforced. As a result, major cities had their red-light districts where perfectly respectable citizens could enjoy gambling, narcotics, and the services of prostitutes. The role of the law enforcement apparatus was not to police the supply of and demand for the means to satisfy personal vice but to guard against any possible anti-social results and to ensure that, whatever criminal consequences followed, they did not spill over into 'respectable' neighbourhoods.

Then, in the early twentieth century, North America was swept by a wave of puritanism made up of several components: emerging female political organizations whose first important manifestation was the temperance movement; a resurgence of support for small-town 'decent' values as a bulwark against big-city cosmopolitan decadence; Anglo-Saxon racism (blacks were associated with cocaine, Mexicans and 'Hindoos' with cannabis, Orientals with opiates, and the Irish with alcohol); and, not least, a movement to disenfranchise immigrant voters by closing the saloons, which functioned as working-men's political clubs.[8]

These political currents were compounded by another. The U.S. Constitution seemed drastically to curtail federal law enforcement powers. Policing serious predatory crime was the preserve of the states. Hence, to assert its presence, the federal government had to find another field of competence. Bolstered by Supreme Court rulings stating that the federal government had the right to regulate everything it had the right to tax, the assertion of federal authority took the form of the regulation, taxation, and prohibition of certain goods and services – in effect, the very creation of the category of market-based crime. Recreational drugs, prostitution, gambling, and even alcohol were criminalized and federalized. Canada and much of the Western world followed the American lead, albeit usually with less intensity.

There were several consequences. One was the extinction of the old red-light districts. Henceforth, the business of supplying and demanding personal vice ceased to respect intra-urban frontiers. Indeed, the criminalization of supply meant that criminal entrepreneurs had to mix deliberately with polite society to lower their profile. A second was the creation of a class of wealthy criminals who could use the profits resulting from criminalization of personal vice to penetrate legitimate parts of the economy. A third was the emergence of a view of 'organized crime' that saw the vice trade as the result of an alien conspiracy, a view that continues to misinform debate to this day.

Who Done It?

With predatory crimes, the popular presumption is that the great majority are the work of individuals or, at worst, gangs, which are regarded, and treated under law, as merely aggregations of individuals. However the rise of market-based offences is inevitably associated in the public (and police) mind with 'organized crime.' This involves applying to a group the notion that the whole is larger than the sum of the parts, with the further proviso that it should be so treated in law. Although members of 'organized crime' groups are quite capable of episodic predatory actions, what seems to produce a compelling need to 'organize' is the fact that market-based offences require a continuous supply of goods and services and, by virtue of being exposed on an ongoing basis, also require an organized interface with police and politicians to ensure protection.

This view seems to justify two legal departures. One is harsher punishments to members of an 'organized crime' *group* than would be received had an *individual* been charged with the same offence. This, in effect, creates two classes of offenders, differentiated not by what they do but by who they are. The second is to make membership in proscribed organizations an offence per se. At that point, association rather than action becomes the crime.

If predatory offences involve gangs defined as merely the sum of their individual members, and market-based ones involve 'organized crime groups' with a collective existence that is more formal than that of a mere gang, commercial crimes are frequently associated with the highest form of collective existence, in which the whole is not merely greater than but qualitatively distinct from the sum of the parts. At this point, the concept emerges of the 'corporate criminal,' a reference not just to individual executives or managers but to the corporate body itself.

The stereotype is correct in one respect – most predatory crimes are the work of individuals or ad hoc groups with no permanence. However, with respect to 'organized crime,' it is seriously flawed. Debate often conflates two quite distinct things – a criminal association and an association of criminals. Time after time, too, serious research has shown that, to the extent that 'organized crime' groups actually exist, they are not economic but political and social in nature. They form a kind of underground government to adjudicate disputes and allocate property rights. But once the rules are set, each individual member operates alone or in partnership with others who may or not be members of the group.

By the same token, criminal markets are not based on hierarchical administrative structures operating on command to monopolize a market, but on loose and ad hoc networks engaged in arms-length commercial transactions. Furthermore, when fact replaces myth, the notion of huge amounts of criminal profit waiting to take over the commanding heights of the legal economy in order to corrupt its functioning also stands repudiated. Some criminals are rich, but most seem to have modest incomes; and when they do invest in the legal sector, they seem more likely to put their money into a registered retirement savings plan than to stage a fraudulent bankruptcy.[9]

Nor does the concept of 'corporate crime' fare much better. There are seemingly intractable problems with defining a corporate *mens rea*, difficulties in determining whether it makes sense to permit jury trials for corporate offences, disputes about whether normal protections afforded to persons facing prosecution should be extended to corporations, and, indeed, a great debate over whether it is even possible for a corporate crime to exist independently of the actions of managers and executives. When it comes to actually meting out punishment, there are even more problems. For an individual, apart from fines, the criminal justice system can impose punishment in the form of loss of liberty or, in some jurisdictions, loss of life. If a corporation is deprived of loss of liberty, its charter is suspended and it is almost inevitably driven to bankruptcy, a punishment that seems to fall as much on shareholders and creditors as on the executives whose decisions were responsible. If a corporation is deprived of life, in the sense of having its right to operate permanently repudiated, the same results clearly follow. Therefore, almost all corporate punishment takes the form of fines. But they, too, fall on the general shareholders, who are powerless, and the executives who made the decisions that led to the charges are almost always indemnified.[10]

A Helping Hand?

There is another form of crime associated with corporations that seems, on the surface, easier to handle – the case where a corporation, or its executives, cooperates with career criminals to advance their joint interests. Take, for example, the notorious case of Ford Motor Company during the 1930s. In the Great Depression, automobile sales in general were sagging, while Ford's main competitors, General Motors and Chrysler, were challenging its traditional industry lead. Survival required cutting costs. And that required both reducing wages and accelerating the pace of work on the assembly lines – at a time of rising labour militancy. Fortunately, help was on hand.

In the past, Henry Ford had been a pioneer in hiring the underprivileged and handicapped. Ford also articulated a philosophy that ex-convicts deserved a second chance, and took them on by the thousands as blue-collar workers. But what began in the 1920s as idealism was soon transformed in the 1930s into opportunism. Using Ford's high-level political contacts, prominent mobsters got early parole and were given supply concessions, management jobs, or distributorships. These served as both a legal source of income and as a cover for rackets. In exchange, they provided security. Partly their job was to protect the Ford family at a time of a wave of kidnappings. Partly it was to protect the Ford facilities from employee theft. But mainly it was to protect the Ford factories from union organizers and sympathizers, who were identified by undercover spies then harassed, beaten, or fired.[11]

It is true that Ford used criminal elements mainly for crude jobs involving muscle, threats, and intimidation. And he could have been prosecuted under existing laws if his political cover had not been so strong. However, when corporations go into partnership with criminals to commit commercial crimes, the lines are not so easy to connect. No better example exists than the situation that prevailed until recently (and to some extent still does) in the toxic-waste business.

For many decades, hazardous wastes were handled just like ordinary garbage. But after major scandals in the 1970s, governments began to toughen up. In the United States, for example, the government implemented a cradle-to-grave manifest system to monitor the movement of toxic, radioactive, poisonous, corrosive, or infectious wastes and to ensure that they were disposed of safely, at a cost many times that of ordinary garbage disposal. For key sectors of the economy, such as the oil, chemical, and pharmaceutical industries, this seemed like a major new regulatory burden. In fact, the regulatory structure was shaped largely to the demands of the chemical industries, which were intent on two things – to make sure there would be no interruption of production, and to guarantee that their liability would be kept under control. They had help.[12]

The trick was to turn the wastes over to licensed disposal companies who would pick up the hazardous material, charging the producing corporations much more than the fee for ordinary garbage but less than the cost of proper disposal. Then they would haul it to a landfill site where the owner would sign off on the manifest. At that point, the companies producing the waste were in the clear. As to the ultimate destination, some of the hazardous waste would be buried with ordinary garbage, while other parts of it were dumped in rivers, down municipal sewer systems, or onto country roads; left stacked in corroding barrels in vacant lots, empty warehouses, or abandoned tractor-trailers; or, even better, mixed with clean petroleum products and sold off as home heating oil, gasoline, or diesel fuel. If and when someone identified the stuff, it was very difficult – often impossible – to trace it back to the company of origin. And if anyone went looking for the disposal company, there was a fair chance that it had already gone bankrupt and that the principals had vanished.[13] It was also the disposal company or its owners, not the corporation that generated the waste, that took the blame.

Partners in Crime?

Not only are the borders between crime and aggressive commerce often blurred, but also, in some cases, explicitly criminal acts and inherently legal ones are entwined in a matrix of economic activity to such a degree that the two, while theoretically distinct, are mutually interdependent.

Consider, for example, the situation that prevailed until recently (and to lesser extent still does) in the garment districts of major urban centres in North America. As a result of pressure from South-East-Asian manufacturers with unlimited supplies of cheap labour, sweatshops, long regarded as extinct in North America, underwent a dramatic resurgence in the 1980s.

Typically, they drew their labour from a number of sources: first-time entrants into the labour force whose lack of documentary history facilitated income-tax and social-security-charge evasion; moonlighters cheating unemployment-insurance agencies; welfare recipients working for cash on the side; and illegal aliens in a state of debt bondage to the gangs that had brought them over. Since the sweatshops often lacked collateral, they could not get working funds from the formal capital market. So some turned to loan sharks engaged in recycling money from drugs, gambling, or other criminal sources. If New York experience is a general guide, these small shops might also have had to pay extortion money to crooked trucking firms that signed sweetheart contracts with the owners at the truckers' expense.

Thus taxes were evaded, social-security charges unpaid, wages reduced, and regulations regarding working conditions brazenly ignored. What the workers lost in wages and benefits and the public sector in revenue turned up on the other side of the ledger as increased profit. Mobsters took their share in the form of usurious interest charges, payoffs from trucking companies, kickbacks from suppliers, extortion payments from manufacturers, and the occasional extra such as the profits from the smuggling of illegal aliens or the privilege of putting an associate or relative on the payroll. Meanwhile, the output (strictly legal) was sold to respectable fashion companies and big department stores who had subcontracted to the sweatshops. These legitimate firms took their share in the form of increased corporate net income resulting from reduced supply costs. Without their active participation, none of the explicitly illegal earnings would have been possible.[14]

Subcontracting Responsibility

When such interrelations occur, it is often difficult for the justice system to allocate responsibility fairly. Seemingly respectable businesses maintain sufficient distance from the explicitly illegal acts of which they are clearly and consciously beneficiaries so that they cannot be judged legally culpable.

Tobacco smuggling provides an example of this problem that has recently received attention. Canada was apparently shocked to discover that its major tobacco producers deliberately set up subsidiaries abroad to link up with career smugglers who would bring cigarettes back into Canada to be sold on the black market and therefore expand total tobacco sales in the face of steadily rising taxes. Yet, in retrospect, what has to be explained is not the apparent unscrupulousness of the tobacco companies but the naïveté or timidity of the Canadian authorities.

Since the Second World War, cigarettes have been the most widely smuggled commodity on the planet.[15] To this day, one cigarette out of every three entering world trade disappears from sight. In total about 300 billion cigarettes per year seem to get smoked by the man-in-the-moon. Around the world, the story is the same. The tobacco companies ship *en masse* to what are euphemistically called 'free-trade' centres and sell the cigarettes, often on credit, to wholesalers. They in turn hire or sell to career smugglers who move the merchandise into the target country, along with loads of whisky, weapons, electronics, and American brand-name jeans. Since any sensible smuggler wants a two-way flow of cargo, on the return leg the small boats or planes typically carry everything from cocaine to illegal immigrants.[16]

Nor does the complicity of the tobacco companies stop there. It was common in places where the Anglo-American tobacco companies were forbidden to sell for them none the less to advertise heavily – to create a market for the merchandise they were supplying to the smugglers. And after smuggling undermined the solvency of national tobacco companies, the big Anglo-American firms were on hand to buy them up and, quite often, close them down, about the most outrageous example of predatory pricing imaginable.[17] This is a pattern begun in South America and subsequently repeated in South-East Asia and Eastern Europe. Yet to this day it is difficult to make a criminal case against the companies (as distinct from having the occasional executive hung out to dry). After all, they insist, they are not the ones who do the actual smuggling.

Diverting Attention

Yet another problem associated with more complex forms of profit-driven crime is the fact that treating them essentially as criminal justice issues, duly resolved when those directly responsible are fined or jailed, may give a false impression of what is really at stake. Take the example of the recent savings and loan bank crisis in the United States, where attention paid to a handful of crooks diverted attention away from the fundamental problem – a combination of serious structural malaise, bad political decisions, and profound weaknesses in the regulatory apparatus.

Historically created to use local savings to finance local housing development, particularly in small-town America, during the mid-to-late 1970s the savings and loan associations got into trouble. Population growth slowed, industrial depression blighted many small communities in the Northeast, and interest rates began to shoot up. As other institutions began offering high and rising interest rates, the savings and loans were drained of deposits, a predicament to which they had to respond by bidding up the deposit rate, while their loans, almost all in the form of long-term residential mortgages, yielded very low returns. Then came 'deregulation' to complete the disaster.[18]

The U.S. federal government decided that the solution lay in freeing the savings and loans to speculate in stocks, play the junk-bond market, and pump money into go-go commercial real-estate areas in the South and West. Simultaneously, it opened the door to the takeover of the industry by a virtual Who's Who of the era's most notorious corporate raiders, real-estate sharks, and bank-fraud artists, plus a smattering of gun-runners.[19]

In short order, the money was pumping with equal ease into empty shopping malls and brimming Cayman Island bank accounts. Every species of bank job figured in the action. There were bust-outs, in which insiders would siphon the money off into phony loans to confederates and then vanish. There were cash-for-dirt deals, in which loans would be made, nominally to finance development, yet actually to speculate on raw land. There were land flips, in which one piece of property was 'sold' back and forth among obliging institutions, with the apparent capital gains siphoned off by the architects of the scheme, leaving the bank eventually to foreclose on worthless collateral. There were linked financing schemes, in which deposit brokers brought in money only on condition that it was to be lent to designated borrowers, whatever their merits – which were, by definition, few or there would have been no need for the link deal. There were nominee loans, in which people, usually lawyers, stood in for the real borrowers, who did not meet minimum standards of credit-worthiness. All these and more became standard operating techniques in what was widely heralded (with considerable exaggeration) as the most expensive financial debacle in history.

In the wake of the collapse, public attention was riveted on high-profile prosecutions of a number of crooked financiers and developers. It was claimed that fraud figured in nearly 75 per cent of the hundreds of savings and loans that had failed. But the crooks who were pros-ecuted accounted directly for a few tens of millions of the hundreds of billions 'missing.' It would actually have been quite easy to find the rest of the 'missing' money. However, it would have been extremely diffi-cult to recover it, since there was nothing illegal involved. For the real problem was not criminality but regulatory failure, which permitted uncontrolled lending and wild speculation. And the main beneficiaries were not the crooks but apparently legitimate borrowers, mainly real-estate developers and construction tycoons, who were operating ac-cording to the deliberately fuzzy letter of selectively enforced law.

Precisely the same kind of problem emerges in the analysis of envi-ronmental crime. For a time it was popular to blame 'the mob' for illegal dumping. In some areas, the ordinary garbage business was already heavily infiltrated by people linked to 'organized crime' groups. They had the trucks, the municipal political clout, and landfill sites owned by themselves, associates, or people amenable to pressure or bribes. They also had the skill to fake manifests and hide the trail. This apparatus, so the argument went, could be readily adapted to a new vocation.

But, in fact, most illegal dumpers were ordinary entrepreneurs al-ready in the trade looking for a fast buck. They knew when inspectors were due, understood well how to disguise the nature of the material they were handling, and also were aware of which laboratories could be most easily induced to issue favourable readings. Furthermore, after the scandals and prosecutions of a few people who, naturally, had Italian surnames, the field was opened to the giant waste-disposal companies – which, in short order, ran up a list of almost all of the offences (bribery of officials, bootlegging tainted gasoline, midnight dumping, etc.) of which the 'organized crime' figures had stood accused.[20]

Thus, the real issue was not the prior existence of a social subset of 'career criminals' willing to apply their existing indifference to law to a new field. That belief served as a dangerous diversion. Rather, the real problem was the criminogenic properties of the industry and its regulatory environment. It was the cost-cutting antics of the chemical companies and the abject failure of the regulatory apparatus to keep it under surveillance that led previously legitimate business people, first, to cut the occasional corner, then, once their confidence and their greed grew, to make violations the norm rather than the exception.[21]

Whose Law? Whose Order?

Given the apparently insatiable urge of the authorities, prodded on by the public, to criminalize, the desire to end social harm easily begins to take second place to the wish to promote hidden agendas. That, at a minimum, makes judgment of success and failure difficult: at a maximum it creates groups with vested interests that will continue to drive a policy even if it seems to be a failure in terms of its avowed objectives.

Thus, it does little good to trot out facts showing that, in the United States – the main driving force for the worldwide 'war on drugs' – despite the hundreds of billions of dollars dissipated, despite the egregious dangers and evident damage to civil liberties, and despite the fact that the average black American male now has a 28 per cent chance of spending time in prison, nothing fundamental has changed on either the supply or the demand side of the drug equation. The reason is not because legislators and policy makers are impervious to facts, but because the 'war on drugs' has in some ways been a brilliant success, provided it is judged in terms of its impact on those constituencies who most benefit.

These constituencies include the military-industrial complex, which reacted to the end of the Cold War by offering services and hardware specifically tuned to the drug war; the intelligence establishment, which saw chasing criminals as a substitute for chasing 'Commies' in order to justify the continuation of a privileged existence; politicians, who prefer to blame 'crack' rather than the flight of industry and destruction of the public school system for the degradation of city cores; and police, who see in the drug war a tool to extract larger budgets and more arbitrary powers. It also included the emergent prison-industrial complex, whose appetite for profit can only be appeased by the construction of new incarceration facilities and the opportunity to fill them with new clientele.

The Law and Unintended Consequences

Another complication derives from the fact that, once beyond the simple, predatory forms of crime – that is, once the problem becomes something embedded firmly within the matrix of conventional economic activity – either by its nature or its magnitude, it may cease to be simply a law-enforcement problem and instead affect larger social, political, and economic variables. Take, as one example, the situation that prevailed in Jamaica during the *ganga* boom of the 1980s.

If, for example, the police in North America had ever been successful in putting an end to the sale of Jamaican *ganga* (marijuana), on the surface they would have solved a serious crime problem. They would have succeeded in taking away from gangs the profits of trafficking, therefore reducing inter-gang violence; and they might simultaneously have reduced any property crime related to the attempts of *ganga* 'addicts' to feed their habit.

But the story would not have stopped there. Deprived of a market, large numbers of Jamaican *ganga* farmers, many of them refugees from the previous collapses of bauxite and sugar, would have been driven out of business. They might have moved *en masse* into the urban slums, swelling an already enormous problem of urban crime that threatened both the country's social stability and its tourism industry, by far the most important source of legal foreign exchange. They would also have emigrated abroad in increasing numbers, joining the ranks of illegal aliens in North American cities and, along with them, the manpower of the exiled 'posses' that would compensate for loss of *ganga* profits by putting more energy into 'crack' and extortion.

Meanwhile, back in Jamaica, banks, drained of liquidity, would perhaps have been forced to cut back loans to legitimate businesses, depleting the country's exchange reserves and forcing it drastically to reduce imports of capital equipment necessary for economic growth. As a further possible consequence, loans extended to Jamaica by both Western commercial banks and international development agencies might have gone unserviced, and exports from other countries to Jamaica might have been slashed because of shortages of foreign exchange.

The possibility of such consequences makes it necessary to ask serious questions about the desirability of a law enforcement response to a complex socio-economic problem.

The Alternatives

When a profit-driven crime such as armed robbery takes place – involving redistribution of existing wealth through force (actual or implied) or deceit – the act, the cost, and the victim are easy to define; and standard methods of crime control will continue to take centre stage. But when a profit-driven crime such as trafficking in some restricted good or service or manipulation of the terms and conditions under which normal goods and services are produced and sold takes place, it usually does so as part of a complex of other, legitimate transactions. True, employee theft can be buried in the mass of normal business activities. But that simply makes the crime more difficult to detect without affecting any of the basic principles involved. When a corporation peddles goods with deceptive product guarantees, there may be a genuine difficulty, except in the most blatant cases, in determining at just what point it steps over the fuzzy border between aggressive marketing and an explicit con-job.

Thus, it is often difficult to be sure where the dividing line between the criminal and the entrepreneurial really is. Furthermore, when criminal activity and legitimate commerce act in mutually complementary ways, it is not always easy to bring to justice those most responsible. When an attempt is made to 'solve' such crime problems, there is a danger of setting off a host of unexpected social and economic consequences that may end up being more of a problem than the designated crime. When crimes involve apparently legitimate institutions used in an apparently illegitimate way, traditional criminal justice methods that focus on bad individuals present the additional danger of distracting attention from deeper causes, such as the need for profound structural and regulatory reform. It is precisely because so many crimes of a market-based or commercial nature involve complex interrelations with the legitimate economy, and can have profound, unintended, and unexpected consequences, that it may be unwise to rely on the criminal justice system alone (or in some cases at all) for their resolution. Even where a particular criminal activity can be isolated, law enforcement action may produce unexpected and costly feedbacks that may generate more crimes than they solve. These can be especially difficult to handle when they manifest themselves on an international scale.

Furthermore, the recent rush to criminalize, fed by the moral panic over a presumed epidemic of profit-driven crime, has led to a rash of new offences. For example, insider trading was first conceived as an offence involving officers of corporations about to merge who took advantage of that knowledge to speculate to their own profit. It was then extended to include employees of law firms planning mergers and acquisitions, merchant banks involved in financing them, reporters for financial newspapers who got leaks, and even janitors who picked up discarded memos in the trash. If any of them, or persons to whom they talked, used such information to anticipate stock price movements for their own gain, they were guilty of insider trading.[22] It thus became unclear just where the frontiers between 'inside information' and the normal search by potential investors for data on which to base a stock purchase really fell. Simultaneously, the core issue ceased to be breach of fiduciary duty and became simply obtaining profit that other people thought should rightfully be *theirs*, from correctly guessing stock price movements. This tendency to seek an ever-expanding mandate while blurring the central moral issues seems a danger inherent in all attempts to use the criminal code for purposes of economic regulation.

However, even if the offence of insider trading were redefined to accord better with its original mandate, its logic could still be open to question. Insider trading is not a predatory crime: it does not involve the forced transfer of property. It is not a market-based crime: the object of the exchange – securities – is perfectly legal. It is not even clearly a commercial crime: to trade on privileged information to capture the profits from market movements that take place for independent reasons is quite different from rigging the market to make it move in a particular direction. With insider trading there is no victim in the classical sense. What is at issue is not a contest between predator and victim over forcibly or fraudulently redistributed wealth but a quarrel between two sets of investors over distribution of profit. In the past (and in the bulk of instances also in the present), most such disputes were (are) left to the civil courts. It is difficult to avoid the suspicion that insider trading was criminalized not for moral but for ideological reasons – it was necessary to convince 'ordinary' investors, particularly at a time when more and more of the money was coming from pension funds and similar collective-investment institutions, that stock markets were something other than crap shoots rigged to benefit a favoured few.

For all these reasons, there is serious need to consider alternatives. These could include better use of the regulatory system, where an *actus rea* suffices to establish guilt while the offence does not lead to sending more people to the glorified crime-schools misrepresented as institutions of penance. It could include much more effective use of the fiscal system to take away the 'proceeds of crime' without trampling on civil rights or burdening the financial system with regulations of dubious efficacy. And it could include a more effective use of the civil courts – basically restoring to them the role of mediating between private parties in disputes about the distribution of wealth, many of which (like insider trading) have been recently criminalized.

Unfortunately, there are constant pressures on the criminal justice system to take on roles for which it has traditionally not been equipped. And, given the popular view that the world is facing a major threat in the form both of new crimes and of an enormous increase in the number and technological sophistication of old crimes, those pressures are likely to increase. Yet there is plenty of evidence that the extent of this so-called new, greatly expanded criminal problem has been exaggerated and that the real challenge is understanding the twilight zone where crime and business interact, often to their mutual benefit. That challenge is clearly one to which a traditional criminal justice system – created largely to deal with the involuntary redistribution of wealth by force and fraud – will always have trouble reacting.

Notes

This material was originally prepared for the Department of Justice in Ottawa as a backgrounder for a panel on emerging crimes of the twenty-first century. The author would like to thank officials of the Department of Justice for their comments and feedback, and for their kind permission to publish the paper in its present form. In particular, thanks are due to Morris Rosenberg, Richard Mosley, Valerie Howe, Paul Saint-Denis, and Stan Lipinski. In addition, the paper was greatly strengthened by comments and suggestions from Alan Block, Mike Levi, Nikos Passas, Francisco Thoumi, and Petrus van Duyne.

1 See, for example, the late Claire Sterling's (1994) *Crime without Frontiers: The Worldwide Expansion of Organised Crime and the Pax Mafiosa*. For a critique see Naylor (1995).

2 For a critique of this kind of techno-hype and the vague and largely useless 'globalism' concept, see Naylor (2002b), 'Introduction' in *The Wages of Crime*.

3 For a detailed analysis of the difference between these three categories, see Naylor (2003, forthcoming).

4 On privateering, see, for example, MacIntyre (1975) and Senior (1976).

5 See Naylor (1999a) and Naylor (2001: chapter 6).

6 See Tremblay, Cusson, and Morselli (1998). Even the concept of 'seriousness' should likely be interpreted differently, depending on the type of crime. With a predatory offence there is likely a wide *moral* consensus based on the act itself, with the sums involved being a secondary consideration, with market-based and commercial crimes, seriousness seems more directly a function of how much money is involved.

7 In addition to the titles cited above, counterculture works such as Morales (2000) and Escohotado (1999) raise some of these issues in an interesting way.

8 These developments are traced in Fox (1989). This is a fairly superficial history that depends heavily on recycling standard anecdotes but that none the less has sensible observations about the emergence of the puritan drive.

9 For an overview see Naylor (1997).

10 There is an enormously contentious literature dealing with the issue of 'corporate crime.' This debate started with the publication of Edwin Sutherland's (1949) *White Collar Crime;* was considerably elaborated in Christopher Stone's (1975) *Where the Law Ends: The Social Control of Corporate Behavior;* picked up steam in Marshall Clinard and Peter Yeager's (1980) *Corporate Crime;* and probably reached its peak with John Braithwaite's (1984) *Corporate Crime in the Pharmaceutical Industry.* Although there has been much literature since, the battle lines were essentially set – between legalists who saw the corporation as unable to commit crimes separate from those of its executives and those who argued for a distinct and collective corporate responsibility. On the notion of a corporate *mens rea* and the various permutations and combinations suggested, see Mokhiber, 1988: 23–4.

11 There are many works detailing the underside of the Ford story. Probably the most comprehensive is Robert Lacey's (1986) *Ford: The Man and the Machine.*

12 See Alan Block and Frank Scarpitti's (1985) *Poisoning for Profit: The Mafia and the Toxic Waste Business;* and Andrew Szasz's (1986) 'Corporations, Organized Crime, and the Disposal of Hazardous Waste: An Examination of the Making of a Criminogenic Regulatory Structure.'

13 Alternatively, the stuff could be shipped abroad and dumped in some developing country where officials were either corrupt or ignorant of the nature of the material, or where the country was too poor to turn down the dumping fees. See, for example, Third World Network (1989), *Toxic Terror: The Dumping of Hazardous Wastes in the Third World*; Jim Vallette (1989), *The International Trade in Wastes: A Greenpeace Inventory*; Center for Investigative Reporting (1990), *Global Dumping Ground: The International Trade in Hazardous Waste*.

14 See Block (1991) for a compilation of official documents and hearings on the resurgent sweatshop phenomenon.

15 This history is best described in E. Clark and Horrock (1973). See also chapter 12 of Timothy Green's *The Smugglers* (1969).

16 *Far Eastern Economic Review* (11 July 1991); *L'Express* (10 November 1994); *Inter Press Service* (10 March 1996); *New York Times* (26 August 1997). There is now a vast amount of information on the Web dealing with cigarette smuggling all over the world.

17 See Shepherd (1986, 1989).

18 There are a number of excellent works on the savings and loan (S & L) crisis. See, for example, O'Shea (1991); Pizzo, Fricker, and Muolo (1989); Adams (1990); Mayer (1990); and Calavita, Pontell, and Tillman (1997).

19 The weakest book on the S & L crisis, Pete Brewton's (1992) *The Mafia, CIA and George Bush: The Untold Story of America's Greatest Financial Debacle*, attempts to deal with this side of the story.

20 See Carter (1999).

21 See the reconsideration of the 'mob' role in Rebovich (1992).

22 For an examination of the Wall Street insider-trading scandals of the mid- to late 1980s, see Naylor (1997 and 1994). The publicity led to a series of copycat cases in other countries, along with a trend towards criminalization of something that had formerly been seen as a regulatory or civil matter.

3 From National to Global, from Empirical to Legal: The Ambivalent Concept of Transnational Organized Crime

Valsamis Mitsilegas

Introduction

The past decade has witnessed the domination of law enforcement, legal, and policy discourses worldwide by the concept of transnational organized crime. Its prioritization has led to the adoption of a multitude of legislative measures, both at national and EU/international levels, with the latest and perhaps most significant measure being the signing of the United Nations Convention against Transnational Organized Crime. The aim of this paper is to assess whether the evolution of these instruments is linked to a clear understanding and acceptable definition of the concept of transnational organized crime, a concept that, while widely discussed, has remained largely undefined, at least until recently. The analysis will assess the evolution of the term in various European countries, focusing in particular on the interaction of law enforcement, criminological, and legal definitions. It will highlight the existence of different national models for understanding and containing the issue, in view of the differences between nations in both the manifestations and magnitude of their organized crime activities and taking into account the diversity of their legal cultures and systems. The national models analysed are of importance as they demonstrate, on the one hand, early attempts in Europe to adopt a comprehensive approach to fighting organized crime (in the case of the Italian anti-Mafia legislation) and, on the other hand, the containment of the phenomenon by 'ordinary' criminal legislation in different legal systems (civil law in Germany and common law in England and Wales). The interaction of these models and their relevance for the development of a 'global' concept of organized crime will then be assessed in view of subsequent international initiatives in the field, which, as will be demonstrated, have to a great extent reproduced these national paradigms.

National Paradigms

Italy: 'Mirroring' Organized Crime in Law

The development of measures against organized crime in Italy is inextricably linked with the proliferation of Mafia and Mafia-type structures in various parts of the country. Already in 1963, the specialized Anti-Mafia Commission was established in response to the escalation of 'Mafia wars' in Sicily. The first major legislative initiative put forward by this all-party body was Law 575 of 31 May 1965 entitled 'Dispositions against the Mafia.' The law, which was the first to use the term 'Mafia,' extended 1956 legislation based on the concept of 'socially dangerous individuals' (Zeid, 1998: 520) to include those 'suspected of belonging to associations of a Mafia type, to the Camorra or to other associations whatever their local name, which pursue objectives or act with methods corresponding to those of Mafia associations.' Although no legal definition of a Mafia-type association was included, the law granted, *inter alia*, special surveillance powers and the possibility of judicial or police identification and freezing of assets belonging to a person suspected of involvement in a Mafia-type association, as well as the power to suspend licences, grants, and authorizations issued publicly. (For an extended analysis, see Jamieson, 2000: 16–23.)

Because of its terminological vagueness and its provisions obliging Mafia members to reside outside Sicily, thus giving them the opportunity to pursue action in different parts of the country, this law was of limited effect (Jamieson, 2000: 18). Until the end of its mandate in 1976, no further legislation was passed by the commission in this respect. However, its final report, published in 1976, identified the following trends in the development of organized crime:

> Organised crime's goal of wealth accumulation is achieved by forms of mediation, by parasitic infiltration, by the systematic use of violence and above all by contact with public power; ... notwithstanding the distinctions between the various clans that divide up territory and responsibilities, there exists a tacit agreement, a criminal structure which, in putting up an impenetrable wall to non-compromised authorities, operates for the support and protection of Mafia criminal activities: a criminal structure

which is not destroyed even by the cruel and ruthless struggles between the clans.' (cited in Jamieson, 2000: 19)

These observations did not influence legislative policy until the beginning of the 1980s. The 1970s witnessed the dramatic expansion of what was called 'the heroin Mafia,' an expansion that was aided in a sense by the emphasis of the Italian criminal policy on anti-terrorism measures, which were considerably prioritized in comparison to anti-Mafia legislation (Jamieson, 2000: 24). In response to that expansion, a draft law, including a definition of a Mafia-type association, was introduced in 1980. However, it was arguably the 1982 Mafia murders of one of its drafters, Pio La Torre, and of the Palermo prefect Alberto Dalla Chiesa, that prompted a swift legislative response in the field: Law 646 was passed on 13 September 1982, only ten days after the murder of Dalla Chiesa (Jamieson, 2000: 26–8).

Law 646, generally known as the Rognoni–La Torre law, was a landmark development to the extent that it modified the criminal code and introduced article 416*bis*, entitled 'Associazione di tipo mafioso,' or 'Mafia-type association.' It was one of the first international attempts to introduce the concept of an organized criminal association in criminal law. According to this new provision, a Mafia-type association consists of three or more persons, and 'those who belong to it make use of the power of intimidation afforded by the associative bond and the state of subjugation and criminal silence which derives from it to commit crimes, to acquire directly or indirectly the management or control of economic activities, concessions, authorizations or public contracts and services, either to gain unjust profits or advantages for themselves or for others.'

In view of a series of Mafia-linked political scandals that shook up the Italian political landscape in the late 1980s and early 1990s, this provision was amended in 1992 to add, in its conclusion, following the reference to the gain of unjust profits or advantages, the aim of 'preventing or obstructing the free exercise of the vote, or of procuring votes for themselves or for others at a time of electoral consultation.'[1]

It is evident that article 416*bis* constitutes an ambitious attempt to translate the social, economic, and political role of the Mafia into a workable legal provision. Starting with membership numbers (three or more), the article describes both the methods of operation of the association and its aims and purposes. Although the provision was systematically included in the 'public order' offences in the criminal code, it has been argued that it is exactly because of the distinct methods and aims of the Mafia-type associations that the provision is needed to protect much broader interests: one of the academic articles supporting the initiative stated that 416*bis* protects both the economic and the political order, focusing also on the protection of the efficiency and impartiality of public administration (Flick, 1988: 853). In furtherance of this argument, other views envisage 416*bis* as protecting interests as broad as personal liberty and tranquillity, highlighting thus the 'political dangerousness' of Mafia-type associations (Crespi et al., 1992: 906).

The special methods used by a Mafia-type association are deemed to distinguish them from common criminal associations, which are also proscribed by article 416 of the Italian criminal code. Central to this distinction are the use of intimidation and the existence of subjugation and criminal silence (*omertà*). Hence, according to Italian jurisprudence,

> The offence of Mafia-type association is characterized by a plural conduct of mixed nature, in the sense that, while for the simple criminal association it suffices to create a stable organization which is directed towards the commission of an indeterminate number of offences, for a Mafia-type, it is further necessary to have achieved within its close environment a real capacity to intimidate, of which its members avail themselves in order to execute their criminal program. (Cass., Sez. VI, 11.2, cited in Pisa, 1997: 546)

The association's power of intimidation is thus viewed as an instrumental part of its existence and an additional element distinguishing it from non–Mafia-type associations. However, no clear definitions of intimidation and its frequent companion, *omertà*, are provided. It has been accepted by the courts that both terms have to be broadly applicable, rather than defined narrowly (Crespi et al., 1992: 907; Pisa, 1997: 548). In the case of *omertà*, it has been accepted that it is 'sufficient' to identify it as a systematic refusal to cooperate with justice and that it is caused by fear of action linked to the Mafia threat (Pisa, 1997: 548–9). Intimidating force, on the other hand, has been broadly interpreted to include even verbal threats. More importantly, it is not necessary for this force to have been exercised, as, according to certain court rulings, it suffices for the association to be known to have the *capacity* of initiating terror, without necessarily doing so (Crespi et al., 1992: 907).

The broad conceptualization of Mafia-type associations is also reflected both in the enumeration of their aims and in the title of 416*bis*. The enumeration of aims is not cumulative, so that an organization having any of these aims would fall within the scope of the legislation. What is of importance here is that, if one goes beyond aims specifically related to the commission of crimes, some of the other aims, especially the economic ones, would appear perfectly legitimate if pursued by a lawful organization. The distinction between the legal and the criminal again rests primarily on the (broadly defined) intimidation criterion (Crespi et al., 1992: 912). The provision further applies to Mafia-*type* associations, with an aim to include structures of similar organizations using the same means, without further clarification (ibid.; Pisa, 1997: 558).

Article 416*bis* criminalizes the promotion, direction, and organization of a Mafia-type association. The *mens rea* of these offences consists in general of the willingness to take part in the association and the knowledge of its aims; and means of intimidation. More specifically, for the promotion one has to establish the willingness to 'give life' to the association and to achieve its aims; while for the direction/organization, the willingness to direct/organize in order to achieve the association's aims is sufficient (Crespi et al., 1992: 913).

More problematic is the criminalization by 416*bis* of the participation in a Mafia-type association. The courts have interpreted 'participation' in a variety of ways, at times under a very broad rubric. According to a recent ruling of the Corte Cassazione, for instance, 'the conduct of participation may, in fact, assume diverse forms and contents and consists of an appreciable and concrete contribution at the causal level to the existence or reinforcement of the association ... or the commission of an offence against the interests protected by this norm, whatever the role of participation within the ambit of the association' (Cass., Sez. II, 15.4, 1994, cited in Pisa, 1997: 579).

In view of the lack of clarity with regard to the level of contribution of a 'participant,' a debate has emerged regarding the distinguishing lines between participation and external complicity within the framework of 416*bis*. Following diverging views of different sections of the Corte Cassazione, the court's united criminal section ruled that while participation involves contributing on a daily basis to the life of the association, external complicity does not amount to membership but to a temporary 'external' contribution helping the association to get through a difficult, 'pathological' phase (Cass., Sez. I, 94/199386, cited in Caraccioli, 1998: 660). The difficulties in drawing a clear line here are evident.

In spite of these interpretive difficulties, the pioneering introduction of the 'Anti-Mafia' association concept in Italian criminal law has been lauded as a powerful weapon against organized crime, as it facilitated a series of prosecutions and convictions of Mafia members and leaders (P. Williams and Savona, 1996: 50–1) and was followed by the extension of prosecutorial and investigative powers in the field (Papa, 1993). At the same time, however, these authors admit that this piece of legislation was born out of emergency (ibid.). The introduction of article 416*bis* is a clear outcome of a securitization process, a response to the demand for the speedy adoption of measures to fight the Mafia at any cost. In this manner, resolving the problem of organized crime is attempted through a recourse to criminal law. As is pertinently noted, 'this phenomenon, reduced to a simple public order issue, forms the foundation of emergency legislation,' which is characterized *inter alia* by improvisation, chaos, repressive rigour, symbolism, and total absence of systematic coordination (Moccia, 1997: 140; see also Romano, 1985: 428).

The symbolic dimension of article 416*bis* becomes evident if one examines the relationship between its systematic introduction to the criminal code and its perception. As noted earlier, although the offence is included in the 'public order' offences, it is deemed to protect at the same time interests as diverse and broad as economic life, the sound functioning of public administration, and political life and the state in general. Various objections can be raised to the vagueness and all-embracing character of such aims, especially those related to the substance of the state (see Moccia, 1997: 141). Their uncritical introduction may amount to the legal enshrinement of a general duty of 'loyalty' to the state, thus infiltrating the criminal code with principles leading to the punishment of 'styles' of behaviour and ideology rather than actions.

The repressive potential of symbolic emergency criminal legislation is also reflected in the all-embracing and vague wording of 416*bis*. The attempt to translate into legal terms the social reality of the Mafia clashes at times with the demands of legal certainty, as the definition of the association contains a series of anthropological, sociological, and descriptive elements (Moccia, 1997: 141, and Palazzo, 1995: 713, versus Flick, 1988: 856). This is particularly the case with the concepts of intimidation and criminal silence (*omertà*), the definition of which largely depends on psychological and social factors. The danger has been highlighted that a general climate of intimidation might suffice to incriminate, notwithstanding the lack of specific intimidating acts (Crespi et al., 1992: 910).

Such problems of legal certainty are inextricably linked with the potential for overextension of the criminal provision, which, going beyond criminal acts, could extend to the punishment of 'styles' of behaviour, or of behaviour that is not precisely described in law (Cesoni, 1999: 164). This danger is exacerbated by jurisprudential tendencies towards what is deemed the 'banalization' of the offence and its application to facts of a scarce 'criminal density' (Crespi, et al., 1992: 910). The broad definition of 'participation' and its conceptual blurring with external complicity provide a good example. On the basis of the current formulation of 416*bis* and its interpretation by the courts, there is still the potential for punishing a person who adheres to the association but does not actively contribute to the achievement of specific criminal goals (see Monaco, 1998: 146–7), or who takes part in legal acts related to the association (Palazzo, 1995: 714). The prospect of confusing the results of a crime with the 'type,' beliefs/ideology, or potential 'dangerousness' of certain individuals is therefore evident (Moccia, 1997: 141).

Germany: Combining Law Enforcement Definitions with
'Ordinary' Criminal Law (Civil Law Systems)

In Germany, attempts to conceptualize organized crime appear for the first time in the 1970s. Following a debate on the potential threat and nature of organized crime in the country, in 1973 state and federal police agencies established a commission whose task was to develop a definition of organized crime in order to revise law enforcement strategies to counter it. The commission's work was influenced by the debate on the existence of organized crime in Germany and on whether it should be conceptualized under the American paradigm or according to the German criminal law concept of the 'gang.' Finally, the commission put forward the following definition (von Lampe, n.d.): 'Organized crime comprises criminal acts which are committed by either combinations with more than two hierarchical levels or by several groups in a division of labour with the aim of obtaining profits or influence in public life.'

It is interesting to note here the adoption of hierarchy/division of labour as structural criteria for organized crime activities and the prevalence of profit or power as their aims. The definition, however, met with mixed reactions from law enforcement bodies, and the commission was disbanded in 1975 without having adopted an organized crime definition (von Lampe). This non-result, combined with a decline in interest in organized crime in the rest of the decade and an increased focus by law enforcement and criminal policy on terrorism, had subsequent repercussions for criminal policy in general in the next two decades (Cullen, 1997: 3–4).

Further attempts to define organized crime were made in the early 1980s, when the concept was back on the agenda of both law enforcement organizations and the press. In 1981, another committee was established to assess new methods of law enforcement, especially regarding undercover policing and the use of informants. According to the committee, organized crime 'is not only to be understood in terms of a Mafia-like parallel society ... but also as a conscious and willing, continuous cooperation in a division of labour between several persons for the purpose of committing criminal acts – frequently with the exploitation of modern infrastructure – with the aim of achieving high financial gain as quickly as possible' (von Lampe).

As is noted by von Lampe, this definition of organized crime extends beyond hierarchical structures and reflects discussions about organized crime networks, especially in the use of the phrase 'continuous cooperation.' Its acknowledgment of the existence of organized crime in the country, however, was exploited in law enforcement, political, and police discourse. Such discourse disregarded the network aspect and highlighted the Mafia threat to German society, causing pressure for more proactive measures against organized crime.

The demand for anti-organized crime measures led to the establishment of another joint working party of law enforcement and judicial officials, which, in 1990, agreed on a working, informal definition of organized crime. The adopted text identified, as distinguishing characteristics of organized crime,

> the pursuit of profit or power by the planned commission of crimes, which looked at individually or in combination, are of a serious nature, involving co-operation by more than two persons working as a team over a long or indefinite period, where such co-operation involves:
> a) the use of commercial or quasi-commercial structures
> b) the use of violence or other methods of intimidation, or
> c) the exercise of influence on the political process, the media, judicial authorities or the functioning of the economy. (Cullen, 1997: 17; Gropp et al., 2000; Levi, 1998b: 335; Sieber, 1995: 760)

It is evident that this definition is very detailed in relation to its predecessors, and it is still the basis on which the Federal Police Bureau

(Bundeskriminalamt [BKA]) compiles its statistics on organized crime.[2] This anti-organized crime impetus led to the adoption, in 1992, of the Law against Illegal Drug Trafficking and other Forms of Organized Crime and, later on, of the Crime Suppression Act of 1994. Both these laws introduced significant amendments to the criminal code and the code of criminal procedure, bending traditional provisions and giving a series of additional investigatory powers to law enforcement authorities (P.-A. Albrecht et al., 1998; Gropp et al., 2000; Meyer, 1997). What is impressive here is that, notwithstanding these developments, none of these laws contains a legal definition of organized crime, although, at the same time, measures such as undercover investigations are permitted for, *inter alia*, any serious punishable acts committed on an organized basis (Cullen, 1997; Meyer, 1997).

In view of this situation, the main legal norm under which organized crime is prosecuted – setting aside article 244 dealing with 'gangs'– is article 129 of the criminal code on 'formation of criminal associations.' This article is systematically introduced under the public order offences of the criminal code, and punishes 'whoever forms an association the objectives or activities of which are directed toward the commission of criminal acts or whoever participates in such an association as a member, solicits for it or supports it.'[3]

Although at first sight the article, which is a traditional 'public order' provision, seems even more general than the Italian 416*bis*, it has been interpreted in a systematic and narrow manner. As far as the definition of an association is concerned, it is accepted that it covers 'a permanent organizational joining together of at least three people who pursue mutual criminal purposes or who develop mutual criminal activity'; in addition, every single member has 'to subordinate to the will of the association and the association has outwardly to appear as a unity' (Lillie, 1998: 143). It is important in this respect that the association is stable and aims at a series of offences and that the members' participation is of some duration (Lackner, 1995: 625–7). Furthermore, with the exception of drug-trafficking offences, which are covered in article 30b of the Narcotics Law, article 129 is applicable only when at least part of the association is based in Germany.

The choice of the German legislature to prosecute organized crime through the general offence of criminal association has been criticized on the grounds that it rarely results in convictions. This is arguably due to the evidentiary difficulties in proving the elements of an association and its structure (P.-A. Albrecht et al., 1998: 96–7, 175; Gropp et al.,

2000). It has been argued that the main use of the provision is to legitimize measures such as wiretapping (Gropp et al., 2000), although, as mentioned above, the reference to organized crime is very general in that case and not confined to article 129. This 'inefficiency' has led at times to the use by prosecutors, instead of article 129, of article 30, paragraph 2, of the criminal code on conspiracy. Conspiracy has a similar range of penalties but is easier to prove: no commission of an offence is required, and no evidence of the existence of a 'structured association' (Lillie, 1998).

Such criticisms are a clear reflection of the clash between the requirements of legal certainty and the pressure for law enforcement/prosecutorial 'efficiency.' Article 129, interpreted in a way that to a great extent avoids the punishment of individuals who have not in reality acted to contribute to the commission of an offence, safeguarding thus the *nullum crimen sine actu* principle, is deemed inadequate to counter the perceived threat of organized crime. Calls have been made for changes to the legislation, but one wonders whether the insertion of a BKA-like 1990 definition would be the right solution.

The 1990 definition is an interesting example of continuity in perceptions of organized crime, to the extent that the commercial orientation of criminality is highlighted (Sieber, 1995: 759). It highlights the concept of a 'continuous criminal enterprise' (Levi, 1998b: 335), and it was deemed an analytically sufficient working definition, 'because it appropriately fits into the dynamics of organizing crime trade' (van Duyne, 1996: 343). At the same time, though, it is generally accepted that it has serious shortcomings. It specifies neither what is meant by 'serious crime' (van Duyne, ibid.; Levi, 1998b: 336), nor what is meant by 'profit or power'; it focuses on a very loose form of cooperation, without the need to prove the existence of structure; and it includes a very broad range of activities, many of them appearing at first sight to be perfectly legitimate.

The result is a vague, catch-all definition that can cover any criminal offence (P.-A. Albrecht, 1997: 230–3; P.-A. Albrecht, 1999: 377–9). It is not really specified what differentiates organized crime from other forms of criminality (Hassemer, 1997: 216), especially politically motivated behaviour, as well as what are its real organizational/structural elements. This is indicative of the pressure to establish broad enough definitions to cover any actual or potential form of organized criminality (Cullen, 1997: 17). The uncritical introduction of a vague BKA-like concept into the criminal law would endanger legal certainty and would feed into the general debate regarding the constitutionality of 'internal security' measures in Germany, a debate that focuses at the moment primarily on the extension of policing powers (Cullen, 1997; Gropp et al., 2000; P.-A. Albrecht et al., 1998; Lisken, 1994; Pitschas, 1993).

The United Kingdom: Combining Law Enforcement Definitions with 'Ordinary' Criminal Law (Common Law Systems)

It is accepted that organized crime in the United Kingdom did not follow the Italian Mafia model in terms of its hierarchical structures and its commingling with legitimate economic or political activities. Rather, organized crime was structured around family bonds and acquaintances in a relatively informal manner, with ad hoc networks, or else 'microstructures,' emerging in response to market needs (Hobbs, 1995: 11). These groups were of short-term duration and drawn together for a specific project, and their links with the legitimate world were limited because a great number of commodities such as alcohol, opiates, gambling, and prostitution 'remain legal but partly regulated' (Levi, 1998b: 338). In terms of duration and structures, this form of criminality appears rather 'disorganized.'

Another specific feature of the U.K. situation is that, until the 1990s, there has been little focus on the definition and characteristics of organized criminality per se. The debate has focused instead on specific types of criminal activities, and on descriptions of the historical evolution of crime from, say, 'the age of the gangster/family firm,' to the 'age of the robber, the fraudster and the dealer' (Levi, 1998b: 339–40). Legislative responses followed this trend, even when such activities started to be perceived as security threats, a characteristic example being the Drug Trafficking Offences Act of 1986.

The situation gradually began to change from the late 1980s to the early 1990s. The concept of organized crime appeared in the policy discourse in order to legitimize legislative measures such as broadly applicable anti–money-laundering legislation, and later on extensive policing powers. At the same time, however, the concept of organized crime served as a legitimizing factor for the pooling of more resources and the restructuring of police and intelligence agencies (Levi, 1998b: 341; Dorn et al., 1992: 203). This has led to the centralization of law enforcement in the field and the establishment in the 1990s of the National Criminal Intelligence Service (NCIS) and the National Crime Squad (NCS), both designed to act against 'serious and organised crime'

(Levi, 1998b: 342; Hobbs and Dunnighan, 1999; National Criminal Intelligence Service, 1999; National Crime Squad, 1999).

In its annual assessment of the organized crime threat for 2000, the National Criminal Intelligence Service (NCIS) conceptualized it as ensuring the availability of illicit commodities, providing an infrastructure that facilitates other serious crime, and being an insidious phenomenon that both meets and creates demand for illicit commodities. A definition is further attempted of organized crime groups, which have to satisfy all of the following criteria:

- they contain at least three people;
- they engage in criminal activity that is prolonged or ongoing;
- their members are motivated by profit or power;
- they commit serious criminal offences (NCIS, 2000).

It is evident that the NCIS approach resembles that of Germany's BKA. The definition is also consistent with that used by the U.K. Organised Crime Notification Scheme and with previous definitional attempts by NCIS and the Association of Chief Police Officers (ACPO), with the latter containing an additional 'transnational' requirement that the activity is being carried out irrespective of national boundaries (see House of Commons, Home Affairs Committee, 1994–5).

As in the German example, however, this definition is not a legal one. Law enforcement organizations and prosecutors agree that a detailed legal definition of an organized crime group would not be beneficial in view of the potential to create legislative voids likely to be exploited and in view of evidentiary difficulties in proving the existence of the group (ACPO and Crown Prosecution Service, both in House of Commons, Home Affairs Committee, 1994–5). These arguments were put forward in the first comprehensive debate over organized crime in the United Kingdom, before the Home Affairs Committee of the House of Commons in 1994. It was accepted then that the existing legal framework, which consisted of the prosecution of membership in an organized crime group by means of the general conspiracy offence, was adequate and that a specific membership offence would be considered should this scheme prove ineffective in containing organized crime (House of Commons, Home Affairs Committee, 1994–5, Recommendation 39). Six years after this report, the situation has not changed; as will be seen below, the United Kingdom supports the introduction of the conspiracy model at the European Union level.

The U.K. preference (in contrast to the German position) for a general legal provision to be applicable to organized crime cases can be explained by the considerable flexibility of the definitions of conspiracy offences. The main offence is the conspiracy to commit criminal offences, introduced by section 1 of the 1977 Criminal Law Act.[4] This section states that,

(1) ... if a person agrees with any other person or persons that a course of conduct shall be pursued which, if the agreement is carried out in accordance with their intentions either
   a. will necessarily amount to or involve the commission of any offence or offences by one or more parties to the agreement, or
   b. would do so but for the existence of facts which render the commission of the offence or any of the offences impossible
   he is guilty of conspiracy to commit the offence or offences in question.

(2) Where liability for any offence may be incurred without knowledge on the part of the person committing it of any particular fact or circumstance necessary for the commission of the offence, a person shall nevertheless not be guilty of conspiracy to commit that offence by virtue of subsection (1) above unless he and at least one other party to the agreement intend or know that that fact or circumstance shall or will exist at the time when the conduct constituting the offence is to take place.'

Conspiracy is thus in essence an agreement between two or more persons to commit a criminal offence (Ashworth, 1999: 471). The very broad scope for criminalization allowed by the section is exacerbated by the even broader interpretation of the offence by the courts. In the much discussed case of *Anderson* ([1986] AC 27), the House of Lords held that 'it was not necessary to establish an intention on the part of each conspirator that the offence or offences in question should in fact be committed,' a ruling that arguably runs contrary to the very concept of the offence and reduces it to a mere agreement (Ashworth, 1999: 480; Clarkson and Keating, 1998: 522; J. Smith and Hogan, 1999: 276–7). This broadening of the offence was counterbalanced in the same case by the contention that a person is guilty of conspiracy if 'he had known that the course of conduct would amount to or involve the commission of an offence or offences and that he had intended to play some part in the agreed course of conduct in furtherance of the criminal purpose that it had been intended to achieve' ([1986] AC 27). This part of the ruling was also criticized in view of its potential to exclude those who plan an offence but do not actually take part in it, in contrast with the purpose of the offence (Ashworth, 1999).[5]

A further extension of the scope of the conspiracy offence occurred not through case law, but by the adoption of the Criminal Justice (Terrorism and Conspiracy) Act 1998. The Act contained amendments to the jurisdiction over conspiracy, justified by the government as 'an unambiguous message to international terrorists that we ... will not allow them to use our country as a base for planning crime ... there should be no hiding place in our jurisdiction for terrorists who traffic in arms, drug smugglers, money launderers or counterfeiters' (cited in Holroyd, 2000: 326). The fusion of terrorism and organized crime in such securitization discourse legitimized the extension of jurisdiction to international conspiracy. The latter, defined in section 5(1) of the act, introduces a new section 1A in the 1977 act identifying an agreed course of conduct that involves at some stage 'an act by one or more of the parties or the happening of some other event intended to take place in a country or territory outside the United Kingdom' (s. 1A[2]).

This jurisdictional extension is subject to the 'dual criminality' test, requiring (1) that the act or event above are criminal offences in both England and Wales and the foreign country involved and (2) proof of a link between the conspiracy and England and Wales. This link is broad enough to include cases when

   a. a party to the agreement, or a party's agent, did anything in England and Wales in relation to the agreement before its formation, or
   b. a party to the agreement became a party in England or Wales (by joining it either in person or through an agent), or
   c. a party to the agreement, or a party's agent, did or omitted anything in England or Wales in pursuance of the agreement. (section 1A95)

As with the BKA definition, the police perception of organized crime in the United Kingdom is broad and has the potential to embrace a wide range of activities. NCIS definitions have not, however, been transposed into domestic criminal law. The main prosecutorial tool against organized crime is the conspiracy offence, which is even broader and deemed easier to prove. Interest by the Home Office in introducing a membership offence into the criminal law is limited because of the increased difficulties of proving membership in a criminal organization.[6] Both law enforcement and Home Office officials emphasize the need for flexibility in this respect, and it is understood that the priority is to achieve judicial cooperation with other countries rather than to focus on organized crime as a concept.[7]

This leaves a situation in which major extensions of police powers are justified in order to combat the vague and broad concept of 'serious crime,' and creates a striking inconsistency between the NCIS definition of organized crime – which requires the participation of three or more persons and implies the existence of a structure or a group – and the conspiracy offence, for the establishment of which the agreement of two people would suffice. In that way, the specific characteristics of organized criminal groups are irrelevant when the criteria of a more general and readily invoked offence are applied.

The existence of the conspiracy offence has been the subject of rigorous criticism. It is a typical 'social danger' offence (Dennis, 1977) and a manifestation of the punishment of dangerousness in criminal law. Like the German article 129 offence, it is largely based on the principle of preventing harm to society. However, in the conspiracy case, the endangerment of society lies in the formation not of an association but of a mere agreement between at least two people. The dangers of drifting away from punishing acts and prosecuting behaviour are evident, especially in view of the procedural convenience of the conspiracy offence and its imprecise scope (Dennis, 1977; Ashworth, 1999). The catch-all potential of the offence, along with the inconsistencies in its use, have led commentators to characterize it the 'least systematic, most irrational branch of English penal law' (case of *D.P.P. v. Bhagwan*, cited in Clarkson and Keating, 1998: 509).

Such concerns become more acute in light of the extraterritorial extension of the conspiracy offence by the 1998 act. It is enlightening to note here that, while the recommendation of a report preceding the act was limited to the inclusion of conspiracies to commit terrorist offences, the act extended jurisdiction to any offence (C. Campbell, 1999: 956). This was justified through a generalized organized crime/terrorism securitization discourse, with the dangerous effect of creating a continuum between these two phenomena. What is even more dangerous, though, is the overextension of the scope of the provisions, which, in disregarding political considerations, have the potential to punish political dissidence (C. Campbell, 1999: 957–8; Holroyd, 2000: 328; C. Walker, 1999: 898). Not only that, but the list may include 'sex tourists, football hooligans, drug traffickers, computer hackers and financial fraudsters' (C. Walker, ibid.). It is evident that the list extends beyond participation in a criminal organization.

International Initiatives

The European Union

> One thing leads to another. This has been a feature of the Community, which is constantly being taken into new areas. One of these new areas is closely linked to the overall concept of security. I am referring, of course, to the consequences of free movement of individuals and the need for joint action, or at the very least close co-ordination, to combat the various threats to personal security: Organized crime, drug trafficking, terrorism ... Political initiatives in this security-related area are another expression of solidarity, a *leitmotif* of the European pact. (Delors, 1991: 103)

These words by the then president of the European Commission reflect in a clear manner both the post–Cold War reconfiguration of the security landscape, which in the early 1990s encompassed non-military threats such as organized crime, and the need for the European Community to provide answers to these threats, especially because of its perceived vulnerability as a result of the abolition of borders in the internal market. Delors's political statement was translated into legal terms with the Maastricht Treaty on the European Union of 1993, whose newly introduced 'third pillar' (title VI) contained a series of provisions in matters related to Justice and Home Affairs. Article K.1 of this title provided that for the purposes of achieving the objectives of the European Union, in particular the free movement of persons, member states should regard as matters of common interest, *inter alia*, 'police cooperation for the purposes of preventing and combating drug trafficking and other forms of international crime, in connection with the organisation of a Union-wide system for exchanging information within a European Police Office (Europol).'

In this manner, the Maastricht Treaty placed 'international crime' directly on the EU agenda and paved the way for legislative action (albeit still in a rather intergovernmental manner) in the field. The Europol Convention, signed in 1995 (OJ C316, 27 November 1995: 1), was an ambitious step in that direction; however, it did not contain any specific definition of organized crime, focusing rather on particular criminal offences. Subsequent European Council resolutions that made specific reference to the 'fight against international organised crime,'[8] contained a series of measures – without legally binding force – on witness protection and the protection of *pentiti*, but still failed to provide a definition of the phenomenon.

An attempt at definition was first made within the framework of a third pillar convention on extradition (OJ C313, 23 October 1996: 12). Acknowledging that differences in legal cultures and definitions between EU member states created obstacles in extradition procedures in cases of organized crime (Explanatory Memorandum, OJ C191, 23 June 1997: 16), article 3 of the convention, entitled 'conspiracy and association to commit offences,' facilitates extradition, under certain conditions, in cases of the lack of uniform definition of conspiracy or association to commit offences in two member states, provided that these offences are aimed at terrorism, drug trafficking, and other forms of organized crime or violent acts. In view of the sensitivity of this provision, paragraph 3 grants to member states a reservation right with regard to the application of this paragraph. In order to avoid rendering the provision ineffective, however, paragraph 4 then states that in the case of such reservations, member states shall make extraditable

> the behaviour of any person which contributes to the commission by a group of persons in the field of terrorism as in Articles 1 and 2 of the European Convention on the Suppression of Terrorism, drug trafficking and other forms of organized crime or other acts of violence against the life, physical integrity or liberty of a person, or creating a collective danger for persons, punishable by deprivation of liberty or a detention order of a maximum of at least 12 months, *even where that person does not take part in the actual execution of the offence or offences concerned*; such contribution shall be intentional and made having knowledge either of the purpose and the general criminal activity of the group *or of the intention of the group to commit the offence or offences concerned*. (Emphasis added.)

Although the convention does not aim at providing a straightforward definition of what constitutes membership in an organized crime association, it is evident that the conceptualization of the latter is broad and is linked with the need to achieve maximum cooperation among EU member states in the field. The political pressure for the intensification of measures against organized crime led, shortly after the adoption of the Extradition Convention, to the introduction, in 1997, of a detailed EU Action Plan to Combat Organized Crime (OJ C251, 15 August

1997: 1). The action plan contains a detailed list of political guidelines and recommendations for legal action in the field, linking such developments to the evolution of the EU into an 'area of freedom, security and justice' (also a key objective of the Amsterdam Treaty). Such measures were justified through a strong securitization discourse in the introduction of the action plan, which opens as follows:

> Organized crime is increasingly becoming a threat to society as we know it and want to preserve it. Criminal behaviour no longer is the domain of individuals only, but also of organizations that pervade the various structures of civil society, and indeed society as a whole. Crime is increasingly organizing itself across national borders, also taking advantage of the free movement of goods, capital, services and persons. Technological innovations such as Internet and electronic banking turn out to be extremely convenient vehicles either for committing crimes or for transferring the resulting profits into seemingly licit activities. Fraud and corruption take on massive proportions, defrauding citizens and civic institutions alike.

This potent securitization discourse led to an ambitious, wide-ranging action plan calling for the adoption at EU level of a series of measures related, *inter alia*, to policing, money laundering, asset confiscation, and judicial cooperation, as well as legislation criminalizing participation in a criminal organization (political guideline 8[1]). This new offence would be introduced by the means of a Joint Action and could consist in the behaviour described in article 3(4) of the Extradition Convention (Recommendation 17).

This recommendation was implemented by the adoption of the Joint Action of 21 December 1998 'on making it a criminal offence to participate in a criminal organization in the Member States of the European Union' (OJ L351, 29 December 1998: 1). Its preamble notes the seriousness of the organized crime phenomenon, highlights the need for a common approach to curb participation in such activities, and envisages the importance of this measure in facilitating judicial cooperation in the investigation and prosecution of such offences (indents 3, 4, and 7). The Joint Action does the following:

PROVIDES A DEFINITION OF A CRIMINAL ORGANIZATION
The latter is defined as 'a structured association, established over a period of time, of more than two persons, acting in concert with the view to committing offences which are punishable by deprivation of

liberty or a detention order of a maximum of at least four years or a more serious penalty, whether such offences are an end in themselves or a means of obtaining material benefits and, where appropriate, of improperly influencing the operation of public authorities' (Article 1). The article further states that such offences are those mentioned in article 2 of the Europol Convention and in the annex thereto and carrying an equivalent penalty.[9]

CRIMINALIZES PARTICIPATION IN A CRIMINAL ORGANIZATION
According to article 2, this covers:

(a) conduct by any person who, with intent and with knowledge of either the aim and general criminal activity of the organisation or the intention of the organisation to commit the offences in question, actively takes part in:
   – the organisation's criminal activities falling within Article 1, even where that person does not take part in the actual execution of the offences and, subject to the general principles of the criminal law of the Member State concerned, even where the offences concerned are not actually committed,
   – the organisation's other activities in the further knowledge that his participation will contribute to the achievement of the organisation's criminal activities falling within Article 1;

(b) conduct by any person consisting in an agreement with one or more persons that an activity should be pursued which, if carried out, would amount to the commission of offences falling within Article 1, even if that person does not take part in the actual execution of the activity.

Article 2 goes on to ensure that, irrespective of the elected conduct, member states will afford one another 'the most comprehensive assistance possible' in respect of these offences and those of article 3(4) of the extradition convention.

INTRODUCES LIABILITY OF LEGAL PERSONS
According to article 3 of the Joint Action, legal persons are held criminally or otherwise liable for offences falling within article 2(1). Such liability is established without prejudice to the criminal liability of natural persons as perpetrators or accomplices. The article reiterates

the clause for 'effective, proportionate and dissuasive' sanctions and considers the possibility of material or economic sanctions.

EXTENDS JURISDICTION
Article 4 extends the possibility of prosecution of organized crime offences (as defined in article 2) that take place in a territory of a member state, irrespective of where the organization is based or pursues its criminal activities or where the activity covered by the agreement of article 2(1)(b) takes place. In case of concurrent jurisdiction between several member states, the article calls for coordination taking into account the location of the organization's different components.

It is evident, by a look at its structure and wording, that the EU attempt to define participation in a criminal organization is the outcome of a compromise among divergent national approaches to the subject. The definition of a criminal organization is largely influenced by the Italian anti-Mafia provision and by the BKA/NCIS policing definitions. Its introduction, however, met with opposition from the United Kingdom, which argued that 'the definition is unnecessarily limiting and rigid; that it fails to address the more sophisticated and flexible way in which much of modern organised crime increasingly operates, where alliances form and re-form for different criminal enterprises; and that a criminal offence defined in terms of Article 1 would impede prosecution because of the difficulty of establishing each of the elements required' (House of Lords, Select Committee on the European Communities, 1997–8).

In view of these objections, article 2 defining participation in a criminal organization was drafted to include two variants: one on actual participation in a criminal organization, based on the article 1 definition; and one criminalizing the agreement between two or more persons to pursue activities falling within article 1. While the first variant reflects the Italian anti-Mafia legislation, as well as the BKA/NCIS definitions, the second is a clear reflection of the common law conspiracy offence.

This reproduction of various national models does little for legal certainty and consistency, while also failing to alleviate the concerns raised at the national level. The broad definition of participation or agreement, both extending in cases when the person involved does not take part in the actual execution of the offences concerned, and in the case of participation, even when the offences concerned are not actually committed, has a clear potential to violate the *nullum crimen sine actu* principle. Moreover, and at the expense of legal certainty, the fundamentally different legal treatment of criminal organizations in different jurisdictions is maintained. None of the previously examined EU member states have changed their legislation to implement the Joint Action, with the exception of the United Kingdom in introducing jurisdiction for international conspiracy in England and Wales. This, however, is not perceived as a problem by EU representatives, according to whom the purpose of the Joint Action was to introduce a concept of participation in a criminal organization in the few countries with no equivalent legal principles and to facilitate the cooperation of member states.[10] The introduction of legislation implementing the Joint Action has been met with strong reactions from various member states, and, four years after its adoption, differences in the conceptualization of organized crime still remain (Mitsilegas, 2001).

In spite of the inability of the European Union to adopt a uniform definition of organized crime, it aspired to emerge as a prominent international actor in the field. This was reflected in EU participation in the negotiations for a major international initiative, the United Nations Convention against Transnational Organized Crime. For that purpose, in early 1999 the European Council adopted a Joint Position on the proposed U.N. Convention (OJ L87, 31 March 1999: 1), calling on member states to ensure that the provisions of the U.N. convention are consistent with those of the EU Joint Action (article 1[2]). By way of ensuring an extended scope for the U.N. convention, the Joint Position attempted a further conceptualization of criminal organizations, going beyond the wording of the Joint Action at times. It was stated that

> In principle, the relevant provisions of the draft convention should encompass the activities of persons, acting in concert with a view to committing serious crime, involved in any criminal organisation which has a structure and is, or has been, established for a certain period of time. They should not be limited to groups with a highly developed structure or enduring nature, such as mafia type organisations; and the organisations need not necessarily have formally defined roles for their participants or continuity of membership. (article 1[3])

The United Nations

Organized crime as a growing security threat was the focal point of the summit meeting of the seven major industrialized countries, held in Naples in July 1994. In their summit communiqué, the G7 heads of state and the president of the European Commission expressed 'alarm about the growth of organised transnational crime and the use of illicit proceeds to take control of legitimate business' and at the same time welcomed the World Ministerial Conference on Organized Transnational Crime, which was due to be held in Naples in November of that year (P. Williams and Savona, 1996: 170). This conference adopted the Naples Political Declaration and Global Action Plan against Organized Transnational Crime, which was approved by the U.N. Assembly one month later (United Nations, 2000). This document expressed the willingness of the participating countries to cooperate against transnational organized crime, affirming the 'responsibility vested in the United Nations in crime prevention and criminal justice and recognizing the need to strengthen its role in the development of a comprehensive programme of action to prevent and control organized transnational crime' (P. Williams and Savona, 1996: 171).

The involvement of the United Nations in the fight against organized crime was linked to the redrawing of the global security landscape. At the U.N.'s fiftieth-anniversary ceremony, held in San Francisco on 26 June 1995, the new role of the United Nations was hailed by then U.S. President Clinton, who called for 'support through the United Nations for the fight against man-made and natural forces of disintegration, from crime syndicates and drug cartels to new diseases and disappearing forests. They cross borders at will. Nations can and must oppose them alone, but we know, and the Cairo conference reaffirmed, that the most effective opposition requires strong international cooperation and mutual support' (quoted in P. Williams and Savona, 1996: 170).

The starting point of the Naples Declaration was followed by discussions regarding possible forms of implementation of its principles. In view of the need to achieve greater international cooperation, emphasis was placed on legal harmonization in the field, possibly through a convention, following the example of the 1988 U.N. Convention against Illicit Trafficking in Narcotic Drugs and Psychotropic Substances. Such an attempt was deemed to be difficult, in view of different national approaches in the field and the open-ended character of organized crime, raising the dilemma of whether one should focus on specific offences or on the threat posed by the organizations per se. It was deemed, however, that an international legal instrument such as a convention would be beneficial at a symbolic level, but also in legitimizing national action in the field. Moreover, an adopted convention would:

- provide a set of standards and expectations that the signatories would have an obligation to live up to;
- have an important regularising effect and provide for a more standardised form of cooperation than the extension of bilateral accords;
- facilitate more systematic assistance in the areas of criminal justice and law enforcement; and
- provide guidance for a programme of implementation that would assist in the dual objectives of harmonising law enforcement risk and making it more difficult for transnational criminal organisations to infiltrate legitimate business. (P. Williams and Savona, 1996: 177–80)

The move to draft a U.N. convention gained momentum through a series of follow-up ministerial conferences from 1995 to 1999. After a series of initiatives, which led to a draft convention, the General Assembly established in December 1998 an Ad Hoc Committee for the elaboration of the U.N. Convention against Transnational Organized Crime and its protocols.[11] The committee approved the convention, after many readings, as early as July 2000, and the protocols in October of the same year. Both were approved by the General Assembly in November and were signed, pointedly, in Palermo in December of that year (United Nations, 2000).

The 'Resolution' preceding the text of the convention reiterates the General Assembly's concern regarding the negative economic and social implications of organized criminal activities and reiterates the 'urgent need' to strengthen cooperation to prevent and combat such activities (doc. A/55/383, indent 7). In order to achieve this aim, the convention includes a series of provisions focusing, *inter alia*, on organized crime, corruption, money laundering, extradition, and forms of judicial cooperation and mutual legal assistance. In relation to participation in a criminal organization, the convention:

DEFINES AN 'ORGANIZED CRIMINAL GROUP'
The convention chose to adopt the term 'group' rather than the term 'association.' According to article 2(a), it is 'a structured group of three or more persons, existing for a period of time and acting in concert with the aim of committing one or more serious crimes or offences estab-

lished in accordance with this Convention, in order to obtain, directly or indirectly, a financial or other material benefit.'

CRIMINALIZES PARTICIPATION IN SUCH A GROUP

Article 5(1) criminalizes the intentional commission of either or both of the following offences, as distinct from those involving the attempt at or completion of the criminal activity:

(i) Agreeing with one or more other persons to commit a serious crime for a purpose relating directly or indirectly to the obtaining of a financial or other material benefit and, where required by domestic law, involving an act undertaken by one of the participants in furtherance of the agreement or involving an organised criminal group;

(ii) Conduct by any person who, with knowledge of either the aim and general criminal activity of an organised criminal group or its intention to commit the crimes in question, takes an active part in:

  a. Criminal activities of the organised crime group;
  b. Other activities of the organised criminal group in the knowledge that his or her participation will contribute to the achievement of the above described criminal aim (5(1)(a)) and organising, directing, aiding, abetting, facilitating or counselling the commission of serious crime involving an organised crime group (5(1)(b)).

Article 5(2) states that knowledge, intent, purpose or agreement may be inferred from 'objective factual circumstances.'

DEFINES THE TERM 'TRANSNATIONAL'

Article 3(1) states that the convention applies in any case to the prevention, investigation and prosecution of, *inter alia*, the participation in an organized criminal group, but that it also applies to serious crime 'where the offence is transnational in nature' and involves such a group. The second paragraph adds the following criteria for the definition of an offence as 'transnational':

(a) It is committed in more than one State;
(b) It is committed in one State but a substantial part of its preparation, planning, direction or control takes place in another member state;
(c) It is committed in one State but involves an organised criminal group that engages in criminal activities in more than one State; or
(d) It is committed in one State but has substantial effects in another State.

EXTENDS JURISDICTION

Article 15 is devoted to jurisdictional matters related, *inter alia*, to the participation in an organized criminal group. Its second paragraph extends national jurisdiction for this offence in cases where it is committed outside the territory of one of the parties to the convention with a view to the commission of a serious crime within its territory (15[2][c][i]).

INTRODUCES LIABILITY OF LEGAL PERSONS

Article 10 establishes the liability of legal persons for participation in serious crimes involving an organized criminal group and for article 5 offences. The provision is open regarding the type of such liability – which may be criminal, civil, or administrative – and without prejudice to the criminal liability of natural persons who have committed the offences. The provision further calls for 'effective, proportionate and dissuasive criminal or non-criminal sanctions, including monetary sanctions.'

The involvement of the United Nations in the fight against organized crime has been hailed both because of the extent of U.N. resources and because of its believed authority 'to attempt not only to bring about more economic equality and less political violence in the world but also to establish democratic constitutional states and/or to induce such states to institute a proper public administration and intensive international cooperation in order to monitor global logistics systems and to track down, prosecute and convict transnational criminals' (Fijnaut, 2000: 125). It was decided that, rather than attack specific offences, the convention would focus on criminal organizations per se, regardless of their activities. Such a focus was deemed essential in order for the convention to 'withstand the test of time,' being effective 'no matter how diverse and sophisticated organised criminal groups are or might try to become' (Vlassis, 2001).

At the same time, however, the attempt to adopt a broad, global instrument against organized crime faces the challenge of accommodating divergent legal and empirical realities in a matter that is notoriously difficult to define. In elaborating global standards, the need to accommodate both the different national approaches and the evolutionary and hybrid character of organized crime has resulted in the formulation of broad, all-encompassing, and at times vague provisions.

This tendency is evident when one looks at the definition of an organized criminal group. The convention provides a detailed, cumulative list of criteria for its establishment, the first being the existence of a structure. Article 2(c) of the convention casts light on this term adding that a structured group is 'a group that is not randomly formed for the immediate commission of an offence and that does not need to have formally defined roles for its members, continuity of its membership or a developed structure.'

Again, as with the EU Joint Position's interpretation of structure, the convention provides a contradictory provision dominated by the oxymoron of a structured group without 'a developed structure.' This approach was obviously selected in order both to avoid limiting the scope of the convention to Mafia-type hierarchical associations and to address the phenomenon of the organized criminal network. This view is endorsed by the convention's *travaux préparatoires*, indicating that the term includes not only groups with hierarchical or other elaborate structure but also non-hierarchical groups. This choice, however, leads to a provision that, apart from its inherent contradiction, is so broad it is almost meaningless.

Similar objections can be raised regarding references to the pursuit by the group of 'a financial or other material benefit.' The introduction of this criterion is essential in order to highlight the enterprise character of organized criminal groups and to distinguish them from forms of political protest or terrorist groups. The exact wording of this criterion was, however, the subject of heated controversy, with participating countries wanting to include either explicit reference to terrorist crimes, or reference to the broad category of 'moral benefit'(doc. A/AC.254/4/Rev.8). In the end, neither was accepted, but the drafters had to take into account the consideration, put forward by the U.S. delegation, that not all relevant crime is motivated by profit or material benefit (doc. A/AC.254/5). According to the *travaux préparatoires*, the provision should be understood broadly 'to include, for example, crimes in which the predominant motivation may be sexual gratification, such as the receipt or trade of materials by members of child pornography rings, the trading of children by members of paedophile rings or cost-sharing among ring members.' As justifiable as such an extension may be, the vague reference to 'other material benefit' does not exclude expressions of organized protest (for instance, political or environmental), and its broad drafting ('other material benefits') necessitates safeguards of restrictive interpretation.

The scope of application of the convention could also be overextended with regard to the activities of organized crime groups. One of the criteria for their existence is the commission of serious crime(s). Serious crime is defined in article 2(b) as 'conduct constituting an offence punishable by a maximum deprivation of liberty of at least four years or a more serious penalty,' following, thus, the example of the EU Joint Action. Rather than including a catalogue of offences, the convention resorts to an all-embracing list of crimes on the basis of their punishability. The utilization of the rather low four-year threshold opens the list up to a very extended catalogue of offences, which may also differ considerably from country to country. Questions about the 'seriousness' of many of these offences remain, and there is the obvious danger that forms of ordinary crime will be perceived in a more extreme manner through their characterization as such by the convention, as the line between ordinary and organized crime is blurred.

The scope of the convention regarding serious crimes may be expanded considerably on the basis of the clause contained in article 3. This provision defines 'serious crime' as transnational, and thus falling within the scope of the convention, if 'it is committed in one state but has substantial effects in another state.' This criterion is also drafted very broadly and has the potential to allow a state to consider as a serious crime an act that is not considered as such in the country where it took place. The *travaux préparatoires* give little guidance in this respect, as they interpret the term 'substantial effects' as covering situations where 'an offence has had a substantial consequential adverse effect on another State Party,' giving as an example a case where the currency of one country is counterfeited in another and put into global circulation by a criminal group. No further guidance is given, however, especially regarding the authority evaluating the inherently subjective concept of 'substantial consequential adverse effect.'

As with the EU Joint Action, major challenges to fundamental legal principles arise from the criminalization of participation in an organized crime group. Article 5 retains the two-variant model of participation, with the parties to the convention having the choice between a conspiracy offence and a 'criminal association' offence. The first variant criminalizes the agreement between two or more persons to commit a serious crime 'for a purpose relating directly or indirectly to the obtaining of financial or other material benefit.' As can be inferred from the wording of the provision, such agreement does not necessarily amount to the undertaking of an act in furtherance of it or involving an organized crime group, as this depends on domestic legislation. The form of participation that is criminalized here is too broad, consisting only of an agreement to commit a crime and nothing more. As discussed in the context of the conspiracy offence, this is a clear reflection of a 'social dangerousness' ideology that may imperil democracy, free expression, and the principle of *nullum crimen sine actu*.

Similar concerns can be raised in relation to the second variant, criminalizing conduct by a person who, with knowledge of either the aim and general criminal activity of an organized criminal group or its intention to commit the crimes in question, takes an active part in the group's criminal activities, or other activities of the group, in the knowledge that such participation will contribute to the achievement of its aims. The formulation of this provision is more systematic in relation to the concept of an 'organized criminal group,' and the explicit requirements of knowledge and active partnership are welcome guarantees. It appears also to be narrower than the EU equivalent, which explicitly extends criminalization in the first case even when the offences concerned are not actually committed. However, the reference to 'other activities' of the organized criminal group may cause serious interpretive problems.

The same may happen with the criminalization, in any case, of organizing, directing, aiding, abetting, facilitating, or counselling the commission of serious crime involving an organized crime group (article 5[1][b]). This provision goes farther than the EU Joint Action and resembles more the Italian anti-Mafia provisions. The terms used here are all subject to judicial interpretation, with some, such as 'facilitating' and 'counselling,' being especially prone to overextension. The danger here lies in the potential criminalization of legitimate activities, bearing in mind the 'financial side' of organized crime activities, such as engaging in legitimate commercial transactions. Unlike the previous subparagraph, this one does not expressly include a knowledge requirement, but only intention.

The Ambivalent Concept of Transnational Organized Crime

Transnational organized crime, a concept rarely encountered in legal texts or even law enforcement guidelines before the 1990s, has become, in less than a decade, a globally defined criminal offence. Superseding diverging national perceptions and competing interpretations, this common concept paves the way for increased international judicial and police cooperation and, potentially, for an extension of law enforcement powers. This has been achieved through a potent securitization process at a global level, which, exploiting the 'emotional kick' of the organized crime imagery and terminology (Levi, 1998b: 336), portrayed organized crime as an ever-growing phenomenon and a global, multifaceted security threat.

But is transnational organized crime a multifaceted security threat? And if so, whose security does it imperil? In spite of the discourse and the adoption of a wide range of legal measures, the picture with regard to the extent and volume of organized crime remains blurred. Efforts by the United Nations and the European Union to 'measure' the scale of the phenomenon have begun fairly recently, and their credibility is challenged by a series of factors, such as the diversity of what is being measured, the overlapping of legal and illegal activities, and the tendency to exaggerate estimates (Beare and Naylor, 1999: 7–8).

Leaving the tricky question of 'measurement' aside, the question is still left unanswered as to whether the threat is from the crimes committed by organized crime groups or from the mere existence of the groups (or both). Taking into consideration the broad definition of serious crime in both the U.N. and EU instruments, on the basis of the four-year deprivation-of-liberty threshold, it is evident that in the first case one has to do with a very extended and wide-ranging list of offences. From their systematic introduction in national criminal codes and the variations in sentencing, it is evident that these offences vary considerably both in terms of the interests they attack and the harm they are deemed to cause.

Regarding the threat posed by criminal organizations per se, the 'social danger' rationale behind such perception is obvious. Organized criminal groups are perceived as a danger to the nebulous concepts of the 'social fabric' and the state itself. Such theorization in the abstract, called pertinently the 'dynamization' of interests protected by law (Baratta, 1991: 9), has the potential to imperil fundamental freedoms. This is achieved through the removal of the punitive level from the act and the subsequent extension of criminalization in cases prior to it or even where no act has been committed, thus potentially punishing political and social beliefs.

Even if it were granted that the offences committed by organized crime groups and the groups' existence per se both pose threats in a variety of ways, can one justify the concept of a 'global' transnational organized crime threat that menaces the international system as such?

And, if it were so granted, which international/global interests merit protection? Under the auspices of the United Nations, organized crime has been broadly perceived to threaten interests as diverse as national sovereignty, societies, individuals, national stability and state control, financial institutions, democratization and privatization, development, and global regimes and codes of conduct (P. Williams and Savona, 1996: 32–9). However, it is clear that some of these interests are threatened only in some parts of the world, or strictly at the national level, while others, such as individual protection and 'safety,' are too vague and difficult to generalize at the global level. In spite of the transnationalization of organized crime, the modus operandi in many instances remains influenced by 'the local,' taking shape according to historical, social, and cultural specificities (Hobbs, 1997: 830).

The 'local' element in transnational organized crime is found not only in its manifestations, but also in national social, economic, and political conditions and legal cultures. One of the paramount difficulties in imposing a global definition of organized crime is that it has to be applied worldwide, to developed and developing countries alike, each of them facing different organized crime phenomena and having different legal systems. The provisions in the U.N. convention were drafted broadly, perhaps in order to accommodate such diversity. But the breadth of the provisions may lead to problems, especially related to the criminalization of participation in a criminal group, which has the potential to include participation in a legal activity if this is furthering the aim of a criminal organization. The effective implementation of such provisions is a major challenge, reflecting the difficulty in distinguishing between licit and illicit activities in developing countries or countries that are in the process of transition to a market economy.

Broad legal provisions pose further problems. The EU/U.N. initiatives provide a definition of organized crime that is a mosaic of national law enforcement and legal responses, an attempt to accommodate a great many different tendencies. The result is neither close to the achievement of legal certainty, nor close to a comprehensive translation of criminological or law enforcement perceptions into law. This may undermine the very aim and operation of these initiatives: it remains to be seen how the U.N. provisions on extradition or mutual legal assistance will be implemented, for instance, in view of the remaining fundamental difference between the concept of a criminal organization and that of conspiracy.

Conclusion

The emergence of a global legal definition of organized crime is a welcome step, not only towards the achievement of legal certainty in this highly empirical field and thus the establishment of accountability mechanisms to regulate extensive police powers, but also towards a better understanding of the concept itself. The dilemma that one faces in such an endeavour is obvious: how to produce a meaningful legal definition, devoid of extralegal, empirical terminology, while at the same time addressing the fluid reality and diversity of worldwide organized crime activities. The response to this dilemma, by both the European Union and the United Nations, has been to translate this reality legally by 'recycling' pre-existing national perceptions and using broad concepts. These choices may have satisfied the participating states and enabled the adoption of the measures; at the same time, however, they have the potential to produce amorphous, catch-all criteria that not only do not provide an accurate legal 'translation' of the organized crime phenomenon but also threaten fundamental legal principles. In view of such risks, much rests on the implementation of the provisions, at both the legislative and the judicial levels. A realistic and effective implementation should be based not on a reproduction of the 'securitization'/'war-on-organized-criminals' discourse, but on respect for fundamental rights and individual freedoms and a shift of focus from uncritical criminalization to an effort, at an earlier stage, to mitigate the criminogenic conditions that nurture organized crime.

Notes

1   As translated by Jamieson, 2000 (28, 42). See also the version of Adamoli et al. (1998: 133), stating that a 'Mafia-type unlawful association is said to exist when the participants take advantage of the intimidating power of the association and of the resulting condition of submission and silence to commit criminal offences, to manage, at all levels, control, either directly or indirectly, of economic activities, concessions, authorisations, public contracts and services, or to obtain unlawful profits or advantages for themselves or for others, or with a view to preventing or limiting the freedom to vote, or get votes for themselves or for others on the occasion of an election.'

2 In the 1999 BKA Annual Report on organized crime, for instance, it was
stated that 396 cases belonged to the first category, 235 to the second, and
88 to the third (Bundeskriminalamt, 1999).
3 Translated by Lillie (1998: 143).
4 Related offences in England and Wales are also the common law conspiracy to defraud, common law inciting offences, and aiding and abetting,
counselling, or procuring the commission of offences contrary to the
Accessories and Abettors Act 1861.
5 The case remains the authority in the field, although two subsequent cases
ruled in a different way. In *Yip Chiu-Cheung* ([1995] 1 AC III), which applies
only to common law conspiracy, the Privy Council has held that the prosecution must establish that each alleged conspirator intended the agreement to be carried out. The Court of Appeal on the other hand held in
Siracusa ([1990] 90 Cr App R 340) that a passive conspirator who concurs
in the activities of the person(s) carrying out the crime, though without
becoming involved himself, is guilty of criminal conspiracy (see Ashworth,
1999).
6 Personal communication with Home Office official, London, September
2000.
7 Personal communication with Home Office official, London, December
2000.
8 Resolution of the EU Council of 23 November 1995 on the protection of
witnesses in the fight against international organized crime, OJ C327,
7 December 1995: 5; and Council Resolution of 20 December 1996 on
individuals who cooperate with the judicial process in the fight against
international organized crime, OJ C10, 11 January 1997: 1.
9 The offences listed in the Europol Convention are as follows: terrorism;
unlawful drug trafficking and other serious forms of international crime
where there are factual indicators that an organized criminal structure is
involved and two or more member states affected by the form of crime
in question (article 2[1]) – initially: unlawful drug trafficking, trafficking in
nuclear and radioactive substances, illegal immigrant smuggling, trade in
human beings and motor vehicle crime; – within two years from Europol's
function: crimes committed or likely to be committed in the course of
terrorist activities against life, limb, personal freedom, or property (article
2[2]); offences against life, limb, or personal freedom (murder, grievous
bodily injury, illicit trade in human organs and tissue, kidnapping, illegal
restraint and hostage-taking, racism and xenophobia); offences against
property or public goods including fraud (organized robbery, illicit trafficking in cultural goods including antiquities and works of art, swindling

and fraud, racketeering and extortion, counterfeiting and product piracy, forgery of administrative documents and trafficking therein, forgery of money and means of payment, computer crime, corruption); illegal trading and harm to the environment (illicit traffic in arms, ammunition, and explosives, in endangered animal species, and in endangered plant species and varieties; environmental crime; illicit trafficking in hormonal substances and other growth hormones; related money laundering and related criminal offences) (annex). Many of these offences enter gradually within Europol's mandate (see, for instance, Council Decision of 29 April 1999 extending such mandate to forgery of money and means of payment (OJ C149, 28 May 1999: 16).

10 Personal communication with official in the Council of the European Union, Brussels, September 2000.

11 The two additional protocols are: the protocol to prevent, suppress, and punish trafficking in persons, especially women and children; and the protocol against the smuggling of migrants by land, sea, and air. A further protocol on the illicit manufacturing of and trade in firearms is under negotiation.

4 The Business of Bribery: Globalization, Economic Liberalization, and the 'Problem' of Corruption

James W. Williams and Margaret E. Beare

Introduction

While available evidence suggests that corruption is an enduring and relatively constant feature of world political systems,[1] the past decade has been witness to a noticeable shift in the treatment of the phenomenon on both academic and policy fronts. Specifically, corruption has emerged within the context of international policy debates as a serious social problem requiring integrated anti-corruption efforts on a global scale. With this international attention, what has historically been defined as a domestic issue, and thus a cost of doing business with a select group of developing nations, has re-emerged as a global political concern. This qualitative shift is captured by Glynn, Kobrin, and Naim (1997: 7) who note that, 'Campaigns against corruption are hardly new. But this decade is the first to witness the emergence of corruption as a truly global political issue eliciting a global political response ... The 1990s, we would predict, are unlikely to pass without the achievement of significant legal and institutional anti-corruption reforms.'

To a large extent, this prediction has been borne out in practice as a number of international economic and development organizations have responded to this perceived 'crisis' of corruption through a myriad research initiatives, policy statements, and legislative reforms. These include the following:

- Proposed legislative and policy reforms submitted by agencies such as the Organization for Economic Co-operation and Development (OECD), the World Trade Organization (WTO), the International Chamber of Commerce (ICC), and the Organization for American

States (OAS). These have largely taken the form of anti-bribery conventions prohibiting the practice of bribery by member nations. The recently approved OECD Anti-Bribery Convention is perhaps one of the strongest statements of this position.

- Anti-corruption initiatives and stricter lending policies[2] on the part of international banking organizations such as the World Bank and the International Monetary Fund (IMF). These have been articulated according to a common, and coordinated strategy to enhance organizational surveillance and governance over the disbursement of funds to client countries (World Bank, 1997d; IMF, 1997).
- The formation of non-governmental organizations such as Transparency International (TI) whose primary mandate is the development and implementation of anti-corruption strategies on a worldwide basis.
- An amassing of research evidence on the part of both academics and policy makers linking corruption to poor economic growth and low political stability to which democratization, liberalization, and privatization are offered as the preferred policy responses (Ades and Di Tella, 1996; Doig, 1998; Elliott, 1997a; Glynn, Kobrin, and Naim, 1997; Hariss-White and White, 1996; IMF, 1997; World Bank, 1997a).

Despite variations in the mandates and strategies of these organizations, their efforts have coalesced into a fairly unitary and cohesive discourse on corruption. This discourse has four dominant attributes: (1) a conviction that corruption has increased to epidemic levels, and that globalization has provided much of the impetus and opportunity for this growth; (2) a high degree of consensus as to the nature, type, and cause of the global 'corruption crisis,' with corruption defined almost exclusively in terms of bribery[3] and attributed to non-democratic and highly centralized political and economic systems; (3) a preoccupation with the effects of corruption on foreign investment, and only a secondary focus on its impacts *within* developing countries; and (4) 'outsider' and top-down policy responses, such as democratization, privatization, free market liberalization, and various forms of institutional and macroeconomic reform, which tend to target the 'demand' rather than the 'supply' side of the corruption equation.

Two crucial observations follow from this discourse and its underlying foundations. First, despite the appearance of an array of separate voices all reaching the same conclusion(s), closer inspection of the corruption 'debate' reveals a clear overlapping of positions and interests. With most of the research on the topic being sponsored and conducted by members of the major economic and development agencies – the IMF, the World Bank, and the OECD – there has been a strong convergence between academic, public policy, and corporate perspectives.[4] This convergence has contributed to a singular and highly politicized account of corruption, its underlying causes, and the necessary policy responses.

Second, these positions and interests have been articulated according to a primarily economic discourse, which attributes the deleterious effects of corruption on domestic economic growth and development to its status as a source of uncertainty in economic exchanges and, thus, a barrier and disincentive to foreign investment (Elliott, 1997a; Glynn, Kobrin, and Naim, 1997; LeVine, 1989; Rodrick and Rauch, 1997). Undoubtedly, much of this effect stems not only from the existence of corruption as a variable cost,[5] but also from its association with non-democratic and non-competitive market structures, which are indicative both of restrictions on foreign trade and investment and of a lack of transparency and accountability in financial transactions. What is of particular interest here are the implicit links between (1) this status of corruption as a form of economic risk and uncertainty and (2) the more general international policy debates surrounding globalization and the professed need for improvements to the accessibility of global capital to foreign markets and the stability and manageability of these markets as they become increasingly global (and, thus, unpredictable in nature). The pre-eminence of economic liberalization and democratization as the preferred policy responses to corruption is particularly telling, given their consistency with the more general interests of foreign investors in greater market penetration and transparency.

An appreciation of this wider political and economic context is critical to understanding the perceived 'crisis of corruption,' as it suggests that the status of corruption as a social problem is founded upon general and profound anxieties concerning the nature, direction, and management of the emerging framework of economic globalization, rather than on more narrow concerns with national economic development and political stability. The implication is that the key change that has occurred over the past ten years is not, as the anti-corruption crusaders claim, the growth of overall levels of corruption or the severity of its effects on domestic economic growth but, rather, the re-framing of corruption as a source of economic risk and uncertainty that must necessarily be problematized according to the objectives and interests of the global economy. Thus, it can be argued that the epidemic of corruption is more perceived than real, and that this perception is conditioned by a broader set of economic and political interests. It is important to note that, in adopting such a position, the authors of this paper are not denying the existence of corruption, or its status as a problem deserving concerted national and international attention; rather, our intention is to provide a context for both the recent emergence of corruption as an object of international concern and the particular manner in which this 'problem' has been defined. Thus, our objective is to provide a critical counterpoint to the corruption discourse that has dominated both policy and academic literatures to date.

These links between the discourse of corruption and the wider context of economic and political globalization are described in three main sections. The first section consists of a general analysis of the international reaction to corruption and its homogeneity with respect to the causes, effects, and policy implications of corrupt practices. The second section contextualizes this discourse by tracing its relationship to the wider framework of globalization. Specifically, it shows that the very same organizations that have emerged as critical players in the anti-corruption crusade are also key proponents of economic globalization in general and of the strategies of capital mobilization and market governance in particular. In drawing together these two apparently distinct and disparate discourses of corruption and economic globalization, the third section reveals that corruption has emerged as a social problem to the extent that it constitutes a potential barrier to the effective implementation of these global economic strategies – and has done so because of its status as a form of economic risk and uncertainty in a market driven by both predictability and unfettered access. The paper then concludes with a brief reflection on the implications of this discussion for the nature of control and order within the emerging global system and, in particular, the growing involvement of non-state institutions and agencies in producing and perpetuating an order based on an explicitly economic and actuarial logic.

The International Reaction to Corruption

The context provided by the studies, reports, and policy statements issued by the key players in global economic and political policy, including the Organization for Economic Development (OECD), the World Bank, the International Monetary Fund (IMF), the Organization of

American States (OAS), and the International Chamber of Commerce (ICC), indicates the existence of a widely held belief that general levels of corruption have increased dramatically in recent years and are continuing to rise.[6] Two specific aspects of this growth have been identified as warranting particular concern. First, there is the growing concentration of corruption in developing countries with fragile or underdeveloped democratic institutions and capitalist market structures (Klitgaard, 1988). In this context, corruption is seen as a serious threat to the objectives of political and economic stability within a liberal-democratic model (Klitgaard, 1988; Meny, 1996). A recent press release from the non-government organization Transparency International serves as a strong testimonial to this concern: 'the impact of bribery on people's lives and on democracy is greatest in the poorest countries and those in transition to free market systems. Here the bribery is like a wrecking ball, destroying good government, a free press and an independent judiciary. Not to mention the destruction of basic health and education services' (Transparency International, 1997: 3).

The second cause for concern is the contribution of globalization to the perceived seriousness of the corruption problem. Globalization, it is argued, has both increased the opportunities for corrupt practices and made detection more difficult because of the proliferation of electronic commerce and off-shore financial centres (Elliott, 1997a; Leiken, 1997; OECD, 1996). This link between the context of globalization and qualitative shifts in the nature and incidence of corruption is directly captured by an OECD policy report stating that 'The expansion and globalization of the world economy have given the problem a fresh dimension. The deregulation of financial markets, the virtual elimination of exchange controls, the spread of new information technology and the development of ever more sophisticated systems of payment are making it increasingly complicated to detect and punish corrupt practices' (OECD, 1996: 9). A similar sentiment is shared by Leiken (1997: 55), who notes that 'a revolution in public opinion is transforming [the corruption] issue. The hardships of global competition have exhausted voters' patience with government excesses and misconduct.' Ultimately, these two dimensions of the corruption debate are highly instructive, as they suggest that the emergence of corruption as a social problem is not merely a case of reported or perceived increases in the frequency of corrupt practices; rather, it is a product of a specific social and economic context, that of globalization, according to which previously acceptable practices have been redefined as objects of international concern and attention. This context is crucial to understanding the nature and significance of the discourse on corruption.

Underlying these general statements concerning the growth of corruption as a global issue is a perception that two specific effects of corruption warrant granting it status as a serious social problem. The first is primarily economic in nature and relates to the deleterious effects of corruption on economic growth and the efficient distribution of economic resources (Doig, 1998; Bray, 1998; Sutton, 1997; Almond and Syfert, 1997; Elliott, 1997a; Rose-Ackerman, 1997; Mauro, 1997, 1998; M.J. Murphy, 1995; Klitgaard, 1988; World Bank, 1997a; World Bank, 1997b; Gray and Kaufmann, 1998; Kaufmann, 1997; OECD, 1996; IMF, 1997). Empirical evidence of these effects is provided by a number of studies that have found corruption to be negatively correlated with both investment and growth (World Bank, 1997b).[7] This economic perspective is clearly assumed by a 1997 World Bank report which argues that

> Global concerns about corruption have intensified in recent years. There is increasing evidence that corruption undermines development. It also hampers the effectiveness with which domestic savings and external aid are used in many developing countries, and this in turn threatens to undermine grassroots support for foreign assistance. Corruption is of growing concern to donors, nongovernmental organizations, and citizens in developing and industrial countries alike. (World Bank, 1997a: 2)

This leads the authors of the report to conclude that 'The international community simply must deal with the cancer of corruption, because it is a major barrier to sustainable and equitable development' (World Bank, 1997a: 2).

The second deleterious effect involves the role of corruption in undermining the legitimacy of both local and national governments (Doig, 1998; Sutton, 1997; Rose-Ackerman, 1997; M.J. Murphy, 1995; Klitgaard, 1988; World Bank, 1997b; Gray and Kaufmann, 1998; OECD, 1996). According to a recent World Bank Report, 'Corruption violates the public trust and corrodes social capital, and it can have far-reaching externalities. Unchecked, the creeping accumulation of seemingly minor infractions can slowly erode political legitimacy to the point where even honest officials and members of the public see little point in playing by the rules' (World Bank, 1997b: 2). This is seen to have serious implications for the political viability and stability of developing nations in particular. In combination, these effects of corruption on economic development and political legitimacy are deemed to be problematic to the extent that they undermine the principles of what has been termed 'good governance':

> The damaging effect of corrupt practices on good governance is well known and applies to all countries. It subverts the governmental decision-making process, distorts development, inducing inappropriate expenditures and waste of needed resources, and undermines the legitimacy of governments. Whatever the economic and political situation of a country, the impact of corruption can be very serious. Policies of good governance which create a favourable environment for the corruption-free implementation of public policy need to be vigorously promoted. (OECD, 1996: 5)

This international perspective on corruption and its effects is telling in a number of respects. First, the entire notion that corruption constitutes a threat to national economic development is based on the assumption that foreign investment is essential to domestic growth. Thus, the central threat is not to the allocation of domestic resources but to the effective, efficient, and accountable capitalization of foreign investment. Second, an explicit connection is made between national development, political stability, and the processes of democratization and liberalization. Here any domestic conception of development is overlooked in favour of policies that are manifestly Western in nature and design, and thus feature the expansion of democratic political and economic structures as the key to prosperity within the developing world – not to mention the greater penetration of foreign investment into new markets. It is these very processes and institutional structures that are assumed by the term 'good governance' and in relation to which corruption is defined as a serious economic and political threat.

The extent to which the international corruption discourse is embedded within the political and economic objectives of the Western nations is even more clearly revealed in discussions of the proposed causes of corruption and their perceived implications for foreign policy. In terms of the former, corruption is largely attributed by OECD, World Bank, and IMF reports to the 'overdevelopment' of the state in developing countries and, hence, to the existence of monopolistic and non-competitive market conditions (World Bank, 1997a; World Bank, 1997b; Mauro, 1998; Gray and Kaufmann, 1998; OECD, 1996). When coupled with a lack of transparency in the political process, this socio-economic context is understood to create widespread opportunities for corruption through both the production of economic rents and the establishment of institutional arrangements that provide government agents with a high degree of autonomy and, subsequently, an absence of accountability requirements in their daily activities. The role of economic rents in corruption is clearly stated by Mauro (1998), who argues that 'A key principle is that corruption can occur where rents exist – typically, as a result of government regulation – and public officials have discretion in allocating them. The classic example of a government restriction resulting in rents and rent-seeking behaviour is that of an import quota and the associated licenses that civil servants give to those entrepreneurs willing to pay bribes' (Mauro, 1998: 1).[8] These factors, combined with the low pay accorded to government officials in many developing nations, are believed to provide ideal conditions for corrupt practices through which political status is translated into economic wealth. For the most part, this etiology is reiterated by the academic literature, which similarly identifies the size of the state, the existence of non-competitive market conditions, and a lack of transparency and accountability in the political process as key factors in the onset and proliferation of corrupt practices (Goudie and Stasavage, 1998; Rose-Ackerman, 1997; Elliott, 1997a; Ades and DiTella, 1996; Hariss-White and White, 1996).

In light of this understanding of the etiology of corruption, the most frequent solution proposed by both researchers and policy makers is the expansion of the processes of democratization and economic liberalization, because, it is argued, these will contribute to a reduction in the size of government, eliminate non-competitive market conditions, and introduce greater visibility and accountability into government practices (Elliott, 1997a; Glynn, Kobrin, and Naim, 1997; Ades and Di Tella, 1996; Hariss-White and White, 1996; World Bank, 1997a; World Bank, 1997b; Gray and Kaufmann, 1998; Kaufmann, 1997; Leiken, 1997; OECD, 1996;). Through the removal of conditions that generate opportunities and create value for corrupt practices, and that provide government officials with the autonomy and low visibility through which they may execute these exchanges, the presumed result will be a significant decrease in overall levels of corruption. This policy stance is most clearly articulated by Hariss-White and White (1996: 2), who note that 'The policy implications of these analyses are that corruption can be reduced by rolling back the state through privatization and deregulation and by introducing more competition, transparency, and accountability into the political process through a transition to a democratic regime.' The implication here is that, 'In the long run, since competitive constraints will destroy the basis of rent-seeking and democratic institutions will create the political constraints necessary to enforce accountability, corruption will wither away' (Hariss-White and White, 1996: 4). The importance of economic competitiveness is also a key element of the World Bank's anti-corruption efforts: 'Any reform that increases the competitiveness of the economy will reduce incentives for corrupt behaviour. Thus policies that lower controls on foreign trade, remove entry barriers to private industry, and privatize state firms in a way that ensures competition will all support the fight' (World Bank, 1997b: 3). Ultimately, it is a very specific, Western-based understanding of market discipline that underlies the bulk of the proposed reforms. This perspective is most clearly revealed in the comments of Robert Leiken (1997) on the benefits of privatization: 'Privatization subjects erstwhile state resources to the discipline of the market and the oversight of investors. Exposing the public sector to internal, domestic, and international competition breaks up state monopolies. The freeing of exchange rates, the reduction of import and export tariffs, and the ending of price controls strip senior officials of the power to determine, for a "fee," the market price of many commodities' (Leiken, 1997: 68).

Overall, the policy reports issued by the major international aid and economic organizations all reiterate a series of widely agreed-upon causes of corruption and its impending policy implications. Paulo Mauro, a researcher and policy analyst for the IMF, makes reference to this developing consensus: 'We have a reasonable theoretical understanding of the causes and consequences of corruption, and have begun to get a sense of the extent of these relationships through empirical research. A consensus is emerging that corruption is a serious problem, and several bodies in the international arena have begun to take policy measures to curb it' (Mauro, 1998: 6). Within this framework, corruption is attributed to authoritative regimes which, through the size and breadth of the state apparatus, are able to create non-competitive economic and political markets that both generate economic rents and provide government officials with a high degree of status, power, and autonomy. With corrupt practices linked to reductions in national economic efficiency, the destabilization, of international trade and capital flows, and the undermining of the legitimacy of newly emergent democratic institutions, the proposed policy response typically includes broad policies of privatization, liberalization, and democratization, to be complemented by more specific strategies such as increases in pay for government officials, the drafting of stricter legislative guidelines and administrative policies, and the general facilitation of greater transparency and accountability in government proceedings. These accounts of the causes, effects, and appropriate responses to corruption are strikingly consistent with the political objectives and foreign policies of Western nations, a link that provides a broad, and potentially instructive, context from which the perceived 'problem' of corruption may be viewed and contemplated.

At this point, based on the preceding review of both policy and academic literatures, we wish to highlight four weaknesses in the dominant international perspective on corruption. First, what is clear in many of these analyses is the disconnectedness of the concept of corruption from the social, political, and economic contexts and conditions of nation states and local communities. Disclaiming statements aside, 'corruption' is most often treated within this discourse as a phenomenon that is uniform in nature and effect and that may be understood independently of variations in national contexts and societal conditions. However, corruption is not only decontextualized within these accounts, it is also defined in extremely narrow terms – most commonly as the acceptance of bribes and kickbacks by foreign government officials. Such a perspective is problematic to the extent that it neglects other forms of corrupt behaviour, ignores the inherent variability in definitions of corruption (Gardiner, 1993; Gibbons, 1989; M. Johnston, 1996) across different nations and cultures, and systematically overlooks the complicit role played by international trading 'partners' – such as corporations that initiate bribes and international banks that facilitate the rapid flight of capital from less developed countries (Hampton, 1996b).

A second weakness is the prevalence of an exclusively economic paradigm. This relates to the fact that, despite general and well-intentioned statements acknowledging the complex and manifold determinants and implications of corrupt practices, the international community views corruption in explicitly economic terms, with little concern for its broader social and political implications. Furthermore, this economic framework is articulated in direct reference to the self-interested Western objectives of democratization and liberalization of world trade and investment. Within this context, corruption is largely viewed as a market distortion – a source of risk and uncertainty to foreign investors – rather than an obstacle to economic growth for developing nations. The predominance of this global economic perspective is made explicit within an OECD report in which it is stated that 'Recognizing that corruption is a many-faceted problem, we were well aware that by reviewing it solely from the standpoint of international trade we would touch upon only one of its dimensions' (OECD, 1996: 10). Any lingering uncertainties as to the economic pragmatism underlying the discourse of corruption are dispelled by Almond and Syfert's assertion that, 'Ultimately, corruption will be contained because, quite simply, it is bad for business' (Almond and Syfert, 1997: 393).

A third concern warranted by the corruption discourse relates to its idealization of the 'resisting forces' ranged against corruption – privatization, liberalization, and democratization. In general, the policy literature is characterized by a naïve and uncritical acceptance of these Western initiatives as the key solutions to the problem of corruption regardless of national circumstances and contexts. One of the key limitations of these policies, as they have been implemented in a variety of countries, is their narrowness and consequent inattention to the need for wide-ranging social and institutional reforms. This exact problem is noted by Kong (1996), who argues within the Korean context that the international trend towards liberalization and democratization has been largely ineffective in countering the institutional foundations of corruption in the country. For him, this reality stems from the narrow framework according to which these efforts are often conceived: 'The evidence from countries where liberalization is advanced is that it is more a formula for promoting efficiency in a very narrow sense than a check against corruption. By contrast, fighting corruption demands effective regulation, the necessary conditions of which are the existence of a genuine countervailing institutional and societal power' (Kong, 1996: 55). Often, the result of liberalization and democratization under these circumstances is the facilitation of corruption. This has been observed by Tarkowski (1989) in Poland and the U.S.S.R., by Flannery (1998) in the African context, and by White (1996: 45) in the case of China, where, he argues, 'Chinese market reforms have created an environment in which an official has greater freedom to abuse his or her position, has more motivation to do so and less motivation not to, and has many well-resourced people willing to join the transaction on terms which offer security as well as material advantage.' What becomes clear from these case studies is the inadequacy of imposing principles of economic and political freedom while systematically neglecting the unique national characteristics and conditions that will determine their viability and reasonableness in practice.

The fourth and final concern precipitated by the corruption discourse is that, while the policies advocated by the international community are extremely narrow in some respects, they are in fact deeply intrusive in others. The international community is seemingly prepared to act with or without the cooperation or consensus of the countries targeted by anti-corruption policies. The invasiveness of this approach is reflected in the following statement made by Kaufmann:

> The time is ripe for a revolution ... The World Bank, which is poised to take concrete action can also deliver technical assistance programs to help reorganize customs institutions, develop transparent and effective treasury departments, and spearhead procurement and auditing reforms within governments ... Finally, international institutions should take steps to encourage participatory approaches in these countries in order to build consensus for anti-corruption drives and associated reforms. Civil society, wherever it is really present, is likely to be a major ally in resisting corruption. (Kaufmann, 1998: 21)

As revealed by this framing of the corruption problem, the participation of targeted countries represents a mere afterthought in anti-corruption initiatives. Once again, this is evidence of the oversimplification of the corruption issue as it is conceived within international debates, as well as of the international community's inattention to local contexts and conditions as they relate to corrupt practices and behaviours.

Overall, what emerges from this critical review of the policy and research literature on corruption is the extent to which the framework through which corruption has been defined, problematized, and remedied reflects the broader interests and demands of the global market system. Thus, corruption is largely conceived of as an economic distortion that is believed to require wide-ranging and highly penetrating campaigns of democratization, privatization, and free market liberalization, initiated almost exclusively by international organizations and agencies and charted within a growing context of foreign aid and investment. Interestingly, the framing of the corruption problem in these terms not only identifies the expansion of the free market as a key anti-corruption strategy, but also requires and legitimates foreign intervention as the basis for the successful implementation of this policy. Clearly, this entire approach both mirrors and supports the reigning

Western agenda for a free and multilateral system of global trade and investment.

In light of this apparent homology, it is our belief that greater scepticism is called for about the assumed status of corruption as a growing social problem. This more critical stance, supported by the lack of credible evidence that corruption has actually increased over the past decade, requires us to reserve judgment about this common assumption of researchers and policy makers and take a closer look at the broader social, political, and, economic contexts and conditions within which the current discourse on corruption has been fashioned. Specifically, the context that must be critically examined is that of globalization as it is represented and defined by the same international agencies and organizations who have become major players in the corruption debate. The rationale for this approach is that it is only with the increasing globalization of capital and investment, and the corresponding demands for access, transparency, and predictability in financial transactions, that corruption has emerged as a critical social, political, and, most importantly, economic issue. An initial sense of this primarily economic link between globalization and corruption is provided by M.J. Murphy (1995: 388), who argues that 'the globalization of trade as evidenced by the formation of the European Union, the signing of General Agreement on Tariffs and Trade (GATT), and, more recently, the ratification of North American Free Trade Agreement (NAFTA), makes the problem of bribery more urgent today than ever before.' Ultimately, what this perspective requires is a re-examination of the anti-corruption crusaders – the OECD, the World Bank, and the IMF – and an analysis of their broader social, political, and economic mandates as they have evolved within the context of economic globalization. It is hoped that such an effort will help to lay bare the underlying nature and dynamics of the global discourse on corruption.

Globalization and the World Economy

According to recent policy statements issued by the key players in the international arena – the OECD, the IMF, and the World Bank – we are currently in the midst of a series of fundamental and profound changes to the world economy. Specifically, it is argued that the forces of globalization, the transformation of political regimes, and the subsequent dismantling of pre-existing social and economic barriers have precipitated a movement towards the globalization of investment, capital, and trade and, thus, the integration of the world's economies on an unprecedented scale.[9] The profundity of these social, political, and economic changes is clearly articulated by Meny (1996: 315) who notes that

> The doctrine of the market has been endorsed by the economic achievements of Japan and the new Asian tigers, and reinforced, conversely, by the collapse of the socialist countries and the growing difficulties of the social democratic governments in coping with their costly Keynesian-based policies. Everywhere, under the impetus of neo-liberals or under the iron rod of the World Bank, or even of OECD, vigorous policies of deregulation and privatization have dismantled the state's legal, economic, and financial control. Everywhere, new rules of the game have been imposed and new players have emerged. Old self-interested coalitions have been challenged under the impact of new ideas and increasingly pressing external constraints bound up with the formation of new regional blocs and the liberalization of world trade.[10]

From the perspective of researchers and policy analysts, this concurrent movement towards the mobilization of global capital and the progressive integration of national economies is understood to require a fundamental shift in the ways in which the economies of the world are managed (OECD, 1997). Specifically, it is argued that future economic growth and prosperity are dependent upon the establishment of a rules-based multilateral system that will permit global capital to flow freely across international borders on the basis of universally binding rules and legislative policies. Such a model is said to be necessary in order both to ensure the growing access of capital to foreign markets and to establish a normative framework of universally agreed-upon rules, policies, and procedures according to which these capital flows may be governed. The intended result is not only the expansion of current levels of economic integration but also the assurance that this integration will be executed under conditions of stability and predictability – key components of the market economy. According to the OECD, IMF, and World Bank, two specific and fundamental conditions must be met if such a global economy is to emerge: economic liberalization, and the establishment of a system of global economic governance.

The first objective, economic liberalization, is based on the principle that future global economic development is dependent upon the unfettered access of foreign capital to domestic markets. The typical rationale for this is that these liberalized economic regimes will generate new opportunities for foreign investment[11] and, thus, attract to developing nations significant capital flows that may be used to finance social and economic development. Typically, this scenario is seen to require a number of fundamental reforms to social, political, and economic institutions – particularly within the context of developing nations – reforms designed to reduce barriers to trade and investment and to enhance the productive capacities of nation states. The pursuit of these policies is seen to be crucial for the successful integration of national economies into the global market system,

> Though the speed and sequencing of liberalization will have to be deter-
> mined by each country in light of its particular circumstances, policies
> should be geared to the ultimate objective of full integration into the
> global financial system. To this end, countries will need to set in place
> forward-looking programmes for the removal of capital controls, the liber-
> alization of cross-border financial services and the abolition of restrictions
> to market access by foreign investors and institutions. (OECD, 1997: 26)

According to the OECD, accomplishing such transformations on an international scale is essential to the maximization of economic growth and prosperity for both developed and developing nations – what it refers to as the high-performance outcome: 'The high performance scenario is not a forecast. It is a realistic possibility for the world economy, if governments undertake a wide range of necessary policy reforms. These include moving towards global free trade and capital movements, fiscal consolidation, structural reform and in the case of a large number of non-OECD economies developing the necessary ca- pacity for development' (OECD, 1997: 7). The dangers of not fulfilling these strategic requirements are also made clear: 'Against that, much worse scenarios could be envisaged, particularly if governments do not proceed with reform or do not resist protectionist pressures. A reversal of globalization could lead down the road of global fragmentation, with adverse effects for prosperity and political stability' (OECD, 1997: 8).

The corollary of this process of liberalization is the establishment of an effective system of economic governance through which emerging market economies may be integrated into the global economic order. The need for such a scheme stems from the reality that rapid economic liberalization has been accompanied by the emergence of a number of new market economies that are now open to global capital flows yet lack the institutional and regulatory frameworks through which these trade and investment flows may be regulated. This dilemma is noted by Jomo (1998: 21), who argues that 'financial liberalization has undermined previously existing governance institutions and mechanisms without creating adequate alternatives in their place.' The absence of such an economic and political infrastructure is problematic to the extent that it allows these economies to operate independently of the principles and discipline of the market system, hence elevating their levels of systemic risk and threatening investor confidence.[12] Within the context of ever-increasing levels of economic integration, this situation makes developing nations, and thus the world economy as a whole, much more susceptible to fiscal shocks and instabilities caused by the constant threat of capital flight.[13]

In response to these concerns, organizations such as the OECD, the World Bank, and the IMF have become increasingly involved in the design and implementation of a system of economic governance whose primary mandate is to introduce greater stability and predictability into the international economic system and, thus, to minimize the risk and uncertainty invariably faced by global capital as it enters into foreign economies currently outside the established market system. This general strategy consists of two key elements. The first is the establishment of stable and sustainable macroeconomic policies and positions. The necessity for these types of reforms – which typically include low inflation rates, a strong and sustainable fiscal position, the absence of large domestic price distortions, and a sound banking system – is clearly stated in a recent OECD policy report:

> It is quite clear that stable and sustainable macroeconomic policy is a precondition for taking advantage of the opportunities provided by globalization, as well as for successful structural reform. This is particularly true for non-Member countries with a history of macroeconomic instability. Low inflation rates and sustainable fiscal positions reduce the riskiness and improve the allocation of savings and investment, thereby stimulating economic development. They also allow economies to take advantage of the opportunities offered by global financial markets. (OECD, 1997: 23)

While from this account developing nations emerge as the primary beneficiaries of this reform, it is clear that the interests of foreign investors are central to the macroeconomic reform effort. This more realistic position is captured in a World Bank report, which argues that

> [developing nations] must implement policy reforms and strengthen institutions to make their markets more attractive to foreign investors and

reduce the risks of capital market instability. While investors are attracted by the potential for rapid growth and high returns, they are discouraged by operating inefficiencies, by the lack of reliability of market institutions and infrastructure, and by regulatory frameworks that increase transaction costs and reduce transparency. Improvements that increase the attractiveness of emerging markets for foreign investors also serve to reduce volatility and risks. (World Bank, 1997d: 55)

Thus, the ability to ensure a stable and predictable investment environment figures prominently in the attempts to manage emerging markets.

The second key component of this loose framework of economic governance is the enactment of institutional reforms designed to introduce greater transparency and accountability into political and economic institutions. A core objective of the OECD (OECD, 1997), the IMF (IMF, 1997; 1998), and the World Bank (World Bank, 1997d), this transparency is believed to be essential to a stable global economy, as it provides a critical flow of information through which levels of economic risk may be ascertained and permits accurate investment decisions to be made. The establishment of an effective system of disclosure also constitutes an important source of accountability through which emerging economies are inevitably subjected to the discipline of the global market. The result is the reduction of systemic risk, the strengthening of investor confidence, and the ensuring of greater economic development and stability. Thus, it is argued within a recent World Bank report that

Constructing and reinforcing the regulatory framework is essential for emerging markets to attract foreign investors and reduce systemic risk. Investors are most concerned with protection of property rights (including minority shareholder rights) and transparency. For example, investors want both macro data on economic prospects and micro data on corporate performance, to be able to make informed investment choices. Improving disclosure will not only address investor concerns but will also reduce the susceptibility of the market to volatility resulting from incomplete or asymmetric information. (World Bank, 1997d: 57)

The establishment of a regulatory system premised upon the principles of transparency, disclosure, and market discipline is also featured in the recent policy work of the OECD. However, the emphasis here is placed more directly on the private sector and the responsibilities of what is termed effective corporate governance: 'If countries are to reap the full benefits of the global capital market, and if they are to attract long-term "patient" capital, corporate governance arrangements must be credible and well understood across borders. Adherence to good corporate governance practices will help reinforce the confidence of investors, may reduce the cost of capital, and ultimately induce more stable capital flows' (OECD, 1999: 2). Once again, the provision of information through clear disclosure practices is identified as a key element of this strategy: 'The corporate governance framework should ensure that timely and accurate information is disclosed on all material matters regarding the financial situation, performance, ownership, and governance of the company' (OECD, 1999: 7).

Overall, what emerges from this review of OECD, IMF, and World Bank policy statements is a clear drive towards the establishment of a global economic order premised upon high levels of economic integration and, thus, growth and prosperity. The pursuit of this global order is understood to entail the upholding of two fundamental principles: access and accountability. Thus, we have an endless number of policy reports issued by each of these organizations detailing the benefits not only of the liberalization of trade and investment but also of the establishment of a framework of economic governance through which these liberated trade and investment flows may be governed in conjunction with the demands of the global capitalist economy. The establishment of clear disclosure practices and transparent regulatory frameworks figures prominently in these efforts. Perhaps the best expression of this dual strategy is the OECD's recent pursuit of a multilateral agreement on trade and investment (MAI), whose objective is both the liberalization of trade and investment and the establishment of a rules-based multilateral system that will provide universal guidelines and protections for financial transactions. The importance of such a strategy is clearly articulated within an OECD policy report stating that

> Widely-accepted and effective international agreements on trade, investment, finance and taxation are essential supports for the multilateral economic system. Internationally-agreed rules of the game limit the scope for domestic regulations to distort transactions. Moreover, without such rules, there is a risk that countries might have recourse to 'selective reciprocity' or opportunistically deviate from internationally-agreed upon principles for short-term advantage through, for example, trade and investment-distorting subsidies, arbitrary treatment of foreign investors, tax competi-

tion between governments, degradation in labour and environmental standards, bribery and corruption in international trade and, more fundamentally, swings between protection and liberalization. (OECD, 1997: 23)

Ultimately, then, it is clear that the international business community
is currently invested in an effort both to expand the reach of Western
nations into developing economies based on the promise of higher
investment returns and diversified portfolios, and to minimize the
systemic risks faced by these capital flows as they enter foreign markets
that have embraced the logic of the capitalist system but have failed to
enact the required institutional and macroeconomic reforms to ensure a
stable investment environment. This framework of global economic
relations is highly instructive, as it provides a fundamental context
through which the corruption epidemic must be viewed.

Globalization and the Risks of Corruption

When the discourse of corruption is juxtaposed with that of economic
globalization, it soon becomes clear that the recent transformations in
the definition of the corruption problem are linked to perceived shifts
in the organization of the global economy. From this perspective, it can
be argued, corruption is problematic to the extent that it represents a
source of economic risk and uncertainty to foreign investment and,
thus, stands in contradiction to the market requirements of stability,
security, and predictability. This very concern is expressed in a 1996
OECD Working Report:

> [Corrupt practices] hamper the development of international trade by
> distorting competition, raising transaction costs, compromising the opera-
> tion of free and open markets, and distorting the allocation of resources at
> the internal level. Corruption is a disincentive to investment: investors
> shun countries where it is endemic. Finally, corrupt practices in connection
> with development assistance cast discredit on the efforts being made, and
> provide justification for drastic cuts in aid budgets in donor countries.
> (OECD, 1996: 9)

Similar views have been expressed in both the general policy literature
and the academic literature, with corruption being identified at various
points as a source of potential risk and uncertainty to the free flow of
international capital (Goudie and Stasavage, 1998; Zedalis, 1998; Al-

mond and Syfert, 1997; Glynn, Kobrin, and Naim, 1997; Rodrick and Rauch, 1997; Elliott, 1997a; Sutton, 1997; Randall, 1997; M.J. Murphy, 1995; LeVine, 1989; Rosenthal, 1989). This is what Goudie and Stasavage (1998: 143) term the disincentive effects of corruption: 'In addition to the distortionary impact that reduces the efficiency of present economic activity, the prevalence of corruption arguably acts on the economic environment in a far more insidious manner through the creation of significantly higher levels of risk and uncertainty in economic transactions.' It is based on this status as a source of risk and uncertainty that corruption is identified as a threat to the stability and integrity of the emerging world economy. This very insight leads Glynn, Kobrin, and Naim (1997: 13) to assert that, 'As a growing number of experts are beginning to recognize, widespread corruption threatens the very basis of an open, multilateral world economy.' This danger is strongly reiterated by LeVine (1989: 687), who, as early as 1989 recognized that 'the new transnational corruption, once revealed, had to be recognized for what it was – a new and dangerous challenge to the stability and predictability of the international market.'

Thus, while national development and social equality are presented as the key issues in the corruption debate, it quickly becomes apparent that these concerns are secondary to a more fundamental and emergent awareness of corruption – particularly in the form of bribery and rent extraction – as a significant barrier to the efforts of Western nations to establish a free and efficient global economic system. Once again, the welfare of developing nations appears as an afterthought to the welfare and demands of international investors.

Despite the general recognition that corruption represents a barrier to trade and a source of risk and uncertainty to international investment, and that this risk has become amplified within the context of globalization, there has been little effort within the research literature to examine systematically these effects and their relation to more general developments within the global economy. In light of the preceding review of the policies of the OECD, IMF, and World Bank, it can be argued that the general category of corruption as a source of risk actually includes three specific elements that undermine or threaten the objectives of economic globalization. The first is most consistent with the dominant view of corruption and relates to the status of corrupt practices as additional and variable costs within financial transactions. This is what Sutton (1997: 1438) refers to as a transactional barrier: 'Transactional barriers play a harmful role in the international market, imposing additional costs on market actors and discouraging transactions from occurring. By forcing producers and consumers to pay higher costs in order to engage in the transaction, corruption functions as a transactional barrier. As such, corruption imposes additional costs on market actors with the effect of deterring market exchanges from ever taking place.' It is important to note that corruption acts as a transactional barrier not only by reason of the elevated costs of investments but also because of the uncertainty about the amount that must be paid, the payment's potential effect on a given transaction, and the added time and expense involved in negotiating with the recipients of the payment (Sutton, 1997). These factors have contributed to the finding by one analyst that the cost of investing in a relatively corrupt country, compared with that of investing in a less corrupt one, is equivalent to an additional 20 per cent tax on the investment (Wei, in Kaufmann, 1997). Thus, in a very basic sense, corruption constitutes a source of uncertainty to investors not only because it imposes an additional cost on financial transactions but also because that cost is variable and indeterminate in nature.

Corruption may also be construed as a source of economic risk and uncertainty to the extent that it constitutes a potential barrier to the free movement of trade and global capital flows through domestic markets. This effect derives from the coexistence of corruption with non-democratic and non-competitive political and economic regimes that are supported by a variety of regulatory and legislative barriers restricting the accessibility of foreign capital to domestic markets. In fact, as previously discussed, it is these closed systems that generate the economic rents upon which corruption depends. Clearly, these forms of economic protectionism stand in direct contradiction to the demands of the global market for unfettered and highly predictable access to domestic markets. In this respect, they are indicative of a critical source of economic risk to foreign investors. From this vantage point, it may be argued that corruption is problematic, not, as is commonly believed, as a threat to national economic development and political stability but rather as an indication of non-competitive, and thus risky, market structures that threaten international investment. In this respect, within the context of international demands for the liberalization and democratization of developing economies, corruption stands as a proxy for a much broader series of economic issues and concerns.

The third element of the corruption–risk equation relates to the status of corruption as an indication of non-transparent and non-accountable market processes. This follows from the reality that the restrictive and non-competitive market conditions typically associated with corrupt regimes not only constitute barriers to market access for global investors but also create conditions in which there is a high degree of secrecy, and a corresponding lack of information, about political and economic activities. This follows both from the considerable authority, autonomy, and discretion with which individuals within corrupt regimes are able to execute their responsibilities and from the systematic absence of independent regulatory bodies designed to monitor these activities. Ultimately, the results of these conditions are a serious restriction on the flow of accurate information to foreign investors and the introduction of unpredictability into the market as investors are deprived of clear information on which to base investment decisions. Uncertainty inevitably undermines investor confidence and engenders market volatility. The importance of transparency in avoiding such a scenario is clearly captured by Kopits and Craig (1998: 13), who argue that 'Fiscal transparency – defined as public openness in government institutions, fiscal policy intentions, public sector accounts, indicators, and forecasts – is fundamental to sound economic policy. Transparency allows the market to evaluate, and impose discipline on, government policy and increases the political risk of unsustainable policies.' Once again, we see that the issue of corruption serves as a proxy for a broader series of issues and concerns. Within the context of this discussion of transparency and accountability, it is clear that corruption is constituted as a form of economic risk because of its association with an economic and political infrastructure that is non-communicative and thus impervious to the demands of the international investment community. The problematic nature of corruption has thus been fashioned within a purely economic logic.

Ultimately, then, the issue is twofold. On the one hand, the global market demands free access to foreign markets. On the other hand, it also requires this access to be governed according to the recognized principles of the free market. To the extent that either of these conditions is not met, the expansion of the global market will be undermined. It is, thus, as a threat both to free market access and to the transparency and governability of this access, once achieved, that corruption has emerged as a critical problem. These links between the liberalization of economic markets, the required transparency and governability of these markets, and the status of corruption as a threat to these twin pillars of the capitalist economy are clearly articulated by

Almond and Syfert (1997), who identify liberalization and governability as two key trends within what they term the New Global Economy,

> One clear trend [in the New Global Economy] is the movement toward
> open markets and free trade. A consensus is emerging among economists
> that free trade benefits all who practice it, even though there remain many
> who do not. Free trade, its advocates relentlessly drum home, is best
> under all circumstances. Another recent trend – slower to develop, but
> potentially as powerful – concerns the darker, sometimes seamy under-
> side of international business. As competition intensifies and margins
> shrink, governments and businessmen around the world are paying closer
> attention to the risks, costs, and consequences of bribery, graft, and other
> forms of corruption in international business. It is increasingly clear that
> these two trends are interrelated and interdependent. A truly open, free,
> and competitive world marketplace requires a trading system character-
> ized by honesty, transparency, and fair dealing. (Almond and Syfert, 1997:
> 391)

The same authors ultimately conclude from this characterization of
the global economy that, 'Corruption is fundamentally incompatible
with international competitiveness; it distorts proper functioning of the
market and drains confidence in a worldwide economic system dependent on tough, but fair competition' (Almond and Syfert, 1997: 403).
Clearly what this suggests is that corruption has become largely defined and problematized in economic terms, and that this economic
framework is not only linked to the broader processes of economic
globalization but also exists independently of any substantive changes
in absolute levels of corruption.

Anti-Corruption Legislation

Another important and informative component of the discourse on
corruption relates to the debates surrounding proposed anti-corruption
legislation, particularly within the context of the OECD.[14] Framed explicitly as a 'supply-side' approach to the corruption problem, the
OECD anti-corruption campaign culminated in December of 1997 in
the signing of the OECD Paris Agreement. Consisting of commitments
by member countries to establish national legislation criminalizing the
payment of bribes by national corporations to foreign governments,
this agreement represents one of the strongest unilateral indictments of

transnational bribery to date and is indicative of at least a symbolic commitment by a number of different nations to combat the perceived corruption problem through the regulation of their own multinationals. The OECD convention entered into force on 15 February 1999, based on the submission of instruments of ratification by countries making up 60 per cent of OECD exports. These included Canada, Japan, Germany, France, and the United States. As of 12 February 1999, the required national legislation had been passed in twelve out of the thirty-four signatory countries.

The OECD agreement is informative to the extent that, in framing the need for anti-bribery legislation in terms of general concerns relating to globalization and the existence of corruption as a threat to the transparency, efficiency, and stability of the global market system, it echoes the more general policy orientation of the organization. However, perhaps more revealing is the legislation's origin in a U.S. effort to multilateralize its own anti-corruption legislation – the Foreign Corrupt Practices Act (FCPA) (Heidenheimer, 1989; Klich, 1996; Roberts, 1989). Initially passed in 1977 as a reaction to a series of political and economic corruption scandals, the FCPA was the first legislation in the world to restrict the ability of domestic corporations to practice bribery in foreign nations. Since its passage, the FCPA has received a considerable amount of scrutiny, given the contention by U.S. business interests that it undermines the competitive position of American corporations operating abroad. Specifically, it has been argued that American corporations are placed at a distinct disadvantage in relation to foreign corporations that are allowed to offer bribes in return for the procurement of lucrative contracts. Losses from this anti-competitiveness of the FCPA have been reported to be as high as $36 billion. This figure, based on a 1995 classified CIA report, represents an estimate of the value of the contracts lost during that year by U.S. companies to foreign competitors who were not bound by anti-bribery legislation. In his comments on these reported losses, Klich notes that they are largely based on anecdotal evidence, and thus do not constitute conclusive evidence of the deleterious effects of the FCPA. This leads him to the conclusion that, 'Overall, studies of the FCPA's impact on the competitiveness of U.S. companies has been inconclusive, frequently reaching inconsistent conclusions. Given such discrepancies, one cannot unequivocally conclude that the loss of business because of the FCPA is material and one cannot assess just how significant that loss is in the grand scale of U.S. investment overseas' (Klich, 1996: 141).

In light of this historical context, the U.S. efforts to introduce internationally binding restrictions against transnational bribery through the OECD may be viewed as part of an explicit strategy to level the economic playing field in response to the perceived anti-competitiveness of the FCPA (Klich, 1996; Mahaney, 1981; Muffler, 1995; M.J. Murphy, 1995; Roberts, 1989). In fact, a key provision of the 1988 Trade Act, which included various reforms to the FCPA, was a request that the U.S. President pursue the multilateralization of the FCPA within the context of the OECD (Roberts, 1989). This call for multilateralization has been echoed on a number of policy and academic fronts (Muffler, 1995).

Overall, a number of insights follow from this relationship between the FCPA and the OECD Anti-Bribery Convention. First, corruption is approached primarily from the perspective of trade. In other words, the OECD initiative grew out of perceived inequalities in trade relations rather than out of any true concern with the implications of corruption for national development and economic efficiency – the most commonly cited motives for the fight against corruption. Despite the narrowness of this initial impetus, the rationale for the anti-corruption legislation has since been expanded to include more general concerns with economic efficiency and equal access to trade markets, hence both legitimating the agreement as a policy that is good for all nations and extending the economic approach to corruption.

Second, the OECD legislation highlights the role of subjective perceptions and opinions in the corruption debate. Almost all the available evidence indicates that the FCPA does not constitute a significant threat to the competitiveness of U.S. corporations. For example, in terms of its actual economic effects, a number of recent studies have found little evidence that the FCPA has had a major impact on U.S. exports and investments abroad (Almond and Syfert, 1997; Elliott, 1997a, Klich, 1996: 141). As Klich (1996) concludes, 'Despite some recent reports, it is not at all clear that American companies are losing substantial investment opportunities because of the FCPA.' Moreover, a number of authors have identified ambiguities within the legislation that make it very difficult to enforce (Meny, 1996; Rosenthal, 1989), and have noted the disinclination of the U.S. government to pursue actual charges and convictions – relatively few prosecutions have been launched under the auspices of the FCPA (Froot, 1998; Randall, 1997).[15] Perhaps the best articulation of the problematic nature of the legislation is provided by Meny (1996: 317), who argues that 'The effectiveness of this policy is

nevertheless doubtful, owing to the many different possibilities of evasion and the difficulty of providing proof of these illegal practices. The
official remuneration of "brokers" or the use of local subcontracted
companies to carry out the "dirty job" are among the objectives sought
without committing a statutory offence.' Overall, the suggestion is that
the restrictive impact of anti-corruption legislation, like the corruption
'problem' itself, is more perceived than real.

Finally, the OECD legislation is an expression of existing inequalities
in economic power and influence – inequalities that may be seen to
underlie the entire corruption discourse. Thus, while the fight against
corruption is presented as a disinterested process designed to benefit
the global economy as a whole, it is clear that these initiatives are
conceived and orchestrated by particular nations (in this case the United
States) that are attempting to further their own economic and foreign
policies under the legitimating guise of international legislation.

Discussion: The Economics of Corruption and Its Control

Taken as a whole, this discussion of the links between recent anti-
corruption initiatives and global economic strategies suggests that the
discourse of corruption must be understood within the context of economic globalization and the management of international capital flows.
More specifically, this discourse emerges as part of a broader strategy of
global economic, political, and social governance articulated through
organizations such as the OECD, the World Bank, and the IMF. The
links between corruption discourses and the forces of global economic
governance have been shown to take two primary forms. First, it is
clear that, to a large extent, anti-corruption platforms have been inspired by the perceived threat posed by corrupt practices to international trade and investment flows. From this vantage point, international
policies designed to restrict these practices may be interpreted as part
of a broader effort to manage investment risk and ensure the stability
and security of international trade. The existence of corruption as a
transactional barrier and, hence, an investment threat is captured by
Sutton (1997: 1439), who argues that 'The uncertainty that producers
face regarding the amount they must pay and the payment's potential
effect on a given transaction, the added time and expense producers
face in negotiating with the recipients of the payment, and the expenditure of an otherwise-unnecessary payment are all additional transaction costs which act as barriers to any investment.' Ultimately, then, it

becomes clear that corruption has emerged as a source of international concern 'because, quite simply, it is bad for business' (Almond and Syfert, 1997: 392). Once again, the well-being of developing nations emerges as a secondary concern within this international discourse.

Second, based on the wisdom that the elimination of non-competitive market conditions, reductions in the size of government, and the introduction of greater visibility and accountability into social and political institutions represent the optimal policy responses to corrupt practices, it may be argued that the discourse of corruption emerges as a central element in the legitimation of the Western agendas of liberalization and democratization – policies that, in reality, have been revealed to increase corrupt behaviours and social inequalities. The explicit link between anti-corruption initiatives and Western political interests is revealed in the recent decision by organizations such as the World Bank and the IMF to make their loans contingent upon the reduction of corruption levels – usually through the fulfilment of directives such as privatization and market liberalization. This corruption-contingent status of loans is explicitly disclosed in a 1997 World Bank press release that makes reference to the new IMF policy:

> The International Monetary Fund, in new guidelines released in August, has warned its member countries that financial assistance may be withheld or suspended if government corruption is preventing their economies from moving out of trouble. The guidelines specifically mention as causes for corruption the diversion of public funds through misappropriation, involvement of public officials in tax or customs fraud, the misuse of foreign exchange reserves, and abuses of power by bank supervisors, as well as corrupt practices in regulating foreign direct investment. (World Bank, 1997c: 1)

This strategy is particularly significant within the context of the 1997 Asian economic crisis, where bail-out packages, sponsored by the U.S.-dominated IMF, were made contingent upon the satisfactory implementation of economic reforms that, in the long run, may be seen to favour Western business and political interests. Given the identification of corruption as a key factor in the collapse of various Asian economies, transparency, accountability, and democratization emerged as important elements of IMF-sponsored reform efforts in countries such as Thailand, Indonesia, and Korea (IMF, 1997). This emphasis upon transparency and accountability in the surveillance efforts of the IMF following the Asian crisis are clearly revealed in a recent IMF report:

> The IMF's work on surveillance issues intensified following the outbreak and spread of the financial crisis to other Asian economies and the subsequent pressures on other emerging market economies. Surveillance was also intensified in recognition that promoting good governance, making budgets more transparent, improving data collection and disclosure, and strengthening financial sectors are increasingly important if countries are to establish and maintain private sector confidence and lay the groundwork for sustained growth. (IMF, 1998: 2)

Ultimately, then, it appears that anti-corruption strategies once again emerge as valuable foils for the promotion of specific strategies of democratization, liberalization, and economic reform (trade and investment liberalization), strategies that, in turn, are supportive of powerful economic and political interests. In the Asian case, anti-corruption initiatives have provided a key opportunity for the penetration of U.S. business interests into the once-lucrative Asian market, primarily through the growing influence and mandates of the World Bank and IMF and their ability to enforce macroeconomic reform through loan conditions. The intersection of these underlying economic and political interests is clearly expressed by Jomo (1998: 21) in reference to the Korean context: 'Almost in tandem with financial liberalization, IMF intervention is generally recognized to undermine and limit national economic sovereignty. Particularly damning is the clear abuse of imposed IMF conditionalities in the Korean aid package to resolve outstanding bilateral issues in favour of the US and Japanese interests. Legislation and other new regulation enabling greater foreign ownership of as well as increased market access to the Korean economy – which have little to do with the crisis or its immediate causes – have been forced upon the Korean government.'

Conclusion

In summary, it appears from the above analysis that the discourse of corruption has emerged as a crucial medium for the articulation and promotion of global economic and political strategies designed both to increase the flow of global capital through the management of potential risks, such as corruption, and to lower trade barriers. Given the links between these strategies and the broader processes of democratization and liberalization, it soon becomes apparent that anti-corruption strategies must be understood within the context of global relations and the efforts made by particular nations to govern the world economy in the interest of promoting specific national economic and political objectives. In this respect, the discourse of corruption may be seen to contribute to the production, reproduction, and legitimation of an ethic of globalization, which itself represents an important form of domination and control. This very point is made by Silbey (1997), who relates globalization to what she terms 'postmodern colonialism': 'I regard globalization as a form of postmodern colonialism where the worldwide distribution and consumption of cultural products removed from the contexts of their production and interpretation is organized through legal devices to constitute a form of domination' (219). As she goes on to argue, the principle of the free market is essential to this vision of globalization: 'Globalization, or what I am calling postmodern colonialism, is an achievement of advanced capitalism and technological innovation seeking a world free from restraints on the opportunity to invent and invest' (219). The extent to which this vision of globalization – as a form of both liberalization and control – is simultaneously endorsed and promoted by organizations such as the OECD, the IMF, the World Bank, and the World Trade Organization is clearly revealed in a 1997 OECD policy statement on the 'New Global Age':

> In the rapidly changing and globalizing world economy, there will be an even greater need for international co-operation so as to realize a 'New Global Age,' and the role of the multilateral system will become even more important. There is a growing internationalization of many policy issues, which were previously more domestic in nature. And countries are increasingly confronted with a common set of policy problems, on which common solutions through identification of best practices and multilateral surveillance can be effective. In this context, the whole range of international institutions – from the UN system and the WTO, to the IMF and the multilateral development banks, and to the many regional groupings – are now working to develop policies that promote economic prosperity, political security (including through enhanced economic interdependence) and sustainable development – policies that would help realize a 'New Global Age.' (OECD, 1997: 36)

Overall, what this discussion suggests is that the issue of corruption must be approached through a critical framework that is cognizant of the broader contexts and conditions by which the corruption debate has been fashioned, and of the interests the debate acts to support. The development of such a critical position has consequences not only for the treatment of corruption as a social issue but also for the response to more general questions concerning globalization and its implications for governance, crime, and social control. Specifically, there is a growing need for criminology to come to terms with globalization as a new conceptual and empirical space that is being used to promote and legitimate a fundamental rethinking of the social order on a global scale. This speaks to the observation by Tita that 'It is a fact that globalization has created a new political and economic space, against which the existing established powers have not yet perfected an adequate response' (Tita, 1998: 48). Based on the foregoing analysis, it appears that this order is increasingly being articulated according to an exclusively economic logic through a series of organizational and institutional intermediaries that transcend the traditional boundaries of the nation-state.[16] In this respect, the problematization of corruption is significant to the extent that it provides a critical perspective on this emerging order and, thus, a point from which criminology, and social theory more generally, may begin to assess the nature and significance of globalization's new space.

Notes

This paper appeared first in *Crime, Law and Social Change* 32 (1999): 115–56, © 2000 Kluwer Academic Publishers, Netherlands.

1 According to one estimate, corruption has existed worldwide in multiple forms from approximately 3000 B.C. to the present day (Noonan, 1984).
2 Both the IMF and the World Bank have recently introduced reforms to their lending practices, making the provision of funds conditional upon the successful implementation of a variety of macroeconomic and anti-corruption reforms. This use of loan conditions to effect desired structural changes in domestic economies has met with severe criticism from a variety of national leaders as yet another form of Western imperialism.
3 The most common definition of corruption applied within the policy and academic literature is 'the abuse of public office for private gain' (World Bank, 1997a: 8), with this abuse understood primarily in terms of the offering and acceptance of bribes by public officials. According to the

World Bank, 'Public office is abused for private gain when an official
accepts, solicits, or extorts a bribe. It is also abused when private agents
actively offer bribes to circumvent public policies and processes for competitive advantage' (World Bank, 1997a: 8).

4 Of the leading researchers on corruption, two are members of international
development organizations: Paulo Mauro, an economist in the IMF's
European I Department, and Daniel Kaufmann, a leading economist in the
World Bank's Development Research Group.

5 Both competitive pressures operating on the initial agreement and the
possible requirement of future payments make corruption a variable
economic cost faced by investors.

6 It must be noted that the evidence for this increase is primarily anecdotal
and subjective in nature. Typically, it is based on corruption indexes
published by organizations such as Transparency International that ask
respondents, primarily from the field of business, to provide ratings of
the *perceived* level of corruption within a number of different countries.
Critics have responded to this methodology by noting that it is virtually
impossible to establish accurate, objective measures of corruption (Rose-
Ackerman, 1997; Meny, 1996). Thus, Susan Rose-Ackerman (1997) has
argued that 'Reliable data on the magnitude of corruption across countries
does [sic] not exist and probably cannot exist in principle' (31). Meny
(1996) comes to a similar conclusion: 'the real or assumed extent of corruption is as much a matter of perception and feeling as a mathematical
measurement of the phenomenon' (310). Nevertheless, even the recognition of these data limitations has not prevented some key commentators
from claiming significant increases in corruption levels: 'However incomplete, data from developing and postsocialist countries confirm the widespread impression that corrupt practices are increasing' (Leiken, 1997: 61).

7 Once again, methodological barriers to the accurate measurement of
corruption levels call into serious question the validity of these types of
studies – all of which rely on subjective corruption indices provided by
organizations such as Transparency International.

8 Additional sources of economic rents include trade restrictions, government subsidies, price controls, multiple exchange-rate systems and
foreign-exchange-allocation schemes, and low wages in the civil service.

9 Indices of this economic integration include the greater contribution of
non-OECD countries to world Gross Domestic Product (GDP) and significant increases in the ratio of trade to GDP and higher levels of Foreign
Direct Investment in developing economies (OECD, 1997: 15–16).

10 As the recent economic crises in Asia, Latin America, and the Soviet Union

have revealed, these developments have not been without their costs. In each of these cases, advancements in economic integration figured prominently in the economic collapse as domestic economies became increasingly dependent upon foreign investments and, thus, subject to the vicissitudes of the market and the possibility of capital flight.

11 According to a recent World Bank report, there are two forces driving investor interest in developing countries: the search for higher returns, and opportunities for risk diversification (World Bank, 1997d). The demand for new investment opportunities is particularly acute given the growing number and strength of institutional investors (e.g., mutual funds and pension funds) who are in search of diversified investment portfolios.

12 According to the World Bank, investor confidence is linked to three main considerations: 'Investors are concerned with the unreliability of emerging markets in three main areas: market infrastructure (where the consequences include high transaction costs, frequent delays in settlement, and outright failed trades); protection of property rights, in particular those of minority shareholders; and disclosure of market and company information and control of abusive market practices' (World Bank, 1997d: 6).

13 This type of effect figured prominently in the 1997 Asian financial crisis.

14 Similar anti-bribery initiatives have been undertaken by the Organization of American States (OAS) with its Inter-American Convention against Corruption, the United Nations, the European Union, and the World Trade Organization (WTO).

15 According to Randall (1997), between 1977 and 1988 the Department of Justice initiated only twenty anti-bribery cases under the FCPA, while the Securities Commission launched only three.

16 Here an interesting parallel is revealed with the work of theorists in the governmentality tradition such as Rose and Miller (1992). Among the various transformations in social control noted by these authors in what they refer to as neo-liberal society, the most significant from our point of view is the shift away from the state as a primary site of governance and control towards a series of intermediary institutions, as well as the growing articulation of social control according to a purely economic and actuarial logic. We believe this to be entirely consistent with the growing influence of organizations such as the World Bank, the IMF, and the OECD in the global social order, and with the organization of this order in conjunction with the principles of economic liberalization and the minimization of financial risk and uncertainty. The governmentality tradition thus emerges as a theoretical complement to our primarily empirical analysis.

5 Against Transnational Organized Crime

James Sheptycki

Every individual is at once the beneficiary and the victim of the linguistic tradition into which he or she has been born – the beneficiary inasmuch as language gives access to the accumulated records of other people's experience, the victim in so far as it confirms him in the belief that reduced awareness is the only awareness and as it bedevils his sense of reality, so that he is all too apt to take his concepts for data, his words for actual things.

– Aldous Huxley (1959)

Introduction

My father, a scholar who takes his wisdom where he can find it, likes to relate parables about experts and their expertise. I recall one occasion when, accompanying me as a young man out shopping for a new suit, he confided that 'Clothiers never make mistakes. If one ever sells you an ill-fitting suit, no matter what he says, he knew what he was doing.' How much simpler criminological policy making would be if social scientists were treated like clothiers. The problem is, however, that whereas tailors have both a recognizable product – clothes – and a recognizable expertise for dealing with the product, in the case of criminologists neither the product nor the expertise comes in such a neat package.

Insofar as criminologists (and social scientists more generally) have a product at all, the product is words. The expertise, such as it is, consists of stringing words together in such a way as to stimulate thought and action. Yet how clearly do we understand either the product itself or the expertise used in delivering it? The limits of our clarity become apparent the moment we attempt to grapple with an arrangement of words such as 'transnational organized crime' (TOC). The very phrase represents an object lesson. In social science vocabulary, the important words are those that set up analytical categories. Apparently, crime is now 'transnational' – rather than 'national' or 'international' – and it is 'organized,' as opposed to 'random' or 'disorganized.' These categories represent an important shift in somebody's thinking. In accepting them, we are accepting not merely their neat phonetic arrangement but, much more importantly, the assumptions built into them. These terms are a way of looking at the world. Their appearance on the criminological scene represents a paradigm shift (Kuhn, 1970). Because this new paradigm is likely to be with us for some time to come, we should subject it to some critical reflection, what Stanley Cohen (1985) referred to as 'third order reflection.' By this I mean we should not simply and unreflexively disseminate and reinforce the use of the term. Trying to understand the institutional processes and hidden biases that lie behind the words – rather than speculating about the cause of a given crime phenomenon, or advancing normative and technical solutions to it – is an important part of the criminological enterprise. Both product and expertise are at issue.

In this chapter I will interrogate the term 'transnational organized crime,' looking especially at its denotative and connotative levels of meaning. We shall also have to consider what is left obscure when that terminology is invoked. The analytical categories that we work with not only focus our thinking by casting light on specific aspects of the social world; they also shape our thinking by what they leave in the dark. In the analysis that follows I will try to show how this term is connected to other terms and to specific institutional practices in the manufacture of what J.G.A. Pocock (1973) called a linguistic authority structure. In so doing we will look at some of the law enforcement and other control practices most implicated in the response to TOC and also at the institution building that goes on in its name. Institution building guided by the conceptual apparatus pertaining to transnational organized crime is global, but this chapter will consider some specific aspects of the phenomenon in the context of Europe and contemporary Latin America, as a way of providing empirical specificity for the general propositions.

Criminologists of a strictly empirical bent might be inclined to impatience with this linguistic analysis. For them, such a pursuit is not a proper scientific one, and they would perhaps be inclined to argue that it is more akin to the kind of intellectual labour favoured by literary critics. To criminologists, who conceive of themselves as social engineers or surgeons with a box of instruments for fixing society, there are more self-evidently important questions. What evidence do we have about TOC? How do we quantify it? By what calculus do we measure its effects? What are the effective interventions against it and how do we evaluate them? In pursuit of an effective policy of crime control, their first reflex is 'to the data!' But before embarking on such a mission, it is wise to remember W.I. Thomas and Florian Znaniecki's (1960) observation that 'all data [are] somebody's data.' Moreover, all definitions are somebody's definitions, and on the meanings of words rest those apparently hard scientific facts that empirical criminologists work with. This is not an attempt to deny or sidestep William James's affirmation that 'evil facts' are a 'genuine portion of reality' (1958). Rather, it is part of the attempt to contribute to pragmatic solutions for crime and injustice that are not themselves part of the problem. It is an article of faith among many proponents of the 'war on crime' that get-tough policies will alleviate the problem of crime. Yet what is the reality behind the words?

Definitions Have Both Connotative and Denotative Meanings

Although by now a somewhat old-fashioned depiction of cognition, the notion of 'lexical look-up,' from psycholinguistics, has supplied a wonderfully graphic image of how our thought processes work (Foss and Hakes, 1978: 99). This image suggests that we are all, in effect, walking dictionaries constantly engaged in the process of referring back to our internalized definitions of terms. Of course, it is not as simple as this picture suggests. At the very least, during social interaction we are constantly adding new definitions and refining old ones. Far from being internalized 'objectively correct' definitions, our terms are experiential, interactional, fluid, and in a sense political. Further, the really interesting terms that we encounter are ones that work on two levels, the level of denotative meaning (the formal definition of the term) and the level of connotative meaning (an implied and less obvious predicate of the term). The dual level of meaning displayed by abstract analytical categories is one reason why the politics embedded in our language can be so emotive.

But words do not mean something by themselves. They take their meaning in the context of other words and in the context of social practices. As William Connolly (1983: 3) observed about the terms of political discourse, 'the concepts of politics are part of the political process itself; they give coherence and structure to political activities in something like the way that rules of chess provide the context that makes "moving a bishop" and "checkmating" possible as acts in a game of chess.' The terms of political discourse are not the only linguistic ensembles that display this feature. All language, and especially the terms of social science discourse, can be understood to work in this way. So the term 'transnational organized crime' is a constituent element in a complex 'linguistic authority structure' that has both connotative and denotative levels of meaning. The first step in coming to terms with TOC, therefore, is to interrogate its dual levels of meaning.

The Denotative Meanings of 'Transnational Organized Crime'

The term 'transnational organized crime' is not one that came naturally to criminologists, whose focus has historically been, in large measure, on the local problems of social order linked with the process of urbanization (Garland, 1997: 25; Emsley, 1997: 61–5). Neither did it come naturally to political scientists working in the field of international relations. In this field, the primary concern has been with affairs between states and, only recently, with other types of transnational institutions (Keohane, 1989). If we were to offer a date for the genesis of the term, a plausible one would be the occasion of the World Ministerial Conference on transnational organized crime held in Naples in November 1994. Definitive historical beginnings are always difficult to establish, of course, and it is true to say that the United Nations and other international organizations articulated concerns about international crime prior to that time, and not only with regard to the specialized field of drug law enforcement (Gregory, 2000). When Hugo Grotius, writing on the cusp of the seventeenth century, declared pirates *hostis humanis generis*, he began laying the foundations in international law for talking about international crime. Earlier manifestations of concern notwithstanding, the occasion of the Naples summit is a good historical moment to fix on because it provided a working definition of transnational organized crime:

> a phenomenon [with] the following qualities [as] characteristic: group organization to commit crime; hierarchical links or personal relationships which permit the leader to control territories or markets; laundering of illicit proceeds both in furtherance of criminal activity and to infiltrate the

legitimate economy; the potential for expansion into any new activities and beyond national borders; and cooperation with other organized transnational groups. (quoted in Gregory, 1998: 134)

Under this definition, TOC is depicted as a variety of pyramidically structured groups that cooperate with each other to infiltrate legitimate economies and control territory. Another way of putting it is that 'transnational organized crime represents a new form of non-state based authoritarianism' (Shelley, 1997).

Experts on TOC recognize that the matter of definition is a controversial one. Definitional debates surrounding the term 'organized crime' are not new, and the addition of the prefix 'transnational' has not simplified matters. With regard to TOC, one way to capture the definitional range is by reference to a continuum: 'at one end of the spectrum are those who see organized crime in terms of large hierarchical organizations that are structured rather like traditional corporations. At the other end are those who contend that for the most part organized crime groups tend to be loosely structured, flexible and highly adaptable' (P. Williams and Savona, 1995: 4). Descriptions of organizational structures from the pyramid to the network are straight out of the textbook of modern management, and on the face of it these metaphors seem to help render the phenomenon tangible. Concretely rendered, transnational organized crime becomes a conspiracy of organizations that law enforcement must disrupt, dismantle, or destroy. And yet this view gives rise to definitional disquiet.

The disquiet arises because, no matter where TOC is said to lie along this continuum, it is the rationality of organizational form that appears as the explanation of, or evidence for, its existence. But the supposed organization of criminal 'syndicates' is, all too often, contradicted by the actual experience of law enforcement: as one U.K. customs officer is reported to have remarked, 'you are never sure where it all leads. Once in a while we arrest someone we are sure is important ... but once we get him, he becomes no more than a tiny cog. Someone else pops up in his place' (quoted in P. Williams and Savona, 1995: 30). All that is solid melts into air and, as Gordon Hawkins (1969: 24) remarked in an earlier period, it 'is almost as though what is referred to as organized crime belonged to the realm of metaphysics or theology.' How many angels may dance on the head of a pin, and how many organized criminals may form a syndicate? However, the problem is not a metaphysical one. Rather, it is simply that the idea of stable and organized criminal structures cannot be sustained in the face of much evidence to the contrary. Careful analysis of the available data tends to show that criminal entrepreneurship is improvisational, opportunistic, and contingent (Fijnaut, et al., 1998; Hobbs, 1995), that it is 'disorganized' (Reuter, 1983; van Duyne, 1996), and that any organization that does appear is as much an artefact of state action as of criminal entrepreneurship itself (Block and Chambliss, 1981; Block, 1994; Bullington and Block, 1990; Chambliss, 1978; den Boer, 1997; Ruggiero, 2000b; Sabetti, 2000, ch. 6; see also Desroches, ch. 10 in this volume).

Despite complications, the specification of transnational organized crime advanced renders it substantiated and substantive as well as substantial. Thus, according to the social theorist Manuel Castells, 'global crime, the networking of powerful criminal organizations, and their associates, in shared activities throughout the planet, is a new phenomenon ... a myriad of regional and local criminal groupings in all countries, have come together in a global, diversified network' (1998: 166–7). Faced with this spectre, the United Nations shifted its emphasis from street crime to cross-border crime (R.S. Clarke, 1995). Over the course of the 1990s, and around the world, law enforcement bodies began to demand the tools for decisive intervention. Defining TOC in terms of a near-corporate structuring principle harks back to arguments made by Donald Cressey – the message is 'loud and clear: criminal organizations should be dealt with as organizations, not merely as collections of individual criminals, and any "attack" on them must deal with organizational structures and the social contexts in which the structures thrive' (1971: 22).

The definitions proffered by the experts are complex. They do not lend themselves to easy classification, but at the same time they have simplicity. As Malcolm Anderson observed, the term is often used 'on the assumption that everyone knows what it means' (1993: 295). Despite the ambiguity that inevitably arises out of thoughtful discussion of the evidence, the established denotative meanings of 'transnational organized crime' tend to treat it as a concrete entity or alignment of entities. This is, of course, a caricature of the phenomenon that experts are attempting to describe when they refer to transnational organized crime. The caricature is even more distorted by the connotative levels of meaning the term carries with it.

The Connotative Meanings of 'Transnational Organized Crime'

Reification – treating abstract analytical categories as if they were real things – is a psychological achievement made all the easier by the fact that concepts are laden with connotative meaning. In the case of a term such as 'transnational organized crime,' when we stretch our processes of lexical look-up for total emotional recall, we find that the words are vividly coloured. It is not just that 'transnational organized crime' conjures up visions of a criminal other; all demonological depictions of crime divide the world into good guys and bad guys. It is that TOC is imbued with the flavour of an alien conspiracy, a foreign contagion, an infectious disease from afar that threatens the health of society.

The list of transnational criminal groups identified in the annual reports of national and international policing agencies gives pride of place to an exotic diaspora of criminality: Jamaican Yardies, Chinese Triads, Japanese Yakusa, the Russian Mafiya (*sic*), Albanians, Turks, and Nigerians. This is not to say that such reports necessarily claim that all transnational organized crime is exclusively foreign; a careful reading will show that some do not. The U.K.'s *Annual Assessment of the Organised Crime Threat* (NCIS, 2000: 41), for example, states quite plainly that 'British Caucasian criminals make up by far the majority of organised crime groups in the UK.' However, the meanings of transnational organized crime are steeped in a lore about ethnic succession up the crime ladder (Haller, 1971), and also in sociological explanations about deviant adaptations to economic strain (Merton, 1949). These sociological observations help to form a background of interpretation that highlights the importance of ethno-religious and class difference in understanding the causes of crime. Such common-sense, often unconscious, sociological assumptions place already established groups or strata above the fray (e.g., see Beare, ch. 8 in this volume). Built into the TOC discourse is the assumption that those who have economically 'made it' do not have the motive to engage in organized criminal activity for illicit gain. And, without a motive, there is no cause for crime.

The notion of transnational organized crime is often read against a background of crude racial stereotyping. Denotative definitions of TOC do not usually hinge on accusations of alien conspiracy; indeed, they may even be explicitly qualified in an attempt to downplay such an interpretation. Nevertheless, the language built up around the concept of transnational organized crime establishes a separate 'criminal class' that threatens the well-being of legitimate citizens, and this tends to chime with connotative levels of meaning that involve an interplay with cultural difference and racism. The result is a vision of the problem as an external threat that needs to be repulsed.

Occasionally, the concept of transnational organized crime will be figuratively linked with infection and disease. Crime of all types can and has been characterized as an epidemic, scourge, or plague. Organized crime is a cancer to be cut from the social body. The stakes are high when the disease analogy is brought to bear. Not only does the 'disease' threaten the health of society; the semantic structure of the terminology connotes transmission from afar. The disease metaphor for TOC harmonizes with the theme of its foreignness. Since it is not *of* the social body, it can be excized *from* the social body. It can be inoculated against or, in the extreme, it can be amputated. The pain of treatment is bearable because the menace of the miasma is so plain. It is notable that, in modern Western medical practice, disease prevention is very often eclipsed by the search for the 'magic bullet' – the surgical or pharmacological intervention that promises a cure after the sickness has set in. This is also the case when TOC is construed as disease.

The interplay between connotative and denotative levels of meaning that is inherent in the term 'transnational organized crime' tends to produce images of an entity that is alien to normal society. That view rests on the fallacious assumption that normal society, even a society that has 'gone global,' can successfully exorcize crime from its midst. The plausibility of that assumption is further enhanced because TOC is constituted in a broader linguistic ensemble that sustains it.

The Terms of TOC Adhere to One Another

Exploring the connotative and denotative meanings that are attached to the concept of transnational organized crime is only the first step in getting to grips with the 'linguistic authority structure' of which the term is a part. Specialized vocabulary of this sort is deployed alongside other concepts, and so the next step is to appreciate how the terms of discourse are used in concert. Experts and policy makers typically articulate their specialist language to the lay public (and to each other) through metaphors. Of all the metaphors used for describing policies of governance during the latter half of the twentieth century, one of the most common has alluded to combat. This habit was started early in the century with 'a war to end all wars.' Since then, governments have announced policies to coordinate the 'fight' against disease, illiteracy, racism, and inequality. There have been a 'war against poverty,' a 'war on want,' a 'war on drugs,' and a 'war on crime.' Martial metaphors are particularly powerful when the object can be constructed as an external threat or a deviation from the norm. In previous sections it was shown how the denotative and connotative levels of meaning that surround the concept of transnational organized crime work to do precisely that. As a result, bellicose governments and transnational institutions alike issue an appeal to arms against TOC.

The concept of transnational organized crime is understood in direct relation to other words, foremost among which are 'immigration' and 'drugs.' With regard to the former, it is striking that the criminological literature in Europe, North America, and elsewhere is preoccupied with the question of whether ethnic minorities commit more crime than indigenous groups, a focus that produces mixed results and a good deal of controversy. It is notable that these debates are most often conducted at the expense of questions about the extent to which those groups suffer from criminal victimization (H.-J. Albrecht, 1991: 86; D.J. Smith, 1997: 711). With rare exceptions (e.g., Björgo and Witte, 1993; Bowling, 1998), criminologists have tended to look at immigrants as a crime problem, and this tendency is compounded in the literature on transnational organized crime. The fusion of immigration and TOC is highly sensitive, and H.-J. Albrecht (2000: 132) observes that 'the issue of ethnic minorities (particularly asylum seekers) and their perceived potential for threatening public safety has become a rallying point for authoritarian sentiments in European societies.' The result has been a process described as the 'fortification of European boundaries' (M. King, 1994), a process that is equally evident in North America (Andreas and Snyder, 2000).

This process of fortification is linguistically embellished: 'illegal immigrants' and 'economic migrants' are vilified for trying to elude the border patrol, while 'bogus asylum seekers' bearing false passports are said to 'flood' across international boundaries. In TOC discourse, the passage of 'illegal aliens' is aided and abetted by 'human smugglers' and 'human traffickers.'[1] As one government-sponsored report on TOC summed it up, 'migrant smuggling has emerged as a microcosm for transnational organized crime. TOC groups have capitalized on profitable illicit services that are inherently transnational in nature, while using existing smuggling "pipelines" and resources to facilitate the transport of and trafficking in people' (Schneider et al., 2000).

It would be naïve to deny that there are those who seek to profit from human misery. What is interesting is how immigration pressures from war-torn and immiserated regions are described in the language of criminal responsibility. Both refugees and those who would bilk them of their meagre financial assets are understood to be different facets of a 'crime problem': the latter because they share smuggling 'pipelines' with other transnational criminals, the former because they bring the seeds of criminality with them, seeds that are expected to blossom into vagabondage upon reaching the fertile soil of the G7 (sometimes G8) nations. Once immigration is construed as a crime problem, there is only one possible response: law enforcement.

The terminology surrounding the 'drug-crime nexus' is even more linguistically embellished. Admittedly, discussion of this language is complicated because drug policy is multifaceted (Bullington, 1993); however, the language of drug war is not. Nor is it of particularly recent vintage. Again it is important to emphasize that our understanding of drug taking is underlined by Robert K. Merton's anomie theory (1949). The drug taker is the archetype of the so-called 'retreatist.' This social type is a moral failure. Thomas Szasz (1975: 11) observed that the word 'addict' was only added to the vocabulary of stigmatizing diagnoses in 1934 and that the word 'pusher' is of even more recent vintage: 'the plain historical facts are that before 1914 there was no "drug problem" ... nor did we have a name for it ... [t]oday there is an immense drug problem ... and we have lots of names for it. Which came first: "the problem of drug abuse," or its name?' His answer is that the slow build-up, over the course of the twentieth century, of negative terminology for talking about drug taking amounted to 'verminization.'

Peter Laurie (1967: 44) remarked that the language surrounding the drug user was a barrier to understanding, but 'if we understand we can hardly condemn.' Jock Young (1971: 215) showed that the words used to describe drug takers set them apart, as anti-social, amoral, disorganized, and outside society; and argued that 'by isolating, alienating and exacerbating the social circumstances of the drugtaker we contribute significantly to the criminality.' More than thirty years ago, he predicted, correctly as it turned out, that criminalization would lead to amplification of the 'drug problem.'

Entwined within the discourse of crime, the immorality of unfettered hedonism, or psychopathology, drug takers become multiple failures. This language is thoroughly entrenched and has become taken for granted. Within these discursive parameters, 'addict populations' are dehumanized and viewed as being 'imbued with treachery'; as individuals, they are described as 'invariably unstable and almost certainly heavily involved in criminal activity' (Bean and Billingsley, 2001: 25). As a consequence, any suffering that they endure in the context of the 'war on drugs' may be rationalized as acceptable 'collateral damage.'

Drug prohibition is the paradigm case for transnational law enforcement (Sheptycki, 2000a), and the equation of drug trafficking with transnational organized crime is largely a product of U.S. foreign-policy thinking in this field (Dorn and South, 1993). It is reasonably well documented that drug prohibition was the primary *raison d'être* for the expansion of U.S. law enforcement abroad (Nadelmann, 1993: 141, 482, Appendix B), a point to which we shall return. The concern here is with how the discourse and terminology that surround the issue of drug use affect our processes of 'lexical look-up' with regard to transnational organized crime. As it turns out, the language of 'international coöperation in the campaign against a common enemy of mankind' is well established, as a document produced for the League of Nations by the Carnegie Endowment for International Peace shows (Renborg, 1943: 1). To quote at length:

> Unless controlled by the authorities, drugs represent a danger to the individual, to the nation and to mankind as a whole. This danger, however, always depends on voluntary acts by individuals or organizations. This characteristic sets it apart from other international dangers, for instance, epidemic disease ... The question arises why drugs must be controlled by international action and why it would not suffice that each government exercize the necessary control in its own territory. The reasons are simple. In the first place, illicit traffic is a very lucrative affair which by its large profits attracts unscrupulous persons and criminals. The drug addict must have drugs to satisfy his craving and is forced to pay any price the trafficker demands. The temptation to engage in illicit drug traffic is thus very strong, and illicit traffic is effectively organized, often on an international basis ... The inevitable consequence of these circumstances is that drugs must be controlled in all countries and territories ... all governments must give their collaboration ... universality is indispensable to international drug control. (Renborg, 1943: 2–3)

Described this way, the drug issue is a result of unscrupulous corrupters preying on an otherwise healthy world society, and the anti-social 'dopehead' is the product of the activities of an international economic Machiavellian trafficker. What is naturalized in the language of 'unscrupulous persons and criminals' is the illicit status of the trade; consigned to the underworld, it remains unquestionably unregulated. 'Narco-terrorism,' a term of much more recent vintage (Griffiths, 1993), fuses the assumptions of geopolitics with those of the 'drug-crime nexus' in a particularly potent mix. Globalizing the terminology of drug prohibition in this way means that other ways of talking about intoxication – religious, spiritual, or medical ones for example – are rendered all but invalid. That is a characteristic of dominant paradigms: alternative terms of discourse are disallowed. The language of 'ceremonial chemistry' (T. Szasz, 1975) is quite different from that of the scapegoat. Unfortunately, there is not room to explore linguistic alternatives to criminalization here. More central for the discussion at hand is to identify specifically criminological lacunae in the standard terms of TOC, and it is to this that we now turn.

The Dominant Terms of TOC Discourse Obscure Alternative Concepts

The problematics of immigration, terrorism, and drugs have been fused together in the discourse of transnational organized crime (Bigo, 2000: 89), and martial metaphors frequently provide the cognitive glue that holds this linguistic *mélange* together. Add the terminology of punishment, deterrence, and law enforcement to the figurative language of fighting, and the paradigm is all but cemented. Punishment is 'pain with a purpose,' that purpose being the general deterrence from criminal law infraction of the population at large (Christie, 1981). The enforcement response is, to paraphrase William Ker Muir, Jr (1977: 145), 'aggressive'; it is 'impatient and unenlightening' and 'unresponsive to what is going on inside the citizen's head and heart.' The words linked to enforcement are 'used as weapons or to incite,' but 'never to probe the soul.' This tough talk is the language of action and so promises viable and quick solutions. The Achilles' heel of transnational drug prohibition is that, despite generations spent pursuing the war on drugs, there is no sign that the problem is decreasing. On the contrary, the situation has worsened, creating live questions about other policy options that are all but obliterated by the preferred terminology of drug warriors (Nadelmann, 1988; Sheptycki, 2000a). Analogous questions might be asked about the words we have for TOC.

One of the most important developments in late-twentieth-century criminology was the rediscovery of crime prevention. Crime prevention had been a founding principle for the London Metropolitan Police in 1829 (Reiner, 2000), but over time, particularly from the 1960s onwards, it seemingly lost ground to the strategy and tactics of criminal law enforcement. Its re-emergence was occasioned by the realization that the tripartite package of law enforcement – police, courts, prison (PCP) – had failed to quell rising crime rates (cf R.V.G. Clarke and Hough, 1984). Given how important crime prevention has been to criminological theorizing, it is striking that the discussion regarding what is to be done about transnational organized crime contains only a meagre component of crime-prevention thinking (see Hicks, 1998, for the only scholarly treatment of the topic that I am aware of). The Swedish Crime Prevention Council survey of European police agencies in the late 1990s, which solicited examples of 'best practice' in preventing organized criminality, provided further evidence of this lacuna. Of the seventeen examples that came to light as a result of this research, most were primarily repressive police operations relying on the use of standard intelligence-gathering methods such as informants, surveillance, and financial investigations, followed by a series of planned arrests. All of the examples were successful law enforcement operations, but few appeared to be looking beyond immediate operational goals towards a lasting reduction in organized criminal activity (Oldfield, 2001).

It would be wrong to argue that TOC requires more preventive thinking, because prevention, unlike enforcement, is a politically neutral social practice. As has been observed with regard to prevention of 'ordinary' crime, such as burglary and theft, when crime control responsibility is outsourced to communities and individuals who have been empowered to make their own crime-prevention precautions on the free market, it often leads to inequalities of security (O'Malley, 1996; Sheptycki, 1997a). Further, situational crime prevention, particularly its surveillance aspects, has given rise to anxieties that much that goes on under its rubric is perhaps rather too Orwellian (Baldwin-Edwards and Hebenton, 1994; McCahill, 1998). Consequently, a vigorous debate about the ethics of crime prevention is underway, but this is with almost exclusive regard to 'ordinary' crime (Felson and Clarke, 1997). It is recognized within the existing crime-prevention literature that the scope of the criminal law is morally problematic and that a society in which crime prevention is maximal is not necessarily a better society (Pease, 1997). With regard to 'ordinary' crime, the prevention discourse is highly developed on all levels, from the utilitarian (what works?) to the ethical (is it good for society?). Trapped within a 'war on crime' discourse, our understanding of TOC has remained retarded, exhibiting neither a refined menu of crime-prevention techniques to apply nor a considered discussion of the political and ethical dimensions of such techniques.

Crime-prevention talk is significantly absent in TOC language, while harm-reduction discourse is positively anathema. The language of harm reduction is associated with drug policy. It is the language of public health. In that context, harm reduction begins by recognizing that the use of intoxicants is a normal feature of human life found in all cultures. It aims to develop a calculus of harm and social cost for different types of intoxicant. On the basis of this knowledge, it derives policies that pursue the least-bad option in reducing socially and individually harmful drug taking. In these terms the war-making approach is seen as a failed strategy 'pursued by those with limited imaginations, punitive inclinations and a desire for quick fixes to social problems' (O'Malley and Mugford, 1991: 60). Strong words, but words that have been shouted down. In many countries across the developed world during the last days of the twentieth century, the drug debate, entwined with the discourse of TOC, became a matter of national, and hence international, security. The vernacular of the security services trumps the idiom of public health (Sheptycki, 2000a). When we think in these terms, harm-minimization strategies to cope with illicit markets become unimaginable.

Another set of terms might also be mentioned: the language of human rights. There is some effort in the critical literature on undercover policing (Marx, 1988) and transnational policing (Brodeur, 2000) to underline the need to ensure that police practice is conducted with respect to human-rights norms. Legal developments such as the European Convention on Human Rights have been quietly acknowledged to affect all aspects of police work, and yet the war-on-TOC rhetoric creates little space for reasoned discussion. Policing should not only be required to respect human rights, it should also uphold human rights (Crawshaw et al., 1998; Sheptycki, 2000c), but the bellicose language built up around TOC focuses all attention on the need to punish and deter the 'Mr Bigs' and disrupt and destroy organized crime groups. Raising questions about the near-absence of the language of human rights in TOC talk is often characterized as an attempt to provide a protective shield to obvious wrongdoers. It is not. Rather, it poses a set of questions about how we ensure the human rights of those who suffer because of unregulated markets and from the, perhaps unintended, effects of heavy-handed law enforcement against them. Disruption may lead to displacement, and enforcement may simply result in amplification. Because TOC discourse largely eschews the language of human rights, it cannot but fail to uphold human rights.

The preferred terminology that surrounds and shapes our concerns about transnational organized crime produces images of suitable enemies. That is why some concepts articulated within the discourse, those to do with financial crime, economic crime, white-collar crime, crimes of the powerful, serious fraud in the private sector, corporate crime and corruption, environmental crime, war crimes, and state crime are only heard *sotto voce*. These alternative words for talking about transnational crime are theoretically profound and practically vital, but they remain rarefied terms used by only a few scholars, fewer of whom are in positions of power within policing institutions or the policy circles that direct the police apparatus (see Naylor, ch. 2 in this volume, for an expanded view of this point). Thus, reportage of the tenth U.N. Congress on the Prevention (*sic*) of Crime (Handelman, 2000) was devoted to a not-untypical list of organized crime types: traffickers in women and children for forced labour, drug smugglers, and, in an interesting variation, 'diamond gangsters.' Faced with such obvious evil, the writers for *Time* magazine could not help but conclude that 'the message from Vienna is hard to ignore: the longer governments wait, the further behind we will fall in the struggle to establish law and order in the new millennium' (ibid.: 58).

TOC discourse drowns out alternative concepts: where theoretically subtle terms could be used, folk devils are projected; where harm could be minimized and human rights upheld, TOC summons forth the dogs of war; and where the social basis of criminal opportunity might be reduced, the enforcers are summoned in a vain attempt to repress, deter, and disrupt. The concept of transnational organized crime, and the linguistic ensemble of which it is a part, holds forth the promise of a simple solution to a complex set of problems; but the solutions of the anti-TOC warriors cannot change the circumstances that produced the problem in the first instance. Indeed, they may make things worse.

The Terms of TOC Implicate Practices

What I have argued so far is that the terms associated with TOC discourse implicate solutions that are the ones least likely to overcome the problems of injustice that overwhelm so many people in so many places. Transnational organized crime, we are told, is a global phenomenon, and indeed, there is human misery and victimization on every continent. Let us look in a little more detail at the practices that are dictated by TOC talk. With so many potential scenarios on which to paste the terms 'transnational organized crime,' the analysis pursued here risks getting bogged down in detail and losing sight of the broader picture. Therefore, in order to focus attention on the general point, one case must stand for all. That case is 'Operation Colombia.'

On 30 June 2000, the U.S. Senate approved a spending bill for approximately $1.3 billion in 'counter drug assistance' to Colombia (IELR, 2000a: 855–6). About 90 per cent of this money was to go towards military assistance, a significant proportion of which was earmarked for the purchase of eighteen Black Hawk helicopters and forty-two Huey II helicopters. This combination of aircraft was the result of a compromise between the House, which preferred the larger and more expensive attack helicopters, and the Senate, which wanted only the less costly Hueys. Neither the intervention nor its character were in question, merely the balance and cost of the technical instruments. This financial assistance to Colombia was an expansion of counter-drug aid (from an annual $58 million in 1998, to $309 million in 1999) at a time when U.S. foreign aid overall was shrinking dramatically. In the 1990s, only Israel and Egypt received more American aid than Colombia. While previously the United States gave counter-drug aid to the Colombian police, the new initiative placed the bulk of the benefits with the military.

Plan Colombia was to include additional money from non-U.S. sources, mainly to provide for public investment to stimulate the country's economy. At a meeting in Costa Rica held in October 2000, the European Union announced an aid package of $250 million, about one-quarter of the amount that Colombian and U.S. officials had expected. According to the American and Colombian architects of the plan, this shortfall would weaken its conceptual basis (IELR, 2000b). The reluctance of the European Union to contribute more arose, apparently, from the predominant emphasis on military action of the U.S. contribution. Spokespersons for the European Union and for Latin American countries other than Colombia denounced the plan, arguing that it would lead to further militarization and spread the fighting to other countries in the region. What money the European Union did put on the table was not to be given directly to the Colombian government. Rather, it was to be distributed mostly to non-profit organizations working for human rights, judicial reform, and economic development. Given the political complexity of Colombia, such caution was well warranted. As the historian Gonzalo Sanchez explained it, the persistence of violence in Colombia is partly due to the fact that there are never only two but always many sides to any conflict there. Finding a way out of the blood hatreds and ideological feuds between ranchers, guerrillas, paramilitaries, the Liberal and Conservative parties, and the army requires real subtlety (Guillermoprieto, 2000c). In historical context, the scale and one-sidedness of the U.S. anti-TOC military intervention seemed destined to undermine efforts at building institutions of civil society and even basic infrastructure.

It is impossible to do justice to the history of conflict in that region of the world in this short chapter (see Ronderos, ch. 9 in this volume for a more lengthy discussion). The complex multisided civil war involves several 'left-wing' guerrilla movements, shadowy 'right-wing' paramilitary units, and corrupt forces within the government itself (Guillermoprieto, 2000a, 2000b, 2000c; *The Economist*, 2001c). The factionalism, violence, and insecurity feed off the cocaine economy, to be sure, but they also gain sustenance from the practices of kidnapping, extortion, and corruption, as violence leaches off foreign assistance and legitimate economic activity. Various left-wing political factions attack the infrastructure of the legitimate economy – chiefly power lines and petroleum pipelines – in a continuing bid to force a degree of political recognition from the government.[2] Right-wing paramilitaries terrorize the countryside in a campaign calculated to deny resources to their political rivals. Military assistance provided to the Colombian government is targeted exclusively at 'left-wing' forces, 'even though paramilitary groups allegedly have been responsible for most of an estimated 35,000 civilian deaths and disappearances since 1987' (IELR, 2000a: 856) and, one might add, even though all sides are equally implicated in the cocaine economy. The one-sided nature of U.S. military aid to the country has a long history – one that has never culminated in a decisive intervention, but rather has tended to reproduce the crisis that lies at the heart of Colombian society at ever higher levels.

Initially, American critics of military aid raised concerns that this would further ensnare U.S. forces in a 'quagmire' not unlike that experienced in Vietnam, Laos, and Cambodia several decades previously. Consequently, the aid bill was careful to ensure that the number of U.S. military personnel operating in the country was limited to five hundred at any one time, unless more were required in a 'rescue mission' (IELR, 2000a). These strictures did not rein in direct U.S. participation in the intervention. On 23 February 2001, it was announced that U.S.

personnel had become directly involved in fighting in Colombia's thirty-seven-year-old civil war for the first time (McDermott, 2001a). At that time, it emerged that the U.S. forces on the ground were being assisted by personnel working for Military Professional Resources Inc. (MPRI). MPRI is a Virginia-based 'military consulting firm' made up of retired senior U.S. military personnel (L. Johnston, 2000). Rejecting the label 'mercenary,' the company takes on only contracts approved by the U.S. government. In Colombia, its personnel arranged 'search and rescue teams' to operate in the countryside – teams made up almost exclusively of former members of U.S. special forces – as well as logistical and surveillance support. The activities of private companies in the context of Plan Colombia are not covered by the rules imposed on U.S. military personnel by Congress, leading some to speak of 'outsourcing a war': 'Human rights groups say the use of private contractors in Colombia is a ploy to ensure actions are carried out that U.S. troops under congressional restrictions cannot perform. They say "deniability" is the name of the game' (McDermott, 2001a).[3]

In its first year, Operation Colombia saw an increase in the amount of countryside devoted to cocaine cultivation (McDermott, 2001b) – an increase of 32 per cent according to U.S. Drug Enforcement Administration (DEA) sources. There was also a displacement of hostilities to bordering regions in Venezuela, Ecuador, Brazil, and Peru (Conteras, 2001). According to the United Nations, the hostilities had resulted in an estimated 2 to 3 million 'internally displaced persons' and an uncounted number of refugees spilling over the border into neighbouring states (*The Economist*, 2001a: 24). True to the language of TOC, developments were described using metaphors of epidemic disease: 'Colombia's drug-fueled (*sic*) civil war is infecting the region' (Conteras, 2001). It might also be observed that the cure – U.S. military intervention – has been iatrogenic. The Black Hawks and Hueys did not stamp out the disease, they merely spread the contagion.

In the early months of 2001, something of a national debate was kindled in the United States upon the release of Steven Soderbergh's film *Traffic*. In the film, Michael Douglas, playing the part of a U.S. 'drug Tsar,' famously says: 'if there is a war on drugs, then our own families have become the enemy. How can you make war on your own family?' This sentiment was articulated by others, among them New Mexico governor Gary Johnson, who said that 'the war on drugs is a miserable failure because it is being waged against 80 million Americans ... this is a war on ourselves.' This prompted Barry McCaffrey, a former 'drug Tsar,' to defend the national strategy in a letter to the *Los Angeles Times*. According to him, 'the fact is our national drug strategy is working' (above quotations from Williamson, 2001). The domestic debate in America touched upon the divisiveness of the 'them-against-us' rhetoric of the drug war, but this focused mostly on the domestic scene. Anti-TOC tactics abroad attracted far less attention from the American public. The newly elected Bush administration was no less committed to the international war on TOC, requesting $500 million in additional funding in early 2001 to fight TOC in the Andean region. The political, social, and economic circumstances present in contemporary Colombia – conditions sustained by global relations, including the U.S.-sponsored fight against transnational organized crime – served to perpetuate the conditions that TOC talk ostensibly aimed at altering. Questions about development, economic dependency, and human rights were shunted to the side by the warlike enforcement practices of Operation Colombia, and the problems there actually got worse.

Operation Colombia is only one example of the war on transnational organized crime, and it exhibits its own unique features. Were other examples to be cited, different contingencies would become apparent. Every day in South-East Asia, the Middle East, Africa, Europe, and elsewhere, the practical implications of the focus on TOC are being implemented, and each locale exhibits its own characteristics. Variations on the theme do not detract from the general point, that our terms implicate the strategy and tactics of intervention. However, neither a critique of the language of TOC nor observations of the paradoxical outcomes of its practices is enough to slow the institution building that is going on under that rubric.

The Terms of TOC Help to Build New Institutions and Refurbish Old Ones

The terms we use shape the way we think. A 'linguistic authority structure' such as that which has been built up around the concept of transnational organized crime is a house in which many of our thoughts about human misery and injustice dwell. Trapped in the house that TOC built, police agencies are becoming proactive, intelligence-led, and perhaps less able to connect with the communities they serve. Of course, we must be careful when thinking analogically about language and human action, because human beings use language as a creative tool in order to shape future action. TOC talk is being used to build new institutions and to refurbish old ones. This is the dynamic aspect of the new discourse of transnational organized crime.

A quiet revolution is currently underway in policing and security services across Europe since, as noted in a previous section, transnational organized crime has been defined as a 'security issue.' The beginnings of this building project, in the early years of the 1990s, were humble. At first there was only a temporary Portakabin in Strasbourg housing a multinational team of fifty police personnel. There, a European crime-analysis project was begun under the leadership of Jürgen Storbeck, a former senior officer of the German Bundeskriminalamt (BKA) who also had experience working within the Interpol framework. The crime analysis undertaken was limited to the drugs field at first, but 'the scope of Europol can be progressively widened so that the experience gained in establishing the drugs capacity can be applied to other relevant types of crime which pose a threat to Member States ... without wishing to prejudice the outcome of future work, it is likely that money laundering and aspects of organized crime linked to drug trafficking would be included' (quoted in Sheptycki, 1995: 624). Europol gained formal legal status in 1994. Its establishment as a transnational policing agency was potentially corrosive of state sovereignty and lacked a clear accountability structure, and this raised questions about the democratic underpinnings of the organization (McLaughlin, 1992). The persistent line of defence against these objections was that Europol would not be an 'operational' police agency; it would be concerned only with the gathering and analysis of information and thus a threat neither to sovereignty nor to civil liberties. This reply was somewhat disingenuous, since crime analysis can be a powerful way of influencing operations, as Storbeck revealed on later occasions. For example, shortly after the Europol convention came into force on 1 July 1999, he stated in terms that were only slightly veiled that since 'we are allowed, under the Europol convention, to establish our own analysis projects, I see us moving progressively to a state where Europol is in a position to take the initiative and make suggestions' (Storbeck, 1999: 10). Crime analysis shapes perceptions about the necessity for law enforcement in Europe. Such analysis is almost exclusively underwritten by TOC discourse, a paradigm that produces images of suitable enemies amenable to a control response by a complex of police agencies acting on behalf of the community of member states in Europe.

By the beginning of the twenty-first century, the creation of a transnational policing apparatus in Europe was well underway. One of the crucial nodes in this network is, of course, Europol. The European policing complex also includes agencies embedded within the constituent states of the European Union (police agencies, customs agencies, immigration police, etc.) networked together both nationally and transnationally. This multi-agency cross-border amalgam of policing-type institutions has been much studied. Less attention has been given to the security services in member states, which have in recent years also been given tasks in relation to organized crime. For example, the possibility that the U.K. security services (MI5, MI6, and GCHQ) might be given a brief to deal with organized crime, transnational and otherwise, was first recognized in 1992 (House of Commons, Home Affairs Committee, 1992). In 1995, the British government made public its intention to draft the security services into the fight against organized crime (House of Commons, Intelligence and Security Committee, 1995). At the end of the Cold War, and at the same time as a seeming diminution of 'the troubles' in Northern Ireland, the security apparatus of the British state was refurbished in order to contribute to the fight against 'the recent growth in serious organized crime, funded significantly by the world wide trade in drugs' (House of Commons, Intelligence and Security Committee, 1998: vi). According to some British parliamentarians, 'the security service can bring a distinct package of skills to this arena (intelligence acquisition, processing, assessment and exploitation); [and] its approach would be characterized by long-term investigation and analysis aimed at gaining a strategic advantage over organized crime targets' (House of Commons, Intelligence and Security Committee, 1995: 3). The National Council for Civil Liberties put forward the view that 'there is a compelling argument that in a truly open and democratic society it should be the responsibility of an accountable police force to investigate crime and not the Security Service which, because its primary role has been to protect "national security" lacks the necessary accountability and openness and is obscured by its culture of secrecy' (Leach, 1996: 224).

Despite such arguments, the perceived threat of transnational organized crime was such that these objections could scarcely prevent the refitting of the security establishment.[4] And so it was that, on 14 October 1996, new legislation extended the security services' statutory remit to include supporting police agencies in work on organized and serious crime. This legislation gave responsibility for work in the TOC area to police agencies, but allowed that the security services could be 'tasked' to undertake intelligence gathering and analysis on a case-by-case basis. Routine liaison with the (newly created) National Criminal Intelligence Service (NCIS) and other U.K. agencies was encouraged under the assumption that these tasking protocols would ensure that police remained the primary competent authorities in organized crime investigation. However, the legislation left room for ambiguity, since the security services (together with the Special Branch) maintain primary responsibility for matters of national security, including counter-terrorism. The distinction between organized crime work and national security work may become blurred in practice, and the concept of 'narco-terrorism,' which features in the academic literature on TOC, allows for this slippage.

The issue of which agency is tasking which agency and for what purpose is difficult to evaluate because of the secrecy that surrounds the work of the security services. Increased levels of secrecy began to characterize mainstream policing as it became 'intelligence-led.' Policing agencies were absorbing other aspects of security-services practice during this period. For example, the newly formed National Crime Squad announced two performance indicators in respect of its work against serious and organized crime. The first of these was in relation to the 'total number of arrests leading to primary detections,' a very traditional police goal. The second performance indicator related to the 'total number of organizations disrupted' (National Crime Squad Authority, 1999–2000: 8). Disruption is not a traditional police tactic. The term refers to the *modus operandi* of security-services professionals who, particularly in the heyday of the Cold War, did not look to law enforcement-directed court outcomes as a measure of their performance, but rather preferred to limit their adversaries' capacities in less obvious ways. The language that has grown up around the concept of transnational organized crime is a hybrid, one that facilitates multi-organizational and transnational institution building. But it is not always easy to see what is happening inside the buildings.

Although it varied according to local legal traditions and institutional conditions, the trend that consolidated TOC as a matter of national, indeed transnational, security was clearly visible across Europe at the end of the 1990s (Bigo, 2000; den Boer and Doelle, 2000; Sheptycki, 1997b). Malcolm Anderson and colleagues (1995: 179) identified a 'gradual transfer of internal and external security control [that] is taking place from the nation state to international institutions.' They warned of the possibility that, as the various security services were brought into play at this transnational level, 'the more secretive and elitist ethos of the security services would gain ground and the ideal of a transparent, rule governed and politically neutral system would become no more than a remote possibility' (ibid., 175).

Conclusion: Against Transnational Organized Crime

The policing apparatus that is being built up around the language of transnational organized crime is opaque. Half a century ago, social scientists began the slow process of making ordinary policing open and visible. The pioneering efforts of scholars such as William Westley and Michael Banton in the late 1950s and early 1960s began a slow incremental process of opening up a secret social world – the world of the police patrol officer – to outside scrutiny. The eventual result was a tradition of scientific research that has made police work more transparent and, in the process, has improved policing in democratic countries, making it more effective and more responsive to the needs of communities.

At the dawn of the twenty-first century, a veil is being drawn over police work as it is progressively redefined through the language of transnational organized crime. That terminology has significant limitations. Through the interplay of both connotative and denotative meanings, it fixates on a limited range of suitable enemies, which are targeted for repressive enforcement. More often than not, such an approach succeeds only in making matters worse. At the same time, TOC discourse precludes a more subtle understanding of the phenomenon it purports to describe and thereby diminishes the effectiveness of the response to it. When we remain trapped within the standard language of TOC, alternative ways of trying to alleviate the effects of a variety of forms of criminality become very difficult to articulate. For these reasons, if for no others, I find the phrase 'transnational organized crime' to be like an ill-fitting suit. No matter how hard I try, I cannot bring myself to put it on. We need to tailor our analytic vocabulary more precisely if we are not to dress up the problems we confront in inappropriate ways. The first step in doing that will be to forswear terms that simply do not fit.

A final thought might be added. Since this chapter was originally written, the world has witnessed one of the most devastating attacks perpetrated on American soil and the resultant declaration of a worldwide 'war on terrorism.' This raises the possibility of a further extension of the linguistic analysis of TOC to encompass the discourse that surrounds terrorism. It may be that, *mutatis mutandis*, the same analysis pertains; only time will tell how closely the interplay of connotative and denotative meanings that pervade our concept of global terrorism parallels TOC talk. What this chapter clearly shows is that the institution building that has been undertaken subsequent to the events of 11 September 2001 was already well underway before that date. Talk about TOC has been supplemented, but probably not altogether eclipsed, by the new threat of international terrorism. Although it is too early to say with definitive certainty, it does not appear that we are witnessing a comprehensive paradigm shift so much as an intensification of already existing practices. What does seem fairly certain is that, because the image of the global terrorist is even more heinous than that of the transnational organized criminal, critical appraisal of our conceptualization of global terrorism will be even more difficult than it is with TOC. Such critical thinking remains important, however, because, as the analysis undertaken in this chapter has attempted to show, the adequacy of our responses to perceived problems rests on the adequacy of our conceptual grasp of the issues. To reiterate a point made earlier, advocating this type of critical thinking is not the same as denying that there are bad people who intend to do bad things. Good people may do bad things with the best of intentions, or with no intentions at all (consider the debates that arose in the United States during the early part of 2002 regarding the usefulness of torture in combating terrorism on American soil). By examining our intentions, and how they are shaped by the cognitive apparatus that we have for describing them, we stand the best chance of ensuring that we do less harm and more good. In short, critical reflection about the terms of criminological understanding remains an essential prerequisite, lest we not only fail to achieve our aim, but even make matters worse.

Notes

This chapter is dedicated to the memory of Professor Ian Taylor (1944–2001), who taught his students to think critically about criminology.

1 The distinction is not always clearly drawn. At the denotative level, the term 'human smuggler' is supposed to delineate someone who takes money from would be migrants in order to facilitate their passage across international boundaries, whereas the 'human trafficker' is understood in

the context of slavery, either sexual slavery or, less often, sweatshop labour. The 'human smuggler' may cheat migrants of their money and merely dump them ashore, or may continue to extort money subsequent to successful passage, thus blurring the boundary with 'human trafficking.' Human trafficking is sometimes no more than facilitating travel arrangements and providing travel documents; the sort of job that a travel agent might do.

2 It is difficult to quantify the cost to the economy of this activity. According to *The Economist* (2001c), the conflict in Colombia adds \$80–100 million per year to distribution costs within the country, while sabotage to the electricity industry cost \$175 million in 2000. Spending by the country's middle class on extra personal security (bodyguards, armoured plating for vehicles, and other protective measures) is incalculable, as are the loss of tax revenue and the loss of economic opportunity resulting from the conflict.

3 The relationship between MPRI and the Colombian military was reportedly severed in February 2001 (*The Economist*, 2001c).

4 At some considerable cost. According to *The Economist* (2001b), the estimated costs of the U.K. security services (MI5, MI6, Military Intelligence, and GCHQ) range from between £1.1 billion and £2.5 billion annually, at least double what the costs were at the end of the Cold War.

6 Discourse, Identity, and the U.S. 'War on Drugs'

Kyle Grayson

Introduction

Both how and why the United States has felt compelled to view drugs as a security issue are questions of the utmost importance to an understanding of the 'war on drugs' and its numerous contradictions. In particular, understanding the notions of security that are employed to justify the war on drugs is of extreme importance. Traditional definitions of security usually concern themselves with 'the absence of military threat or the protection of the nation from external overthrow and attack' (Krasna, 1999: 47). Such definitions, though, seem to fail to provide the necessary imperative for waging a war on drugs. Do drugs in and of themselves pose a military threat to the United States? Do drugs have the potential to overthrow the U.S. federal government? One's initial reaction would probably be to say no.

To overcome this natural scepticism, one response by policy makers to this disjuncture between the threat posed by drugs and the official position taken has been to emphasize the vital importance of the production and distribution of illegal narcotics for transnational criminal organizations. Mirroring Karl Marx's comments on the significance of the opium trade to the early development of capitalism, it is often argued that the drug trade is currently the linchpin of transnational crime. Thus by employing this rationale, the war on drugs becomes a proxy for the global battle against transnational crime and the nefarious individuals involved. Yet, despite this claim, the vast majority of those being arrested for and convicted of drug violations in the United States are simply users or small-time dealers rather than high-level criminal kingpins. From a critical perspective, there are two key questions: how does this type of war on drugs become possible, and what purposes does it serve?

This chapter examines both the U.S. 'war on drugs' and the 'security-threat' rhetoric that justifies this war. The two terms are interrelated – understanding the use of either term in reference to drugs is necessary in order to understand the other. We have become so used to hearing the phrase 'war on drugs' that it takes its place alongside other war situations – and yet there is little similarity. Critics of the 'war' termi-nology argue that few, if any, of the conditions of more traditional definitions of security threats, such as the potential for external over-throw and attack (ibid.) are met. Supporters of the 'war' approach bemoan the failure to launch an actual all-out military response. The general public, however, is swayed by these arguments. By invoking these traditional definitions of security in framing responses to the international drug trade, policy makers have led many Americans to believe that the dangers posed are so great that 'war,' traditionally con-sidered the last recourse of political activity, is the only way to address the issues of drug production, trafficking, and consumption. Under-standing this seemingly no-win strategy is the task of this chapter.

Perceptive war theorists have argued that, throughout the ages, war and the conduct of warfare have had both ontological and strategic purposes.[1] While wars are fought for reasons such as territory, eco-nomic disparity, and geopolitical calculations, all wars may serve to shape the identity of those who have fought in them. Victory in war, while providing certain spoils, also reinforces a state's sense of identity. Conversely, defeat in war not only requires costly concessions but also calls into question a state's national identity (e.g., the United States and Vietnam) (Shapiro, 1997). While we may falsely assume that these are 'secondary' benefits or costs, some wars are waged specifically to rein-force boundaries, sense of sovereignty, and a moral imperative rather than for any of the more traditional war booty.

As an example, Shapiro singles out Aztec society as being unique in that the majority of the Aztecs' 'Flower Wars' – wars that took the form of highly ritualized combat with weapons that required a high degree of expertise – were largely ontological rather than geostrategic in na-ture (ibid. 50–1). In contrast to regular wars over territory, the primary purpose of Flower Wars was to demonstrate martial skills and serve the resulting prestige structure.[2] While Flower Wars sometimes changed into wars of territorial conquest, they were primarily used to secure captives and to provide combat training to the warrior class (Hassig

1988: 128–30).[3] The taking of captives was a means of upward social mobility, and the total number of captives taken over a lifetime of combat was a determinant of status in Aztec society. Unfortunately for the captives, they were almost always sacrificed. According to James Ingham, 'the sacrificing of slaves and captives and the offering of their hearts and blood to the sun thus encoded the essential character of social hierarchy and imperial order and provided a suitable instrument for intimidating and punishing insubordination' (quoted in Shapiro, 1997: 51).[4] Therefore, Aztec warfare, through the practice of Flower Wars should be seen as a method to strengthen Aztec identity and to demonstrate that a particular way of life was justified and good.[5]

The war on drugs is perhaps best understood as the closest thing that modern industrial societies have to a 'Flower War.' The war on drugs has been primarily about distinguishing the American national identity from that of 'others' (outsiders) who, by producing and using drugs, engage in hedonistic, medically unsafe, and morally corrupt behaviour.[6] In addition, the war on drugs has been in part about demonstrating martial skill, whether it be by intercepting drug shipments at the American border, eradicating drug cultivation in foreign countries, arresting a local street dealer, or capturing the president of a sovereign state. By being able to show the public these accomplishments through the media, American 'true' and 'good' foundations are legitimated. A difficulty arises, however, in that, unlike the Flower Wars, the war on drugs does not have a clean start and finish or a clear victor. Despite the barrage of 'successes' touted in the media, there is concern among both analysts and policy makers that at best the war on drugs is a stalemate.[7] It is likely to be a war that the United States will ultimately lose – or will need to redefine. How is it, then, that the United States finds itself engaged in a war that it probably cannot win, and where losing the war may place aspects of the American national identity at risk?

Writing Security and the U.S. War on Drugs

Drugs discourse within the United States is conducted within very limited parameters.[8] Drugs are assumed to be harmful in and of themselves and potential catalysts for the creation of other security threats. Neither the harm nor the link between drugs and other security issues are questioned or problematized. The enemy is clearly defined – that is, it is found to be outside the United States and to be exploiting the weaknesses of U.S. citizens. On occasion, the 'enemy' may be within –

but is then typically a problem for marginalized segments of the wider population. Every nationality, from Afghani to Nigerian, is blamed for America's drug problem. Locating the drug problem 'outside' (i.e., defining it as 'alien') speaks to solutions that reinforce the status quo at home.

In *Writing Security: United States Foreign Policy and the Politics of Identity*, David Campbell argues that the war on drugs, in the absence of the Communist threat, has formed a new discourse of danger to reproduce American identity. Because the state has never been a stable ground to anchor national identity against ontological threats, foreign policy as a practice must both 'reproduce and contain challenges to the political identity of nations such as the United States,' thereby preserving socially constructed national identities (Campbell, 1997: 196). He argues that, regardless of the hype, the rationales behind the war on drugs (i.e., levels of drug consumption, deaths from drug consumption, and the crime-drug nexus) provide actual levels of danger far below what one would think necessary to surround the drug issue with an 'evangelism of fear' (ibid. 200). Therefore the war on drugs must be about a different issue; that issue is keeping the American national identity at the status quo in the face of 'foreign' challenges.

The strategy being utilized is a familiar one. The war on drugs has borrowed many of the practices employed during the Cold War in the domestic battle against Communism – including language (the normal versus the pathological), targets (e.g., minorities and subcultures), methods of exposure (e.g., testing for deviance), and threat formulation/ reaction – in order to maintain a 'society of security' that defines an 'increasingly narrow optimal mean in the tolerable bandwidth of normal behaviours' (ibid. 207–9). A policy of drug containment is deemed essential in order to prevent the occurrence of the 'domino effect.' Innocuous drugs are seen to represent the 'slippery slope' into addiction, and entrepreneurial drug suppliers are seen to be the visible limb of vast organized crime empires. The domestic *and* international policy response is seen to rest on a combination of discipline and surveillance. By constructing a system of social discipline (rather than social control), policy makers create a standard by which attitudes and behaviour can be authorized or proscribed as legitimate or illegitimate (ibid. 209).

In Campbell's analysis, the war on drugs bears all the hallmarks of a morality play designed to reinforce the ethical boundaries of identity and demarcate the boundaries between 'foreign' and 'domestic' (ibid. 210). Therefore, within the United States, drug users are considered to be un-American/foreign and/or diseased. This is replicated at the international level, where Campbell illustrates that 'the discursive practices of the "War on Drugs" which focus on the external element of the danger, serve to illustrate the frontiers of America' and sustain the notion of sovereignty through the creation of a 'geography of evil' (i.e., drug-producing and transit countries), (ibid. 210, 214). The war on drugs 'replicates earlier narratives in American history which have identified un-American behaviour at home and abroad' (ibid. 215).

While Campbell's analysis of the U.S. war on drugs provides an excellent starting point and guide for re-examining drugs as a security issue in the post–Cold War era, we must understand in greater detail where the U.S. 'knowledge' about drugs comes from and why it has taken the form that it has. It is imperative to discover how a 'regime of truth,' to use Foucault's phrase, has been established within the drugs discourse. When the myths produced by the regime of truth surrounding the drug discourse are compared to the available empirical evidence, it becomes clear that the war on drugs is a war that the United States is doomed to lose.

More attention must be paid to the disciplinary techniques utilized in the war on drugs. Campbell is able to illustrate at the domestic level how disciplinary techniques such as drug testing and surveillance have affected not only those considered to be targets (e.g., minority groups) but also 'normal' Americans, who fear that these techniques may be used against them. This analysis can be extended to show how, at the international level, disciplinary techniques have been utilized and how these have affected America's enemies/allies and reinforced notions of hegemony.

At the domestic level, the war on drugs has been a tool used to silence alternative views within the United States. At the international level, the war on drugs is an ideal arena in which the United States may demonstrate its leadership and skills, as Aztec city-states did during Flower Wars. Moreover, by formulating a low-level crisis in which it must take the leading role, the United States is able to reproduce itself and its hegemonic position in the absence of other significant threats through the utilization of disciplinary techniques (e.g., certification and invasion) that are given 'justification' by the pursuit of a war on drugs.

The Process of Prohibiting Drugs

The fact that drug prohibition is itself seldom seen to be problematic limits the approaches the state can take to the war on drugs. Prohibition is uniformly taken as the starting point for many analyses of international drug trafficking or government responses to drug-related criminality. In *The History of Sexuality*, Foucault argues that prohibition is a powerful discursive ruse for this very reason. Prohibition becomes the basic and constituent element that one must work from when discussing topics such as drugs (Foucault, 1990: 12). Despite the fact that the United States presents itself as a country where individual freedom is paramount (often beyond levels some would consider to be practical – as, for example, with the right to bear arms), drug laws are to a large extent about power relations and controlling the individual body. In addition, they are also ontological in that they have been used to define the American national identity, often in combination with a racist ideology.

The history of American drug laws is relatively brief – the earliest legislation being around 130 years old. The Opium Laws in the late 1870s served to marginalize Chinese immigrants by restricting their ability to import and use opium. Laws against opium smoking were one of the methods used to legally target the Chinese population and as a way to distinguish them from Americans 'proper.' The racial-targeting aspect of drug laws continued with the first laws restricting the use of cocaine, in the wake of many newspaper reports in 1914 concerning the bizarre criminal behaviour of the 'Cocaine Negroes' of the American South (E.H. Williams, 1914). Furthermore, early marijuana laws were directed against Mexican migrant workers, who at the turn of the century began to migrate to states of the American Southwest. When one looks at the legislative records of these states, it becomes clear that the prohibitions against marijuana had nothing to do with the drug per se but were motivated by hostility towards the new Mexican communities (see Whitebread, 1995).

Counter-cultures have also been the targets of American drug laws. The jazz musicians of the 1940s, the Hippies of the 1960s, and current-day ravers have all found themselves victims of U.S. drug laws. And, as with the targeting of other minority groups, health has not been the primary concern. For example, it is debatable how much the scheduling of LSD in the most-dangerous drug category at the height of the Vietnam War had to do with its chemical properties and how much it was motivated by a University of Southern California study that showed it was making graduate students more open-minded to other viewpoints and less materialistic (McGlothlin, 1967: 14).[9] Anything that might make Americans even more anti-war (such as LSD) would likely have been seen as threatening by the U.S. government.

Until 1969, U.S. drug laws were, in fact, tax laws. One would be charged for not paying a flat tax of several thousand per cent on a drug purchase or sale. Before the law was changed in 1969, it was not uncommon for an individual in the United States found guilty of possession of marijuana to face a twenty-year minimum sentence with no chance of parole, even though this was technically a sentence for tax evasion.

Despite the existence of punitive drug laws that found their inspiration in racial bigotry rather than public safety, the full fury of American opposition to drugs and drug use did not fully manifest itself until Ronald Reagan launched his 'official' war on drugs in 1982 by securing an amendment to the Posse Comitatus Act. This amendment allowed for military involvement in civilian law enforcement for the first time in more than a hundred years (Bertram et al., 1996: 112). In his 1983 State of the Union address, Reagan proclaimed: 'It is high time that we make our cities safe again. This administration hereby declares an all-out war on big time organized crime and the drug traffickers who are poisoning our young people' (quoted in ibid: 113). The war on drugs was unique because it involved a two-pronged approach to dealing with America's drug problem.[10] The first prong was traditional in that it concentrated on the domestic level. Cocaine became the primary target as it began to flood the U.S. drug market in response to increasing demand, primarily from white middle- and upper-middle-class citizens who saw it as fashionable. During the mid-1980s, media reports from urban ghettos on the growth of crack, a potent and cheaper derivative of cocaine, created a panic.[11] The perception of an increase in drug use was the motivation for increasing drug penalties for dealers and consumers. Harsher drug laws and sentences caused prison populations to sky-rocket to the point where almost 5.7 million Americans are either currently on probation, in jail, in prison, or on parole.[12] Sixty per cent of federal prisoners are serving time for non-violent drug offences.[13] Furthermore, despite the fact that it was the demand of 'white' America that fuelled the 'cocaine boom' of the 1980s, minority group members have borne the brunt of the war on drugs, particularly African Americans.[14] While incarceration rates for both whites and African Americans have skyrocketed since the beginning of the war on drugs, the rate for African-American males is 7.0 times that for whites.[15]

Another important aspect of the domestic war on drugs (besides increasing levels of incarceration) was the introduction of asset forfeiture and seizure laws. Under the civil forfeiture provisions of the RICO statutes, law enforcement agencies were given the civil power to take away any financial assets or property that appeared to be involved in, or a result of, criminal activity, without having to file criminal charges against an individual. The idea was to provide a financial discouragement for engaging in criminal activities, to limit the power and influence that drug dealers would be able to exert on the justice system through their personal wealth, and to redistribute resources to the various branches of law enforcement involved in the war on drugs (Bullington, 1993: 53–61). While the American government has considered asset seizure to have been an overwhelming success, in part because it has helped to fund the war on drugs, the policy has facilitated serious abuses of power by law enforcement agents.[16] For example, evidence has shown that fewer than 20 per cent of those who have assets seized are ever convicted of a crime.[17] Moreover, the majority of asset seizures are for under $1,000, contradicting the belief that these laws target big-time criminal enterprises.[18]

The second prong of the war on drugs concentrated on reducing the supply of drugs from countries identified as drug producers and traffickers.[19] While interdiction efforts had always had a primary role in drug enforcement, the war on drugs demanded that America take a more proactive role in reducing the supply of drugs available. The United States, through government organizations such as the Drug Enforcement Administration (DEA), began operations within an assortment of countries identified as drug producers and traffickers in Latin America, the Caribbean, and South-East Asia. Military equipment was often donated to assist in efforts to eradicate the cultivation of illegal drugs and to fight powerful drug cartels, which often had their own large, privately financed armies. Furthermore, the United States tried to pressure foreign governments to sign extradition treaties so that high-ranking members of drug cartels could receive a 'fair' trial in the United States. Many of these American-sponsored policies were vehemently opposed, not only by the drug cartels but also by the populations at large within these countries.[20] As pressures mounted, these policies began to be seen as issues of sovereignty and imperialism in producing countries.[21] Opposition in Colombia to extradition was so fierce that a paramilitary force sponsored by the Medellín Cartel and led by guerrilla activists attacked the Colombian Supreme Court, killing all but one of the justices. There was less public outcry than one would expect, primarily because of the widespread support for the anti-extradition position.[22]

As the war on drugs continued, the process of militarization became more and more pronounced. What had begun under the guise of a law enforcement exercise began to turn into a military campaign. While countries of Latin America requested police equipment, intelligence-gathering devices, and technical assistance in establishing judicial systems free of corruption, the United States sent them conventional arms (Bagley, 1992: 5). The full-scale militarization of the war on drugs was best demonstrated by President Bush's unilateral decision to invade Panama with American troops in order to capture President Manuel Noriega (a CIA informant), who had been implicated in drug-smuggling and money-laundering activities (ibid. 5). Militarization has continued to the present day, with a gigantic aid package to Colombia that focuses on supplying military aid and arms rather than improving social, political, and economic institutions, as many Colombians had requested.

Despite the militarization of the war on drugs, it became obvious that eradication and interdiction efforts against foreign producers were not reducing the quantity of drugs available in the United States. Furthermore, estimated levels of drug use that had dropped in the early years of the war on drugs, as many middle-class and upper-middle-class individuals found that the potential costs of drug use (i.e., jail) outweighed the benefits, once again began to rise (Bullington, 1993: 64–5). Confronted with evidence that the war on drugs was 'addicted to failure,' the United States pointed to corruption and a lack of cooperation from producer countries, placed all of the blame on them, and utilized a new technique to try and ensure compliance with American drug-control efforts.[23] Known as the 'certification procedure,' this technique, which began to be used in the late 1980s, involved several processes. First was the creation of a yearly International Narcotics Control Strategy Report, which identified all of the major drug-producing and transit countries with the aid of gathered intelligence. Second was the creation of Section 490 of the Foreign Assistance Act, which requires the U.S. President to certify on an annual basis that each major country has cooperated fully or has taken adequate steps on its own to meet the standards of the 1988 United Nations Drug Convention. Governments that the President feels have not met the standard lose their eligibility for most forms of U.S. military and economic assistance. They also face an obligatory 'no vote' by the United States government for loans in six multilateral development banks.[24] Regardless of the certification process, the volume of drugs available and drug consumption have continued to flourish in the United States (U.S. General Accounting Office, 1997).

The failure of the war on drugs is most often addressed as a technical issue. Experts lament that not enough money is being spent on reducing supply, while others argue that more should be spent on reducing demand. As a result, the war on drugs is viewed as an equation that, in order to be balanced (i.e., successful), needs certain variables to be added, some to be subtracted, and others to be manipulated. There is, however, an alternative way to view the war on drugs.

America's War on Drugs from a Foucauldian Perspective

In his own work, which has covered topics as diverse as sex, madness, and criminality in Western societies, Michel Foucault expresses a common underlying theme: what is defined as deviant behaviour within a society is not the result of an objective assessment of the potential harm of a particular act.[25] Instead, deviant behaviour is defined subjectively by societies through an interplay of various (often unequal) societal actors and institutions in the form of power relations that deem certain actions to be legitimate and others to be illegitimate. Therefore, deviance plays a functional role in society by legitimating state interference, proscribing behaviour within certain boundaries that serve particular social hegemonies, and masking both the nature and power of these social hegemonies. With regard to the war on drugs, the Foucauldian concepts of power, regimes of truth, Panopticism, and docile bodies help to demonstrate the socially constructed nature of deviance and the social interests that this construction serves. By targeting minorities and various American counter-cultures, drug laws and the war rhetoric serve a deep ontological purpose in that they help to form the American identity by demonstrating what is not 'American' and what activities are not pursued by 'real Americans.'

For Foucault (1990: 93), power is everywhere and is being exercised from innumerable points in the drug discourse – not merely from the top down; in fact, power can also come from below (ibid. 94–5). From this perspective, the American government, law enforcement agencies, medical practitioners, drug users, drug producers, and 'average' citizens are all involved in a set of power relations that has defined the 'truth' regarding drugs. Spaces that might have facilitated a radical rethinking of the war on drugs have been filled via the manipulation of the drug discourse towards exclusive concern with issues of prohibition.

In *The History of Sexuality*, Foucault (1990: 11) speaks of the power–

knowledge–pleasure nexus that shapes who is allowed to speak, from what positions and viewpoints they may speak, the institutions that prompt people to speak, and the institutions that store and distribute what they have to say. Not surprisingly, he feels that 'truth is not outside of power or lacking in power ... truth is a thing of this world ...' (Foucault, 1977: 131). In other words, truth does not exist independent from society and its institutions. It is generated by these institutions based on prevailing ontological interests.[26] Therefore, in order to be able to establish what is true, Foucault argues that 'each society has its regime of truth, its general politics of truth: that is the types of discourse which it accepts and makes function as true; the mechanisms and instances which enable one to distinguish true and false statements; the means by which each is sanctioned; the techniques and procedures accorded value in the acquisition of truth; the status of those who are charged with saying what counts as true' (ibid.). These have all been operationalized within the drug discourse. 'Facts' regarding drugs are determined by the interwoven power relations and ward off the degree of debate that would challenge the prevailing rhetoric. As Foucault has shown with sex, 'facts are often servile with respect to the powers of order rather than being amenable to the requirements of truth' (Foucault, 1990: 54). Hence, in the public arena (facilitated by media reports and political rhetoric), rather than the illegal status of particular drugs being blamed for creating conditions that foster health risks and violence, drugs are seen to be by their very nature the major killer in American society.

The drug discourse has therefore created its own regime of truth based on a loose adherence to the scientific method as presented by doctors, research scientists, lawyers, law enforcement officials, and state bureaucrats.[27] According to this regime,

- Drug use is inherently bad as it is medically unsafe and morally corrupt.
- Real Americans do not use drugs.
- Foreigners and other deviants use, traffic in, and produce drugs.
- Prohibition is the natural conditon for drugs.
- Drugs are the major source of criminal activity.
- Drugs are a major killer of Americans.
- Drugs have the potential to destroy the current international system.
- Science is the only measure that can determine the potential value of drugs.

Although those who disagree with the current drug laws and the war on drugs are often allowed to speak in opposition, they must frame their arguments within the parameters dictated by the regime of truth that operates within the drug discourse.[28] For example, if one wants to argue that marijuana should be legalized and be taken seriously, one must present 'scientific' evidence that demonstrates that it is helpful in curing particular diseases. Other systems of knowledge (e.g., religious and/or non-Western) that might inspire similar claims do not hold enough legitimacy within the drug discourse (or American society for that matter) to be given due attention.

The power relations manifested within the drug discourse also keep the majority of discussions on the use of drugs centred on those that have been made illegal. We speak of drugs and use drugs without realizing that we are doing so (e.g., caffeinated beverages such as coffee and tea, over-the-counter medications such as aspirin, Tylenol, and codeine, and legal recreational drugs such as alcohol and nicotine). Hundreds of such drugs are advertised daily in the media. We encourage those with mental disorders to take certain drugs. We sedate our children who have been diagnosed with attention deficit disorder with drugs. When we encounter health problems, we take drugs to treat the condition almost without thinking. When we cannot sleep we take drugs and when we cannot stay awake we take drugs. Far from being repressed, drug use is rampant in modern Western societies such as the United States, yet the repression and prohibition of certain drugs is still embedded in our thinking as the primary condition of existence.

Furthermore, because repression and prohibition are our starting reference point when engaging in the drug discourse, the war on drugs becomes an inevitability. Most people feel that at least some drugs must be completely prohibited, thereby maintaining a role for the war on drugs.[29] Very few (if any) involved in the drug discourse advocate the complete dismantling of the war on drugs.[30] Positions critical of the war on drugs usually focus on making technical improvements to the anti-drug machine (e.g., Falco, 1996).

From the Foucauldian perspective, America's drug laws and the war on drugs have expanded the operation of American Panopticism at the national and international levels. 'Panopticism' refers to processes of surveillance that appear to be so overt that those who believe they may be subjects of surveillance modify their behaviour at all times because of the expectation that they are probably being watched (even though they may not be). The purpose of Panopticism is to maintain asymmetrical power relations between the observer and the potential subjects of surveillance.[31]

At the national level, drug laws and the war on drugs have served as justifications for increasing levels of surveillance on American citizens, particularly those who are members of minority groups. At the most overt level, in the name of protecting society from the drug scourge, the privacy of individuals in the United States has been invaded through electronic listening equipment, video surveillance, phone taps, and police searches backed by 'probable cause.' At a more covert level, America's drug laws and the increasing rates of incarceration under the war on drugs have created a whole class of people with permanent negative documentation. A criminal record for non-violent drug offences brands an individual potentially for life and makes it hard for him or her to find gainful employment. Probation and parole also operate as panoptic monitoring systems making a sizable part of the American population aware that their movements may be monitored.[32] With the vast numbers of minority males being found guilty of drug offences in the United States, the asymmetrical distribution of power between them and the 'Anglo-American' establishment is able to entrench itself further within American society.

However, it is not just at sites of incarceration that docility is manufactured. As mentioned earlier, David Campbell (1997) has argued that the drug prohibition and the war on drugs have aided in the maintenance of an American 'society of security' where behaviour is increasingly constrained within a shrinking tolerable bandwidth. For example, the use of peyote by Native Americans in religious ceremonies had been tolerated in the United States for most of the past century and became legal for members of the Native American Church with the passage of the American Indian Religious Freedom Act in 1978. However, in 1990, this freedom became bounded as a result of a decision rendered by the Oregon Supreme Court and upheld by the U.S. Supreme Court holding that 'peyote's sacramental character could carry no weight against "neutral" laws passed by the state against "criminal" activities' (Stewart, 1991: 58).

Reflecting the society of security in a subtler manner, many leaders of African-American communities have found themselves in a bind. Holding the initial perception that their neighbourhoods were being ravaged by illegal drug use, many supported the war on drugs. As time has passed, however, many now realize that the consequences of this effort have been extremely damaging. At the same time, trapped within the regime of truth surrounding the drugs discourse, many are still not ready to accept the position that the drug prohibition must be re-examined (see Freedman, 1998). Atlanta mayor Bill Campbell (an African-American Democrat) has argued that 'We must reject all proposals to legalize illicit drugs, because it is morally reprehensible to consider an action that would (a) erode our children's anti-drug attitudes of risk and social disapproval and (b) make harmful and addictive drugs far more accessible' (ibid. 37). By having in place a 'legitimate' legal inroad to target counter-hegemonic groups as well as the social apparatus (i.e., the regime of truth) to constrain behaviour, the state can pre-empt great debates and silence alternative voices.

At the international level, the war on drugs has also facilitated the processes of surveillance, although in a much cruder manner. Unlike Foucault's Panopticism, which in its ideal form does not necessarily need an observer, countries know that they are being watched and who is doing the watching. Numerous countries identified as major drug producers and traffickers are monitored by the United States to see if they are complying with the American drug-control regime.[33] Military surveillance equipment is used to track drugs as they move through their distribution network.[34] Intelligence is gathered on the levels of cultivation, trafficking, corruption, political will, domestic drug use, and the effectiveness of domestic law enforcement (U.S. General Accounting Office, 1997).

As mentioned earlier, the certification process is the primary technique of Panopticism used by the United States. This process has allowed the United States on the one hand to maintain its asymmetrical economic power relations with several regions by tying economic development aid to effective participation in the 'war on drugs.' On the other hand, certification has caused the United States to separate foreign development from the U.S.-waged drug war by failing to recognize that engaging in drug production and trafficking is often the very result of regional economic underdevelopment.[35] Moreover, the war on drugs has legitimated American interference (in the eyes of the American public) in the internal affairs of other states such as Colombia, Bolivia, Peru, and Panama. This, of course, has served to reinforce and remind both citizens of the United States and others of American hegemony.

The certification procedure has also had implications for developed countries of the Western world such as Canada and has produced a more nuanced form of Panopticism that has helped maintain the drug status quo. Well aware that they are being monitored for drug-related activities, countries such as Canada are encouraged to turn drugs into a major domestic and international issue (Alexander, 1990: 24). For example, Canada has recently been threatened by the United States for not being proactive in the fight against marijuana cultivation. Hal Klepak has argued that 'for the United States, the issue [i.e., drugs] has even become something of a touchstone for testing the loyalty of other countries in the post-Cold War era' (Klepak, 1993–4: 67), and many countries seem to agree with this assessment as they pursue policies similar to or congruent with the war on drugs. With the exception of the Netherlands, few Western countries administer a domestic drug-control regime markedly different from that of the United States.[36]

From a Foucauldian perspective, the ultimate goal of American's drug laws and the war on drugs has been the production of docile bodies. Western societies such as the United States have attempted to increase both physical productivity and obedience to authority.

At the domestic level, individuals involved with prohibited drugs are thrown into prison, perhaps the harshest form of discipline available in Western societies. Moreover, those found guilty of drug offences in U.S. District Courts tend to get longer sentences than those charged with crimes such as rape, fraud, and civil-rights violations.[37] Drug users and dealers are considered to be society's deviants. As Foucault has illustrated, medicine of the Victorian era wove an entire network of sexual causality to explain deviant behaviour; today it is prohibited drugs that have taken over the bulk of the responsibility for playing this role (Foucault, 1990: 65). For example, look at the number of crimes reported in the media as 'drug related.' Yet the relationship between crime and illegal drugs is not as strong as these reports would suggest. Although 35.6 per cent of inmates have reported using an illegal drug at the time of their offence, an average of 30.6 per cent of those in the criminal justice system (i.e., on probation, in jail, or in prison) reported consuming alcohol at the time of their offence. Therefore, the link between crime and illegal drugs is not as dominant as is suggested, especially if one considers that a significant percentage of the American prison population is in for drug-possession charges (and would likely be using drugs around the time of their arrest). It is also difficult to ascertain what role (if any) these substances might have played in anti-social behaviour (see U.S. Department of Justice, 1998).

To facilitate processes of depoliticization, several states have laws that disenfranchise those who are convicted felons and are in prison or on parole.[38] It is no wonder, then, that minorities and members of counter-cultures are those that tend to be targeted by drug laws and the war on drugs.[39] By having a legal inroad that facilitates the incarceration of those who may be politically active, engaging in counter-hegemonic social discourses, and presenting challenges to the prevalent notion of American identity, it is probably hoped that the spirit of dissension can be broken, counter-hegemonic movements destroyed, and 'trouble-makers' assimilated into what has been decided upon as the 'American way of life.'

At the international level, the war on drugs is a catalyst in the creation of 'docile countries.' Arguments are made that eliminating the drug economy in regions such as Latin America and South-East Asia will make them economically efficient and more profitable as sites for American foreign investment.[40] Yet neoliberal reforms tend to contribute to the economic, social, and political circumstances that encourage drug production.[41] At the same time, manipulating these countries into pursuing the war on drugs through processes such as certification ensures political obedience and recognition of American hegemony. Essentially, these countries are co-opted to an extent into becoming 'quasi-American.' This process, though, still creates enough difference within the international drug discourse to allow the American government and the American people to distinguish themselves from those they have identified as the major drug nations. As mentioned earlier, the international aspect of the war on drugs is also able to keep countries that might not be susceptible to American influence in line with American hegemonic aspirations by ensuring that they pursue particular drug policies.[42]

The Foreign Policy of the U.S. War on Drugs

I have demonstrated through the utilization of Foucauldian concepts, theories, and techniques, that America's drug laws and the war on drugs are not about protecting the public safety and health of Americans. Rather, all those elements that compose the American drug-control regime should be seen as issues of ontology and American identity. Returning to David Campbell (1997), we see that his argument that an important link exists between national identity and the practice of foreign policy is extremely significant.

The practices of foreign policy are seen to help to hide the socially constructed character of identity within societies such as the United

States. Therefore, the successful and effective practice of foreign policy requires that internal threats to identity be attributed to factors external to the state and that they be managed without creating the opportunity for the political contestation of national identity. It is little wonder, then, that America's drug problem is blamed on 'other' nationalities and 'other' countries.

A new reading can be made of the progression of American drug laws. First, there appears to be a correlation (with the exception of the Marijuana Tax Act) with increasing levels of immigration to the United States and the composition of 'others' within these migrations.[43] There also appears to be a correlation between American drug laws and situations of flux and uncertainty. For example, turn-of-the-century drug laws such as the Harrison Act were passed at a time when the United States was having to deal with the outbreak of the First World War. Finally, it also does not appear to be a coincidence that drug laws were traditionally introduced into regions along the frontier. After all, these are the geographical locales in which the 'national identity' would have been perceived as being the most vulnerable to the influences of the 'other.'[44]

Campbell maintains that the link between foreign policy practices and national identity is especially evident in the foreign policy history of the United States because it represents to a certain extent Benedict Anderson's 'imagined community par excellence' (D. Campbell, 1997: 11). From the brief genealogy of American drug laws presented earlier, it is quite apparent that, from the beginning, these laws were about distinguishing Americans from those perceived to be inferior and morally corrupt.[45]

From an international perspective, the war on drugs has been about distinguishing the American system of governance and American society in general from 'others.' Certain countries are identified as having a major drug problem that they have tried to export to the United States in order to weaken America and change its identity. These states are identified as having characteristics such as ineffective control over their territory, scarce national resources, weak economies, corrupt law officials, widespread crime, traditional cultivation and use of drugs, and a lack of political will.[46] If the United States does not try to combat this situation, it is implied that Americans, too, will soon live in a country with these sorts of problems. Given how this danger has been constructed, the certification process solidifies American ontology and identity in two different ways. First, it serves to reinforce American hegemony by having the United States elect itself as the judge, jury, and execu-tioner in the trials of those countries that it believes to be major drug states. Second, the process implies that the only way for these countries to join the ranks of the civilized world is willingly to participate in the war on drugs and do exactly what the United States says they should do. For example, the International Narcotics Control Strategy Report, 1998, states that 'The United States will continue to provide necessary leadership and assistance to our partners in the global antidrug effort. As one of the countries most affected by illegal drugs, we cannot afford to give up any of the ground gained in the last decade. The success of this effort, however, depends not on one country but on the coopera-tion and commitment of our allies in the worldwide drug control effort' (Bureau for International Narcotics and Law Enforcement Affairs, 1999: 8). The foundations of American hegemony (which play a major role in the ontology and identity of the United States) are therefore further strengthened through the war on drugs.

Conclusions

Sun Tzu, a military general and philosopher, outlined what he believed to be the keys to military success in *The Art of War*. He advised that war be only a means of last resort; however, there are further words of wisdom that are of utmost importance to the American war on drugs. Sun Tzu stated that 'If you know the enemy and know yourself, you need not fear the result of a hundred battles. If you know yourself but not the enemy, for every victory gained, you will also suffer a defeat. If you know neither the enemy nor yourself, you will succumb in every battle.'[47] Given the centrality of identity issues in the war on drugs, it is obvious that this is a war that the United States cannot win because its knowledge of both the self and the 'enemy' is lacking.

Because the use of drugs is not considered a part of the true American identity, its prevalence in American society is downplayed or ignored. 'Others' (e.g., Latinos and African Americans) are the ones who are seen as using drugs and having the drug problem. Yet the fact remains that the United States is the world's number-one consumer of illegal drugs and also one of the biggest producers of illegal drugs. U.S. government statistics that have been cited by the DEA show that about 12.7 million Americans have used an illegal drug within the last month, between 30 to 40 million Americans have used an illegal drug within the past year, and 70 to 90 million Americans have used an illegal drug during their lifetime.[48] These statistics are considered to be conservative estimates, as they are the result of monthly telephone surveys; after all, how many people would willingly admit to an illegal act over the telephone to a stranger? Moreover, as drug use in the United States continues to rise, it has been fuelled not by members of minority groups or the counter-culture but by white, middle-class Americans.[49]

In terms of production, Uncle Sam is the Pusher Man. Marijuana continues to be the biggest cash crop in California, Kentucky, and Georgia, forming a multibillion-dollar underground enterprise (Jennings, 1998).[50] In 1998, close to 1,700 illicit drug laboratories were seized in the United States (Bureau for International Narcotics and Law Enforcement Affairs, 1999). Despite the overwhelming evidence that America is a 'junkie,' the myths that drugs are a preoccupation of the 'other,' that drugs have been pushed (rather than welcomed with open arms) on American society by the 'other,' and that 'real' Americans do not use or produce illegal drugs continue to shape the American world view and the national identity.

While the United States suffers from the denial of its prohibited drug problem, it at the same time does not recognize its rampant use of unprohibited products that are drugs (Parascandola, 1995). Many of these substances – including nicotine, alcohol, and caffeine – are considered as medically dangerous as those drugs that have been prohibited (and in some cases more dangerous).[51] Because Americans do not perceive these products to be drugs, the non–drug-user aspect of the American national identity remains intact.[52]

Knowledge of the enemy in the war on drugs is also lacking. This is compounded by the fact that the war on drugs seems to be fighting several different enemies at once: drugs themselves, the 'marginalized other' represented by drug users in the United States, and the 'foreign other' represented by major drug states in the international system. In terms of drugs, what is considered to be knowledge is part myth and part 'bad science.' Science in the Western world is equated with civilization and progress. Therefore, a scientific regime of truth that steers the drug discourse prohibits the introduction of arguments from other modes of rationality (e.g., issues of drugs, religion, and the human spirit). This, then, makes all questions about the American drug-control regime seem like technical issues and masks their true ontological and identity-based roots. What is desperately needed in terms of public health and safety (and not necessarily to make the war on drugs winnable) is research into drugs, their uses, and their potential long-term liabilities. This research does not have to be confined to the natural sciences. Other fields, including anthropology, criminology, sociology, economics, political science, and security studies, should re-examine drugs and the discourse of drugs, free from the yoke of prohibition as a starting point.

In terms of knowledge of the 'other' represented by drug users in the United States, America has to understand that it is itself the 'other.' The use of prohibited drugs is not an activity confined to minority populations or counter-cultures; currently in the United States, significant numbers of the white middle-class establishment have used or are using prohibited drugs.[53] Richard Lawrence Miller has argued that 'drugs do not threaten the American way of life; they are a part of it' (Miller, 1994: 154). Therefore, the non-drug component of the American national identity is false; it is a myth that was formed by a racist ideology at the turn of the century. Charles Whitebread has speculated that, as increasing numbers of white, middle-class Americans are arrested for violations of drug laws (particularly marijuana), prohibitions might fall. After all, 'no prohibition will stand, ever, when it comes back and penalizes our children, the children of the U.S. who enacted it' (Whitebread, 1995).

At the international level, the United States suffers from a lack of knowledge of the 'other' represented by those it has deemed to be major drug-producing states. Few involved in the war on drugs examine how these countries got to the point where producing and trafficking drugs became a viable and often essential economic activity. Instead, these countries are seen as evil drug pushers contaminating American society with their seditious wares. William O. Walker has argued that 'supply-side policy makers in the United States have historically assumed that narco-traffickers were national actors' (Walker, 1993–4: 40). Therefore, drug production and trafficking are viewed as conscious attempts by these states to destroy the American 'way of life.'

If America's drug warriors began to ask 'how' certain states reached the point where large-scale drug cultivation was a viable option, I believe that a different enemy would become the target of the war on drugs. As has been argued within the United Nations literature, drug production, drug trafficking, poverty, and economic underdevelopment are connected and mutually reinforcing. If the United States wants to stop drug production in these countries, it must address issues of poverty and international economic inequality. However, this places the United States in a 'Catch-22' situation. If the major drug-producing countries are able to develop economically and their populations are able to enjoy a higher standard of living, much of the basis for America's ontological outlook will be lost.[54] In essence, the United States needs these countries to be economically underdeveloped and involved in the drug trade in order to maintain its hegemony, keep its national identity intact, and maintain faith in its chosen 'way of life,' which perceives no legitimate role for 'illicit' drugs. Therefore, the national and international drug problem has been constructed by American policy makers as a means to other identity-based ends.

At the same time, American policy makers have been able to merge drugs, transnational crime, traditional conceptions of security, and all of the images, symbols, and feelings that these conceptions evoke through their associated discourses, thereby constructing the drug trade as a paramount issue for American national security. Yet it is not the cumulative direct physiological effects of drugs and the drug trade itself that pose threats to the United States. Rather, it is the American identity and its foundations that are at risk if the United States loses its war on drugs. As such, the war on drugs paradoxically appears to be a vicious circle from which drug users, drug producers, and those charged with the task of eliminating the (inter)national drug trade will be unable to escape.

Notes

This paper is a shortened version of the Major Research Paper requirement for my Master's degree. I wish to thank my two supervisors, David Dewitt and David Mutimer, for their help, guidance, and support during all of the stages of this project. I also wish to thank the Nathanson Centre for the Study of Organized Crime and Corruption for financial support while conducting further research on this paper, and the York Centre for International and Security Studies for providing the opportunity to have this paper initially circulated in a draft form. Any errors, though, are my own responsibility.

1 See for example, Michael J. Shapiro (1997).
2 Ross Hassig (1988: 128–30) warns against overemphasizing the ontological nature of Flower Wars (a mistake that appears to be present in Shapiro). In many respects, he argues, they were also about exerting dominance over another city-state without having to engage in a full-scale territorial battle.
3 The combat on the battlefield was usually non-lethal. The types of weap-

ons used in 'Flower Wars' were designed to require a high level of skill in order to effectively injure opponents.

4 See also John Ingham (1984: 369).

5 In other words, victory in a Flower War provided 'proof' that a particular city-state (including its way of life) was better than its opponent.

6 The general idea here is that, according to the accepted view of the American national identity, Americans do not use drugs.

7 Gains made in one area are often balanced by setbacks in another. For example, the *International Narcotics Control Strategy Report 1998* indicates that while opium cultivation in the Western Hemisphere is on the decline, there is little that the United States can do to curb cultivation by the major Asian producers, who account for 90 per cent of the world's supply. See Bureau for International Narcotics and Law Enforcement Affairs (1999).

8 For examples of this type of literature see Stephen E. Flynn (1994); Ivelaw L. Griffiths (1993); and Mathea Falco (1996).

9 In another report prepared for the U.S. Justice Department's Bureau of Narcotics and Dangerous Drugs in 1969, the authors state that 'LSD has become a rallying point for some young adults, particularly those who denounce the dominant values of American society.' See Richards, Joffe, and Spratto (1969: 27).

10 For a discussion of the approach of the war on drugs see Bullington (1993).

11 Despite the stereotype that the typical crack user is African American, statistics show that two-thirds of crack users identify themselves as white or Hispanic; however, 84.5 per cent of those who are convicted of possession of crack are African American. Moreover, sentencing guidelines for crack are far harsher than those for powder cocaine (5 grams of crack worth about $200 is considered equivalent to 500 grams of powder cocaine worth about $20,000). See *The Sentencing Project* at *http://www.sentencingproject.org/*. Retrieved June 1999.

12 Approximately 1.6 million Americans are in jail or prison. No other 'democracy' in the world (with the exception of Russia) approaches these levels of incarceration and surveillance. See U.S. Department of Justice (1998) and *The Sentencing Project* at *http://www.sentencingproject.org/*. Retrieved June 1999.

13 See Clifford A. Schaffer, 'Basic Facts about the War on Drugs,' at *http://mir.drugtext.org/druglibrary/schaffer/library/basicfax.htm*. Retrieved March 1999. Twenty-three per cent of those in state prisons are serving time for drug offences. See *The Sentencing Project* at *http://www.sentencingproject.org/*. Retrieved June 1999.

14 Although African Americans make up only about 12.4 per cent of the

population, they represented 38.4 per cent of those charged with drug violations in 1998. In a broader context, while African Americans are arrested (for all violations) at 2.5 times their representation in the general population, they are imprisoned at 4.5 times their overall representation. In addition, African Americans and Hispanics are more likely to receive a court-imposed mandatory minimum sentence for drug trafficking (35.2 per cent and 37.8 per cent respectively) than their white counterparts (25.1 per cent). See U.S. Department of Justice (1998); Coffin (n.d.); and Schiraldi, Kuyper, and Hewitt (1996).

15 See Schaffer, at *http://mir.drugtext.org/druglibrary/schaffer/library/basicfax.htm*, March 1999.

16 The sheer monetary value of these seizures is astounding. In 1997, asset seizures by the Drug Enforcement Administration (DEA) alone accounted for $551 million. For the time period 1993–7, the DEA confiscated more than $3 billion in assets. See U.S. Department of Justice (1998).

17 See Schaffer, at *http://mir.drugtext.org/druglibrary/schaffer/library/graphs/22.htm*, March 1999.

18 A and E Investigative Reports, *The Crystal Methamphetamine Epidemic.*

19 In the 1970s, the United States had 'assisted' Turkey in trying to combat opium cultivation and heroin smuggling.

20 For critical discussions of the foreign component of the U.S. war on drugs see Gugliotta and Leen (1990); Perl (1994); and W.O. Walker (1993–4).

21 Many arguments were made that the United States should first deal with the issue of American demand rather than foreign supply.

22 For a first-hand account of the incident see Gugliotta and Leen (1990: 402–18).

23 The term 'addicted to failure' is borrowed from Mathea Falco (1996).

24 For an official discussion of the certification process see Bureau for International Narcotics and Law Enforcement Affairs (1999).

25 This argument is meant to counter those who claim that certain acts (e.g., illicit drug use) can be objectively considered deviant by their very nature.

26 For example, in medieval Europe, the Catholic church was empowered to decide what could be considered true and created a methodology to determine truth. This methodology and the decisions that resulted from it were obviously based on a particular reading of biblical texts that predetermined what could be said to exist.

27 It is interesting to note that, at first, the prohibition against certain drug activities was couched in terms of morality. As we saw earlier, to use certain drugs was to be like the Chinese, Mexicans, or African Americans, and to be devoid of morality and decency. Slowly, starting with the Mari-

juana Tax Act, officials had to begin to provide scientific evidence (however flawed) in order to justify prohibitions. This is not to say that the moral aspect of prohibitions against drug use has disappeared (one need only look at how drug addicts are portrayed in the media to see that it is still framed as a moral issue), but that to a certain extent, prohibition has supposedly become more about using science to protect the human condition from the dark side of human nature.

28 Usually they must be a lawyer, judge, scientist, doctor, or law enforcement agent. Even then, those who are engaged in the 'war' against the war on drugs are usually unable to initiate changes in the policy community's discursive practices, even though these critics are fellow members of the élite (e.g., George Soros, Milton Friedman, George Schultz, Mathea Falco). Therefore, one cannot underestimate the embeddedness of the drug discourse within American policy circles.

29 In stark contrast to reality, prohibition is seen as being the natural state of affairs when discussing drugs.

30 For example, in a survey of American opinion leaders, only 24 per cent of respondents favoured the legalization of drugs. See Holsti and Rosenau (1996: 36).

31 See Foucault (1984a: 217–18) and Michel Foucault (1984b: 212).

32 The infrastructure and equipment needed to administer the programs aimed at targeting criminals and monitoring their activities also serve to condition the behaviour of ordinary citizens towards societal 'norms,' as they may feel that these surveillance techniques are also being directed against them.

33 The audacity of the world's biggest illicit drug consumer and fellow producer state in passing judgment on others almost needs no comment.

34 Yet military surveillance has not led to any reduction in the estimated flow of illegal drugs into the United States. See Rodrigues (1993).

35 United Nations analysts have concluded that 'debt, falling commodity prices, poverty, and drug trafficking are interconnected and mutually reinforcing.' Quoted in Jamieson (1990: 3).

36 Recently, the Netherlands has come under increasing fire from the United States and Great Britain (both of which are prime destination points for Dutch-produced synthetic drugs) for its liberal drug-control regime. See L. Collins (1999).

37 The median sentence for rape is 50 months; for fraud, 14 months; for civil-rights violations, 27 months; and for drug offences, 60 months. See U.S. Department of Justice (1998).

38 *The Sentencing Project*, a prisoner advocacy group, estimates that one in

seven African-American males in the United States are prevented from voting by these laws. In seven states that deny the vote to ex-offenders, one in four African-American men are permanently disenfranchised. Given the current rates of incarceration, three in ten of the next generation of African-American men can expect to be disenfranchised at some point in their lifetime. In states that disenfranchise ex-offenders, as many as 40 per cent of the African-American men may permanently lose their right to vote. See *The Sentencing Project* at *http://www.sentencingproject.org/*, June 1999.

39 More shocking is that it is not high-level dealers within these groups that seem to be the targets. Instead, 75 per cent of arrests are for possession. Most possession arrests (36 per cent) are for marijuana. See U.S. Department of Justice (1998).

40 Some of this persuasion might also argue that eliminating the production of drugs would stop flows of migrants into the United States from Latin America.

41 For a discussion of the contradictions between neoliberal structural adjustment and drug cultivation in Latin America, see Peter Andreas (1995).

42 For example, British moves to remedicalize the drug issue in response to HIV in the mid-1980s were subverted by DEA officials, who helped to create a 'crack scare' in the United Kingdom by 1989. This led to the adoption of stricter drug laws and a reorganization of drug enforcement in a manner similar to that of the United States. See Dorn and South (1993: 76–7).

43 For this analysis, 'others' were defined as people who immigrated to the United States from Asia, Mexico, and the Caribbean. Although for most of the time periods the 'other' represented only a small percentage of the total volume of immigrants, drastic increases in their numbers were perceived as threatening. For example, in a treatise that claimed to be sympathetic to Chinese immigration, Rev. O. Gibson used a pestilence metaphor when he referred to the Chinese as 'the vast population of heathen, now our near neighbours, and swarming on our shores ...' (see Gibson, 1877: 6).

44 The history of American drug laws also points to the fact that the discourses of foreign policy can be applied domestically.

45 While one might argue that American distrust of hedonistic activity can be traced back to its Puritan roots, historical evidence suggests that the Puritans had absolutely no inhibitions about getting drunk, and that they treated alcoholics with compassion. See H.G. Levine (1979) (Also available at *http://www.lindesmith.org/library/tlclevin.html*.)

46 An example of this type of text is the following: 'other significant, long standing obstacles also impede U.S. and drug producing and transit

countries' drug control efforts; in the drug producing and transit countries, counter-narcotics control efforts are constrained by competing economic and political policies, inadequate laws, limited resources and institutional abilities, and internal problems such as terrorism and civil unrest; moreover, drug traffickers are increasingly resourceful in corrupting the countries' institutions' (see U.S. General Accounting Office, 1997). Yet, many of the same problems (e.g., terrorism, corruption, and civil unrest) are also inside the United States.

47 Quoted in Clavell (1983: 18).

48 See Schaffer, at *http://mir.drugtext.org/druglibrary/schaffer/library/basicfax.htm*, March 1999); and U.S. Department of Justice (1998). To give some perspective, the number of Americans who have used an illegal drug in the past year is greater than the total population of Colombia!

49 For example, according to the *Sourcebook of Criminal Justice Statistics 1998*, 40.5 per cent of white high school students have tried marijuana and 24.6 per cent currently use the drug. See U.S. Department of Justice (1998).

50 Estimates of the total value of America's marijuana crop range from $4 billion to $24 billion. For comparison, the value of the largest legal cash crop (i.e., corn) in 1993 was $16 billion. See Eric Schlosser (1994).

51 In terms of the potential for dependence (i.e., the difficulty in quitting or staying off the drug and the number of users who eventually become dependent), nicotine has been ranked number one by several research studies. In terms of withdrawal effects (i.e., the severity of withdrawal symptoms produced by stopping the use of the drug), alcohol has been ranked number one (even higher than heroin). In several categories, including withdrawal, tolerance (i.e., the user's need to have ever-increasing doses to get the same effect), and dependence, caffeine ranks higher than marijuana. See Schaffer, at *http://mir.drugtext.org/druglibrary/schaffer/library/ basicfax.htm*.

52 Borrowing from D. Campbell's argument (1997) that even technical language contains formulations of identity, it is interesting to note that drug users are labelled addicts but that addiction is not used to describe the high consumption levels of certain products (e.g., non-renewable resources) by the United States (e.g., imagine 'oil addicts').

53 The majority of drug violators who are caught and charged in the United States are white (60.4 per cent).

54 It is little wonder, then, that the *International Narcotics Control Strategy Report 1998* has argued that 'our partners themselves must lay the political and economic groundwork for development programs to provide legitimate alternatives to farmers now raising illegal crops.' See Bureau for International Narcotics and Law Enforcement Affairs (1999).

7 Global Markets and Crime

Vincenzo Ruggiero

Variations in the organization of crime are associated with variations in the conditions of social control. This claim, which may sound 'truistic,' struggled for decades before gaining acceptance, though reluctantly, in the criminological community. The official wisdom tended to reject the notion that criminal organizations are rationally geared to confronting problems of social control. Traditionally, social control was regarded as a reaction to crime rather than a determinant of its evolution (McIntosh, 1975). Similarly, the notion that legitimate markets shape the way in which illicit goods are simultaneously marketed found it very hard, and perhaps still does, to gain currency. Admitting to such close connection between legitimate and illegitimate commercial undertakings amounts, in some quarters, to acknowledging that economic development brings, along with wealth and social opportunities, parallel opportunities for the acquisition of illegally produced wealth.

In the current debate on globalization, this admission may sound like an implicit endorsement of the view that the expansion of markets is accompanied by a simultaneous expansion of crime, and that economic development is far from bringing harmony, progress, and legality. This view, in its turn, is an extension of analyses focusing on business as criminogenic, namely that the structure of organizations and the culture of those who operate in them create an environment in which opportunities for misconduct constantly arise (M. Clarke, 1990; Punch, 1996). Are we faced with increasingly powerful criminal organizations and corporate actors who are poised to take advantage of the openings of markets and international deregulation?

This article starts with a brief discussion of the concept of globalization and attempts to identify some of the new social and economic features that such a concept implies. It then hypothesizes that these new features are associated with specific forms of social control that shape patterns of transnational criminal activity. After the presentation of a number of cases, the argument is put forward that such patterns, together with the social actors involved in transnational criminality, prompt a reconsideration of the concepts of organized and white-collar crime.

Global Elites and the Localized Rest

A key word of the present, 'globalization' is also, and inevitably, a contested term. Some commentators focus on revolutionary developments in communication and transport, on internationalization of trading and labour, as well as on growing coordination of tasks performed by groups and individuals worldwide (A.D. King, 1991). With organizations attempting to position themselves globally, whether in relation to markets, media, or politics, enthusiasts claim that the world is becoming a single space in which new opportunities arise for all.

Critics, however, argue that this process mainly involves the most advanced countries, namely countries engaged in all sorts of international interactions and exchange. Therefore, the benefits of this interconnectedness are rarely shared with developing countries and, when they are, the unequal terms in which benefits are shared make globalization seem in large part synonymous with *Westernization*. According to Hannerz (1996: 18), globalization should be stripped of its awesome character and be brought down to earth: 'Globalization, all this goes to say, is not brand new, it can move back and forth, it comes in many kinds, it is segmented, and it is notoriously uneven; different worlds, different globalizations.' In brief, the term implies a generalization, is suggestive of a radical change, a dramatic shift between 'before' and 'after' (Harvey, 1996). But how new is interconnectedness around the world? Did exchange and interactions at the international level not occur in the past, though designated with the more humble term 'international'?

It is true that geographical expansion is one of the historical necessities of business, the result of a constant urge to establish new markets. However, the intensification of this process and its effects can hardly be denied. These include the formation of networks and interdependencies forging a world system, the corrosion of borders, and the increasing 'placelessness' of the economy (Knox and Taylor, 1995). World flows of information, which constitute pivotal elements of economic growth, epitomize the growing mobility of goods and finances (Castells, 1989).

There is, on the other hand, an in-built contradiction in this process: while mobility is granted to goods and finances, it is strictly denied to certain groups of people. Perhaps it is the immobility of these groups that guarantees the free movement of others. Immobility, in this context, is tantamount to lack of resources: 'Being local in a globalized world is a sign of social deprivation' (Bauman, 1998: 2). Current forms of social control are aimed at favouring the movement of certain goods and people while impeding the movement of others.

The forms of social control fostered by globalization make centrally structured hierarchies redundant, as power relationships tend increasingly to be embedded not in organizations and institutions but in networks in which instructions are processed. While globalization implies the weakening of localized sovereignty and structures (Beck, 2000), contemporary networks of capital, production, trade, science, and communication by-pass the nation-state (Castells, 2000).

Criminal business responds to the new forms of social control and the reorganization of sovereignty by establishing networks that by-pass national regulations. This response gathers momentum as demand for prohibited goods increases along with the demand of localized people for mobility. Transnational crime, in sum, appears to be a specific variant of illicit business that mirrors the current, specific forms of social control.

Developing versus Developed?

It is perhaps for this reason that official concerns about transnational crime appear to be centred on the feeling of vulnerability that developed countries harbour towards criminal activity originating in other countries. This manifests itself through fear that illicit goods and unwanted people may destroy the citizens and institutions of the 'civilized' world. In this sense, 'transnational crime is new only for the manner in which law-enforcement and international agencies have recently identified it as a priority' (Findlay, 1999: 51).

Official concerns address with particular vehemence the trafficking in illicit drugs, to the point that transnational crime is almost coterminous with the drug trade (Farer, 1999). However, many commentators from Western consuming countries fail to take into consideration how a pre-existing pharmacological culture in advanced countries partly allowed a culture of illicit drug use to develop. The demand side is also over-looked, as concerns mainly address 'foreign' producers and distribu-tors. Migrants building bridges with their countries of origin are depicted as a threat to the national security of the host country. Thus, 'One factor that has led Colombia to become the centre of the cocaine production industry is the strength of its ties to a large immigrant community in the United States, which was established well before the drug trade was significant' (Reuter and Petrie, 1999: 20).

Foreigners are also singled out for the detrimental effects they might produce on the national economy because of their potential ability to manipulate funds for criminal purposes and to disrupt the legitimate creation and distribution of wealth. This concern is based on the as-sumption that proceeds generated by illicit drugs are appropriated only by foreign producers and large distributors. This selective concern omits to consider the considerable revenues generated by illicit drugs within the consuming countries themselves, and the significant aggre-gate income shared by indigenous users and local distributors.

Transnational organized crime, in the main, seems the result of the growing numbers and variety of individuals and groups reaching ad-vanced countries. Because such individuals and groups arrive from places scattered around the world, and often from countries in transi-tion or in turmoil, they are perceived as being increasingly 'illegible,' problematic to control and impervious to integration.

In sum, what is meant by 'transnational crime' is not criminal activity crossing borders, but rather criminal activity originating in developing countries that crosses the borders of developed countries. For example: 'Organized crime in the post–cold war era presents an array of complex and novel challenges to United States security interests' (Lee, III, 1999: 6). These challenges are said to call for a re-examination of legal sys-tems and of the role of law enforcement, along with the deployment of military power (Viano, 1999).

The cases listed below show how criminal activity conducted by 'aliens' needs a receptive environment, along with a range of indig-enous partners and agents, in countries in which it operates. They also show that crime may originate in developed countries and impact on developing ones.

Brief Phenomenology

Case 1: In 1999, a partnership among members of Russian syndicates, politicians, and New York bankers carried out money-laundering operations. Finances lent to the Russian government became intermingled with other furtive money, totalling about $7 billion. Without the participation of legitimate actors and their willingness to utilize the services and practices of illegitimate partners, the laundering operations would have been impossible (*La Republica*, 30 October 1999).

Case 2: A group of illegal migrants were arrested in 1999 while working on British North Sea oil rigs. They were given 'slave wages' and forced to work twenty-eight-day stretches without a break (Nelson, 1999). To enter the United Kingdom they had paid a fee to an organization that had established a partnership with an official employment agency operating in Britain. This agency provided regular work for registered individuals and, on the side, offered jobs 'off the books' for illegal migrants. Similar agencies operating in the country recruit illegal labour for the food industry.

Case 3: In March 2000, a group of Italian businessmen operating in Albania were charged with promoting illegal migration. They offered false employment contracts to local residents in exchange for an agreed sum. The migrants were then left with the choice of entering Italy 'legally,' and once there 'disappearing' in the country, or contacting traffickers who would bring them to their destination at a lower price (Mastrogiacomo, 2000).

Case 4: Here I would like to group a number of case studies conducted in Germany, according to which most episodes of trafficking in human beings that were brought to court involved legally registered firms and individuals without a criminal background. These included transport companies and travel and tourist agencies in partnership with employment operators (Dietrich, 1999).

Case 5: Journalists posing as illegal migrants in Calais found a number of van drivers waiting to be approached and prepared, for a fee, to hide the migrants and take them over to Britain. The journalists who experienced the uncomfortably cramped journey described how 'The transaction is carried out with an almost matter-of-fact simplicity; few questions are asked, and no consequences are discussed. The money, it seems, will encourage the driver to turn a blind eye as we climb on board the truck' (Wazir, 2000). These drivers are in Calais on business, and 'moonlight' in human trafficking.

Case 6: Premier Oil, a British petroleum company, was involved in a legal action after being accused of human rights abuses in Burma. Nobel prizewinner Aung San Suu Kyi called on the company to withdraw from the country in order to bring pressure to bear on Burma's military junta. Premier Oil was also charged with using forced labour and committing offences against the environment (Macalister, 2000; World Development Movement, 2000).

Case 7: A case brought to light by investigators across Europe showed how alliances among a variety of actors, both legitimate and illegitimate, are required for transnational crime to occur. A group of cocaine wholesalers bought quantities of the illicit drug from South American producers and sold consignments to distributors operating in Europe. The group had business links in Germany, Spain, France, Switzerland, and Italy. Payments for consignments took place courtesy of the mediation performed by European financial institutions. Importers included legitimate entrepreneurs who 'mixed' the drugs with the legitimate goods of their trading activity (*Il Corriere della Sera*, 1999).

Case 8: A number of cigarette-producing companies are under investigation for selling quantities of their goods to international smugglers. Producers are accused of establishing partnerships with international distributors and of sharing with them the profits generated by tax evasion (see *The Guardian*, 23 March 2000).

Case 9: Research conducted by Interpol shows that seemingly aboveboard entrepreneurs and politicians are prime actors in the illegitimate transfer of money abroad. Despite permissive rules legally allowing them to move capital across borders, they find ways of increasing the sums moved by resorting to illegal practices. 'Hot money,' which is commonly and almost automatically associated with the laundering of criminal proceeds, in reality includes money earned, legitimately or otherwise, by official actors (Arlacchi, 1993). This money includes flight capital, proceeds from tax evasion, bribes, and illicit transactions in licit goods (such as arms transfers), illegal funds provided to political parties, the furtive return to the developed world of money lent to developing countries, and so on. Credible estimates suggest that the proportion of money laundered by organized crime constitutes only around 10 per cent of the overall amount of 'hot money' (Walter, 1989; Hampton, 1996a; Banca d'Italia, 1999).

Case 10: Research into illegal arms transfers suggests that a variety of organizations are involved and that international criminal groups may form business partnerships with producers and the political lobbies supporting them. While the expertise of intelligence agencies may be of paramount importance, 'such trafficking is scarcely the work of one or two individuals in government or the private sector' (Martin and Romano, 1992: 68). In varying degrees, it requires the cooperation of diverse actors, including organized crime, on an international level (Phythian, 1998).

Partnerships

The cases listed above would suggest that transnational organized crime is not to be exclusively identified with the illegal activities of notorious large crime syndicates. These may perhaps constitute the most powerful groups engaged in transnational criminal activity, but they are far from monopolizing such activities (P. Williams, 1998). Rather, the cases above show that transnational crime may well transcend conventional activities and mingle with entrepreneurial and, at times, governmental deviance. This occurs when legally produced goods are illegally marketed, or when the illegal marketing of goods produced in one country is supported by the complicity of corrupt politicians in a country in which those goods are officially banned. In this respect, it is appropriate to identify transnational organized crime as the result of partnerships between illegitimate and legitimate actors. In other words, as stressed earlier, criminal activity conducted by 'aliens' needs a range of indigenous partners and agents, along with a receptive environment in which that activity is carried out. Partnerships with legitimate entrepreneurs of the host country, in sum, may offer larger guarantees that, along with official commercial consortia, effective smuggling lines are also set up.

The notion of partnership implies that organized criminal groups both teach and learn from their legitimate counterparts in the economic arena. By investing illicit proceeds in the official economy, for example, they learn the techniques and the rationalizations adopted by white-collar and corporate offenders, thus being, in a sense, corrupted by the economy rather than corrupting it. In a variety of ways, organized crime may learn criminal techniques from fraudulent white collars rather than the other way around (Ruggiero, 2000a). For example, investment of criminal proceeds in the financial market forces organized crime to open up to and establish connections with mediators and agents who make 'pecunia non olet' their favourite motto. In brief, the encounter between organized crime and the official economy is not the result of an unnatural relationship between a harmonious entity and a dysfunctional one. Rather, it amounts to a joint undertaking of two loosely regulated worlds, both deviating from the rules they officially establish for themselves. For example, the rules of fair competition are often disregarded by those very legitimate entrepreneurs who claim their universal validity; similarly, the rules of 'honour' are often ignored by criminal entrepreneurs who claim their unconditional faith in them (Ruggiero, 1996).

Among the effects of partnerships between illegitimate and legitimate actors, one deserves particular attention for its potential impact on the international community. It is a classical sociological tenet that the more a social group extends its relationships outside its specific enclave the more it tends to lose its distinct identity and culture (Simmel, 1971). If we consider relationships among groups, and their potential evolution, we can hypothesize developments of global crime in current and future times. In societies where contacts between groups are limited, the outcomes of such contacts are also highly unpredictable. These societies are highly programmed and structured within groups but are loosely structured among groups. Because of the weak bonds between the different social enclaves, groups see little advantage in establishing cooperation and tend to act in isolation. In societies in which relationships between groups are mainly affected by competition, those endowed with more material and symbolic resources are able to set the moral tone of the community through the establishment of precise boundaries between acceptable and unacceptable conduct. Finally, in societies inspired by a prevailing sense of mutuality, groups are prevented from acting alone; their behaviour is harnessed and called to account. Mutuality, however, makes relationships between groups predictable in their effects and also contributes to the blurring of the boundaries between controller and controlled, insider and outsider (Hood, 1996; Douglas and Ney, 1998).

The globalization of markets encourages both competition and mutuality, thus simultaneously favouring clashes and alliances between groups. It is against this background that the development of transnational organized crime should be analysed, as in the example that follows.

Victimization of Humans

Among the illegal activities attributed to transnational organized crime, those associated with trafficking in human beings are paramount. In this respect, different analyses are put forward, and controversial points come to the fore. Some authors appear to assume that trafficking in humans is conducted by structured enterprises engaged in specialized, long-term activity. Related to this assumption is the implicit association of this type of activity with 'organized crime,' therefore conveying the notion that those thus engaged are full-time criminal entrepreneurs who have developed expertise and accumulated resources in previous

illegal activities. Are we faced with groups formed by 'full-time miscre-
ants,' namely, individuals with a criminal curriculum vitae who have
gone through the different stages of criminal apprenticeship in order,
finally, to engage in big-time crime? Other commentators, however,
suggest that many of those involved in trafficking in humans have no
previous criminal record and derive their skills and expertise from the
licit arena of business in which they operate (B. Anderson, 1993;
Ruggiero, 1997; Bales, 1999). The cases presented above indicate that
travel agencies are involved, along with transport companies, often in
connection with informal employment agencies. Usually, the staff of
such agencies and companies do not have criminal records; nor do they
have a stable and organic association with members of organized crime.
While committing offences that organized criminal groups also commit, such companies may become partners of the latter without sharing
their overall culture and strategies. They may also clash with criminal
groups, which they may see as competitors in the remunerative market
in which they operate.

According to other analyses, traffickers frequently maintain control
of illegal migrants once they reach the destination country and force
those trafficked to commit crime, engage in prostitution, or work for
low wages (Shelley, 1998). It is also assumed that girls and women
recruited in their home country and promised jobs abroad are later
forced into prostitution. Finally, it is remarked that illegal migrants who
use the services of traffickers experience debt bondage; that, in addition
to the cost of transportation, smugglers charge exorbitant rents for
substandard, abandoned, or even condemned housing; and that debts
force immigrants to work in sweatshops (Reuter and Petrie, 1999).

It is extremely controversial to portray this illicit business as one
exclusively characterized by a victimizer/victimized relationship. As
van Duyne (2000) warns, one should be aware that there are willing as
well as unwilling victims in this business, and that the very concept of
trafficking needs to be carefully unravelled in order to bring other
dynamics to light. According to representatives of the International
Migration Organization, for example, many women illegally entering
developed countries are fully aware of the type of job for which they are
destined. Some women know that their work in the host country will
be in the sex industry. Many choose to pay a fee to traffickers who, in
this context, could more appropriately be described as 'illegal' migration operators (Gramegna, 1999).

As for the conditions under which illegal migrants are forced to work, this seems hardly attributable to the traffickers, as responsibility for such conditions lies with the very labour market in which migrants are mainly employed. In this respect, it should be noted that the increase in flexible and casual work in most Western countries has created a situation where workers who display low social and economic expectations are highly desirable. Among these workers, illegal migrants seem to have a formidable advantage, because as soon as their expectations become higher employers may always report them to the police as illegal. In sum, trafficking in human beings should be analysed within a demand-supply framework, as illegal migrants employed in the hidden economy, including the sex industry, meet a specific demand in economically advanced countries. Invisibility characterizes the condition of these migrants, an invisibility informing both the way in which they migrate and the way in which they are required to work and live in the country of destination (Ruggiero, 1999). Strict immigration policies, in this context, do not limit the flow of people seeking relocation in rich countries, but only contribute to lowering the expectations and demands of those who migrate. Paying a fee to traffickers is part and parcel of this strategy, as migrants are taught that it is a privilege to enter an advanced country and that, once there, they had better not blow such a unique opportunity by demanding too much.

Conclusion

Globalization moulds business networks and, at the same time, shapes new forms of social control. Transnational organized crime, in response, establishes criminal networks that transcend centralized and highly structured organizations. Dispersed participants and diverse social actors are involved in these networks, in which opportunistic chances are taken and short-time alliances are set up. I have argued that, with globalization, both partnerships – inspired by mutuality – and clashes – governed by competition – may occur between different social groups. These groups include not only established criminal syndicates and large organizations but also a variety of legitimate entrepreneurs and first-time offenders who seize on the unprecedented opportunities offered by global markets. This leads to some final considerations.

It is true that transnational organized crime is the result of new criminal opportunities. However, the nature and features of these opportunities deserve brief examination. According to a distinction suggested by Albanese (1999), there are opportunities that provide 'easy access' to illicit earnings with relatively low risk and there are opportunities 'created' by offenders. The former include provision of illicit goods and services that are in high demand, but also opportunities made available by social and technological change. Opportunities created by offenders often involve bribery or extortion. Examples, in this case, include protection rackets and frauds involving otherwise legitimate business enterprises. The criminal activities examined in this paper make this distinction extremely blurred, if not redundant. Transnational organized crime seizes 'easy' opportunities and 'creates' new ones at the same time. Its *modus operandi* is such that criminal acts become increasingly interdependent and multifaceted (Adamoli et al., 1998). Skills acquired in one field are utilized in new markets, while partnerships are established with a variety of actors, be they legitimate or otherwise. This movement from one activity to another crucially entails an intermittent shift from areas that traditionally pertain to organized crime to areas that are the traditional preserve of white-collar or corporate crime. In brief, organized crime possesses some of the features of white-collar crime. The notion of transnational crime encapsulates this mixture of criminal behaviour.

I have argued that transnationality makes partnerships between these different ideal typical criminal figures easier. The cases listed above testify to the possibility that offences may be committed by gangs, professional criminals, organized groups, and white-collar offenders, who may at times act jointly and at times compete in illicit enterprises. This raises serious concerns, which I would identify as follows.

There is a widespread feeling that white-collar and corporate crime are less stigmatized and penalized than conventional organized crime. With the interconnection of the two types of criminal behaviour, the relative tolerance normally accorded to white-collar criminals may be extended to members of conventional organized crime. What might happen if the development of transnational organized crime led white-collar and organized criminals to blur their distinctive traits? I suggest that we may have to face two possible developments.

First, one may presume that both types of criminals – now become one – may be met with very mild social disapproval. In this respect, a celebrated Durkheimian formulation should be borne in mind. Traditional organized crime, with its visible, horrifying, violent conduct, elicits a powerful social reaction that reinforces feelings of belonging and cohesion among law-abiding people. White-collar and corporate offenders do not cause such social reaction. The blurring of the distinctive traits of the two, namely the coalescence of organized and white-collar crime encouraged by transnationality, may make social reaction disappear.

Second, developments of transnational crime may follow a more selective trajectory. In order tentatively to sketch this trajectory, we need to bear in mind the concepts of 'innovation' belonging to economics and to the sociology of deviance, respectively. When Schumpeter emphasized that economic systems develop thanks to new combinations of productive factors, he meant to warn that lack of such new combinations would lead to static equilibrium and therefore to economic stagnation. Innovative action, in his view, distinguishes real entrepreneurs, who express with their initiative a degree of 'discontinuity' with respect to stagnant economic operators. Entrepreneurs, therefore, distance themselves from their conservative peers when they manage to supersede old combinations of productive factors. In Merton's celebrated conceptualization of 'innovative' behaviour in crime, illicit actors who innovate are identified as those who pursue officially shared goals with constantly new illegitimate means. The cases listed above, along with the partnerships between organized and white-collar crime examined, appear to suggest that successful groups will have to *innovate* both in Schumpeter's sense and in Merton's sense. Deviant entrepreneurs, in other words, will have to introduce new combinations of productive factors, while devising deviant adaptations to economic strain, therefore pursuing legitimate goals through illegitimate means. This, presumably, will enable successful groups to remain aloof from sanctioning, especially if they manage to repel the criminal label from their activity while directing it to competitors. This ability is yet another aspect of *innovation*, and entails changes in the perception of business whereby those who, indeed, *innovate* successfully claim their activities and practices to be ethical and those of competitors to be unethical. This type of innovation entails the vindication of one's economic activity as value-bound and the displacement of the criminal stigma onto the activity of others as value-free. It consists of decreasing marginal morality while criminalizing others as responsible for such decrease, and promoting an 'ethical race to the bottom' while deflecting moral judgment from oneself. Future developments, therefore, may lead to the production of a new market *Weltgeist* whereby those illicit partnerships that better succeed in criminalizing others will also claim that their own interests correspond to those of the collectivity.

8 Organized Corporate Criminality: Corporate Complicity in Tobacco Smuggling

Margaret E. Beare

Scenario: The mayor of the small Canadian town of Cornwall, Ontario, goes into 'hiding';[1] nightly shootings occur across the waterways of the St Lawrence River; smuggling-related killings take place; rumours exist of tobacco company complicity, but fears of a growing organized crime network focus on Aboriginal communities, armed and potentially violent 'pirates,' Asians, and other profit-seeking racketeers. Another major organized crime market is created. The policing and political response targets the most vulnerable criminals while the media focus on the spread of various types of ethnic-based organized crime. The cigarette companies walk away ... almost. Seven years later the attention turns toward the corporate 'suppliers' of the illegal commodity – giving new meaning to the phrase 'targeting upward.'

Organized Criminals with White Collars

Despite much evidence to the contrary, organized criminals are still perceived to be distinguishable from 'ordinary' criminals by the possession of various mythical qualities. Corporations typically do not qualify as 'organized criminals' for a variety of reasons – not least of which is that they have the financial backing to sue anyone who would try to extend a definition of serious, continuous, organized criminal activity to include their corporate business policies. While we may question the police preoccupation with bikers and other 'outsider' criminal groups, the police are not alone in their selection of visible and vulnerable targets. Governments, the media, and the public appear to feel most comfortable with a moral order that is divided with a degree of certainty and clarity between the legitimate and the illegitimate – with a minimum of blurring between the two.

The Racketeer Influenced and Corrupt Organizations (RICO) statute in the United States has become the model for anti-organized crime law enforcement among Western countries. Many countries have replicated this legislation, in part or in whole. While there has always been some criticism that RICO was introduced for one purpose and then used against other groups, Robert Blakey, the main drafter of the statute, could not have been more clear that racketeers exist in all professions and all social classes and that the statute was intended to target all such criminals: 'There is nothing in RICO that says that if you act like a racketeer you will not be treated like a racketeer, whatever the colour of your shirt or your collar ... people who run groups by extortion or violence or fraud ought to be called racketeers. And what they engage in is racketeering.'[2]

While many people have now written about cigarette smuggling between Canada and the United States and internationally in the early to mid-1990s, the continuing unfolding dynamics of this criminal activity warrant another look. The process of labelling activity as criminal rather than merely naughty or nice is complex. Understanding cigarette smuggling requires more than a simplistic 'state'-interested interpretation, or a focus strictly on the most visible criminal activities, or a preoccupation with the attempts of law enforcement to 'handle' yet another impossible situation.[3] The money available is a tremendous inducement for corruption and greed. As was reported in the *Globe and Mail*, evidence of corruption by officials was readily documented, but corporate greed was initially harder to identify: 'Mounties have been charged with selling information to Indian smugglers and stealing impounded cigarettes. Customs officers have been bribed. Two recent killings in Montreal and one near the Akwesasne reserve have been linked to the trade' (Moon, 1993: A1–A2).

It has become obvious during the last few years that the driving force behind the criminal industry was organized corporate crime. However, the interwoven interests that knit corporations – even when they are acting irresponsibly or criminally – into the larger society meant that the law enforcement mechanisms and government policy options were restricted through a kind of blindness, wilful or otherwise.

The cigarette-smuggling industry illustrates the dynamics of a manufactured organized crime problem *and* the reluctance of the state and state agencies to challenge the role played by powerful 'suppliers' of the illicit commodity. An analysis of this market shows how the political interests and sensitivities surrounding the competing discourses resulted in the quite inappropriate definition of the problem as a traditional 'law enforcement' problem, with interdiction and seizures of the contraband being the key strategies of control.[4]

Defining it in this manner not only allowed the smuggling and its accompanying violence to continue – and continue to 'organize' – but also avoided challenging any of the powerful lobby groups: the tobacco lobby, the anti-smoking lobby, the Aboriginal rights lobby, the governmental and public deficit-reduction lobby. Perhaps most significantly, it avoided redefining either the role of the corporations or the identity of the criminals.

The Market

The facts of this issue are fairly straightforward and are surprisingly widely agreed upon. During the early 1990s, the U.S. taxes on cigarettes and cigarette tobacco were much lower than those imposed in Canada. The differential was significant and in some areas accounted for a Canadian cigarette price three times higher than the price across the border. As Akwesasne chief Mike Mitchell stated, 'The money – it's unbelievable the money you can make and it's so easy ... You can buy a pack of cigarettes on the American side of the reservation for $1.58 and you go across here in Cornwall and you have to buy it for close to $7.00 a pack, same pack, within a short distance of each other, so no one is surprised that all this is happening' ('Cigarette Smuggling at Akwesasne,' 1991).

In economic terms, the cigarette trade was comparable to drug trafficking. An automobile crossing into Canada with ten to fifteen cases[5] of cigarettes had a potential to make in a single trip a profit of $14,250. A single tractor-trailer loaded with 1,200 cases of cigarettes could make a profit of $1,140,000.[6]

Canadian cigarettes are sold 'duty and tax exempt' for export to foreign jurisdictions such as the United States, St Pierre and Miquelon, and Europe, where they are subject to foreign taxes. Tax-exempt cigarettes are also sold within Canada and elsewhere through duty-free stores and to special categories of customers such as embassy staff. As the price differences widened, the tax-exempt status became increasingly valuable and hence vulnerable to exploitation. As with the bootleggers in the 1920s, the public felt some sympathy for the entrepreneurs who chose to turn a 'bad' tax into a 'good' profit. Only the incidence of violence served to lend credibility to the need for enhanced action of some sort by government and/or police.

The statistics that were not so well known were the huge profits that the smuggling market brought to the tobacco companies. While the tobacco companies joined in demonizing the 'criminals' who were exploiting the various loopholes (i.e., the export conditions and the jurisdictional divisions), their own financial gain from the criminality, even if the smuggling was not of their own doing, tended not to be reported in the media. The emphasis was on the huge export sales to the United States and the unusually large numbers of cigarettes passing through the embassies and off the under-the-counter shelves of local corner stores.

Successful law enforcement requires an adequate level of support and compliance from the public. There was little compliance from the public during this period. The 1992 Linquist Avey Macdonald Baskerville study of contraband tobacco illustrates the widespread lack of good faith among all of the tax-free groups, including the diplomatic service, the armed services, and the travelling public. Diplomatic sales totalled 18.7 million cigarettes, in 1989; 22.8 million in 1990; and 111.4 million cigarettes or approximately 557,000 cartons, in 1991. Unless one believes that there was a rampant increase in smoking among the diplomatic corps, this growth indicates, in keeping with the Linquist report, that the diplomatic community was/is illegally selling its cigarettes (Linquist Avey Macdonald Baskerville, 1992: 16).[7] Publicity and government pressure on this group reduced but did not eliminate illicit tobacco sales during 1992. It is estimated that, in 1986, 1 in 176 cigarettes was contraband; in 1990 the estimate was 1 in 45; and in 1992 the estimate was 1 in 6.

The larger amount of contraband resulted after export from Canada as Canadian tobacco was smuggled back across the 7,000 kilometre U.S.–Canada border and through the French-owned islands of St Pierre and Miquelon off the coast of Newfoundland. Of perhaps greatest concern was the key role played by the three Indian reserves that are located along the U.S.–Canada border – the Akwesasne reserve that straddles the Ontario/Quebec–New York state border; the Kahnawake reserve in Quebec; and the St Regis reservation in New York state.

In order to stem the tide of smuggling, the Canadian government introduced an $8 per carton export tax in February 1992. This export tax had three immediate consequences: it served as the apparent cause of threats from the tobacco companies that they would move out of Canada; it reduced the number of cigarettes exported *officially* out of Canada; and it created an illicit market of generic low-priced tobacco products.

These illicit products were either produced in Canada from raw tobacco grown in Canada, or were 'imitation' Canadian cigarettes produced in the United States and smuggled into Canada or across the Indian reserves.

As a result of intensive lobbying by the tobacco manufacturers, the export tax was removed after a mere six weeks. The power of the tobacco lobby had been demonstrated by what was termed 'brass-knuckle lobbying' (Alaton, 1993: D3) by manufacturers, culminating in the government's withdrawal of the tax. By the time the export tax was suspended on 8 April 1992, critics claimed that the predictable, but still somehow unanticipated, consequence of this export tax included the development of a 'parallel tobacco industry.' This secondary industry involved the setting up of new repackaging plants, new tobacco sources, and different and possibly expanded two-way smuggling strategies (Linquist Avey Macdonald Baskerville, 1992: 62). Hence, what had been a major problem with the smuggling of cigarettes back into Canada (minus the various Canadian government taxes) after they had been legally sold into the United States for distribution there – and, in some regions, with the simple smuggling of U.S. cigarettes into Canada – was now complicated by strategies to negate the export tax. There thus came to be four types of contraband cigarettes: Canadian-manufactured cigarettes exported and then smuggled back in; duty-free cigarettes intended for a restricted group being sold for profit; American-produced cigarettes (either Canadian look-alikes or otherwise); and 'generic' Canadian products.

The debate regarding the merits, or intended merits, of the export tax is clouded slightly by the fact that the Linquist Group, whose findings are quoted and requoted, was in fact retained by Imperial Tobacco Limited to produce the 1992 and 1993 reports.[8] Supporters of the export tax focus, not as the Linquist reports did, on the 'accommodations to' (or techniques for avoiding) the export tax by the illicit trade, but rather on the decrease in official exportation during this period. The number of cigarettes exported went from a low of under 0.2 billion cigarettes during the export tax to a high of 1.2 billion three months later.[9]

Competing Discourses

Government policy regarding tobacco sales, advertising, and taxes was driven by five opposing lobby groups – the tobacco companies with their own interests to protect; political jurisdictions with tobacco as their main income-generating crop; grass-roots anti-smoking groups supported by health-oriented government departments and various international health organizations; Aboriginal rights and Aboriginal sovereignty activists; and the deficit-reducing/revenue-producing interests among government and the general public.

While policy decisions are often difficult, they become more so when the issue is one that involves debate about self-government within Aboriginal communities versus discrimination and oppression; 'health' issues versus individual choice; and the rights of capitalism versus the influence exerted by capitalism. I am arguing that these voices were so equally matched, in terms of the potential political consequences, that none could be ignored by the policy process. It might have tipped the balance if the role of the corporations had been defined as criminal – but that did not happen until years later.

The tobacco companies threatened to leave the country if taxation strategies became too inhospitable for them to conduct business in Canada as they wished to conduct it. There was some evidence to suggest that they might have been actively looking for an excuse to relocate. Likewise, the anti-smoking lobby is powerful and has political influence derived from direct lobbying with the government. Any reduction of the taxes would have been seen as putting economic concerns ahead of health concerns. The unique smuggling route through the Akwesasne community added to the policy nightmare. Aboriginal self-government issues involve extremely complex negotiations, with the smuggling questions being only one small part of a larger national issue. Aggressive policing by federal or provincial forces within the Aboriginal communities was not seen to be an option for the government.

Alternative policy responses, which were never seen to be politically viable, would have included a serious consideration of the following:

• reduce Canadian taxes to the level of taxes in the United states;
• hold tobacco manufacturers accountable for the excessive exporting of cigarettes and raise export taxes while monitoring or reducing the number of classifications of tax-free cigarette distributors;
• clarify land rights and law enforcement relationships regarding the policing of the reserves – potentially involving the saturation policing of Aboriginal reserves.

We were 'left with' a government response based on the rhetoric of control of smuggling via traditional law enforcement and targeting the importers of the contraband. Newspaper headlines focused on 'the guy on the snowmobile' hauling a sleigh across the frozen water between Canada and the United States on his way to pick up a shipment of contraband cigarettes. These people became the 'organized criminals.' Less picturesque but more dramatic was the rhetoric about the tentacles of organized crime spreading out from the border-crossing points and reaching into the ethnic communities to supply cigarettes and fund other illicit activities, including political protests and, at the extreme point of the rhetoric, terrorism.

Smuggling Activity

This is Cornwall ... and this is 1993 ... It is not Chicago during Prohibition Days and I will not be intimidated by lawless individuals who have no respect for either law and order or the lives of innocent people. (Cornwall mayor Ron Martelle)[10]

Every province was experiencing an increase in smuggling activity. The main movement was, first, across the U.S. border into Quebec, Ontario, and British Columbia[11] and, second, into the Maritime provinces via the French islands of St Pierre and Miquelon.[12] Cross-border smuggling became the first step in what in some areas was a highly sophisticated distribution network with links to other provinces and even across Canada. Separate criminal groups forged partnerships with the smugglers to improve efficiency and broaden the market. Competition among numerous 'independent' smuggling entrepreneurs resulted in corruption and violence, both actual and potential.

Ontario and Quebec perhaps provided the greatest variety of cigarette-smuggling activity. In Ontario, the prime smuggling area is around Cornwall and was linked to organized criminal elements within the Aboriginal communities, the Asian community, and other independent groups. Of particular concern to the police was the evidence that Aboriginal criminals in Ontario were beginning to assist Aboriginal communities in western Canada to set up smuggling and distribution organizations (Canadian Association of Chiefs of Police [CACP], 1993: 75). The Akwesasne reserve and St Regis reservation are ideally situated, since they straddle the U.S.–Canada border in both Ontario and Quebec. Residents of Akwesasne can use their Aboriginal status to buy Canadian duty-free cigarettes legally exported to the United States and have them delivered to the U.S. side of the reserve. They can then move tobacco easily from New York to Ontario through this reserve. Special roads were built to connect to docks along the south side of Cornwall Island, where the cigarettes were loaded onto fast boats and carried across the St Lawrence River.

Police intelligence reports such as the 1993 *Organized Crime Report* of the CACP indicated that the Mohawk Warriors supplied Asian Canadians in Toronto with both smuggled exported Canadian cigarettes and American cigarettes, and that the huge profits were being used by the Warriors to buy such things as AK-47 assault rifles.[13] As the report stated, a Warrior could make $30,000 tax free with just one car delivery of 1,250 cartons of cigarettes.

The point was made that there was a tendency to think in terms of unsophisticated smuggling operations, while in fact the police had seized scanners and night-vision devices as well as powerful weapons. The enormous profits from cigarette smuggling were seen to initiate a cycle – with the illicit profits going into weapons' purchases, casino operations, and sophisticated political lobbying activities. The police had observed that outlaw motorcycle gangs, members of the drug-trafficking trade, and key Montreal-based organized crime families had all become involved in the cigarette-smuggling 'business.' As a CACP report noted, cigarette smuggling as a criminal activity has many advantages over drug trafficking – there is a greater demand for cigarettes than for other drugs, and the sentences given if caught are less. In addition, there are ready sources that are easily and more cheaply accessible.

The superficial parallels to the Prohibition era are obvious. A market was created via government taxation policy. When the prices on either side of the border were close to equivalent (until about 1983), smuggling was not a money-making enterprise. Even the significant differential that existed up to the mid-1980s was tolerated. After a certain point, however, the public no longer viewed the taxes as legitimate, and hence the legalities set up to collect the tax became hurdles to avoid rather than moral imperatives to obey.

The point has been made by law enforcement officials that, when the government increases the resources available to the police to enable more seizures of cigarettes, this law enforcement activity actually results in more tobacco sales and therefore more profit to the corporations, who then receive additional orders to compensate for the seized quantities. And, as in New Jersey when the government decided to crack down on illegal gambling,[14] a direct result of the enforcement efforts was the removal of vulnerable, unsophisticated individuals and groups – rather than of the organized gambling operations that were of particular concern to the public. As Rod Stamler[15] stated, 'the RCMP are powerless to act. Politically it's dynamite. Enforcement looks good. They're arresting the novice, the inexperienced, but they can't tackle the professionals and they're certainly not going to go after the Indians on the big reserves. This is a losing battle.'[16]

Stamler's affiliation with the tobacco companies may have caused him to fail to acknowledge the 'other' professionals – the corporate criminals who were not being tackled by law enforcement. While wealthy entrepreneurs had entered into this illicit trade, the industry also supplied work and income to segments of the population that had suffered particularly from unemployment and underemployment. In describing the comparable Prohibition period, Michael Woodiwiss noted that 'Along the coasts, rivers and the Great Lakes, fishermen, tugboat operators, shippers and dockworkers gave up their normal occupations and entered the smuggling trade ... Bootlegging was so much better paid.' (Woodiwiss, 1988: 13).

In the case of some of the smugglers from the Aboriginal communities, they had very limited opportunity for lawful employment, which made the enormously lucrative opportunities of the tobacco trade irresistible.

Industry Complicity

Canadian tobacco manufacturers exported 1.8 billion cigarettes in April 1993 – more than four times the figure exported in April 1992.[17] During the first four months of 1993, exports had increased over 300 per cent from the equivalent rates during the first four months of 1992. Given that the foreign market had not increased by this margin, or likely at all during the year, the excessive exported amount of tobacco ought to have been 'explained.' One obvious explanation was that it was 'intended' for smuggling back into Canada for profit to the smugglers and, of course, for the profit from the initial sale for the tobacco company. It is estimated that 80 to 95 per cent[18] of all exports to the United States re-entered Canada. The remaining small percentage (between 5 per cent and 20 per cent) was consumed by Canadian tourists or nonresidents. The point to be emphasized is that manufacturers realized that Americans smoke American cigarettes not Canadian brands.

The act of exporting excessive tobacco products outside of Canada could be interpreted as a significant 'cause' of the tax avoidance, criminal violence, and wasted enforcement resources. It was not until much later that the emphasis shifted to the attempt to hold the tobacco corporations accountable for complicity in the growth of an organized crime enterprise around their products. Less powerful, less 'legitimate' players in the smuggling scenario were targeted as renegades, racketeers, or plain ordinary criminals.[19] In her study of tax evasion and tax avoidance, Doreen McBarnet (1992) states that 'To suggest then that the key to staying on the right side of the line is "not what you do but the way that you do it," is not to imply simply a distinction in style, a matter of cleverness or moral choice, but to underline the significance of opportunity and resources. Manipulating the law to escape control yet remain legitimate is an option more readily available to large corporations and "high net worth" individuals than to the mass of the population' (71).

Private gains are made at the expense of public tax loss. The Linquist studies put this loss of tax dollars to the federal and provincial governments in 1992 at $1.6 billion and the loss to the legitimate Canadian retail trade at $2.3 billion. In addition, there was the cost of the resources consumed by an ongoing RCMP–Canada Customs Joint Force Operation, a newly created OPP–RCMP–Cornwall Police 'Regional Task Force on Smuggling and Related Criminal Activity,' plus enhanced border and investigative resources, in addition to ordinary levels of policing that target the border (Small, 1993).

The tobacco corporations argued that their sales for export were indisputably lawful. In response to the argument made in the early 1990s that, because of their involvement in 'supplying' the smuggled commodity, the tobacco companies should have been charged with offences such as conspiracy and possession of the proceeds of crime, Rob Parker, president of the Canadian Tobacco Manufacturers Council, stated that 'If she has any evidence of that ... she should make it public and bring it to the attention of the authorities. It is simply not true.'[20]

Before the decade had ended, the accuracy of this rhetoric was seriously challenged. The Canadian Tobacco Manufacturers Council was named in the Canadian federal government's lawsuit. By 2001, tobacco companies had been named in legal action alleging their involvement in smuggling operations in Canada, the European Union, Colombia, Ecuador, Honduras, and Belize.

Tobacco companies exported their cigarettes knowing that others would commit the crime of tax evasion by smuggling the same commodity back into Canada. What was not immediately clear – and what the Canadian government was not intent on discovering until much later – was how 'close' the tobacco companies and the smugglers were. The Department of Justice appeared to accept as irrefutable that as long as the exported cigarettes were going into a licensed warehouse in the United States, the extraordinarily large amount of cigarettes and the reality of the smuggling activity were in no way the responsibility of the tobacco companies. This period is interesting historically in light of more recent attempts to hold the tobacco companies accountable.

The sense of the tobacco companies' near-total immunity during this period is instructive. In defending the industry against the anti-smoking lobbyists, the tobacco lobby countered with the compelling argument that 'If tobacco generates health problems, the premature death of smokers would yield savings in health care and disability.'[21] The vice-president of the Canadian Tobacco Manufacturers Council (CTMC) maintained that 'There are statistical indications of risk but they do not reach the level of a causal relationship between smoking and disease.'[22]

This reminds one of the role of the North American tobacco industry abroad. Stan Sesser documents the deliberate and aggressive foreign strategies that U.S. tobacco manufacturers were using to introduce American cigarettes to all age, sex, and economic groups in Asia. Evidence presented by Sesser illustrates the North American tobacco industry's willingness to advertise to a market that can only afford to buy on the black market; to employ children as the sellers of American cigarettes in the Manila streets; and to propagate the belief articulated by Joaquin Ortega, head of the National Tobacco Administration in the Philippines: 'I don't think smoking affects a person unless he's genetically disposed to concur ... Should you tell a seven year old boy to stop eating sugar since sugar can cause diabetes?' (Sesser, 1993).

The model who appeared as the 'Winston Man' for the R.J. Reynolds Tobacco Company (RJR) asked a group of executives if any of them smoked. The executive shook his head: 'Are you kidding? We reserve that right for the poor, the young, the black and the stupid.'[23]

In 1993, the federal government acknowledged the seriousness of cigarette smuggling by amending the Excise Act and the Customs Act, making it an offence to be in possession of the proceeds of cigarette smuggling. The Proceeds of Crime provisions of the *Criminal Code* were made applicable to the Excise and Customs Acts. Smuggling cigarettes was therefore recognized as an enterprise crime, and possessing the proceeds of smuggling and laundering these proceeds also became criminal offences subject to seizure and forfeiture of these proceeds to the government undertaking the prosecution. Nevertheless, attention was still not directed at the tobacco companies. The profits accruing to the tobacco manufacturers from excessive exports are in a real sense the profits of crime since they are dependent on the existence of a smuggling industry. Just as in drug trafficking, in cigarette smuggling there are suppliers, importers, and a distribution network. Tobacco manufacturers are the corporate entities that knowingly export close to 90 per cent more cigarettes than they know there is a foreign market for and that have been active players in supplying the commodity for the smugglers.

With the amount of money that was available and the willing complicity of the suppliers, law enforcement efforts were practically futile. Police targeted the non-Aboriginal retail distributors – an activity that proved to be non-productive; used the rhetoric of 'targeting upwards' to disrupt the organized smuggling operations, but with little impact because of their number, diversity, and the reserve-based factor; and worked collaboratively with both customs and U.S. enforcement agencies to carry out numerous successful seizures – but all with no sign of any reduction in the criminal activity. What was required was to stop – or slow – either the supply or the demand. The demand was not budging, and the corporations were seemingly 'untouchable.'

Much of the debate regarding imposing sanctions against or controlling corporate behaviour is centred on the issue of applying criminal code or administrative/regulatory sanctions for corporate violations.[24] The potential for using the seizure and forfeiture laws was not adequately explored. Corporations have much to lose from a successful 'Proceeds of Crime' prosecution. The insignificance of a typical fine given to these corporate entities or the difficulty in identifying 'a' guilty individual to sentence to jail for criminal corporate violations can be compensated for by the ability of this legislation to strip the illicit proceeds from the criminally involved corporation.[25]

The Current Situation

The situation at the end of the 1990s was quite different from that of a mere six years before. Detailed reports had by then documented the complicity of the tobacco companies. Claims made by the companies that they could not be responsible for what happened to their cigarettes after they were sold or exported were destroyed by allegations that they had built the smuggling operations into their business plans. The acknowledged complicity of the RJR company with cigarette smuggling over the Canadian border was claimed to mirror situations in Europe, China, South Africa, Latin America, Vietnam, and elsewhere.[26] RJR's Canadian affiliate, Northern Brands, and its president, Les Thompson, pleaded guilty in 1998 to charges of being involved in illegal smuggling.

Internal correspondence from the tobacco corporations has now been made public as a result of the various health-related court cases and reveals an established vocabulary to manage the illegal cigarettes. Legal imports were either 'DP' (duty paid) or 'DF' (duty free). However, corporate documents also referred to 'DNP' (duty not paid), 'transit,' or 'GT' (general trade) shipments. These euphemisms for smuggled cigarettes also included 'the parallel market,' 'second channel,' and 'border trade' (Beelman et al., 2000: 2). An internal British American Tobacco document stated that an office in Bogota, Colombia, should be purged of any reference to smuggled cigarettes: 'documents dealing with DNP have been separated and should now be forwarded to Caracas. A good quality safe and shredder are required.'[27]

In a statement that served to blame both the competition and the government for making it necessary for his company to form an alliance with smugglers, Kenneth Clarke, deputy chairman of British American Tobacco, said that it was the government's unwillingness or inability to stop smuggling that made it necessary for his company to be 'available alongside those of our competition in the smuggled as well as the legitimate market' (Maguire, 2000: 2). Corporate involvement in smuggling was therefore merely 'business.'

On 21 December 1999, the Canadian government filed a lawsuit in the United States against R.J. Reynolds Tobacco Holdings Inc., several related companies, and the Canadian Tobacco Manufacturers Council. The suit was launched in the United States under the RICO statute. The case claimed an alleged conspiracy to defraud Canada going back to 1991 and spoke of the elaborate network of smugglers and offshore shell companies that were put in place by the tobacco companies to ensure an abundance of cheap cigarettes on the Canadian market.[28] Canada was seeking more than $1 billion in damages – namely, lost revenues – resulting from the evasion of duties and taxes and the increased law enforcement costs arising from the need to combat smuggling operations.

As described by the government's lawyer to the U.S. Federal Court judge: 'This is a case of legitimate business that hooked up with organized crime.' It would have been more precise to describe it as *white-collar organized crime*. In a case brought against the tobacco companies by the European Union and Colombia, their attorney perhaps more accurately described the criminal operation in the following manner: 'What you have is one big smuggling conspiracy from the standpoint of the cigarette manufacturers, their distributors, the money launderers; it's the same people doing the exact same thing.'[29]

As outlined in the *Attorney General of Canada v. RJ Reynolds Tobacco Holdings* (30 June 2000),[30] the allegations were as follows:

- *FTZ Scheme* – Officials from RJR-Macdonald met with the LBL Importing (Larry Miller and Robert and Lewis Tavano) and devised a scheme whereby RJR-Macdonald would ship tobacco from Canada through 'foreign trade zones' (FTZs) in Buffalo, New York, to LBL and other customers who would then ship the tobacco through the U.S. reservation to be smuggled back into Canada. Rather than 'not being able to control what happens to the tobacco after it is originally sold' (which was the frequent claim by the corporations), evidence produced indicated that this 'scheme' was worked out to offset declining profits. During 1997, Miller and the Tavanos were among more than twenty-one individuals indicted in the United States. They pleaded guilty to smuggling and money-laundering charges.
- *False Packaging Scheme* – When Canada imposed a new export tax, the 'threats' made by the tobacco companies to move out of Canada were in part realized. RJR-Macdonald moved two production lines for Canadian cigarettes from its plant in Montreal to RJR-PR (a Delaware corporation with its principal place of business in Puerto Rico) – thereby avoiding the export tax. The tobacco manufactured at RJR-PR allegedly was packaged in RJR-Macdonald packaging, sold to Caribbean intermediaries, shipped through FTZs to the U.S. reservation and then smuggled into Canada.
- *NBI Scheme* – Under the alleged Northern Brands International Inc. (NBI) scheme, RJR-Macdonald established NBI. Tobacco products manufactured by RJR-Macdonald in Canada were exported to FTZs in New York. LBL then placed an order with NBI for the tobacco and wired the money for the tobacco from the LBL account in New York to the NBI account in North Carolina. NBI paid a portion of the proceeds from LBL to RJR-Macdonald. After receiving payment, RJR-Macdonald notified the FTZs to transfer title to the customer (such as LBL), who then shipped the product to the U.S. reservation

for smuggling back into Canada. Hence, based on these allegations, RJR-Macdonald was intricately and knowingly a party to the smuggling operations. NBI pleaded guilty to aiding and abetting others to violate 18 U.S.C., section 542 (Entry of goods by means of false statements). Leslie Thompson, ex-RJR-Macdonald employee went to work for the alleged 'shell company,' NBI. He was nicknamed the 'Indian Trader' because of his ability to generate the black-market smuggling business and is serving a seven-year sentence in the United States for his role in it.[31]

The case that Colombia brought against the various Philip Morris and British American Tobacco companies and subsidiaries alleges that the tobacco companies 'conceived, directed, controlled and implemented an international conspiracy.'[32] Colombian officials allege that the tobacco companies:

- sell cigarettes directly to persons or to entities that they have reason to know are smugglers;
- sell large quantities of cigarettes to entities or destinations even though the defendants know that the legitimate demand cannot possibly account for the orders;
- knowingly label, mislabel, or fail to label their cigarettes so as to facilitate and expedite the activities of smugglers;
- generate false or misleading invoices, bills of lading, shipping documents, and other documents that expedite the smuggling process;
- engage in a pattern of activity by which they ship cigarettes designated for one port knowing that, in fact, the cigarettes will be diverted to another port;
- make arrangements by which the cigarettes in question can be paid for in such a way as to be virtually untraceable;
- make arrangements for payment into foreign accounts, including Swiss bank accounts, to shield smugglers from government investigations;
- have formed, financed, and directed the activities of industry groups in order to disseminate false and misleading information.

Colombian officials emphasize that, without the active and knowing assistance of the tobacco companies, the smugglers could not have obtained, smuggled, or sold such large quantities of contraband cigarettes. The tobacco companies are alleged to have controlled, directed, and facilitated the smuggling operations. Many of the activities, such as the false invoicing, would be criminal by themselves. The intent, however, was specifically to assist the organized criminal smuggling operations. The Colombian affidavit builds a case for the existence of a hierarchical organized criminal operation that consisted of the tobacco companies and co-conspirators (i.e., associated distributors, shippers, currency dealers, currency brokers, and lobbyists). They speak of the network as being an association-in-fact that constituted a criminal 'enterprise.'

Attempts to Redefine the Role of the Tobacco Corporations

Headlines around the world 'exposed' the complicity of the tobacco companies in criminal operations. Few countries were any longer accepting the 'didn't know/wasn't directly involved' rhetoric of the big tobacco companies.[33] A large newspaper file existed for countries as diverse as Colombia, Australia, the United States, and England. Given all of this, what has been the outcome to date from these numerous lawsuits? With the exception of one case in Syracuse, New York, where the defendants pleaded guilty to smuggling-related charges, the tobacco industry has not faced criminal prosecution.[34]

Canada lost in the U.S. court based on the eighteenth-century 'Revenue Rule,' which states that the revenue laws of one state have no force in another, and that 'the tax laws of one state cannot be given extraterritorial effect so as to make collections through the agency of the courts of another state.' The court concluded that the Revenue Rule precluded Canada from pursuing a RICO claim seeking damages for lost tax revenue and that the law enforcement costs did not constitute a RICO injury to Canada.[35] Canada appealed, and the European Union filed a supporting brief.

In February 2002, the tobacco companies scored another major legal victory. Based in part on the Canadian decision, a Brooklyn judge threw out the federal lawsuit by the European Union that alleged smuggling sponsored by the tobacco companies into Europe. This same decision served to dismiss a similar suit filed by the governors of twenty-two states in Colombia.[36] Again, a couple of weeks later, a U.S. federal judge dismissed lawsuits brought by Ecuador, Belize, and Honduras.[37] The judge is quoted as saying 'This is precisely the type of meddling in foreign affairs the Revenue Rule prohibits.' It may be reassuring to some people to know that there is at least one area of 'meddling' that is prohibited by the United States!

It seemed somewhat incredible that all of the enhanced money-laundering and financial-tracing legislation and powers following 11 September could still not touch the tobacco companies. While the decision did not absolve the cigarette makers of the charges that they took part in a global smuggling conspiracy, it found that they were immune to being pursued by foreign governments for unpaid taxes in U.S. courts. The judge argued that the 'money-laundering' aspect of the cases could be examined only if the smuggling aspect was allowed. Since the Revenue Rule forbids the U.S. court to try the smuggling case, the same rule bars the court from hearing the money-laundering claim, since 'to show harm [from money laundering] will cause this court to adjudicate the smuggling scheme.'[38]

As of March 2002, Canada was still in the process of appealing and must now gain leave to be heard by the U.S. Supreme Court. The European Union and some of the other jurisdictions have said that their cases are not over and believe that at least money-laundering cases can in fact proceed. In November 2002, the U.S. Supreme Court upheld the lower court's decision and refused to hear the Canadian case.

Whether or not these cases have a degree of success in the future, two questions are interesting: first, why did it take them so long to come before the courts; and second, how, in fact, did they ever make it as far as they did? In answer to the first question, some of the previous immunity came from the difficulty of 'tracing' white-collar criminality. The tangle of subsidiaries is itself enough to form a protective wall around some of the operations. In a letter about the Canadian smuggling allegations from R.J. Reynolds Tobacco Company to the Center for Public Integrity, we get a hint of the maze that was created:

> It is important to clarify that R.J. Reynolds Tobacco Company and its employees were not involved in the day-to-day business operations of its international operations including Canada. Those businesses were operated by R.J. Reynolds International and its subsidiary, RJR-Macdonald. (Northern Brands International Inc. a subsidiary of RJR Nabisco, happened to be located in Winston-Salem, as were the headquarters of R.J. Reynolds Tobacco Company and R.J. Reynolds International at that time ...)[39]

However, in addition to any difficulty with proving these cases, the power and influence of the corporations has been a major factor – and perhaps continues to be. Everyone agrees that victory will not be easy. Influence, intimidation, the ability of the corporate entities to restructure and relocate, and the resources available to the tobacco companies all mean that the opposition is immense.

In answer to the second question – how the cases ever came to be brought at all – we need to look beyond criminal justice issues. The health-related lawsuits have revealed a wealth of information that was not previously available. What was revealed so contradicted the rhetoric of the tobacco corporations as to challenge their credibility not only on health issues but also with respect to their wider corporate policies. The presence of insider informants, of course, helped to link ongoing business practices with the smuggling businesses. Once information began to be leaked or uncovered, it led to more inconsistencies and lies.

The tobacco companies' role in facilitating the criminality of a few smugglers has been overshadowed by the demonstrated links between the corporations and the laundering of drug money in Colombia. The 2000 report of the Center for Public Integrity[40] states that the 1998 Colombian governors' report and two independent studies have reported that smuggled cigarettes have become a vehicle for money laundering in Colombia. Cigarette smugglers are also claimed to be instrumental in the black-market peso exchange in which peso brokers exchange U.S. dollars from drug traffickers for clean pesos from the smugglers, who need U.S. dollars. The 2001 report of the Center for Public Integrity presents additional evidence about the extent of the complicity of the corporations. And in 2002, the European Union linked cigarette smuggling with terrorism, submitting documents to show the circuitous route of cigarette shipments from the United States to Spain, Cyprus, and Turkey, and into Iraq, with a link to the PKK (Kurdistan Worker's Party), which the United States has labelled a terrorist group.[41]

Conclusion

Even with all of this information, it remains tempting to view the alleged corporate criminals in these criminal processes as somehow still 'outside' organized crime – useful to organized crime but 'different' from it. However, the conduct that has been alleged, if proven in court, *is* organized crime activity. There is no justification for separating off the suppliers of the illegal commodity – categorizing the other 'players' as organized crime while the tobacco companies are viewed as merely neglectful or, at most, occasionally guilty of 'white-collar crimes,' but always less guilty than organized criminals.

We have yet to see what will come of this redefining of the tobacco companies' 'organized crime' conduct. The current lawsuits are taking place within the United States, and the immense lobbying powers of the tobacco companies cannot be ignored. President Bush and Attorney General Ashcroft are considered to be 'friends of big tobacco.'[42] While the 'lost revenue' cases appear to have failed, more recent cases brought by the European Community allege money laundering, involvement in drug trafficking, and corruption.[43]

While this paper addresses the issue of the role of corporations in criminal activity, the additional facilitating conditions were the different tax structures and the invisibility offered by cross-jurisdictional trade. In our 'global community,' law enforcement and the justice systems alone will not be sufficient to combat these forms of transnational crimes. International agreements must address the need for some degree of uniformity of commodity costs, taxation, and regulatory efforts in order to block potential criminal conduct and the exploitive, lucrative financial manipulations open to transnational corporations.

As Sutherland made clear in 1968, white-collar criminality – in this case white-collar organized crime – arose from opportunity, greed, and an ambiguity about how the society was prepared to view the behaviour (see Yeager, 1975). Grass-roots groups and numerous governments have determined for themselves that corporate complicity in tobacco smuggling deserves to be subject to the mechanisms that are in place to combat other forms of organized crime. Hence, as Robert Blakey suggested, the individuals who orchestrate and carry out the transactions, if they are convicted, *are* organized criminals.

Notes

A version of this chapter was published in *Crime, Law and Social Change* 37 (2002): 225–43, Kluwer Academic Publishers, Netherlands. We thank that journal for permission to include this updated version here.

1 Threats and the shots fired into the civic complex were interpreted as a direct attack on the mayor. However, after he went into hiding, the local activity seemed to be to play 'spot the mayor,' since hiding in a small town is not the easiest of tasks. The mayor called the smugglers 'trigger happy renegades,' which, as of 16 October 1993, caused the residents of the Akwesasne reserve to boycott shopping in Cornwall – even though apparently the mayor had his speech notes approved by communications

officials from the reserve who determined that these comments were not
discriminatory to the reserve members since 'renegades' could be from
any group.

2 Taken from a transcript of proceedings that included a presentation by
Robert Blakey at a June 1982 Symposium on Enterprise Crime, hosted by
the solicitor general, in Ottawa. Quoted in Beare (1996: 150).

3 Canada Customs is responsible for the interdiction of smuggling at all
U.S.–Canada official points of entry. The RCMP is responsible for smuggling investigations that take place at other locations along the border.
Because of the location of the majority of tobacco-smuggling operations,
the RCMP Customs and Excise Section is the main enforcement agency.

4 RCMP and Canada Customs officials have stated publicly that tobacco
smuggling is not an 'enforcement problem and therefore law enforcement
will not prove to be the solution.' It is not customary for the police in
Canada to resist taking ownership of a crime problem – regardless of its
nature. The uniqueness of this recognition by a police organization that its
involvement will prove futile is noteworthy.

5 Quantities used are: 25 cigarettes per cigarette package; 200 cigarettes per
carton; 50 cartons per case.

6 As estimated by the RCMP and Customs Canada. Comparison may be
made with the appropriate Canadian charge for cigarettes. Even if the
customer of contraband cigarettes is able to buy them slightly cheaper,
there is still a wide profit margin to be shared among the smuggler, the
retailer, and the customer.

7 The RCMP reports of seizures in Ottawa support their assumptions that
members of the diplomatic community were reselling their supplies.

8 These reports are fairly well researched. The problem lies with what is
avoided – chiefly, any implication about the complicity of the tobacco
companies in the smuggling situation.

9 The decision was made by the Linquist group that they could no longer
continue to produce an objective report – one that would be seen to be
objective – when in the employ of such a potentially 'interested' party
(conversations with Mr Rod Stamler, spring 1993). However, Rod Stamler
eventually joined FIA (International Group of FIA companies), and FIA
was then hired by the National Coalition against Crime and Tobacco Contraband (the Coalition) to study 'Organized Crime and the Smuggling of
Cigarettes in the United States.' Updated reports were produced through
1999. Once again, organized crime – the exploiter of the contraband cigarettes market – was seen to consist of criminals unrelated to the tobacco
companies.

10 Quoted in *Whig Standard*, 25 September 1993: 1.

11 In British Columbia, the smuggling trade tends to be in American cigarettes from the source states of Maryland, North and South Dakota, Nevada, Montana, Idaho, California, Oregon, and Washington. Police intelligence indicates that Vietnamese criminals are heavily involved in the smuggling of cigarettes into British Columbia. The smuggling in the province seems to be one-directional – American cigarettes, rather than the exported tax-free Canadian brands, are smuggled from the United States into Canada. See, Canadian Association of Chiefs of Police (August 1993: 72).

12 In keeping with the romantic Prohibition-era smuggling history of these French islands lying off the coast of Newfoundland, St Pierre and Miquelon have apparently re-entered (or are merely continuing in) the smuggling trade. Alcohol and cigarettes pour into the Maritime provinces from these islands. See Andrieux (1983).

13 The report describes an incident where, after being tipped off about a shipment of tobacco crossing the St Lawrence River, the RCMP were forced to back off because of the Warriors' use of these weapons.

14 See Morin (1976). See particularly also Reuter (n.d.), 'An Analysis of the Characteristics of Arrested Gamblers in the State of New Jersey.'

15 Rod Stamler, formerly an assistant commissioner of the RCMP, became the chief forensic investigator for Linquist, Avey, Macdonald, Baskerville Forensic and Investigative Accountants and is responsible for the 'Linquist' reports that are quoted throughout this paper.

16 See Moon (1993: A2).

17 Customs intelligence reports and Statistics Canada figures released in May 1993.

18 Estimates from law enforcement and from the Non-Smokers Rights Association, using different strategies. These estimates are only that and cannot be assumed to be as accurate as those making the claims may argue. However, there is no doubt that a large majority of exported Canadian cigarettes arrive back into the Canadian market.

19 David Friedrichs encourages the reader to acknowledge the importance of the perception of respectability or legitimacy in discussions regarding white-collar crimes or corporate crimes; in the case of cigarette smuggling, we must ask whether the corporate 'suppliers' would be seen as culpable if they were less powerful. See Friedrichs (1992: 18).

20 Quoted in *Globe and Mail*, 28 January 1994 (see McInnes, 1994). Comments made in response to a paper prepared by Margaret Beare.

21 Quoted in Alaton (1993: D3), from a report by André Raynauld and Jean-

Pierre Vidal entitled *Smokers' Burden on Society: Myth and Reality in Canada*.
22 Ibid.
23 Quoted in *New York Times*, 28 November 1993 (see Herbert, 1993).
24 See Pearce (1992). See also Pearce and Tombs (1990) and Snider (1992).
25 *Martin's Annual Criminal Code* (1993: 52–5). The Canadian *Criminal Code* defines 'abetting' as follows:

> Section 21(1)(b) makes an accused liable as a party for acts or omissions which are done 'for the purpose' of aiding a principal to commit an offence. It is not sufficient that the acts had the effect of aiding in the commission of the offence – the purpose must be proven.

> Section 21(1)(c) makes an accused liable as a party to the offence if that accused 'abetted' the principal. Abetting simply means encouraging ...

Likewise, the *Criminal Code* has extensive conspiracy provisions encompassing the notion that 'a person is a party to the offence of conspiracy (as opposed to a participant in the conspiracy), if for example the accused having learned of the conspiracy at any time prior to the attainment of its object, encourages the conspirators to pursue its object.'
26 See National Center for Tobacco-Free Kids (2000), 'The Big Cigarette Companies and Cigarette Smuggling.' 2 March. Retrieved from *http://www.tobaccofreekids.org*. Pages 2–3 of 7.
27 Taken from National Center for Tobacco-Free Kids (2000), p. 2, quoting from Beelman et al. (2000), International Consortium of Investigative Journalists, Part 1 of the *Report of the Center for Public* Integrity, 'Major Tobacco Multinational Implicated in Cigarette Smuggling, Tax Evasion, Documents Show.' For full details of this source, see note 34.
28 See Harper (1999), 'Lawsuit Links Sales to Top Brass.' *Toronto Star*, 22 December.
29 See International Consortium of Investigative Journalists (2001), Part 2 of *An Investigative Report of the Center for Public Integrity*, 'Tobacco Companies Linked to Criminal Organizations In Lucrative Cigarette Smuggling' (March). For full details of this source, see note 34.
30 *Attorney General of Canada v. RJ Reynolds Tobacco Holdings*, U.S. District Court, Northern District of New York, 30 June 2000.
31 Harper (1999).
32 *The Departments of the Republic of Colombia* [separately listed] *v. Philip Morris Defendants* [BAT Defendants], U.S. District Court, Eastern District of New York, Docket No. 00 Civ. 2881 (NGG), 6 November 2000.
33 Samples of articles include: William Marsden, 'Tobacco Insider Talks: Major Firms Were Deeply Involved in Cross-Border Smuggling Former

Executive Says' (*Montreal Gazette*, 18 December 1999); 'RJR Affiliate Pleads
Guilty to Cigarette Smuggling' (*CNN* 23 December 1998); Maguire and
Campbell (2000), 'Tobacco Giant Implicated in Global Smuggling Schemes'
(*The Guardian*, 31 January); Griffin (2000); 'BAT Accused of Criminality'
(*The Guardian*, 22 September); Raymond Bonner, 'Racketeer Cases Shed
Light on Cigarette Smuggling in Italy' (*New York Times*, 2 September 1997);
Beelman et al. (2000), 'Major Tobacco Multinational Implicated in Cigarette
Smuggling, Tax Evasion, Documents Show'; Harper (1999), 'Lawsuit Links
Sales to Top Brass' (*Toronto Star*, 22 December 1999).

34 See two Reports (Part 1 and Part 2) completed by the International Consor-
tium of Investigative Journalists for the Center for Public Integrity. One is
listed on the Internet by specific author, the second is by the consortium:
Maud Beelman, D. Campbell, Maria Ronderos, and Erik Scheizig (2000),
'Major Tobacco Multinational Implicated in Cigarette Smuggling, Tax
Evasion, Documents Show' (International Consortium of Investigative
Journalists; Center for Public Integrity [*wysiwyg://5http://www.publici.org/
story_01_013100.htm*, retrieved 1 March 2001]); and International Consor-
tium of Investigative Journalists (2001), 'Tobacco Companies Linked to
Criminal Organizations in Lucrative Cigarette Smuggling' (Report written
by William Marsden. Contributors include Maud Beelman, Bill Bimbauer,
Duncan Campbell, William Marsden, Erik Schelzig, and Leo Sisti.
Center for Public Integrity [*wysiwyg://6/http://www.publici.org/
story_01_030301_txt.htm*, retrieved 6 March 2001]).

35 *Attorney General of Canada v. RJ Reynolds Tobacco Holdings*, paragraph 93.

36 See AP Online, Financial News, 'U.S. Judge Dismisses EU Tobacco Suit,'
19 February 2002; 'Tobacco Companies Win as Smuggling Suits Dismissed,' *Chicago Tribune*, 20 February 2002. Actual judgment is titled *The
European Community, et al., Plaintiffs, v. Japan Tobacco, Inc., et al., Defendants.
The European community, et al., Plaintiffs, v. RJR Nabisco Inc. et al., Defendants.
Department of Amazonas, et al., Plaintiffs, v. Philip Morris Companies, Inc., et
al., Defendants.* 2002 U.S. Dist. LEXIS 2506, 19 February 2002, Decided.

37 Reuters (2002), 'U.S. Judge Dismisses Suits over Cigarette Smuggling' (28
February). Available at *http://6.z.yahoo.com/rf/020228/n28119704_1.html*,
retrieved 12 March 2002, p. 1 of 2.

38 *The European Community, et al., Plaintiffs, v. RJR Nabisco Inc. et al., Defendants. Department of Amazonas, et al., Plaintiffs, v. Philip Morris Companies,
Inc., et al., Defendants.* 2002 U.S. Dist. LEXIS 2506, 19 February 2002, Decided. Page 10 of 12.

39 Letter to Maud Beelman, the Center for Public Integrity, from R.J.
Reynolds Tobacco Company, 28 January 2000.

40 From Beelman et al. (2000), 'Major Tobacco Multinational Implicated in Cigarette Smuggling, Tax Evasion, Documents Show.' *Report of the Center for Public Integrity.* p. 11 of 15.
41 Maud Beelman, 'U.S. Tobacco Companies Accused of Terrorist Ties and Iraqi Sanctions-Busting,' *An Investigative Report of the Center for Public Integrity*, 22 February 2002.
42 International Consortium of Investigative Journalists, 'Part 2: Tobacco Companies Linked to Criminal Organizations in Lucrative Cigarette Smuggling,' *An Investigative Report of the Center for Public Integrity* (2001), p. 24.
43 See *The European Community v. RJR Nabisco Inc. et al.* Filed in U.S. District Court, Eastern District of New York, 30 October 2002. Brooklyn Office.

9 The War on Drugs and the Military: The Case of Colombia

Juan G. Ronderos

Introduction

This chapter examines the international effects of using wartime tactics to deal with criminal activities and the way in which this practice distorts their real origins and consequences by failing to address the social factors that create the perfect settings for crime.[1] In particular, it looks at the problems created by the U.S. 'war on drugs' policy and the effects of the policy on foreign countries and their legal systems. This focus will require an examination of the historical process by which the drug-trafficking problem was turned into a warfare scenario, taking as an example the relations between the United States and Colombia. I shall attempt to show that Colombia's sovereignty has been violated through U.S. pressure on the country to adopt and change internal legislation by a process called 'legal acculturation.' In pursuit of its war on drugs policy, the United States has also fuelled Colombia's internal armed conflict and created an excuse to intervene in it. Yet this intervention has so far not alleviated the drug problem in any way. Instead, it has diverted attention from the real humanitarian problems that underlie drug trafficking – problems such as poverty, lack of education, and lack of basic health services that are the real causes of most of the criminal activity.

I first analyse the U.S. war on drugs policy, reviewing both the policy's history and its military implications. I then explain how those practices generated by the war on drugs discourse legally acculturate other countries' legal systems and customs. In the second part of this paper, I recount the recent history of drug-related activity in Colombia, and the legal changes that have occurred in response to it. This part identifies two different types of U.S. intervention in Colombian internal affairs that have led to what has been described as legal acculturation. Also in this second part, I discuss the increasing militarization of Colombian society and the U.S. military intervention in Colombia's civil conflict, as well as the realities and consequences of the Plan Colombia. As will become clear from the discussion, drug-related transnational crime in Colombia is the result of a very complicated historical situation that embodies social struggle and guerrilla fighting. It will also become clear that U.S. policy has played, and continues to play, a key role in the emergence of these problems and constitutes an obstacle to their solution.

The U.S. War on Drugs

The U.S. policy regarding drug trafficking has been driven by a particular approach that can be summarized as follows: drug trafficking is no longer a traditional criminal activity but a threat to the nation-state. In U.S. Senator John Kerry's words, 'a new criminal order is being born, more organized, violent and powerful than the world has ever seen. Its goals are more malevolent, too: It aims at nothing less than taking over entire governments' (Kerry, 1997: 27). Hence, the United States has assumed the responsibility for, and has mainly directed, the war against drugs. As Senator Kerry expressed it, '[j]ust as it is abundantly clear that America cannot go it alone against global crime and terrorism, it is equally obvious that only America has the power and prestige to champion that cause, forge the alliances, lead the crusade' (ibid. 193). Such bravado might be inconsequential if Kerry were an unknown academic. However, his position as a U.S. senator and a member of both the Senate Foreign Relations Committee and the Senate Intelligence Committee gives him considerable power to influence public and government opinion.

Policies of the U.S. Congress and government have not only fuelled conflicts in Latin America. It is also evident, from an examination of U.S. international legal policy and U.S. Supreme Court decisions,[2] that the United States, especially its judiciary, has generated a unique understanding of the extraterritorial applicability of U.S. laws. Within the U.S. international legal policy on drugs, the U.S. government has been establishing rules for its agencies in foreign jurisdictions governing their interaction with foreign law enforcement agencies in gathering evidence and capturing offenders. Judicial decisions have supported this policy. The Alvarez-Machain case[3] illustrates the U.S. understanding of the extraterritoriality of law.[4] It addresses the issue of the abduction by U.S. authorities of foreign citizens in their countries in violation of both their countries' laws and international law. On 21 July 1989, the Office of Legal Counsel of the U.S. Department of Justice presented a secret document entitled 'Authority of the FBI [Federal Bureau of Investigation] to Override Customary or Other International Law in the Course of Extraterritorial Law Enforcement Activities.' This document proposed that 'FBI agents have the legal authority to seize and arrest U.S. fugitives in another country without the permission of that country's government' (Tokatlian, 1997: 475–6). Moreover, the Drug Enforcement Administration (DEA) would use all those tools with the acquiescence of the U.S. judiciary. Thus, for example, in the Alvarez-Machain case, Dr Alvarez-Machain was allegedly involved in the kidnapping and killing of DEA agent Enrique Camarena Salazar. In order to bring Dr Alvarez-Machain to U.S. justice, '[o]n April 2, 1990, a team of men alleged to be hired by DEA agents working in Mexico, abducted Dr Alvarez-Machain from his office in Guadalajara.'[5]

The U.S. Supreme Court 'ruled that American courts had jurisdiction to try the case, even if the U.S. [government] had violated international law by abducting Alvarez-Machain in disregard of an extradition treaty with Mexico' (Teson, 1994: 551). In this case, the U.S. Supreme Court decided, on a writ of certiorari, the question of whether or not the district court that tried Dr Alvarez-Machain had jurisdiction over the case when he was abducted in violation of an extradition treaty between Mexico and the United States. In searching for an answer to the question, the U.S. Supreme Court found that the treaty does not refer to the obligation of the parties to abstain from forcible abduction of people in the other country's territory. The court agreed that the reason for the existence of extradition treaties is to 'impose mutual obligations to surrender individuals in certain defined sets of circumstances, following established procedures.'[6] However, the court maintained that the treaty does not forbid 'abductions outside of its terms.'[7] This interpretation of international law and the powers of the United States to extend the authority of its laws abroad shows a very complicated picture in which the United States is not willing to respect the jurisdiction of other countries. It is important to highlight that this type of extraterritorial application of U.S. laws arises within the context of the war against drugs.

Drug trafficking has been a concern for the United States since the beginning of the century, but it has not been seen as a 'war' until recent years. It was with Operation Intercept (W.O. Walker, III, 1994: 18, 25–6) in 1969, under the Nixon administration, that the United States declared a 'war' against drugs. In the beginning, the war was primarily viewed from a law enforcement perspective (see Rosenberger, 1996: 30). The military approach to the war on drugs had been planned since the early 1980s. In 1981, the hundred-year-old Posse Comitatus Act (enacted in 1878; see ibid. 30), which regulated civil–military affairs and prohibited the use of the military within U.S. borders for purposes other than protection from foreign threats, was amended by Public Law 97–86. This amendment allowed the U.S. Department of Defense to share intelligence information, training, and some resources with law enforcement agencies. This was a response of the U.S. Congress to the federal law enforcement agencies' perceived failure to combat drug trafficking (Drucker, 1997: 55; see also Rosenberger, 1996: 30).

This new understanding of the drug problem and the new policy of the United States towards the matter became more evident when, on 8 April 1986, President Ronald Reagan 'issued a national security decision directive to the effect that drug production and trafficking constituted a grave threat to the hemisphere's security' (W.O. Walker, III, 1994: 30).[8] The strategy that was outlined at that moment consisted of fighting the war against drugs first in the Andean countries, with advice, support, equipment, and training from the United States, and second in international waters (ibid. 31). Hence, this policy fixed the war to be fought primarily in the producer countries (see Marbry, 1994: 102). This crucial moment in U.S. policy created a formal linkage between drugs and national security (W.O. Walker, III, 1994: 23).

Military intervention in the war against drugs formally started in August 1986 when U.S. troops were authorized to provide temporary logistical support to the National Police Corps in Bolivia (see Mendel, 1992). By the end of the 1980s, the United States was beginning to see drug trafficking as a national security problem and therefore a military one. Hence, some committee leaders of the House Select Committee on Narcotics Abuse Control (HSC) 'encouraged a militarization of the so-called war on drugs' (W.O. Walker, III, 1994: 27–8). As some scholars have argued, '[t]he U.S. military became an instrument of drug foreign policy because civilians could not stop the importation of illicit drugs' (Marbry, 1994: 101). In 1989, under President Bush's administration, the secretary of defense, Dick Cheney, declared in a directive to the military that 'detecting and countering the production and trafficking of illegal drugs was a "high-priority, national security mission" for the Pentagon' (Bagley, 1992: 4; see also Drucker, 1997: 62; Rosenberger, 1996: 29). In addition, the 1989 National Defense Authorization Act laid the foundation for the role of the military in the war on drugs (Drucker, 1997: 63). In September 1989, President Bush's National Drug Strategy, known as the Bush–Bennett Plan, was launched with comprehensive military components for the Andean region (Lessmann, 1997: 59). This plan included military aid to Peru, Colombia, and Bolivia, as well as a regional call for the presidents of the Americas to implement an economic, military, and law enforcement plan in drug-producing countries (Chepesiuk, 1999: 83). Such a plan materialized in 1990 with the Cartagena Declaration (del Olmo, 1998a: 81; see also Chepesiuk, 1999: 84). In 1989, after Secretary of Defense Cheney's directive was issued, 'it was determined that DIA [the U.S. Defense Intelligence Agency] would concentrate on developing the necessary data bases, automation, communications, and collection management necessary to improve the foreign intelligence contribution ... DIA intelligence support would be provided, as required, to any of the participating law enforcement agencies (LEAs)' (Drucker, 1997: 65). It was in the same year that the only real military battle in the war on drugs was fought. On 20 December 1989, U.S. Operation Just Cause was launched. The objective of this operation was to overthrow Panama's head of state, General Manuel J. Noriega, and bring him to U.S. justice (ibid. 71).

Once the war against drugs was declared, it was understood that it was not going to be a conventional war, for drug traffickers cannot be catalogued in military terms as single visible enemies that can be fought under conventional war assumptions. Rather, drug traffickers are in most cases independent, 'organized' delinquents who are moved not by political[9] but by illegal entrepreneurial motives. Because of this, the United States has since applied the Low Intensity Conflict (LIC) doctrine (see for example, J.M. Collins, 1991: 10; García-Sayán, 1990: 30; del Olmo, 1994). LIC doctrine is 'a sophisticated and far-reaching theoretical framework constructed by the U.S. military-security establishment' (Dunn, 1996: 13). This war method became more evident towards the end of the 1980s and in the early 1990s (W.O. Walker, III, 1994: 28; see also Dunn, 1996: 20). The LIC is a non-conventional irregular war strategy linked to Third World disorders and insurgency.[10] The objective of the LIC doctrine is to neutralize and debilitate an enemy that is usually hard to identify. The LIC doctrine is a very complex war strategy that uses both military and non-military combat methods in pursuit of a global objective that encompasses a political, economic, military, and psychological program with a regional dimension. Under the LIC doctrine, the military gains a broader latitude for its activities, as it performs tasks usually reserved exclusively for police forces (i.e., drug enforcement) (see Collins, 1991: 50; del Olmo, 1994: 27–8; Dunn, 1996: 21; Teson, 1994: 556).

The implementation of the LIC doctrine implies the use of propaganda and other media to persuade and influence the opinions, attitudes, and conduct of friendly, neutral, and hostile groups. These kinds of operations are part of the U.S. Special Operation Forces (SOF), the Civic Action Unit (CA), and the Psychological Operations Units (PSYOPS) (del Olmo, 1994: 42; see also Dunn, 1996: 28).[11] LIC doctrine has three central points: '(1) an emphasis on internal (rather than external) defense of a nation, (2) an emphasis on controlling targeted civilian populations rather than territory, and (3) the assumption by the military of police-like and other unconventional, typically nonmilitary roles, along with the adoption by the police of military characteristics' (Dunn, 1996: 21). Having this broad mandate, the U.S. military has determined the following LIC mission areas: foreign internal defence, proinsurgency, peacetime contingency operations, terrorism counteraction, anti-drug operations, and peacekeeping operations (ibid. 21–2). Within these types of operations, the U.S. military has instructed Third World military personnel on not only 'military matters but also virtually all aspects of social, economic, and political life' (ibid. 23). As noted by Dunn, this '"new professionalism" led third-world militaries to intervene with increasing frequency in domestic politics and social issues in the name of "national security"' (ibid. 23). These operations included military aid in training and equipment, as well as economic assistance with collateral requests related to social and political reform. The LIC doctrine uses different methods to fight against drugs. On one hand, it has a military or paramilitary component to it, in which there are operations against drug traffickers. On the other hand, there are civic and psychological actions used to support military operations that are taking place in Latin America (see del Olmo, 1994: 41–7). The level of secrecy of these methods and operations is a barrier to determining the nature, extent, and implications of CA and PSYOPS operations (ibid. 45). It is, however, under the umbrella of psychological operations and civic actions[12] that the non-military component of the LIC doctrine can be found in U.S. international policy on the drug war. The U.S. certification process provides an example of how this policy is put to work.

The U.S. drug policy in the 1980s was driven by diplomatic pressure and sanctions against Latin America and the Caribbean (Bagley, 1992: 2). U.S. policy on drug trafficking comes from two different sources: the executive power and the legislative power. However, perhaps the most powerful tool in enforcing U.S. policy is derived from a combination of the two powers in the shape of what is known as the annual certification process.[13] The certification process was created in 1986 as a method to ensure that producer countries would comply with U.S. narcotics policy. The certification is a procedure by which the United States acknowledges the cooperation of producer countries in fighting drug trafficking and money laundering. This requires that countries be certified as cooperating with U.S. authorities 'in the areas of crop eradication, narcotics seizures, money laundering and asset forfeiture legislation, a crackdown on drug corruption, prosecution of drug kingpins and destruction of drug cartels' (U.S. Senate, 1996: 1). Within this process, the U.S. President produces a list of the primary drug-producing and transit countries. In relation to these countries, the U.S. President can certify that a state has fully cooperated with the United States, that it has not fully cooperated but will receive a waiver, or that it has not fully cooperated. A country that receives a waiver is certified as being of vital national interest to the United States, so that its government can receive preferential assistance and trade treatment. If the country is not certified, 'all money, except that for humanitarian and counter-narcotics purposes, is cut, and the U.S. representatives to the World Bank and six regional banks – Inter-American Development Bank (IDB) in the case of Colombia – are directed to vote against loans to that Government' (ibid.). Notwithstanding the U.S. President's decision, Congress can disagree and, within the next thirty days, may issue a certification or non-certification of a producer or transit country.

The United States is the major business partner for the region and the largest importer of Latin American products. Thus, any possibility that certification will be withheld creates great stress for many Latin American countries. Non-certification means not only that they may lose economic aid to fight against the narcotics trade, but also that they risk economic ruin or – perhaps equally serious – the fear of economic ruin. In some instances, the psychological pressure on Latin American governments and constituent groups is greater than the damage caused by the actual withdrawal of economic support to a non-certified country. In the case of Colombia, the certification with a waiver means nothing other than a moral reprimand to the government. However, decertification generates distrust in the minds of international investors and is therefore bad for business. It becomes a stigmatizing tool used to designate countries as undesirable. This problem is ultimately reflected in the performance of the country's government, as it generates discontent within the citizens. Therefore, the government is caught by a combination of U.S. pressure and electoral pressure. It is, however, fair to say that problems of governance in the Andes are not solely the result of the certification process. These problems are fuelled by other internal factors such as guerrilla warfare, weak democracies, corruption, and unstable economies – factors that are not analysed in this chapter. However, the various factors are linked. The United States not only has contributed to the problem of governance in Latin America but also has contributed to the instigation of internal problems in the name of the drug crusade.

As argued by Teson (1994: 558), '[l]ow-intensity conflict is a form of international coercion. This coercion may involve varying degrees of violence. At the very least, low-intensity operations involve violation of the sovereignty of another state.' Those actions cannot be justified, especially with regard to the misinterpretation of international criminal and public law as in the Alvarez-Machain case. The only way in which the United States could justify its activities was by bringing the drug-trafficking problem into the warfare scenario. This placed the drug discourse on a different footing, allowing anti-drug forces to bypass the rule of law in order to grapple with the national security threat allegedly posed by drugs. As explained above, LIC doctrine is the best way to justify the military approach to the war on drugs. However, it seems that LIC as a doctrine involves not only the military but also other agencies and branches of the state law enforcement apparatus. As the enemy is not clearly identifiable in this type of warfare, it requires a whole range of agencies to tackle the threat from different perspectives. The military, the DEA, the FBI, the Internal Revenue Service (IRS), the Bureau of Alcohol, Tobacco and Firearms (ATF), the Central Intelligence Agency (CIA), Congress, the judiciary, and the General Accounting Office, among others, are involved in this war. The result is a war being coordinated by the executive with a doctrine designed to override general principles of international law.

The U.S. War on Drugs, Legal Acculturation, and Legal Transplants

The process by which one legal culture is exhorted to change by an external culture, resulting in the alteration of some legal institutions, can be called 'legal acculturation.'[14] This process is often driven either by the external culture's distrust of local legal systems in managing certain legal issues or by its lack of willingness to understand and respect the rule of law in other jurisdictions. This is the case with the U.S. war on drugs and its accompanying legal battle. On the one hand, the United States has been applying its law with extraterritoriality as in the Alvarez-Machain case. On the other, it has been urging different countries to change their laws by exerting pressure through the certification process. One example of this process would be the U.S. request for Colombia to re-establish extradition laws. In this case, the objectives of extradition were twofold. The first objective was to apply the U.S. law to fugitives from U.S. justice. In addition, the United States sought to avoid the application of the other jurisdiction's laws, namely Colombian laws, to these fugitives, as it appears that the U.S. government does not consider Colombian laws appropriate. This process of legal acculturation is often carried out by means of indirect pressure, mainly generated by threats of economic sanctions and diplomatic intervention, as will be described in the next part of this paper, with Colombia as the chief example.

This drug-related legal acculturation process often advocates the homogenization of the law, a fact that is openly acknowledged by some North Americans. For example, in his book *The New War: The Web of Crime That Threatens America's Security*, U.S. Senator Kerry states: 'We simply must recognize that the world's patchwork quilt of legal systems is as much an anachronism as carbon paper. A working system of laws to combat transnational crime must be hammered out among nations of good will' (Kerry, 1997: 171). Senator Kerry believes that U.S. law enforcement should be able to investigate outside U.S. borders whenever crimes against Americans are being perpetrated or Americans are in danger from an external threat, as in the case of drug trafficking. Senator Kerry thinks that there is an existing gap in the U.S. legislation that does not allow U.S. law enforcement to conduct investigations freely overseas (ibid.).

This pressure for homogenization of the law via legal acculturation constitutes part of what can be called a U.S. attempt to 'manufacture consent' around the issue of drugs and the national security threat. This process of manufacturing consent is analogous to the media's role as described by Noam Chomsky. When Chomsky alludes to 'manufacturing consent,' he is referring to the use of the media to shape and control both the knowledge that people have about some matters and their total ignorance about other matters. This is accomplished by an indoc-

trination effected through control of topic selection, the distribution of
concerns, emphasis, issue framing, the filtering of information, and the
limiting of debate. In manufacturing consent, the media determine,
select, shape, control, and restrict information in order to serve the
interests of dominant élite groups in society (Chomsky, 1992). If someone goes against what the institution says, he or she is likely to be
excluded. In the case of the war on drugs, the official U.S. discourse,
which describes drug trafficking as a threat to national security, has
permeated the media and government policies around the globe. This
discourse can be found not only in books such as Senator Kerry's, but
also in official discourse when U.S. officials refer to the drug problem,
as will be examined in the next part of this paper. Legal acculturation
thus becomes a method by which the United States manufactures a
universal consent, not only in identifying threats but also in identifying
how to counteract them. The media serve as prime supporters of U.S.
initiatives and endorsers of its actions against drugs. With spectacular
and endless stories about drug seizures, drug barons, and countries
with weak democracies where drugs, crime, and violence are the rule,
the media persuade the public of the great danger posed by drugs not
only to society but also to the United States as a nation. Furthermore,
U.S. officials have been pressuring other countries to fight against
drugs for almost three decades. The 'seriousness' of the drug threat is
further 'sold' as having caused the United States to threaten withdrawal of economic and political support. With the nature and the
gravity of the threat agreed upon, there must be a final consensus
concerning the 'appropriate' response. U.S. law enforcement agents
travel to other countries such as Colombia and instruct local officials
about how to investigate and prosecute drug trafficking, sometimes
regardless of local legal tradition. All this manufactures consent for
the war against drugs and contributes to the legal acculturation
phenomenon.

The Influence of the U.S. War on Drugs on
Colombia's Political and Legal System

In the first part of this study, it was shown how the U.S. war on drugs
has been fought inside and outside the United States, using a variety of
tactics that potentially violate other countries' sovereignty and help
fuel internal conflicts without addressing the social and economic problems that foster criminal activities. Colombia has probably suffered

more than most countries from this type of warfare, since it has been the focus of the U.S. drug war for the past thirty years. U.S. policy has affected Colombia in several ways. It has especially contributed to the breakdown of Colombian institutions and has resulted in the death of many civilians, law enforcement officers, judges, journalists, soldiers, and politicians. Thus, Colombia has been negatively shaped by both external and internal forces into one of the most violent countries in the world, dominated by polarized violent factions.

Colombia has been described as one of the 'oldest and strongest democracies' in South America. This description fails to acknowledge that this 'democratic tradition' refers to the formality of constitutional rule, as opposed to real democracy. The country's supposedly democratic institutions have been distorted throughout this century by factors such as a closed political circle, the domination and oppression of peasants and workers, the undeclared civil war, and ongoing corruption. In addition, some legal institutions are being eroded by the effects of the U.S. war on drugs. In order to demonstrate the effects of the U.S. war on drugs within the Colombian political system and legal institutions, I will examine two examples. The first is the certification process and its implications within the Colombian legal system. The second is the involvement of the military in the war on drugs. This involvement threatens civil rights and undermines constitutional provisions, especially the one that prohibits the military from engaging in judicial police (law enforcement) work. Finally, the implications of the Plan Colombia will be reviewed in light of the U.S. military involvement and the refusal of some European governments to participate in this American crusade.

Although Colombia has had a long-lasting democratic tradition, it has also had violent periods in its history that have given the country its reputation as 'the most dangerous nation on earth' (Francis, 1999: A14). Despite some periods of peace, most of the country's history in this century has been tainted with violence and death, starting with the 'Thousand Days' War' at the beginning of the 1900s. Thirty-five years of peace ensued,[15] followed by a violent period known as *la Violencia* ('the Violence'). This civil war, fought by liberals and conservatives, between 1946 and 1964, claimed 200,000 lives and displaced 2 million people (Pécaut, 1996; Human Rights Watch, 1996: 10). To end the war generated by la Violencia, the liberals and conservatives made a pact to alternate power from 1958 until 1974, a period that was called the National Front (Human Rights Watch, 1996: 10). Beginning in 1977, political violence coming from the guerrillas was again perceived as a threat to the nation (Pécaut, 1996). By 1980, Colombia had eight active guerrilla movements, only a few of which remain active today. Among them are the pro-Soviet Revolutionary Armed Forces of Colombia (FARC) (established in the 1960s and now the oldest guerrilla group on the continent), and the 'Cuban style *foquista* guerrillas,' the National Liberation Army (ELN) (Tirado Mejía, 1998: 113).

In 1981, the first known paramilitary group, called MAS (death to kidnappers), was formed. This group was created by approximately 223 drug traffickers, and its main objective was to fight against the guerrillas who had kidnapped the relatives of drug traffickers (Human Rights Watch, 1996: 17). The MAS model was adopted by an army battalion in a province of Colombia (ibid. 17).[16] By the mid-1980s, a new paramilitary group was founded, with the name Peasant Self-Defence Group of Cordoba and Urabá (ACCU). This right-wing group remains today one of the major actors in Colombia's armed conflict.[17] As described by Michael Reid, during the 1970s and at the beginning of the 1980s, the violence related to drug trafficking was limited to the wars between rival drug bands (Rid, 1989: 144–5). During this period, drug trafficking was not considered to be a big threat. Drug trafficking was so accepted that, in 1982, Pablo Escobar, head of the so-called Medellín Cartel and known as one of the most violent criminals of this century, was elected as a substitute deputy for Congress (ibid. 144). However, by 1986 the relations between drug traffickers and the rest of the actors in Colombia's conflict dramatically changed. The Medellín Cartel's death squads went on a rampage of killings that included the slaughter of, among others, Colombia's minister of justice, Rodrigo Lara Bonilla; Colonel Jaime Ramirez, director of the Counter-narcotics Police; Guillermo Cano, director of one of the most prestigious newspapers in the country; Hernando Baquero, a Supreme Court justice; and, in January of 1997, the attorney general, Dr Carlos Mauro Hoyos.

As Alvaro Tirado Mejía (1998: 111) has pointed out, '[i]t is estimated that some 165,000 people met a violent death between 1980 and 1990.' By 1990, violence had become the primary cause of death in Colombia (ibid.). This violence cannot be attributed to a single factor, as explained by Tirado Mejía. Rather, it is the different *violencias* (plural for 'violence') generated by various actors that created such a climate (ibid. 112). However, it can be argued that the violence produced by the narcotics traffic is not the main cause of death. As Rodrigo Uprimi has said, during the most violent period (1989–90) of what was called 'narco-terrorism' (ibid. 113),[18] when bombings orchestrated by the Medellín Cartel took place in the main cities in Colombia, 227 people were killed by bombs. While this number is not small, it should be noted that, during the same period, a total of 2,969 people were killed as a result of what Uprimi calls a 'dirty war.' This was the war against left-wing militants by the paramilitary, with occasional help from the military (Uprimi, 1994: 75). Clearly, although narco-terrorism was a threat to Colombian security, it was not the main violent threat that the country was facing.

Perhaps the most shocking moment of this war occurred on 18 August 1989, when the leading presidential candidate, Senator Luis Carlos Galán, was assassinated by Medellín Cartel *sicarios* (Bagley, 1996: 201).[19] Galán's assassination was the last great political killing done by the Medellín Cartel to achieve impunity and defeat extradition efforts by Colombian officials. After the assassination, the government of President Virgilio Barco (1986–90) declared war on the drug cartels and launched an intensive campaign to arrest and punish drug traffickers (ibid. 203–5). The Medellín Cartel created a movement called *Los Extraditables* ('The Extraditables'), to which most of the terrorist acts conducted since 1987 have been attributed (McRae, 1995: 239). Their sole objective was to attain the assurance that they would not be extradited to the United States.

While between 1986 and 1990 the drug-trafficking problem was turning into narco-terrorism, Colombia was searching for a political solution to its guerrilla problems. Whereas drug trafficking and narco-terrorism were perceived as criminal problems, it was clear that the guerrilla problem was political and socio-economic in nature. Hence, by this time it was acknowledged that the country needed deep political and structural changes. During the first period of Cesar Gaviria Trujillo's presidency (1990–4), a peace agreement was reached with four main guerrilla groups (M-19, EPL, PRT, and Quintín Lame). At the same time that these peace agreements were being negotiated, a profound political reform was taking place in Colombia. A National Constitutional Assembly was elected, and a new constitution was enacted (Tirado Mejía, 1998: 116). This new constitution was the result of a process that Manuel José Cepeda calls, 'the most open, pluralistic and democratic in Colombia's history' (Cepeda, 1998: 71). This process renovated almost all the country's institutions, created new ones such as the Constitutional Court and the Ombudsman's Office, and established a special procedure to protect fundamental rights called *acción de tutela*. Other changes were also included, such as the prohibition against extraditing Colombian nationals.

During President Gaviria's tenure, Pablo Escobar, Rodriguez Gacha, and the Ochoa clan were defeated.[20] The president's task then became to fight against the 'Cali Cartel' and the Rodriguez Orejuela brothers. This task would not be completed until President Samper's term (1994–8). During almost all this period, Colombian President Ernesto Samper Pizano was fighting accusations of accepting more than $6 million from the Cali Cartel (Schemo, 1996: 1). For this reason, in 1995 Colombia was certified with a waiver by the United States, as were Bolivia, Paraguay, and Peru (Jaramillo, 1998); then, in 1996 and 1997, Colombia was decertified (Clinton, 1997). In 1998, the certification was given with a waiver, because of U.S. national interests (Clinton, 1998). This certification, as explained by the U.S. sub-secretary of narcotics, did not imply either that the United States trusted the Colombian government or that the Colombian government had been fully cooperative. Instead, it meant that U.S. interests would be undermined if it kept decertifying Colombia. In Mr Beers's words, 'Colombia did not [deserve] to be certified this year' (*Semana*, 2 March 1998: 829).[21] Samper's visa to the United States was revoked, and he was declared *persona non grata* in that country (Hufbauer, 1998). His term of presidency was probably one of the most scrutinized in Colombian history. The Colombian Congress opened an impeachment process against him, though he was absolved of wrongdoing. Ironically, during his stay in office, his government managed to incarcerate the Cali Cartel's kingpins, the Rodriguez Orejuela brothers, while also losing U.S. support. By the end of Samper's term, Colombia was in bad economic shape, international relations with the United States were at the lowest point in decades, and illicit drug production was on the rise.

In January 1998, a set of articles in the Colombian magazine *Semana* explored the probable outcomes of the presidential campaign of 1998 in which the controversial President Samper was to be replaced. The relative chances of becoming president of the two candidates from the two main political parties were analysed: Horacio Serpa for the Liberal party, and Andrés Pastrana for the Conservative party. With regard to the former, the articles in *Semana* were quick to notice that his biggest problem as a presidential candidate was his involvement in President Samper's government and the fact of his being investigated in what became known as the '8,000 Process.'[22] These two points inevitably placed him in a difficult position, requiring him, according to the magazine, to win in two constituencies: the Colombian ruling class, and the United States (*Semana*, 26 January 1998: 24). *Semana* was correct, and Pastrana was elected in 1998. U.S. sanctions against Colombia had succeeded in influencing the election to prevent Serpa from being elected. Gary Hufbauer considers the U.S. sanctioning policy against Colombia to have been a success, for it brought about a change in government from Samper to Pastrana (Hufbauer, 1998). President Pastrana was facing the dual challenge of fighting the drug traffic and negotiating peace with the guerrilla groups at a moment when the United States claimed that there was no distinction between the two. It was a moment when Colombia was also facing its worst economic situation in decades as well as unprecedented levels of crime and violence.

By 1999, Colombian and U.S. relations had changed. The elected Colombian president, Andrés Pastrana, had been in office since mid-1998 and had officially visited the United States on various occasions. This change in Colombia's government led to a new phase in which Colombia was to be certified for its 'cooperation.' Nevertheless, it appears that Colombia's cooperation was not being measured by its success in eradicating illicit crops (Bustos, 1999; see also *Cambio 16*, 8 May 1999). Hence, it is legitimate to ask: What exactly constitutes cooperation for the United States? The U.S. attorney general, Janet Reno, visited Colombia in 1999 after Colombia was certified and, in an interview with *Cambio 16*, mentioned that the United States was pleased with President Pastrana's efforts to formulate a strategy against drugs and to review Colombian legislation in order to improve its criminal justice system. She was positive about her visit and said she expected to see concrete results very soon (*Cambio 16*, 8 March 1999: 298). However, we need to ask what kind of results she was referring to.

In early 1999, the United States sent a letter to the Colombian minister of foreign affairs in which the U.S. government established seven issues for the Colombian government to address in order to attain full certification (*El Tiempo*, 10 August 1998). All the requirements outlined in the letter were covered under what the United States called a need for the 'implementation of an integral anti-drug strategy' by Colombia (ibid.).[23] Although some of these requirements appeared not unreasonable, such as the need for the army and the police to give priority to the development of human rights policies, others were not. One requirement that encroached on Colombian sovereignty was the U.S. demand for a Colombian government budget increase to expand eradication programs and other aspects of the fight against drugs. This clearly impinged on

Colombia's right to determine its own budgetary priorities. In addition, the United States requested the strengthening of investigations into and punishment of corruption related to drug trafficking. This was a method of pressuring the Colombian government and the Colombian judiciary to provide concrete results in U.S. terms. These terms could be translated into more people in jail and tougher sentences. The United States also demanded a more effective extradition mechanism so that people serving sentences in Colombian jails who were wanted by U.S. authorities could be sent to the United States to be judged by U.S. justice. As explained by *El Tiempo*, this meant that the United States was insisting on the extradition of the Cali Cartel clan, who were already in jail serving sentences predating the enactment of the extradition law. In other words, the United States wanted retroactive application of extradition. For the United States, the penalties imposed on drug traffickers convicted in Colombia do not reflect the magnitude of their crimes. Again, the United States insisted on the implementation of tougher penal legislation that would include enhanced penalties for drug-related crimes. Finally, the U.S. government warned that the certification process for 1999 would depend heavily on whether Colombia implemented major prison reforms. This would ultimately mean legal reforms to laws governing the penal system (ibid.).

As the evidence presented shows, the United States has been using the certification process to make Colombia change parts of its political and legal system to conform to U.S. wishes. Although various reasons were cited for the decision to decertify Colombia, most of them were related to U.S. discomfort with aspects of the Colombian legal system and Colombian leadership. While the existing Colombian laws might have needed some amendments, it is troubling when one country uses methods not ratified in international law to force legal changes in a foreign jurisdiction. As the above examples show, international cooperation between Colombia and the United States appears to be a one-way street. In this regard, it is interesting to observe that Colombia has requested information from the United States about various criminal cases 731 times, but has received replies to only approximately 3.8 per cent of them (Moncayo, 1998: 228, 230). As a matter of fact, Attorney General Reno admitted that the United States had decided to limit its cooperation with Colombian judicial authorities beginning in 1994. This was because information provided by the United States often resulted in only 'minor' penalties that, by U.S. standards, did not adequately reflect the seriousness of the crimes committed (*Cambio 16*, 8 March 1999: 298).

Military Aid and Military Policing: The Militarization
of a Social and Criminal Problem

The U.S. military has recently been advocating the involvement of the Colombian military in the fight against drug trafficking and has recommended the creation of special anti-narcotics brigades. For example, in December of 1998, in the Cartagena bilateral agreement, the United States agreed to increase military aid and training to the Colombian army in exchange for the establishment of anti-narcotics brigades. In the short term, this initiative will affect the Colombian legal understanding of drug trafficking as a crime, and will nourish the Colombian civil conflict. It will alter the legal understanding of drug trafficking, since it creates an appearance of political subversion. Hence, drug trafficking ceases to be an ordinary crime and becomes a threat to state stability and, therefore, the main cause of the war. Since it becomes a matter of war, then ordinary criminal law no longer applies to drug-trafficking offences, and the law of war as understood by the military will be imposed. In order to clarify this problem, I will first examine the history of the guerrilla conflict and its nexus with drug trafficking, as well as the U.S. initiative to create anti-narcotics brigades. Subsequently, I will discuss from a legal perspective the involvement of the Colombian military in the fight against drugs. Finally, I will analyse the Plan Colombia.

Guerrillas, Narcotics, and the U.S. Military Initiative:
The Plan Colombia

Colombia has been fighting an undeclared civil war since the mid-twentieth century. The major actors during the past forty years of civil warfare have been the guerrillas, the paramilitary groups, and the army. Guerrilla movements in Colombia have been mainly left wing; paramilitary groups, on the other hand, have been right wing, and their main purpose has been to defeat the guerrillas. Meanwhile, the army has been fighting against the guerrillas and, in recent times, occasionally against the paramilitaries. FARC, the main and oldest guerrilla group in Colombia (and in Latin America),[24] has taken the jungles of the southern part of the country as its centre of operations and as a shelter for most of its troops. During the last two decades, this area has also been dedicated to the production of coca leaves. Until approximately 1990, cocaine crops were situated mainly in Peru and Bolivia, with Colombia serving to process the coca paste and ship the final product to the United States and Europe. However, in recent years this area of Colombia has suffered an increase in quantities of illegal crops as a result of the reduction in cultivated areas in Peru and Bolivia (Farah, 1998b). This reduction could be considered an effect of U.S. eradication policies in those countries.

The expansion of coca-leaf plantations in Colombia was made possible by a large number of internal migrants who left the cities and the main populated areas for the southern jungles in search of prosperity in what can be called the expanding agricultural frontier (Vargas and Barragán, 1996: 4). Since this area is isolated from the rest of the country, there being no roads to bring products into the central part of Colombia and other populated areas, peasants had to look for alternative crops. Because coca was more profitable than legal crops, it replaced most of the small, subsistence crops. The drug traffickers who processed the leaves and produced cocaine to be exported did not require roads to export their product, since they were using airplanes. Even today, the areas of the country where coca is being cultivated and processed remain isolated from the rest of the country. Physical infrastructure to transport conventional crops to markets where they can be sold for enough profit to generate sustainable development does not exist. There is also a lack of state presence at every level. Most of the coca plantations belong to small farmers and peasants. Those who work in these areas are peasants who have no option but to work in the coca business.

It is this isolation that led guerrilla groups to operate in these regions. Not only can they count on the support of the people, but in some cases they even play the role of the state. The interrelation between the guerrilla groups, the coca growers, and the drug traffickers is not a simple one. Guerrilla groups have operated in the country for the last forty years, whereas coca growers and drug traffickers in these areas have operated on a large scale for only the past two decades. On one side, guerrilla groups and drug traffickers were enemies by the mid-1980s. On the other, paramilitary groups were created by drug traffickers in association with some members of the army. In the 1990s, the relationships among these groups changed. As mentioned by del Olmo (1998b: 275), 'while it is true that there are guerrillas in this region, the situation is much more complicated since this is an area that has a long tradition of peasant struggles to win social concessions.' Paramilitary groups detached themselves to some extent from the military and the drug traffickers. Guerrilla groups started their involvement with the drug traffic in the southern part of the country as part of their insurgency, because the government was eradicating the peasants' illegal crops. They also seized the opportunity to impose a kind of taxation on the narcotics operations to finance their insurgency. Their involvement, according to the authorities, now includes offering protection to drug traffickers. In short, as explained by Ricardo Vargas and Jackeline Barragán, 'illegal cultivation in Colombia is a part of a conflictive scenario which should be seen as a part of the so-called "agrarian problem." This is characterized by, among other things, an unequal distribution of land ownership which has been the historical cause of frustrated attempts at agrarian reform' (Vargas and Barragán, 1996: 4).

The crop-eradication campaign by U.S. and Colombian authorities remains very difficult in these areas of the country since the guerrillas continue to defend coca growers from fumigation. Fumigation airplanes need to be escorted by armed helicopters in order to respond to the guerrillas' gunfire. It is because of this complicated relationship among all the actors that the United States started to refer to insurgency groups in Colombia as narco-guerrillas. This has served as an argument to allow the U.S. Congress to give military aid to Colombia to fight against the guerrillas.

The U.S. Defense Intelligence Agency went even further, saying that, unless Colombian armed forces are drastically restructured and the government regains legitimacy, the 'Marxist insurgency financed by millions of dollars from the cocaine and heroine trade ...' could win the war, turning Colombia into a 'narco-state' (Farah, 1998a: A17). Intelligence agencies in Colombia and the United States have estimated that two-thirds of both main guerrilla groups are involved in the narcotics trade in a country where, according to the same authorities, 80 per cent of the world's cocaine is being produced (ibid.). General Charles Wilhelm, commander of the U.S. Southern Command, warned in a letter to the general commander of the Colombian armed forces that 'at this time the Colombian armed forces are not up to the task of confronting and defeating the insurgents ... Colombia is the most threatened in the area under the Southern Command's responsibility, and it is in urgent need of our support' (ibid.). These assertions have created fears in the U.S. political environment about insurgency groups in Colombia, and have strengthened the link between the military and the 'war' against drugs. In fact, up to 1997, the United States was cautious about giving any type of military aid in the fight against insurgency. However, because of pressures in the U.S. Congress, such as the campaign led by Republican Dan Burton, there has been an increasing clamour to increase U.S. military aid to Colombia. This military aid includes Black Hawk helicopters. Other equipment, including used radios, a thousand M-16 A1 rifles, five hundred M-60 machine guns, and 1.1 million rounds of ammunition, was ready to be sent to Colombia by mid-1998 (ibid.; Priest, 1998a). The Colombian government responded furiously to the U.S. assertions. President Samper stated that Colombia was not seeking any military aid from the United States to fight the guerrillas (*El Tiempo*, 13 April 1998). The guerrillas' response to the U.S. intelligence report was that they wanted to internationalize the solution to the internal conflict, while the United States wanted to internationalize the war (ibid.).

In 1998, it was somewhat clear that the United States was not going to give any military assistance for counter-guerrilla efforts in Colombia. To this effect, a senior State Department official stated that the U.S. policy in Colombia 'is to assist in fighting narcotics production and trafficking ... When our personnel and equipment are attacked during counter-drug operations, they will return fire. We do not, however, provide assistance for offensive counter-guerrilla operations' (Farah, 1998a: A17). In 1998, warnings were already being issued about the U.S. involvement in Colombia. By that year, military aid had 'risen to an estimated $195 million annually' (Diebel, 1998: A14). In addition, by that time, 'the number of military advisers – from Green Berets to Navy SEALS – [had] doubled to about 225, according to reports' (ibid.). The initiatives to train police forces in the Andes started in Peru and spread into Ecuador with what has been called the 'most ambitious anti-drug programs the Pentagon has ever undertaken in Latin America' (Farah, 1998c: A01). A five-year program, involving U.S. Navy SEALs, Army Special Forces, Marines, and the Coast Guard in training the Peruvian police force, took place in the Amazon jungle near the Colombian border (Efe-Reuters, 1998; Farah, 1998b). In addition, the CIA was appointed to provide intelligence training to the same Peruvian forces in order to fight drug trafficking. One of the trainers interviewed by the reporter said that there was little difference between the counter-insurgency training in Central America and the current initiative. In his words, 'It is exactly the same thing ... All of this is the same counterinsurgency stuff, now useful for fighting drugs' (Farah, 1998b: A01).

Meanwhile, the Colombian guerrillas had been complaining that the U.S. military advisers were working with the army to fight against guerrillas rather than against narcotics (Diebel, 1998), despite statements by U.S. officials that the U.S. involvement was strictly anti-drugs oriented and would not support any counter-insurgency operations (Bajak, 1998). Although it had been suggested in early 1998 that the United States would not become involved in counter-insurgency warfare, such a development became a real possibility in March of that year, when Clinton administration officials began to consider an increase in U.S. military assistance to the Colombian government (Priest, 1998a). By then, U.S. national security officials were starting to acknowledge a blurry link between fighting drug traffickers and fighting rebels in Colombia (ibid.). In 1998, after Colombia had been decertified for two consecutive years, U.S. military aid to the Colombian military was boosted again 'under a program that avoids restrictions imposed on military aid by the Clinton administration in response to Colombia's abysmal human rights record and drug-related corruption' (Priest and Farah, 1998: A01). This aid consisted mostly of training, involving hundreds of U.S. troops, that 'allowed the U.S. military to play a much more direct and autonomous role in Colombia than officials have publicly acknowledged' (ibid.). This training was made possible through a program known as Joint Combined Exchange Training (JCET), the very same program that allowed U.S. troops to conduct forty-one military training sessions with Indonesian troops, although the U.S. Congress believed it had banned any military tie with that country on grounds of human rights violations.[25] Under this program, U.S. Special Forces are allowed to conduct training in certain countries, notwithstanding a State Department ban, even in spite of human rights violations by the receiver country (Priest and Farah, 1998).[26] The use of JCET forces needs the approval of the U.S. Embassy and the Special Operations Command in Florida. In addition, a new approval level is being created at the 'Office of the Secretary of Defense that will be done in the Special Operations / Low Intensity Conflict area – SOLIC' (Bacon, 1998).

In October 1998, the United States gave Colombia the first military aid directed to support joint anti-narcotics operations. A total of $20 million was allocated as part of a $41.1 million package that was approved by the U.S. Congress International Relations Commission (Gomez, 1998a). On 29 November 1998, the Third Conference of Ministers of Defense of the Americas took place in Cartagena (Pastrana, 1998). At the end of the conference, Colombia and the United States signed an agreement establishing a bilateral working group that would hold meetings twice a year in order to evaluate U.S. military aid and options. The objective of the working group, according to officials, is to improve human rights and to fight drug trafficking. The discussions between the Colombian minister of defense and the U.S. secretary of defense included proposals for the creation of a military battalion of about 1,000 soldiers to be established by mid-1999. 'The unit's sole function will be to assist police in anti-narcotics operations' (Kotler, 1998). Because of the Colombian army's poor human rights record, the U.S. military aid is tied specifically to anti-drug operations. The U.S. military also acknowledges that it can support the police only in counter-narcotics operations. Within the terms of the agreement, the United States sent to Colombia a delegation of U.S. Department of Defense officials in order to review Colombian military criminal justice. Their study was to concentrate on an evaluation of the bill presented to the Colombian Congress. The bill would amend the Military Criminal Code and would advise different methods for expediting the prosecution of human rights violations (Char and Arcieri, 1998). This military agreement caused great concern in the United States. The *New York Times* dedicated a whole page to the Third Conference of Ministers of Defense of the Americas in which it warned that the military aid to Colombia could result in full-blown U.S. involvement in Colombia's counter-insurgency war (Schemo, 1998: A14; Myers, 1998: A14; Gomez, 1998b). The Center for International Policy in Washington, Human Rights Watch, and the Washington Office on Latin America (WOLA) expressed their concern about any military aid to the Colombian military, given its deplorable human rights record – one of the worst in the world (Gomez, 1998c; Colombian Human Rights Network, 1999).

In June 1999, the U.S. General Accounting Office (GAO) acknowledged that the line between counter-narcotics and counter-insurgency operations was becoming a policy problem for the United States (Kushner et al., 1999: 2–3). When referring to the Colombian drug strategy, the GAO said that, according to the U.S. State Department, the strategy 'does not precisely define the military's role in reducing drug-trafficking activities' (ibid. 11). With respect to the Colombian military's counter-narcotics initiatives, the GAO said that both U.S. and Colombian drug strategies, 'recognize that the Colombian military needs to become more involved in counternarcotics operations, particularly in areas not under government control' (ibid. 12). It mentioned the creation of the counter-narcotics battalion and said that it 'will be dedicated to conducting its own counternarcotics operations and supporting CNP [Colombian National Police] operations' (ibid. 12). Finally, the GAO said that in order to achieve U.S. counter-narcotics goals for Colombia, it would be necessary, among other things, to determine 'when it is appropriate to share information with the Colombian military on insurgency activities for planning counternarcotics operations' (ibid. 16). In June 1998, it was decided that there was a restriction on sharing information on guerrilla activities between the U.S. and the Colombian armies unless the information was to be used in counter-narcotics operations. However, as explained by the GAO, 'within the area where most drug-trafficking activities occur, U.S. embassy officials stated that the drug traffickers and the insurgents have become virtually indistinguishable' (ibid. 21). Consequently, in March 1999, new guidelines on information sharing with the Colombian military were issued, allowing the exchange of 'information with the Colombian military on insurgent activities within the drug-trafficking areas' (ibid.). In fact, intelligence sharing between the U.S. and Colombian military have helped the Colombian military to defeat recent attacks by FARC. In mid-July 1999, rebels from FARC conducted attacks in various parts of the country but were overwhelmingly defeated for the first time in four years by the Colombian army. But the Colombians were not alone, as became clear from General Wilhelm's comments at Fort Benning, where he 'acknowledge[d] that U.S. and Colombian military officials had been in constant communication throughout the weekend ...' when these events occurred (Rohter, 1999).

In July 1999, General Barry McCaffrey submitted a report to his superiors in which he proposed that there should be $1 billion 'in emergency assistance available to the Colombian government to strengthen its efforts against drugs' (ibid.), going beyond even what the Colombian government wanted from the United States (ibid.). McCaffrey's proposal was based on his claim that the guerrillas were being financed through drug trafficking and that one cannot differentiate 'between anti-drug programs and the Colombian government's counterinsurgency war against the guerrillas' (Drug Reform Coordination Network [DRCNet], 1999). Meredith Tate of the Washington Office on Latin America (WOLA) commented that '[t]he real danger of Barry McCaffrey's remark is that it completely delegitimizes the concerns and interests of the peasant population, who live in that part of the country' (ibid.). While not supporting civil disobedience of any sort, we are suggesting, however, that riots, drug production, migration, and mass street criminality might be seen as the only means available to the very poor to articulate a need for change. For example, in August 1996, a stigmatized southern community in Colombia that represented a significant part of the province, but that was also engaged in one way or another in growing or producing drugs, demonstrated against the government. As del Olmo (1998b: 275) described it,

> more than 50,000 well-organized peasants began a series of protests and mobilizations in the southern part of Colombia, against aerial fumigations. These protests lasted through three months of intense confrontation with the armed forces and left several persons dead or wounded. The Government considered such confrontation a public order and criminal problem and, following the official, simplistic 'narcoguerrilla' discourse, blamed guerrillas for the conflict.

In July 1999, General McCaffrey publicly used the term 'narcoguerrilla' when referring to insurgent Marxist groups, labelling them as common delinquents dedicated to trafficking in narcotics and to attacking counter-narcotics police and military posts (*El Tiempo*, 1999). During the previous month, a study published by the U.S. General Accounting Office revealed that Colombia receives the third-largest amount of U.S. military aid after Israel and Egypt (Pizarro, 1998).

This military understanding of the drug problem became ever more evident by 13 July 2000, when President Clinton signed 'Plan Colombia,' the aid package to Colombia. This controversial plan was originally published in Spanish on the Internet in 1998, and introduced President Pastrana's social investment strategy for conflict zones in Colombia. That was the first version of four that were presented to the public. The second document – undated – is the translation of a document that was elaborated in collaboration with advisers from the U.S. Department of State. There is, however, a final English version, dated October 2000, that was distributed in anticipation of a meeting of the United Nations General Assembly. What is really relevant in these documents is that, though they are all called Plan Colombia, they differ considerably in substance, as Professor Aileen Tickner explained to a Colombian reporter (Sanchez, 2000). The English version presented to the U.S. Congress has an emphasis on counter-narcotics that the others, circulated in Colombia, do not have. The order of the chapters of these papers also differs. While the chapter on peace appears last in the version presented to the U.S. Congress, in the other documents, it appears first. There are also differences in the tone and language of these documents. The version presented to the U.S. Congress speaks of the plan as the main counter-narcotics strategy for Colombia, whereas the versions that circulated in Colombia mention the counter-narcotics offensive as one part of the overall plan. In addition, parts of the version circulated in the United States do not appear in the versions distributed in Colombia. Finally, the plan that was presented in the United States was never presented for consultation or approval to the Colombian people.

What is the relevance of this plan? From the perspective of this author, the plan is worrisome. It provides an aid package of $862.3 million to fight the drug traffic in Colombia alone, out of a total of $1.3 billion approved by the American Congress to deal with the war on drugs in the whole of the Andean region. In the Colombian portion, a total of 81 per cent of the aid is dedicated to military assistance, police assistance, judicial reform, and law enforcement. For example, $328 million is dedicated to buying helicopters. Out of the $512 million allocated for the military forces, $416.9 million is to fund a combined military and police operation called 'Push into Southern Colombia' to eradicate illicit crops in the southern part of the country. In contrast, the plan provides a mere $3 million to support efforts at making peace between the guerrilla movements and the Colombian government. This money is to be used on negotiation seminars for government officials to deal with the guerrillas. In the area of social and economic assistance, $68.5 million is allocated for alternative development and crop substitution, $22.5 million to assist the 1.5 million people displaced internally by the armed conflict, and $51 million for several initiatives to improve human rights in the country (Center for International Policy, 2000). The amounts allocated to deal with the root causes of the problem are so small that it raises questions about the U.S. government's real intentions.

Many critics have raised such questions. Chomsky, for instance, has pointed out in a recent article that Plan Colombia is designed to fight guerrilla movements in the southern part of Colombia but not paramilitary forces that have publicly stated that they are being financed by the narcotics trade (Chomsky, 2000). In addition, Chomsky quoted Vargas's comment that '[t]he counterinsurgency battalions armed and trained by the U.S. do not attack traffickers ... [they] have as their target the weakest and most socially fragile link of the drug chain: the production by peasants, settlers and indigenous people' (ibid. 30–1).

Conclusions

Defining drug trafficking and drug-related crimes as threats to national security is, in most cases, inappropriate. While it is true that, during the late 1980s and early 1990s, drug trafficking and narco-terrorism were a serious threat to Colombian police and law enforcement officials in major cities, as well as to bystanders, it is not true that the so-called drug cartels threatened the existence of Colombia as a nation-state. In fact, the dirty war between right-wing death squads and left-wing activists killed more people during the same period than narco-terrorism activities. Hence, if there is a threat to national security, it would be from the dirty war.

Unlike guerrilla movements, drug traffickers and related offenders do not have a political agenda to seize power and dominate the state with a particular ideology.[27] As criminals, they try to acquire as much legal protection for their illegal activities as they can buy, creating an ideal scenario for social, official, judicial, and political corruption. Hence, corruption threatens the rule of law and justice. However, since the existence of the state is not being jeopardized, it cannot be generalized that drug trafficking and its inherent corrupting practices are national security matters. Understanding drug trafficking as a threat to national security situates legal policy discussion on different grounds than if it were viewed as a widespread and serious criminal matter. It may lead to the adoption of measures such as the ones taken by the United States in Operation Just Cause, the Alvarez-Machain case, and the certification process, as explained above. The only way in which the United States could justify such activities was by bringing the drug-trafficking criminal problem into the warfare scenario by 'manufacturing' a national security threat.

This national security threat discourse placed the drug problem on a different level, allowing the application of the LIC doctrine in order to approach the war on drugs in military mode. However, the LIC doctrine involves not just the military but also other U.S. governmental agencies and branches. This war against drugs is being coordinated by the U.S. executive with a military doctrine designed for situations where the enemy cannot be clearly identified. This national security-cum-military approach to the drug problem has as one of its outcomes the U.S. acculturation of other countries' legal systems through demands for changes to their laws and direct intervention in domestic issues related to social and economic policy.

Colombia serves as a perfect example of how the U.S. war on drugs affects another country's social, political, and legal institutions. The certification process assists U.S. demands for legal changes in foreign jurisdictions by threatening withdrawal of economic aid. These legal changes and 'improvements' are sought by the United States from its perspective of what ought to be, on legal and moral grounds. Hence, the United States becomes a world moral arbiter in its global fight against drugs. In this war, certification was a useful tool, allowing the United States to force Colombia to change and enact laws related to drug trafficking, organized crime, extradition, and related fields. The certification process was complemented by psychological pressure from U.S. officials in the form of repeated and strong suggestions (closely resembling demands) about changing Colombia's laws and legal system. Continuing declarations by U.S. high officials and the ostracizing practice of certification brought about changes in discourse within Colombian politics. This pressure has affected the Colombian political and legal environment in such a way as to allow the manufacturing of consent in favour of the U.S. approach to the war on drugs.

As mentioned before, U.S. intervention in the Colombian extradiction law is clear. After the Colombian constitution was enacted, the United States demanded that a provision proscribing extradition be changed, making the change a requirement for permitting Colombia to be fully certified. Finally, after two decertifications and much pressure from the United States, Colombia acceded to the demand and amended its constitution. This amendment did not permit retroactive extradition, however, to the annoyance of U.S. officials, who once again pressured the Colombian government. The U.S. justified the demand by claiming that extradition is the only legal instrument for bringing real justice – that is, U.S. justice – to bear against the narcotics traffic. While it is legitimate for one country to disapprove of another country's legal system, it is not legitimate for that country to impose its legal values and systems on other jurisdictions, especially when the laws and the legal system have been legitimately adopted by a democratic process within such foreign jurisdictions.

The U.S. intervention in Colombian affairs has been possible because of the militarizing of the war on drugs. Considering drugs a threat to national security allows the application of military strategies in the fight against drugs. Under this perspective, militarization should not be understood only as the involvement of the military but also as the underlying rhetoric of war within the parameters of the LIC doctrine. The danger of this military perspective is that it is used to legitimize the deployment of force and violence against problems that are social in essence. This will even further aggravate the undeclared civil war that has racked Colombia for the past forty years. This war has resulted from decades of class conflict, political corruption, intolerance, violence, and lack of opportunities for the people. While guerrilla groups have coexisted with drug traffickers, they have not been linked to them until recently. In short, drug trafficking and guerrillas are different and should be treated differently. A military approach does not touch the social, economic, and political problems that generate the narcotics traffic in Colombia. As has been shown, the military approach short-sightedly views the drug problem as a battle that can be won by the use of force.

Following 11 September 2001, there have been some particularly frightening developments. First, the peace negotiations between the government and the FARC guerrillas broke down, and the war resumed. Second, the U.S. government declared that Colombian guerrilla groups *and* paramilitary groups are to be considered terrorists and treated as such. Finally, after much consideration, the U.S. Congress is contemplating aiding the Colombian government in fighting the guerrilla groups as part of the 'war on terrorism' (Gomez Maseri, 2002). If this happens, it will be the end of the traditional U.S. policy – in part, a recognition of the Colombian army's record of human rights violations – of aiding the Colombian government in fighting narcotics but not in fighting the guerrillas. This escalation of the conflict will have a devastating impact – making it still more difficult to combat the real causes of the narcotics traffic. Priorities will be shifted to fight what is deemed to be 'a terrorist threat,' and the real social and economic dimensions of the drug problem will be obscured by yet another rhetoric of 'war.'

Notes

This article is based on my Master of Laws' thesis, which was the result of two years of research and work that attempted to explain what I had witnessed over the three years I worked for law enforcement agencies in Colombia. During those years I met wonderful people who blindly believed that there is a war against drugs that must be fought and won. Many of them have died fighting in this war, which was invented and fomented by the United States. Out of the thousands of people who have suffered through this war, I want to dedicate this paper, as I did my thesis, to Mardoqueo Ćuellar, a very good friend and a counter-intelligence officer at the Administrative Department of Security, who was tortured and killed because he was conducting investigations related to allegations of drug corruption within the force. His family, as is the case with all law enforcement officers in Colombia, was very poor. He was twenty-nine years old, and he left behind a wife and a three-month-old daughter. I also want to dedicate this paper to all of the children who live in the southern part of Colombia. I hope one day they can forgive the Colombian ruling class.'

1 This understanding about the drug war is disclosed in, and perhaps started with, President Reagan's secret directive No. 221 (April 1986), in which the drug conflict was referred to as a threat to democracy: del Olmo (1994: 31).
2 For an overview of U.S. extraterritorial application of the law see R.D. Gregorie (1991).
3 *United States v. Alvarez-Machain*, 112 US S. Ct 2188 (1992) [hereafter *Alvarez-Machain to S.Ct*).
4 For a discussion of the Alvarez-Machain case and LIC doctrine see Teson (1994).
5 *Humberto Alvarez-Machain v. United States of America et al.*, 97 Cal. Daily Op. Serv. 1109. (9th Cir. 1996) at 699.
6 *Alvarez-Machain to S. Ct*: 664.
7 Ibid. 666
8 See also del Olmo (1998a: 79), Drucker (1997: 58), and Dunn (1996: 25). Decision Directive No. 221. J.J. Veloz (1998: 241).
9 By 'non-political' it should be understood that the intent is not to occupy a territory or change its government. It can be said that drug traffickers do not want to change the status quo. See Tokatlian (1998: 8).
10 See Dunn (1996: 20). 'The term *low-intensity conflict* is derived from the Pentagon's abstract division of the 'spectrum of conflict' into three levels: 'high, medium, and low.'
11 For new proposals within the U.S. Army for police–military services to conduct LIC operations, with PSYOPs and CA, see Demarest (1996, 1999).
12 del Olmo (1994: 41) explains in her work how civic and psychological operations within the LIC doctrine imply the use of political, economic, and social means to achieve U.S. goals.
13 *Foreign Assistance Act*, Pub. L. No. 87–195, (S.1983), 75 Stat. 424, approved 4 September 1961, I 8 s. 490.
14 'Acculturation' is a term used by anthropology to describe 'the process of culture change set in motion by the meeting of two autonomous cultural systems, resulting in the increase of similarity of each to the other ... Acculturation subsumes a number of different processes including DIFFUSION, reactive ADAPTATION, various kinds of social and cultural reorganizations subsequent to contact, and "deculturation" or cultural disintegration.

The range of adjustments that results includes ... the assimilation of a
weaker by a stronger contacting group ...' (Barfield, 1997: 1).

15 Between 1910 and 1945 Colombia passed through what was known as an
epoch of tranquility.

16 '[T]he town's military mayor, Capt. Oscar de Jesús Echandía ... convened a
meeting of local people, including local Liberal and Conservative party
leaders, business[people], ranchers and representatives from the Texas
Petroleum Company. They found that their goal went far beyond protecting the population from guerrilla demands. They wanted to "cleanse"
(*limpiar*) the region of subversives. To do so, they agreed to gather guns,
clothing, food, and a fund to pay young men to fight. Money came from
business [people] and ranchers, while the military committed tactical
support' (Human Rights Watch, 1996: 17).

17 For a complete description of how paramilitary groups and the army have
been operating in Colombia, see Human Rights Watch (1996: 67).

18 Tirado Mejía (1998) describes narco-terrorism as the 'use of political
assassinations and an army of terror ...'

19 '*Sicario*' is the word used in Colombia to refer to paid assassins.

20 Although these drug traffickers were defeated, the so-called Medellín
Cartel is still operational today. See Johnson (1998).

21 Translated by the author.

22 The '8,000 Process' is the Colombian presidential campaign criminal trial
against former President Ernesto Samper and his aides. See Comisión
Ciudadana de Seguimiento (1996).

23 Translated by the author.

24 Revolutionary Armed Forces of Colombia

25 JCET operations are permitted under section 2011 of title 10 of the United
States Code.

26 For more information about JCET operations around the world see Priest
(1998b: A01).

27 See note 9.

10 Drug Trafficking and Organized Crime in Canada: A Study of High-Level Drug Networks

Frederick J. Desroches

Drug Trafficking and Organized Crime

High-level drug trafficking is typically viewed as an activity dominated by organized criminal syndicates. There is no consensus among academics or law enforcement organizations, however, on how to define or describe the structure of organized crime. A traditional view depicts it as an underworld monopoly called the Mafia or La Cosa Nostra controlled by a powerful group of Italians through a national syndicate with international connections (Cressey, 1969; Maas, 1967). Many criminologists contend that the popular Mafia image of organized crime is fictional and inaccurate and argue instead that organized criminal syndicates encompass a wide variety of cultural backgrounds, are loosely organized, decentralized, informal, coalitional, and situational, and compete with one another for business (Beare, 1996; Adler, 1985; Adler and Adler, 1982, 1983, 1992; Mieczkowski, 1990; Jenkins and Potter, 1987; Chambliss, 1978; Reuter, 1984, 1990; Reuter and Haaga, 1989; Dubro, 1985; Pennsylvania Crime Commission, 1991).

Beare offers the following definition of organized crime: it is an ongoing criminal conspiracy, with a structure greater than any single member, and the potential for corruption and/or violence to facilitate the criminal process. Beare notes that these 'requirements' do not include a formal hierarchical structure as depicted on the charts of mob or Mafia 'families' (1996: 15). It can also be said that organized criminals operate secretly to avoid arrest and conviction, that they insulate their leadership from direct involvement in illegal activities through their organizational structure, and that they pursue financial rewards as their main objective. Organized criminals frequently use the services of

238 Frederick J. Desroches

lawyers, accountants, and financial institutions to establish legitimate businesses and to launder their illegal profits. In some countries, the massive profits generated by drug trafficking allow them to corrupt government officials, including law enforcement officers (Garcia Marquez, 1990).

Organized criminal syndicates are attracted to commercial activities that produce the highest profit with the least amount of risk. The most lucrative and safest crimes involve consensual-type activities such as drug dealing because they generate revenue over an extended period of time and there are no victims to complain to the police. Becoming a drug dealer is not simply a matter of choice, motivation, or volition. Harvesting and moving drugs from the fields of Colombia or Afghanistan to the streets of Toronto, Vancouver, and Montreal requires access to capital, knowledge of the drug trade and law enforcement strategies, reliable and trustworthy associates, and a network of suppliers, distributors, and couriers willing to transport drugs across international borders. Clearly, some form of organization is required to conduct a large-scale illegal business on an ongoing basis.

The focus of this study is on the criminal organization or networks engaged in high-level drug dealing. The following analysis attempts to describe how drug syndicates in Canada are organized and operate and their connections to criminal syndicates both inside and outside the country. The analysis also attempts to capture the fluid, dynamic, and opportunistic interactions that characterize this type of criminal activity.

Sample and Research Methodology

The data for this study were gathered through interviews with fifty high-level drug traffickers: importers, manufacturers, and wholesalers of large quantities of illicit drugs. The subjects were all men serving time in federal penitentiaries in Canada for drug-trafficking offences and were selected from police and correctional files and inmate referrals. Offenders were members of forty-two drug-dealing syndicates that operated in Nova Scotia, Ontario, Quebec, Alberta, and British Columbia from 1990 to 2000. In eight cases, interviews were conducted with two members of the same crew. Additional data were gathered through interviews with three drug couriers, six drug investigating officers from the Royal Canadian Mounted Police (RCMP), and three officers from a large municipal police department. Police interviews and files generated important information about the investigation and acted as a means for testing the accuracy of subject interviews.

The fifty subjects had an average age of forty years and represent a number of racial and ethnic categories. Most convictions involved conspiracy charges, and sentences ranged from two to seventeen years and averaged approximately seven years. The majority of dealers (36 of 50) began trafficking at a wholesale level, and only fourteen subjects (14 of 50) retailed drugs before moving up the ladder. A significant minority (15 of 50) reported that, although their business was primarily wholesale, they occasionally sold drugs to users. Six (6 of 50) were former retailers who had retained some of their better clients. The vast majority of subjects specialized in one drug only: thirty sold cocaine; seven distributed heroin; four manufactured designer drugs; four dealt in marijuana/hashish; and five subjects sold a variety of illicit drugs. A majority (38 of 50) of high-level dealers reported that they were non-users; some (5 of 50) smoked marijuana recreationally; and seven (7 of 50) men admitted to heavy drug usage/addiction – three of whom were non-users when they began trafficking drugs.

The present study indicates that high-level traffickers work in small groups, are flexible in their organization and division of labour, deal with a small number of clients, insulate themselves from their illegal activities, maintain a low profile, collect tremendous profits, and function as independent entrepreneurs. Members of high-level drug syndicates are secretive, security conscious, and operate on a need-to-know basis. An average of eleven persons were charged for each of the forty-two drug networks in this study, with the number of accused varying from one to fifty-two offenders. Most of the fifty respondents had been dealing in illicit drugs for several years and had realized huge profits. For many, their arrest occurred only after the police had undertaken a sophisticated and proactive criminal investigation and prosecution that in some cases cost millions of dollars and took years to complete.

High-Level Drug Traffickers: Suppliers and Wholesalers

Drug dealing is a hierarchical system in which high-level dealers sell their product to lower-level distributors, who, in turn, sell to other distributors or to users. Traffickers use the terms 'supplier' or 'source' to refer to the person above them in the distribution network and from whom they purchase their drugs. High-level traffickers are defined as importers, growers, manufacturers, or wholesalers who market large quantities of high-quality illicit drugs. Importers typically have connections in source countries and smuggle drugs such as cocaine, heroin, hashish, and marijuana into Canada. Growers produce marijuana crops, often through sophisticated hydroponic operations, while manufacturers produce methamphetamines and other designer drugs in laboratories. The terms 'distributor' or 'wholesaler' are used to describe dealers who purchase drugs in large quantities and sell them to other distributors or dealers down the chain. Dealers who sell directly to drug users in the retail market are referred to as 'retailers,' 'pushers,' or 'street-level dealers.'

Drug Trafficking as a Business Enterprise

All traffickers in this study viewed drug dealing as a business that requires knowledge, business sense, and connections. To be successful, traffickers must provide a quality product at competitive prices and maintain a reputation for reliable and trustworthy service. A forty-two-year-old career criminal serving seven and a half years for conspiracy to import cocaine operated his illicit drug business for several years.

> 'I referred to this as a business and it was a business. It started small and we built it up and expanded the business. I had employees and all the problems of handling people's personalities and quirks. You have to keep on top of your employees and as the employer, I had to deal with them. The RCMP have me on tape as referring to the "business." I was in a hotel room and I was talking to someone who should have been taking this more seriously. I was trying get him to act more cautiously and professionally. They have me on tape saying, "If you're going to be in this business ..."'

One surprising finding is that 60 per cent (30 of 50) of the subjects in this study operated small businesses prior to moving into drug dealing. These included an auto body repair shop; an auto mechanic shop; a money exchange; a fruit and tobacco business; a used car dealership; trucking companies; a fishing boat; a lumber company; clothing export companies; a beauty salon; food importing/exporting businesses; a mushroom export business; a paint and decorating company; and a construction machinery dealership. Six men owned and operated liquor establishments. Other subjects operated subcontracting businesses involved in picking worms, cutting lumber, installing roofs, landscaping, pipe fitting, and industrial painting.

The 'crime as work' nature of drug trafficking has been noted by several researchers and theorists (Hafley and Tewksbury, 1995; Langer, 1977; Letkemann, 1973; Redlinger, 1975). The fact that so many of the high-level drug traffickers had earlier operated small businesses indicates that entrepreneurial attitudes, skills, and experience are variables that significantly influence the decision and the opportunity to engage in drug trafficking. A strong work ethic and legitimate business experiences also contribute to the relative success of the drug-dealing enterprise.

It is clear that opportunity theory (Cloward and Ohlin, 1960) is relevant to high-level drug trafficking, since all subjects emphasized the necessity of having connections in order to enter this closed and secretive world. While some traffickers make their drug contacts through known criminals (sometimes in prison), others are asked to participate because they have legitimate businesses and knowledge that traffickers need to import and distribute drugs and/or to exchange and launder money. For example, several offenders used their trucking company, fishing boat, or import/export businesses as a cover for smuggling drugs into Canada. Reuter and Haaga also noted that being 'a good businessman' was a term of praise among drug traffickers and that many in their sample had entrepreneurial and business experience:

> The dealers who had important or organizing roles in remunerative schemes tended not to have extensive prior criminal records; many had done well in some legitimate sales-type profession (real estate in at least two cases, and import/export, which provides good training as well as good cover) ... Four of our respondents were owners or managers of bars, nightclubs, or restaurants before becoming dealers. (1989: 35–6)

Friendship, Kinship, Race, and Ethnicity

Drug-dealing crews in this sample consist of people who have known one another for many years. Partners and associates are typically chosen on the basis of family ties, friendships, and/or past criminal involvements. Race and ethnicity factor into the structure and dynamics of drug crews, since friendship and kinship networks are often culturally based. Information networks within ethnic communities allow traffickers to assess a person's character and trustworthiness. There is also a tendency to define members of one's own race and/or ethnicity as trustworthy and to view other groups as outsiders.

More than half of the drug syndicates in this study involved persons primarily from the same ethnic background. One subject convicted of importing heroin, for instance, had eight co-accused, all of whom were Sri Lankan. Another subject and his brother immigrated from Guyana as children, established cocaine connections on return visits to Guyana, and operated primarily although not exclusively, within the Guyanese community in Canada. Another crew of marijuana smugglers consisted of six co-accused all of Mexican Mennonite origin. Four had immigrated to Canada, and the other two maintained residence in Mexico and fled this country before being arrested. Other drug-trafficking crews in this study consisted mainly or exclusively of people of British, French and English Canadian, Jamaican, Italian, Irish, East Indian, Chinese, or Vietnamese origin. Although many of these groups purchased from and/or distributed drugs to persons of other ethnic origins, the composition of their own small crew was restricted by common ethnic background. Redlinger reports similar findings among street-level heroin dealers, who define trust along ethnic lines and limit their associates to other Mexican Americans (1975: 343).

Not all drug-trafficking crews exclude others on the basis of ethnicity or country of origin. Several crews incorporate persons of diverse ethnic backgrounds but restrict membership to persons they know and trust. The limited data available on outlaw motorcycle gangs indicate that membership is restricted to Caucasians, although they too purchase from and/or distribute to various racial and ethnic groups.

The racial and ethnic composition of high-level drug crews in Canada reflects the fact that most illicit drugs come into this nation from source countries. Many of the subjects in this study are immigrants to Canada from such countries. Because of the connections afforded them through ethnic communities and friends and associates 'back home,' opportunities are available for them to engage in drug trafficking at a relatively high level as importers and/or wholesalers. Many of the dealers in this sample, like those in other studies (Adler, 1985; Adler and Adler, 1983; Redlinger, 1975; Reuter and Haaga, 1989; Sorfleet, 1976), began their criminal involvement at or near the top of the drug hierarchy. This occurred in some cases because criminal organizations in source countries actively solicit kinship and/or ethnic connections in Canada to expand their business. Subjects know that, by creating a closed and loyal criminal syndicate based on friendship, kinship, and/or cultural ties, they make it difficult for law enforcement officials to investigate and penetrate their organization. A cocaine smuggler who worked with his brother, his best friend, and boyhood friends from the same town and high school was arrested only after the police set up a currency-exchange sting. As he states, 'That's the only way they could have busted us. Exchanging money was our biggest problem and our down-fall. The police could never have penetrated us. We were just too tight an organization. I was involved in the trade for twenty years before being busted. I have no criminal record prior to this beef, and I'm forty-five years old.'

Hafley and Tewksbury (1995: 216) similarly observed that business within the marijuana industry in rural Kentucky is primarily if not always restricted to participants who know one another well. Here, too, the recruitment of workers is closely connected to the structure of kinship networks. There is a mistrust of outsiders, since their family origins and reputation cannot be adequately determined.

Size and Composition of Drug-Dealing Syndicates

There is no evidence in this study of a Mafia-style monopoly, near-monopoly, or cartel in the Canadian drug market. The organizational structure of high-level drug trafficking syndicates typically includes the dealer and a handful of paid employees. Some crews will operate as an equal partnership of two or three members who employ others to perform certain tasks. High-level drug dealers operate in small groups referred to as a crew, gang, family, cell, business, or syndicate. Each of the forty-two crews was relatively small in size, and each operated as an independent business. Like the marijuana growers in rural Ken-tucky (Hafley and Tewksbury, 1995: 206, 212), drug dealers in this sample view drug trafficking as a business and do not conceptualize their activities as organized crime. U.S. studies of high-level smugglers and wholesalers similarly note that dealers view themselves as busi-nessmen and operate in small crews and a variety of partnering arrangements (Adler, 1985: 105; Adler and Adler, 1992: 264–9; Reuter and Haaga, 1989: 36–40).

One marijuana/hashish importer described his crew as consisting of himself, a boat captain who smuggled his drugs into the United States from Jamaica, a pilot who flew them into Canada, and an associate who received and distributed the drugs in Canada. He also worked with three independent drug wholesalers who purchased his drugs and passed them on to their own distributors. In addition, he occasionally employed couriers who drove the product from Florida to northern U.S. states where it was picked up and flown into Canada. This dealer defined his crew as consisting of four people: himself, his boat captain, his pilot, and his 'right-hand man.' Although his three distributors had dealt exclusively with him for several years, each was fully independent and free to deal with whomever they chose. Even his captain and pilot occasionally moonlighted by transporting drugs for other importers.

In his latest indictment, thirty co-accused were arrested including all members of his crew, his three distributors, a lawyer who helped him establish legitimate fronts for laundering money, several independent smugglers of American citizenship who shared the cost of importing drugs into the United States, his boat captain's girlfriend and assistant, lower-level dealers, and some of their clients. His suppliers in Jamaica were not arrested or charged. The police investigation that led to his arrest took two years to complete; it was coordinated by the RCMP and involved Canada Customs, two Canadian municipal police departments, and the Federal Bureau of Investigation (FBI) and Drug Enforcement Administration (DEA) in the United States.

Another drug-dealing crew was run by a career criminal who sold three to five pounds of methamphetamines per week through a network of low-level dealers. His crew consisted of himself, an associate, who received 25 per cent of the profits, and three persons who transported drugs on a fee-for-service basis. Drugs were sold to a network of fifteen distributors, all of whom were independent entrepreneurs who cut and resold the product to their own clients.

The remaining drug-dealing crews in this study ranged in size from three to nine members and consisted of the dealer, one or two close associates or partners who oversaw the distribution of drugs, and paid employees who moved the product and performed other tasks. Typically, the dealer and his partner or associate used trusted workers to insulate themselves from any physical contact with the illicit drugs.

The small size of drug-dealing crews can be explained in several ways. For one thing, the illicit drug market is open to individual entrepreneurs, and this means that new persons enter the drug trade on a regular basis. These businesses are typically small in size and remain so for several reasons. A small group has safety advantages, since crew members can be chosen from trusted and known associates; associates and employees can be monitored more closely; and the organization is difficult to penetrate by law enforcement organizations. The use of informants by the police in drug-dealing investigations is less effective against small tight-knit criminal syndicates. Several dealers indicated that one reason for not expanding their drug business or joining other crews was their belief that, by being independent and maintaining a small crew, they were better insulated against informants and police infiltration. In addition, a large organization is not needed in order to run a drug-trafficking business, since drug shipments are relatively small in size yet can reap millions of dollars in rewards.

Several traffickers resisted joining other crews to form a larger organization because they valued their independence and autonomy. A major marijuana importer stated that he turned down offers to become partners with an American drug-smuggling crew and an outlaw motorcycle gang because of safety concerns and because he preferred being his own boss. 'I always chose to be independent. I didn't want to be hooked in with a whole bunch of other people. I operated in a small cell. I didn't want to be a part of anybody else. I wanted to make my own decisions and reap my own rewards and accept my own mistakes and downfall if it came.'

Dorn and colleagues interviewed twenty-five convicted male and female drug traffickers in Britain and report similar findings. Drug-trafficking crews were relatively small in size and operated as independent businesses. The researchers found no cartels, no Mafia, no drug barons, and little corruption (1992: x). Dorn and South (1990) argue that large drug cartels are likely to attract the attention of police organizations from various jurisdictions and to be targeted for aggressive law enforcement. Because covert police operations are risky, time-consuming, and expensive, they tend to be mounted against larger rather than smaller drug enterprises. This results in a fragmentation of the drug-dealing market into small syndicates. 'New emphases in law enforcement, such as covert operations and surveillance of cashflow, tend to structure the market into a series of smaller and flexible enterprises ... Smaller is safer as far as drug-distribution enterprises are concerned. Within this general tendency, there is considerable variation in organization of drug-distribution enterprises, reflecting their diverse origins and local or regional circumstances' (Dorn and South, 1990: 176).

Modus Operandi and Security

The modus operandi of high-level drug dealers functions to protect them against robbery, diminish losses through bad loans or police seizures, shield their clients from competitors, and insulate themselves from arrest and conviction. The division of labour compartmentalizes tasks in such a way that the arrest of one person does not necessarily implicate others. In addition, the movement and storage of drugs and money are organized so that a police bust will result in seizure of only a portion of the assets. Most respondents indicated that their drug-dealing operation tended to operate on a 'need-to-know' basis (see Reuter and Haaga, 1989: 46–7). In other words, knowledge was not shared among all members of the crew or other criminal associates. As one dealer states, 'If someone in my crew has no need to know something or someone, they are not allowed that privilege. Only me and my partner knew who our source was. Most of the people who worked for me did not know who my clients were. We always used nicknames when discussing clients.'

High-level drug dealers are aware that the police attempt to infiltrate drug syndicates through the use of informants and undercover officers. To protect themselves, dealers will often refuse to meet people they do not know and will require that new clients go through a trusted associate who knows and vouches for them. 'If I didn't trust you, I didn't do business with you. Another principle I followed was to keep to a minimum what people knew about my business. If you had a friend who wanted to buy drugs, he would have to go through you. I would never meet with him directly.'

In one cocaine syndicate, the 'financial manager' was responsible for money laundering and setting up legitimate fronts. He knew nothing about the drug-distribution activities and was never allowed to meet anyone but the dealer and his closest associate. Most subjects report that clients will meet only one or two crew members and would not know the identity of others. It is common in a large investigation of drug traffickers for several of the co-accused never to have met. For example, a police investigation into a cocaine importing ring led to the arrest of twenty-eight persons. One of the kingpins behind this smuggling operation stated that he knew only six of his co-accused: his partner, two persons who acted as runners and couriers, and three clients. The other co-accused were persons employed by his partner and lower-level drug dealers and users whom he had never met. Individuals employed on a fee-for-service basis typically know even fewer of their co-accused and little about the structure and functioning of the business.

Drug Trafficking as Independent Entrepreneurship

High-level drug traffickers typically work within small groups, often in ad hoc partnerships. In most crews, one or two persons will be in charge and will employ two or three others who work on a commission or a fee-for-service basis. These 'employees' are delegated high-risk tasks such as crossing national borders or moving drugs from storage areas to distributor clients. The association between suppliers and distributors, however, is not an employer–employee relationship in which the upper-level dealer controls his underlings. Rather, it is a financial arrangement in which participants operate as independent business persons and maintain a high degree of personal autonomy. The normative system that exists and is understood by the players is that clients can change suppliers and take their business elsewhere if they so choose. A common scenario is for a dealer to approach his supplier and ask for better-quality products and/or price discounts to match those offered by other suppliers. If he cannot obtain this, the dealer is free to buy drugs elsewhere.

> 'The drug business is like the legitimate business world. If your supplier is providing an inferior product at too high a price, you'll find a better source to stay in business.'

> 'We're all independent. It's all market value, it's all free market. It's product, price, reputation, and service. Absolutely! And with the people I dealt with, there are no guns and no intimidation.'

> 'You're basically an individual entrepreneur. Even though I supply them with product, they're not working for me. They're working on their own and I'm just their supplier. But there is a lot of loyalty. Believe me, you want to be able to trust people, and you get used to dealing with people.'

Dorn and South describe high-level drug trafficking in Britain in similar terms: it is a competitive market inhabited by a range of small, flexible organizations the structure of which varies and reflects their diverse origins and local or regional circumstances (1990: 176). Studies

248   Frederick J. Desroches

of high-level drug traffickers in the United States (Adler, 1985: 63–82; Reuter and Haaga, 1989: 40–7) similarly describe an open market and informal relationships between suppliers and clients that are sometimes long term but rarely exclusive. Research on street-level drug sales has also emphasized the entrepreneurial and competitive aspects of the trade (Dorn and South, 1990; Mieczkowski, 1988, 1990, 1994; Reuter, 1990). An entrepreneurial market is controlled by no single organization but instead is open to individuals and groups who have the personnel, skills, and products that will make them competitive. An entrepreneurial model of drug dealing is consistent with opportunity theory, since the process of becoming a drug dealer is often an opportunistic extension of a person's life experiences.

Criminal and Non-Criminal Drug Networks: Violence among High-Level Traffickers

A major distinction can be made between criminal and non-criminal drug traffickers and drug syndicates. The majority of the offenders in this study (35 of 50) were relatively law-abiding men who had little criminal involvement apart from drug-dealing activities. These 'non-criminal' traffickers typically have extensive employment histories, associate with other law-abiding persons, begin their criminal career later in life, operate primarily at the wholesale level, and eschew the use of violence. Most of these men have families, live in upscale neighbourhoods, and present themselves as successful businessmen. Partners and associates have similar backgrounds and lifestyles, and most do not use illicit drugs. Other studies (Reuter and Haaga, 1989: 35–6; S. Murphy et al., 1995) also comment on the otherwise law-abiding lifestyle of many of the dealers in their sample: 'Our respondents came to see selling cocaine as a job – work, just like other kinds of work save for its illegality. For most, selling cocaine did not mean throwing out conventional values and norms. In fact, many of our respondents actively maintained their conventional identities' (S. Murphy et al., 1995: 484).

A small number of men in this study (15 of 50) were committed to a deviant lifestyle, and all fifteen reported that they never or rarely worked at legitimate employment. These 'criminal' dealers typically have extensive criminal records for a variety of offences, began their criminal career at a young age, admit to using drugs, sold drugs at the retail level, and became high-level dealers by moving up the ladder. The members of their crew have similar values and criminal careers. 'Criminal' drug-dealing crews are generally willing to use violence in dealing with problems in the drug world.

Many theorists see violence as intrinsic to organized crime and characterize this violence as systemic (Goldstein, 1985, 1989). Some 'criminal' dealers in this study believe that violence is required in the drug business to enforce normative codes. Violence is typically aimed at other criminals and is used to extract revenge for rip-offs, to collect debts, and to silence or punish informants. Several dealers report that a reputation for violence will prevent problems and diminish the need for coercion. A career criminal and methamphetamine manufacturer argued that a dealer cannot climb the ladder unless his reputation is one that guarantees him respect: 'It is not a game for wimps. You cannot expand your business and keep your connections unless you are willing to use violence. A dealer who cannot protect himself is a joke, and nobody wants to deal with a joke.'

Although some 'criminal' drug dealers occasionally use force – primarily to collect debts – most emphasize that threats alone will usually convince clients to pay. 'Non-criminal' dealers report that they sometimes presented themselves as violent persons but rarely used force in their business dealings.

All subjects in this study stated that their goal was to make money without the use of violence. They also emphasized that primarily market forces rather than coercion govern business relationships in the drug trade. Most subjects reported that they seldom or never used violence in their drug transactions; nor were they victims of violence. Violence is considered harmful to business, since it gains significant media play; it draws unwanted attention from the police; it can lead to retaliation; it can damage reputations and business relationships; and a violent conflict between drug syndicates requires time and resources that are more profitably invested in dealing drugs.

The relatively non-violent nature of high-level dealing is also reported in studies done by Adler (1985: 119) and Reuter and Haaga (1989: 25). Most traffickers are highly selective about the people with whom they deal and avoid persons and situations they perceive as dangerous. Subjects also reported that, by treating and paying people well, they gain the loyalty of associates and that this prevents problems from developing. In addition, many traffickers simply write off bad debts and refuse to deal with clients who owe them money. 'If it was clear that this guy had messed up and I wasn't getting my money, I'd just write it off. I never used violence because money is only money and

I made it so easily. I wouldn't sell to them anymore and that would be their punishment.'

The marijuana and hashish market, in particular, appears to attract a variety of middle-class dealers who are not part of the criminal world and who are typically non-violent. Other researchers have similarly noted that marijuana-dealing subcultures are characterized by ideologies that frown on the use of violence (Adler, 1985; Hafley and Tewksbury, 1995; Langer, 1977; Sorfleet, 1976; Weisheit, 1990). Several respondents in this study indicated that 'hippie' types still operate in the marijuana market and differ significantly from career criminals. Police also reported that violence is uncommon in the marijuana and hashish trade. One major marijuana importer claimed never to have used violence in his twenty-two years of dealing drugs: 'The pot business has no guns and there is no intimidation. I never had a gun and my friends never had guns. The drug business lures all sorts of people of less character. But they're not in it long if they rely on muscle. I've never had a gun stuck in my face and been ripped off.'

A cocaine importer with no past criminal involvement also repudiated violence. 'We had no guns. That was a total no. We would never do any business with anyone who used a gun. Why should I? If you have to use a gun, then you don't trust me. And I don't want to deal with anyone who's into guns and violence. There is no trust when guns are involved.'

The almost unanimous consensus among higher-level dealers is that violence is largely unnecessary and that market forces, not coercion, govern business relationships in the drug trade.

> 'There were never any guns involved. The deals took place in nice restaurants and ended with a handshake. The guys I dealt with have millions of dollars pass through their hands and I bet they have never held a gun in their lives.'

> 'There are not many thugs at the higher levels. It takes too much business sense.'

> 'I've been in front of a lot of money and I've never seen a weapon put in front of a deal. There was no violence with any of the people that I dealt with.'

> 'You don't give anyone a reason to be violent. We were honest just like any other business. We were interested in doing repeat business.'

'We never used guns and would not deal with anyone who used guns. It's much easier to have a meal at the Park Plaza Hotel and discuss business. It was totally non-violent.'

'There were no weapons charges laid against anyone. That was a norm for us, don't play with them. If you have to pack guns, you're dealing with the wrong people.'

'Criminal' drug syndicates are more prone to violence, and these include outlaw motorcycle gangs. The sample contains only three biker associates, but information from the police and other traffickers indicates that motorcycle gangs are committed to a deviant lifestyle, engage in a wide variety of criminal activities, and are known to use violence in their illicit dealings.

Data gathered from the police and traffickers also indicate that regardless of the type of illicit drug being dealt, high-level drug traffickers typically conduct their business without resorting to violence. It is a different story at the retail level, however, where both dealers and investigating officers are at higher risk of injury. An experienced RCMP undercover officer offered the following assessment:

'The most dangerous undercover operations are not the high-level ones, but the ones that occur on the street where you deal with substance abusers and desperate people dealing for money for their habit. The street is a foreign environment and you're on their turf. They could pull a gun in a second ... At the higher levels, the guy wants longevity for doing business tomorrow and next month. They don't want to harm anyone because that will only bring heat to themselves. You make your deals in a hotel restaurant and not some back alley. There is some physical danger in all of it, but it's less likely at the higher level.'

Organized Drug Syndicates and Territoriality

Previous scholars have suggested that organized criminal syndicates grow so large that they are able to gain monopolistic control of illicit goods and services within certain geographic areas (Cressey, 1969; Maas, 1967). The present study indicates that drug traffickers in Canada operate in small independent crews that compete but sometimes cooperate with other syndicates to maximize profits and minimize risks. These groups may operate in one city or defined geographic area, but without controlling the territory. Just as drug trafficking is an open market in which anyone can participate, towns and cities in Canada are open to the independent drug entrepreneur. In high-level drug trafficking, geographic territories are not controlled by drug cartels. Although drug trafficking within certain areas of the city often reflects the race and ethnic composition of the population, various independent crews are likely to operate in competition with one another. 'Somebody trying to muscle has never been a concern of mine at that time or even now. Like I would move in myself but I wouldn't come in like with guns and all that. I'd come in with a proposition. Using muscle is thinking along the French mentality, Quebec thinks like that. I'd find out what they want. "Give me a wholesale price and forget about marketing. It's done. I take complete distribution."'

Drug traffickers who were also career criminals were particularly resistant to the idea that someone would attempt to muscle them out of a city or geographical area. They all stated that they would use violence if threatened and would not be intimidated by other criminals. 'The bikers tried to muscle me in the early days but nobody ever tried to use muscle when I moved up the ladder. I've never heard of it happening. The only people I've seen try to muscle are the bikers, and they don't have the etiquette.'

Both police and inmate respondents agreed that outlaw motorcycle gangs attempt to control territory by the use of force. In particular, bikers often own or control various bars and strip clubs and use these as locales to sell illicit drugs. Several police noted that bikers would soon threaten or use violence against anyone who entered one of their establishments to sell drugs.

Organized Crime and the Corruption of Public Officials

Subjects reported instances of airline employees, truckers, and ordinary citizens accepting money to store, hide, transport, and courier drugs. Lawyers, bank employees, and accountants are also used to establish legitimate businesses, launder money, and facilitate foreign exchanges. Although this type of corruption is common, there is very little evidence in this study of corruption of public officials. Only one syndicate reported bribing a law enforcement employee – a secretary who worked in a police department and provided information on car registrations. Three drug-dealing syndicates reported bribing officials in source countries to assist them in exporting illicit drugs and/or to avoid criminal prosecution. Apart from the police secretary, subjects made no attempt to bribe or corrupt public officials in Canada. Most held the belief that police and customs officials were difficult and dangerous to bribe and that business can function without official corruption. Reuter and Haaga (1989) and Adler (1985) also found little evidence of official corruption in their studies: 'Because Southwest County drug traffickers were entrepreneurial and disorganized, their ability to corrupt drug agents was insignificant at best' (Adler, 1985: 119).

Dorn and colleagues (1992) similarly report a relative lack of corruption among public officials in their interview study of twenty-five drug dealers incarcerated in British prisons. This contrasts starkly with the widespread and systemic corruption of politicians and public officials in developing source countries such as Colombia, where the loss or weakness of the authority of the central state has been a precondition for the emergence of drug trafficking on a large scale (Garcia Marquez, 1990).

Several hypotheses may explain the relatively corruption-free status of public officials in Canada. In addition to the strength and moral authority that government institutions in Canada enjoy, Canadian cultural values and traditions instil a pride in the civil service. Strong values not only help prevent criminal behaviour, they also help to ensure that the public and public officials learn to value the work that is done. Related to this are the relatively high salaries and benefits paid to civil servants. This, too, helps to create job satisfaction and offers a measure of deterrence against corruption, since public employees have much to lose.

The small size of drug syndicates also helps to explain why they seldom corrupt public officials. Independent drug traffickers keep a low profile, have a closed network, and avoid contact with public officials or law enforcement personnel. They also lack the resources that huge foreign cartels have to corrupt high-ranking public officials. Drug syndicates in this study rely on secrecy and caution rather than corruption to conduct their illicit business and protect themselves from arrest.

Summary and Conclusion

This study of high-level drug traffickers was conducted through interviews with a sample of fifty inmates representing forty-two drug syndicates. The data show that the illicit drug trade in Canada is not dominated by drug cartels that secure geographic territories and control the importation, manufacturing, and distribution of narcotics. Rather, there is open competition among a large number of small criminal networks that vary in size, race and ethnicity, criminal background, types of drugs sold, profits, and modus operandi.

The present research indicates that opportunity theory is highly relevant in explaining entry into high-level drug trafficking. In particular, family and friendship relations in source countries outside Canada give many of the dealers in this sample access to high-quality drugs at low prices. Drug traffickers prefer to work with people they know and trust and often choose associates and partners from their own cultural group.

The study describes drug dealing as a business and illustrates how entrepreneurial skills are necessary to succeed. Supplying high-quality products at competitive prices is the cornerstone of a successful drug-dealing enterprise. Dealers in this study emphasized how a reputation for quality, reliability, and trustworthiness helps to secure and retain clients. The illicit side of the business enterprise requires secrecy, caution, and a sophisticated modus operandi. A significant finding is the fact that 60 per cent of the sample operated small legitimate businesses prior to entering drug trafficking. Few respondents in this study advocated or admitted to using violence to settle business disputes, and most said they were careful to avoid situations where violence could occur.

Most dealers work in loosely structured small groups – referred to as a gang, organization, family, crew, syndicate, or cell – and operate on a need-to-know basis. Even though there was an average of eleven arrests for each of the forty-two crews in this study, subjects appeared to know and work closely with only three to six associates. It is common in a large police investigation of drug traffickers for several of the co-accused never to have met. Beyond this small syndicate are users, dealers, suppliers, ex-convicts, and other criminals who make up the drug/criminal underworld. This loosely organized subculture supplies the drug trafficker with illicit drugs, users, and dealers, and acts as a source of information about the ever-changing drug scene. The association between higher- and lower-level dealers is a loose business arrangement in which independent dealers maintain a high degree of autonomy.

The small size of drug-dealing crews provides safety advantages: crew members can be chosen from trusted and known associates; associates and employees can be closely monitored; and the organization is difficult to penetrate by law enforcement agents. A large organization is not necessary to run a drug-trafficking business, since costs are relatively low and small quantities of product can be easily handled by a few people and yield millions of dollars in rewards.

There was very little evidence of corruption of public officials in this study. Because independent drug traffickers operate in a relatively small, secret network, they are unlikely to have close contacts with public officials or law enforcement personnel. Drug syndicates in Canada rely on secrecy and caution rather than corruption to conduct their illicit business and protect themselves from arrest.

11 Follow-the-Money Methods in Crime Control Policy

R.T. Naylor

Introduction

Over the last fifteen years there has been a quiet revolution in law enforcement. Instead of just closing rackets that generate illegal income, the objective has become to attack criminal profits after they have been earned, on the theory that taking away wealth accumulated by criminals removes both the motive (profit) and the means (operating capital) to commit further crimes. A new crime – money laundering – has been put on the books of many countries. New reporting requirements have been imposed on financial institutions. And law enforcement agencies host special units responsible for arresting, not malefactors, but bank accounts, investment portfolios, houses, cars, even Rolex watches. These initiatives are closely related. Anti–money-laundering rules require detailed records that create a paper trail to aid in tracing and seizing criminal money. They also create new offences to justify such seizures.[1]

To varying degrees in various places, the new laws have undermined traditional presumptions of financial privacy, muddled civil and criminal procedures, and opened previously confidential tax records to police probes. Furthermore, the laws have been accused of reversing the burden of proof, smearing citizens with the taint of criminality without benefit of trial, and converting police forces into self-financing bounty-hunting organizations.[2]

Clearly, these new legal initiatives are powerful weapons. It is reasonable to ask that they not be deployed unless and until the need for them has been unambiguously established, their objectives have been clearly delineated, and the public has been well informed both about their actual (as distinct from nominal) purposes and about any 'collateral damage' their use might entail. It should be convincingly demonstrated that any perceived failure of existing methods of crime control results from deficiencies of existing laws rather than from deficiencies in the application of existing laws, that a crisis of sufficient order of magnitude exists to require radical alternatives, and that such alternatives have a good chance of being effective in rectifying those deficiencies.

Yet, despite the rapid spread of anti–money-laundering regulations and asset-forfeiture laws around the world, no one really knows how much criminal income and wealth actually exists, how illegal gains are distributed, or how (if at all) deleterious their impact on legitimate society really is. Nor can anyone say with any degree of confidence what impact a follow-the-money strategy might really have on its intended target, though they can point with considerable confidence to some of its pernicious side effects.

A Solution in Search of a Problem

Contemporary laws that facilitate the confiscation of criminally derived assets are of two main types. Some involve *in personam* procedures – an individual must be charged with a crime, and that crime must be proven beyond a reasonable doubt, before specified property, also proven on criminal criteria to be the proceeds of that crime, can be seized. Standard safeguards – the presumption of innocence, the right to counsel, and protection against double jeopardy or disproportionate punishment – apply. Others involve *in rem* procedures – property can be seized if it can be established by civil criteria (balance of probabilities) that the property was the proceeds of or provided the means to commit a crime. Sometimes property can be frozen in advance of a trial and, if an individual is found guilty under criminal criteria, that property can be forfeited if it is determined, on civil (balance of probabilities) criteria, that it is likely the proceeds of a crime.[3] However, in the more extreme versions, as in the United States today, there is no need to charge the owner with, let alone prove, a crime. Once probable cause to freeze property is established, the burden of proof is shifted onto the owner, who has no protection against double jeopardy or disproportionate punishment.[4]

Although both criminal and civil forfeiture have only recently assumed a prominent place in the roster of modern law enforcement methods, they have deep historical roots. The obvious precursor of civil forfeiture is the medieval notion of *deodand* ('gift to God'). If an object (anything from a runaway horse to a flying axe blade) was deemed to have done injury (usually fatal) to a person, the object itself was adjudged guilty and therefore forfeit. Originally, the guilty property was destroyed in elaborate rituals, or used for compensation to kinfolk of the victim.[5] Later, the forfeited property began to be appropriated by the Crown. But, whatever the fate of the property, from very early times there were protests that the procedure really involved punishment of the owner without benefit of trial. None the less, the fiction was maintained that property, rather than a person, was guilty, and that the procedure was therefore remedial rather than punitive.

The spiritual antecedents of today's criminal forfeiture can also be found in early modern Europe. Anyone found guilty of treason was stripped of chattels and estate – the first became Crown property, and the second reverted to the individual's liege lord. Later, that process was applied to all convicted felons – with the number of felony offences rising *pari passu* with the Crown's need for revenue. Unlike modern criminal forfeiture, there was no need to establish any relationship between a specific crime and the lost property – a felony conviction could lead to the loss of all chattels and estates, even those of completely legitimate origin.

In Britain, there was also a third method by which assets could be seized, one that, though technically quite distinct from either civil restitution or criminal enforcement, would in some ways prove more influential in shaping modern proceeds-of-crime methodologies. The tasks of enforcing the Navigation Acts (which regulated trade within the British Empire) and of assuring collection of the customs duties and excise taxes were assigned to the Vice-Admiralty and Exchequer courts. The overwhelming share of state revenues came from indirect taxes, mainly on imported goods. Since owners of cargoes, and of the ships, were often unknown or unavailable, captains were expected to prove that all taxes had been paid. If a ship and/or cargo lacked proper customs stamps or tax receipts, it could be impounded. The Vice-Admiralty court would determine if there was probable cause for proceeding. If there was, the court ordered the ship and cargo appraised. Notice went out to those with a stake in the ship and cargo to show why their interests should not be forfeited. If there was no contest, a summary forfeiture occurred. If there was a contest, the burden of proof shifted to the party contesting the forfeiture (Levy, 1996: 44).

Of course, the actual administration was not so tidy. Customs officials were rewarded with a share from confiscated cargoes. Therefore, corrupt officers collected kickbacks from merchants seeking to evade taxes, employed networks of paid informants, and falsified the value of seized inventories.[6] These abuses aside, however, the basic operating principle seemed reasonable enough.

Deodands eventually died out and were formally abolished in Britain in the mid-nineteenth century. Forfeiture of estate, already de facto abandoned, was legally repealed in 1870, though maintained in cases of 'outlawry' (i.e., fleeing justice) for some decades further. What was left in Britain (and its colonies) was the device of enforcing tax law through *in rem* procedures in Exchequer Court. It would be left to Yankee ingenuity many decades later to combine the superstitious spirit of deodands, the moral absolutism of forfeiture of estate, and administrative procedures created originally for fiscal purposes, to give birth to the modern principles and practice of asset forfeiture.

Extortionists or Entrepreneurs?

To be fair, the United States was not the only place to experiment with asset seizure as a tool of crime control. In 1982, in the wake of a series of assassinations of prominent public figures by 'the Mafia,' Italy passed its Pio La Torre law, popularly named after the murdered head of the Sicilian Communist party who had campaigned for action on the financial front.[7] This widely heralded (and generally misunderstood) law introduced to Italy two fundamental legal departures. It created a new crime, the Mafia conspiracy. And it opened the books of the Italian financial system to police probes. It waived bank secrecy in the event of a criminal investigation and allowed the courts to seize the assets of persons belonging to a 'Mafia conspiracy' as well as those of any relatives or associates suspected of fronting for them. The two initiatives were linked – anyone guilty of Mafia conspiracy could lose the right to financial privacy and have his or her assets seized without any need by the state to demonstrate the person's participation in any specific criminal act.[8]

The law was intended to address certain fundamental underlying realities. Traditionally, the Mafia (which Italian investigators had long identified as a mode of behaviour rather than an organization in any strict sense of the term) was seen as a Sicilian problem, and a symptom of cultural isolation, social introversion, and economic backwardness. But during the 1970s, a new 'entrepreneurial Mafia' allegedly emerged.

This transformation was reputedly fuelled by the burgeoning drug trade. Not only did a drive for wealth displace the traditional concern with 'honour' among Mafiosi, but the availability of drug-derived wealth permitted members to infiltrate deeply into the economy of certain southern areas (in Sicily and Calabria, reputedly, 15 to 20 per cent of all economic activity came to be controlled by Mafia-linked firms and individuals), and to spread throughout Italy. Most alarming was the alleged tendency of Mafia entrepreneurs to take control of businesses offering legitimate goods and services and to apply to them criminal principles of operation. Given the supposed ability of Mafia-linked firms to tap great pools of underground cash, push down wages, corrupt government functionaries, and employ violence to drive out competitors, Mafia entrepreneurs were perceived to be a serious threat, not just to this or that local firm, but to the entire Italian economy.[9]

The Pio La Torre law therefore attempted to deal with both the flow of new criminal money and the stock of accumulated criminal wealth. Against the ongoing flow, it hoped to deter mob money from taking control of legal businesses, as well as to stop legal money from moving into illegal activity where higher rates of tax-free return were available. Against the accumulated stock of criminally derived wealth, it was the explicitly stated hope of the intellectual author of the law that the threat of asset seizure would lead not so much to actual confiscation of huge amounts as to encouragement of a rapid and massive asset transfer. Mafia money would shift from illegal businesses (including legal ones operated in illegal ways) into the strictly legal economy. It would also shift from the ownership of assets such as land and commercial property into passive financial holdings. The result would be that the money accumulated through criminal means could be made accessible to the legitimate economy through passive investments without bringing with it the threat of criminal takeover (and criminalization) of actual businesses. Needless to say, most of these subtleties escaped the notice of North American enthusiasts for asset forfeiture.

There are many points at which the underlying theory of the Pio La Torre law could be subject to criticism.[10] Did the theory exaggerate the overall amount of criminal money actually pouring into the Sicilian economy? Did it put too much emphasis on the role of drug money in the transformation from 'men of honour' to criminal entrepreneurs? Indeed, was the typical Mafioso really becoming a criminal entrepreneur, or did he remain essentially an extortionist, simply shifting, as the economy itself changed, from draining money out of agriculture and construction to milking the commercial and financial system as well?[11] In creating a Mafia conspiracy offence, was the new law in danger of accepting, even implicitly, the fundamental American error of seeing Mafia as an 'organization' instead of a pattern of behaviour? If so, was there really any advantage to be gained from criminalizing association, particularly in light of the potential human rights abuses doing so might permit? Furthermore, was the crucial distinction between legal and illegal sectors, the logical foundation of the law, really a matter of black and white, or was the situation better seen as a continuum of various shades of grey?

Indeed, it could be further asked how many of the murders that finally galvanized Italian public opinion to permit the passage of the law were really attributable to the new flood of underground wealth from drugs and other illegal economic activities rather than to attempts to settle accounts by political factions, secret societies, and the intelligence services that simply hired Mafiosi on occasion to do the dirty deed. It was hardly a secret that Italian politics had less to do with electoral contests between legitimately structured, publicly functioning parties than with acts of corporate corruption, conniving by the Vatican, and underground plots by a bizarre amalgam of crooks, spooks, and secret parapolitical organizations. Even Pio La Torre's assassination may have been a contract hit instigated by those seeking to silence his opposition to the deployment of NATO cruise missiles in Sicily, rather than a murder by Mafia bosses to stop his agitation for a financial attack on Mafia wealth.[12]

None the less, at the end of the day, in Italy asset seizure was conceived not as an end in itself, or as just a deterrent in the standard sense of the term. Rather, the threat of seizure was to work as an incentive for a long-term change of economic behaviour. These objectives were quite different from those espoused in the United States, and in other countries that followed the American lead. There the principle was 'find it and grab it,' without putting any real effort into determining whether the assets of criminals were really the same thing as criminal assets. And the main tool for doing so was not criminal forfeiture but a remarkable proliferation of laws facilitating civil forfeiture – to the point where the sheriff of every sleepy one-store town and the customs chief of every grassy one-runway airport could use them for their own purposes, be they crime control or ego enhancement, be they harassing ethnic and political undesirables or padding the local law enforcement budget.

Licensed to Loot?

Several factors drove U.S. law enforcement to its present fixation on the money trail. One was the apparent failure of the traditional strategy of 'targeting up.' This theory held that it did little good to nail and jail easily replaced subordinates in hierarchically structured criminal organizations. Instead, the target became the top management (Beare, 1996: 191). The only problem was that jailing capos did not seem to make much difference either. The resilience of the criminal marketplace might have convinced some that the notion of crime controlled by a grand conspiracy of swarthy men whose names were suspiciously difficult to pronounce was pure fiction. It might have suggested that the crime world was really populated by an anarchic collection of small-time operators, more intent on ratting out each other than on laying tribute at the feet of a local godfather. It might have conveyed the notion that, rather than huge amounts of capital under the control of great criminal 'cartels' that stashed it in obliging financial institutions, most illegal profits were distributed in small amounts among a host of petty wheeler-dealers who kept them in cash stuffed in socks under their beds – when they did not immediately fritter away the money on booze, drugs, and flashy living. And, just maybe, the appropriate deduction might have been that, as long as a demand for illegal goods and services existed, someone was going to find it profitable (thanks to the way that criminalization drove up the price) to supply that demand.

Instead, the accepted explanation became that, not only were mob bosses, too, more replaceable than previously thought, but even if not replaced, they had little problem continuing to run their businesses from prison.[13] That seemed to argue in favour of arresting and de facto jailing the one thing presumably indispensable – the money that provided the motive (personal enrichment) and the means (investable capital) for further crimes. This theme was repeated by law enforcement officials with a vehemence that contrasted remarkably with the lack of evidence offered to support it.[14]

The second reason for shifting attention to the money trail was the conviction that the Western world was being flooded with 'narcotics,' and that, as a result, the world-wide drugs trade raked in gross earnings of at least $500 billion per annum, of which the United States alone accounted for $100–120 billion.[15] These startling figures about megabillions of dirty dollars seemed to be confirmed, before televised

U.S. congressional committee hearings, by hooded witnesses who, after privately striking deals for sentence reductions, went on to publicly dazzle their audience with tales of loading cash by the baleful into cargo planes en route to Panama, the Bahamas, or the like.[16] Indeed, this great wealth in the hands of alien 'cartels' posed a threat way beyond the merely economic. For example, Colombia's so-called Medellín Cartel (whose members demonstrated their aptitude for criminal conspiracy by routinely murdering each other and competitively flooding the market with their product) was described by influential *Washington Post* columnist Jack Anderson as 'a subterranean superpower that threatens U.S. security ...' Anderson further insisted that the U.S. government should 'call upon' all other countries to adopt emergency laws and treaties to confiscate drug money.[17]

Added to this presumably enormous take from drugs were the proceeds from a host of other rackets – old ones such as the flesh trade and new ones such as the traffic in endangered species; stalwarts such as rum running and newcomers such as the smuggling of nuclear materials; vintage businesses such as loan-sharking and innovative ones such as international securities fraud. Police intelligence units, academic crime experts, and high-price-tag research institutes competed to churn out big numbers reputedly representing the amount of ill-gotten gains. Their ultimate triumph came in 1996 with the construction of a world Gross Criminal Product of $1.1 trillion.[18]

Of course, there was (and is) lots of funny money washing around the world economy. Most, though, comes not from peddling kiddy porn or designer drugs but from tax and exchange-control evasion on money of legal origin.[19] All that those frightening statistics about a deluge of 'narco-dollars' or a burgeoning world Gross Criminal Product really prove is that it is not necessary to take the square root of a negative sum to arrive at a purely imaginary number. But the objective was not to illuminate the shadowy world of crime so much as to enlighten politicians about the need for larger law enforcement budgets and more arbitrary police powers. Therefore, those magic numbers assumed the status of religious cant and were rarely revised, except heavenward.

A third reason for the new law enforcement approach was the triumph of the ideology of 'fiscal restraint' – Wall Street's term for a combination of tax cuts for the rich and government expenditure cuts for the poor. During the 1980s, out-of-control military spending combined with burgeoning tax evasion (much of it legal) had driven the

U.S. budget deficit to record highs. Simultaneously, drug consumption, and therefore the presumed untaxed wealth of drug barons, supposedly hit its peak. It was also a time when the principle of universality of access to public services, the idea that all citizens had a right to have their basic needs met regardless of economic status, was under attack, and when 'user fees' for things the government had formerly provided for free were becoming more common. Along with that trend came demands for the privatization of public functions. If users were to be expected in the future to pay full cost for hospitals, schools, and other services formerly considered a public responsibility, it took only a small shift to apply that principle to crime control. This was clearly articulated in 1982 before the U.S. Senate Judiciary Committee by a senior official of the attorney general's office:

> Official: The potential in this area is really unlimited. My guess is that, with adequate forfeiture laws, we could ...
> Senator: We could balance the budget.
> Official: ... There clearly would be millions and hundreds of millions available ...[20]

Closely related was a fourth factor, a change in attitude towards the causes of crime. For decades, academics and activists alike had urged, with some success, that the focus should be on eradicating the environmental factors that drove people to crime. But in the new era of free marketeering, the rhetoric changed to favour the punishment of individual evildoers. If economically motivated crime was the consequence largely of an imbalance of income and economic opportunity, the government should correct the balance. But if it was the work merely of bad people, there was no need for a fundamental alteration in the status quo distribution of wealth and power. On this view, the criminal should be seen not as a complex product of psycho-socio-economic conditions but as a simple cost-benefit calculator. It followed that crime could be addressed by merely tilting the likely outcome of such a calculation to reduce the potential profitability of the criminal's actions and to incapacitate (by stripping away economic assets as well as by imprisonment) those who failed to heed the initial warning (Brake and Hale, 1992).

These four factors account for the enthusiasm with which the United States embraced the follow-the-money doctrine. But to these four must be added a fifth influence to explain why it was so imperative for the rest of the world to follow suit.

On the Track of the Black Greenback

Across the world, U.S. notes, especially the $50 and $100 denominations, are greatly in demand for conducting covert transactions, for hiding international financial transfers, and for underground savings parked in a safety deposit box, stuck in a wall safe, or buried in a garden. By the late 1980s, it was estimated by the Federal Reserve that perhaps 75 per cent (by value) of all U.S. $50 and $100 notes were in circulation outside the United States.[21]

That presented a golden opportunity. The cost of printing a $50 or $100 note is a few cents. Therefore, exporting cash has been by far the cheapest way to finance U.S. government expenditures. As other countries suffer increases in black marketeering and tax evasion, as they watch their own currencies displaced and, along with them, the ability of their national governments to finance public-works expenditure through the printing press, the benefit pours into the U.S. Treasury at a rate of $10–20 billion per annum – the amount in interest that the United States would have to pay on the equivalent amount of borrowed money. This neatly returns to the U.S. government a good chunk of the money it pays out in foreign aid to poor countries whose tax cheats and smugglers are particularly hungry for U.S. dollars. The United States also gains indirectly – persons habituated to thinking of the physical greenback as their primary haven against political and financial uncertainty would, by inference, come to see U.S. dollar deposits and investments in American securities as the most logical place for their longer-term savings as well. Furthermore, by raising the prestige of the U.S. currency, the greenback's role encourages more legitimate trade to be financed through dollar-denominated bank instruments. That reinforces the competitive position of U.S. banks and pays additional returns to the United States in the form of increased 'invisible' earnings on its international balance of trade.

Yet, simultaneously, the export of U.S. currency makes U.S. antilaundering initiatives more difficult.[22] The simplest way to bypass U.S. reporting requirements is to take cash, especially in high-denomination notes, load it into a suitcase or stuff it inside some commercial cargo (outbound loads of U.S. bills have turned up in everything from Monopoly boxes to the lining of microwave ovens to cryogenic containers of bull semen), and fly it (drive it, float it) abroad. The greater the acceptability of the U.S. dollar internationally, the easier it is to exchange the dollars for other assets.

Added to that, for decades American exports of goods had been sagging relative to imports. The gap in the commodity trade account had to be covered by importing capital (much of it based on capital flight from and tax evasion in other countries) or by running a large and growing surplus in services – the payments earned by U.S. consulting firms, insurance companies, banks, and other institutions all over the world. At the same time, the biggest growth sector in financial services has been 'private banking,' managing the portfolios of what are euphemistically called 'high-net-worth individuals.' Traditionally dominated by Swiss and British banks, by the 1980s this was a field major U.S. banks were eager to exploit. Standing in the way were those pesky anti–money-laundering rules, which made the United States the least attractive of the major jurisdictions to foreign clients seeking confidentiality.

Therefore, the United States faced a dilemma. The U.S.-dollar was supreme, meaning that the world's super-rich wanted to hold the bulk of their assets in U.S.-dollar-denominated form. But banks of virtually any other major Western country could offer more discreet service while still providing clients with a wide variety of dollar instruments. To the rescue rode Senator John Kerry with an amendment to a 1988 money-laundering law that required the U.S. Treasury to negotiate with other countries the imposition of rules similar to those in force in the United States. Senator Kerry was clear about the danger: 'If our banks are required to adhere to a standard, including offshore, and other banks do not and rush for deposits in those [U.S.] banks, we will have once again taken a step that will have disadvantaged our economic structure and institutions relative to those against whom we must compete in the marketplace' (U.S. Senate, Committee on Banking, Housing and Urban Affairs, Subcommittee on Consumer and Regulatory Affairs, 1990: 3). Thus, instead of restricting the export of U.S. bank notes – so beneficial to the Treasury – or watering down the U.S. reporting rules to attract more foreign fund-management business to U.S. banks, the strategy was to force other countries to impose on their own banks the administrative costs and competitive disadvantages of U.S.-style reporting rules. Initially, those reporting rules were demanded for all cash transactions conducted by foreign banks in U.S. dollars over the $10,000 threshold. More recently, other countries have been pressed to adopt such rules for all cash deposits and withdrawals.

Nor was it merely moral exhortation. Behind the Kerry Amendment and subsequent measures stood the threat that foreign banks would be barred from use of the American-controlled international wire transfer

(CHIPS) system, something that would have crippled their international competitive position. As President Clinton declared to the U.N. General Assembly in 1996: 'We will help nations to bring their banks and financial systems in conformity with international [sic] anti-money laundering standards, and, if they refuse, apply the appropriate sanctions' (Courtenay 1996: 71). Therefore, with the enthusiastic support of their police forces, country after country 'herd' the message.

Right on the Money?

The theory behind the proceeds approach to crime control is based on four premises. First, since profit is the motive, eliminating criminal gains acts as a powerful deterrent. Second, taking away ill-gotten income prevents criminals from being able to infiltrate and corrupt the legitimate economy. Third, removing the money also takes away the capital essential to commit future crimes. To these could be added the fourth, the moral principle that no one should be permitted to profit from commission of a crime. Together they appear to provide a compelling rationalization. But appearances can be deceiving.

The deterrent theory seems at best an oversimplification. Professional criminals are often motivated by factors other than money – the sheer thrill of the act or the desire to show off their cleverness or daring. Moreover, most professional criminals seem to be profligate spenders. That reflects partly inherent hedonism, partly the urge to impress peers and partners, and partly the fact that they always operate under the threat that their careers might be shortened by competitors or regulators. Likely, the stronger the asset-seizure provisions of law, the stronger this already inherent propensity to earn and spend, leaving little for law enforcement to seize. Furthermore, since it is no mystery that the bulk of the class of career criminals is made up of down-and-outs rather than billionaire narco-barons, seizure of assets might well simply force them to repeat the acts that generated the money, since professional criminals tend not to have a particularly wide range of vocational alternatives. Granted, some certainly save. But criminals, no less than other entrepreneurs, have a learning curve – being burned is as likely to motivate them to learn better techniques for hiding and laundering as to switch careers.

Furthermore, asset-seizure laws discriminate in favour of a criminal who spends all his or her money on high living, against the one who, while committing the same offences, might use the proceeds to buy a house for aging parents or invest in U.S. Treasury bills to help finance the war on drugs.

Perhaps the ultimate repudiation of the deterrent notion is the simple fact that the United States, the country in the world where the proceeds approach is used most intensely, boasts a higher percentage of its population behind bars than any other country except Russia. Yet it remains the world's richest market for the forbidden products enterprise criminals energetically peddle.

The second rationalization is that seizing proceeds stops criminals from infiltrating and corrupting legitimate businesses. But this, too, is at best an exaggeration. First, a rather obvious question – just how much criminal money is out there? – has to be answered before any rational judgment can be made about the threat it poses. Second, it is also necessary to ask just why criminals would wish to invest in the legal economy. There are actually several reasons, with radically different consequences.[23]

One is that some criminals, especially aging ones, want to provide for the future. Not only is their reason for investing in the legitimate sector benign, but so too are their methods. They will work through bona-fide investment houses to make passive investments in high-quality securities that convey no control over the issuing enterprise. There may be a moral objection to the principle of the criminal so securing his or her profits. But there is no reason to suspect that, in so doing, the criminal will control or corrupt legal markets.

A criminal may also decide that, in anticipation of death, arrest, or retirement, he or she wants to transfer wealth to members of his or her biological rather than criminological family. Ensuring an inheritance requires, first, moving assets into the legal economy. Although the actual investments may be slightly different from those chosen for the entrepreneur's own retirement, the reasons, the methods, and the consequences are equally harmless to the legal economy.

Alternatively, the criminal entrepreneur might seek to reduce risk to his or her income stream by diversification into an active legitimate business. Presumably, the more insecure the source of illegal income, the greater the strictly financial need for an independent source of legal income, and therefore the greater the incentive to create a legitimate alternative. For this strategy to be effective, however, the business must be run in an impeccably clean manner – criminal methods should be avoided; and the business is unlikely to be used as a front for illegal operations or for laundering criminal money.

In all three cases, the integration of criminally earned assets into the legal economy does not threaten the integrity of legal markets. That poses a dilemma for crime-control policy. If the objective is to punish past acts committed by the criminal entrepreneur, the logical policy is to take away from the criminal those legitimate assets acquired using illegitimately earned income. (Precisely how they should be taken away is a separate issue.) If the objective is to prevent recidivism, there is actually a case for leaving the criminal in possession of those assets, along with measures to encourage a shift from illegal to legal activity. Similarly, if the objective is not to address this or that malefactor but to attack the criminal marketplace as a whole, the correct policy might be actively to encourage the movement of criminal assets into the legal economy. These kinds of transfers represent a process of legitimization, not merely of laundering. They simultaneously reduce the assets of the underworld economy, while raising those available to the legal one.

On the other hand, some of the reasons criminals choose to shift their money to the legal parts of the economy are not so benign. A legitimate business might be used, for example, to support underworld operations. That, in turn, can take three different forms.

One is to provide laundry facilities. By running illegally earned income through a front company, the criminal entrepreneur gives that income an alibi. However, money laundering is a means not of *earning* criminal profit (except by a professional launderer) but of redirecting profit after it has been earned. Once laundered, the money might be used to bribe a judge or hire a professional assassin. Or it might be used to make payments into the criminal's retirement savings account. Yet, in actual crime-control measures, no distinction is made.

Another possibility is that a front business provides the underworld entrepreneur with tax cover. By itself, this introduces no serious distortion into the operation of illegal markets. Indeed, on one level it is beneficial, since otherwise untaxed income becomes exposed to the fiscal authorities.

Yet another possibility is that a front operation directly supports underworld rackets. It might function as a place to sell stolen or smuggled merchandise, traffic drugs, sell snuff movies, or operate an illegal gambling enterprise. However, what is involved is a veneer of legality to disguise continued illegality. Whether used for laundering, tax-cover, or logistical support, the front company, which appears to be part of the legal economy, operates in reality as part of the apparatus of crime. Therefore, it can hardly be said to be corrupting the legitimate sector.

Where the threshold is unambiguously crossed is when the criminal uses investments in the legal economy not as cover for ongoing crimes but as a direct source of criminal profit. The criminal takes into the legal economy underworld techniques – a reputation for violence, a willingness to bribe regulators, the capacity to extort kickbacks from suppliers, and the means to reduce through intimidation both labour costs and competition – in order to squeeze higher profits out of the legal business than would be possible using strictly legitimate methods. Here (and only here) is it possible to say with absolute conviction that criminal assets corrupt a legal business. However, it still cannot be said a priori that career criminals do more to undermine the integrity of legitimate businesses than do legitimate business people who employ illegal means to achieve the same ends. Yet no one suggests preemptively seizing their assets to head off that result.

The third reason for attacking proceeds is based on the premise that, deprived of financial resources to maintain a constant flow of product to their customers, crime 'cartels' would be quickly put out of business. There is an obvious problem with this theory. Asset seizure targets the firm, not the industry. For every firm knocked out, others are eager to enter or expand. It is not clear that the extent to which any particular criminal firm is affected will reduce the scope of a criminal market; it merely changes the identity of those who earn the profits.

None the less, money is a necessary, even if not a sufficient, condition for enterprise crime. Unlike the deterrent and corruption-of-legal-business arguments, the notion that depriving a criminal of operating capital will serious impair illegal markets does merit further consideration.

The Numbers Racket

To determine if an attack on proceeds truly has any discernible impact on the criminal marketplace requires some basic calculations – and a preliminary clarification.

It is necessary to differentiate criminal *income* (i.e., proceeds) from criminal *wealth* (i.e., assets). Although the first is necessary to produce the second, its existence is not sufficient. Income is what is earned from rackets, much of which is dissipated in costs. If the objective is to stop criminal income, then the only way to do it is to close the rackets – which makes the 'new' law enforcement method really no different from the old. But if the objective is to deter through eliminating motive and means, the focus must be on net income or profit, and the target must be the accumulated *wealth* in which that net income or profit is held pending reuse.

Therefore, to determine the effectiveness of a profits-of-crime policy, it is necessary, first, to find the ratio of seized criminal *wealth* to total criminal wealth, both at the beginning and again at the end of the test period, in order to assess how big a dent is being made in underworld resources. Properly speaking, that ratio should be calculated for every year in the period under review to reduce the possibility that the first and/or final years are for some reason anomalous. If the ratio is rising, then net assets available to criminals are falling. But by itself that does not suffice to prove the success of the policy.

Second, it is also necessary to make a comparison between the rate of growth of criminal *income* relative to legal income to ascertain if the chunk being taken out of criminal wealth is actually adversely affecting the ability of illegal markets to service their clientele. If the growth of criminal income begins to slow relative to legal income, or if it falls absolutely, then clearly something besides general economic conditions has affected the criminal sector. If nothing else has radically changed on the law enforcement front, it might be reasonable to impute that change at least partially to the net loss of criminal assets.

Without both types of data – about changes in the amount of available criminal wealth, and about the relative growth of criminal and legal income – no defensible conclusion about the impact is possible. The question is, can those two calculations actually be made?

The first piece of data required is the value of seized assets. In theory, that should be simple to find. In fact, it is not. The figures announced by the police are generally their guess about the value of properties frozen. Asset values must be deflated to take account of outstanding debts – this is particularly a problem when dealing with mortgaged property. In general, the (rarely reported) value of the actual forfeiture is usually substantially less than the (enthusiastically reported) value of the initial freeze, for a variety of reasons: the initial amount was exaggerated for public relations purposes; some assets presumed to exist could not be found; some depreciated in police custody; or it ultimately proved impossible to establish any link between the assets and the crime. Furthermore, all innocent property inadvertently (or, sometimes, deliberately) caught in the net should be deducted. Obviously, if a teenager is caught smoking a joint in the backyard and the parents' house is forfeited as an instrumentality of crime, it makes little sense to include the value of the house in a calculation purporting to show how much criminal wealth is being taken out of circulation.[24]

Assuming that the value of seized criminal *wealth* could be satisfactorily calculated, it has to be compared with the total amount of criminal wealth in existence. Even the roughest guesstimate requires several steps. First, it is necessary to arrive at some approximation of total criminal *income* flows. Second, a certain profit rate must be imputed to those flows. (This is especially problematic, since profit rates in practice will vary widely, not only among different rackets, but among different practitioners of the same rackets.) Third (particularly tricky given the propensity of criminals to blow all their earnings), a certain percentage of the profit must be assumed to be saved and therefore be available to accumulate as assets each year. (Why not the magic 10 per cent?) Fourth, those assets must be accumulated over time, while imputing a certain rate of return (if held in financial form) or depreciation (if held as durable goods) or potential speculative gains/losses (if held as things such as precious stones, high-priced art-work, or mink stoles). Difficult though steps two through four might be, they are useless unless the first step is taken. The simple fact is that getting a reasonable estimate of criminal *income* flows is virtually impossible.

Finally, with respect to macro data problems, aggregate figures, even if reasonable, are simply that – aggregate. By themselves they give no clue as to the number of beneficiaries or the distribution of the sums among them. Therefore, they can provide little or no information about how criminal enterprises are structured or how criminal markets actually work. Clearly, even large amounts of criminal income distributed among a host of petty wheeler-dealers pose much less of a potential threat to the integrity of legal markets than massive infiltration of money in the hands of a few criminal titans. The more widely distributed the proceeds, the greater the likelihood that they will stay on the street or be blown on the purchase of flashy goods, frittered away in prestige-enhancing entertainment of peers or playmates, or lost by gambling. In the absence information about the nature and size (and the strategic objectives) of the criminals earning the money, even establishing that the ratio of seized assets to total criminal assets was rising would not allow us to know whether the criminal market was adversely affected by a policy of targeting illegal wealth. For example, if seizure values are skewed upwards by a few large catches in a marketplace dominated by many small operators, there is likely little impact on the ability of the criminal marketplace to satisfy its customers; other operators will simply expand to fill the void.

In all likelihood, the criminal marketplace probably has both types of operators represented, though in what proportions no one has the faintest idea.

Finally, nothing can be concluded without taking account of the intent of the criminal entrepreneur. If the objective of accumulating criminally derived assets is to further a life of crime, taking away those assets might have a positive effect – even if it does not go beyond merely changing the identity of the players in the criminal marketplace. But if the objective is one of the more benign possibilities, such as investing in the creation of an alternative and legal source of income as a prelude to retirement from the underworld, seizing those assets can hardly be construed as an unambiguous contribution to crime control.

Up Close and Personal

Even if little can be accomplished with the macro approach to estimation, surely effective data on a local or regional level can be obtained from particular incidents? By inference, these should also give some clues about the distribution of criminal income among various enterprises and individuals. This kind of data can come from informants, actual cases, or sting operations.

Informant-derived information is especially problematic. The criminal milieu has more than its share of people who have lived so long in the shadow world of deceit and deception that they cease to recognize any border between fact and fantasy. This is particularly true when informants have a vested interest (in terms of direct payment, licence to continue their own rackets, or reduced sentences) in exaggerating the importance of the information they are peddling.

Case-driven information should, in principle, be more reliable. But there is a major distinction between predatory and market-based enterprise crimes. With predatory offences, establishing the value of misappropriated property is fairly straightforward. The victim has an incentive to report – with some danger of exaggeration if an insurance company is expected to cover the bill. What the victim loses, the perpetrator gets – although, if it is physical property, the returns to the perpetrator from resale to a fence are likely much lower than the replacement cost to the victim (or insurance company). But with a market-based offence, that is not true. There is no victim to complain. If caught, a perpetrator has a vested interest in minimizing the amounts earned. The accused will face charges for the particular incident for which he or she was caught, not for the sum total of all the income he or she might have earned over a career in crime. Yet while a particular heist in a predatory crime might generate a very large sum – and be rarely repeated – in an enterprise offence, the predominant pattern is for most incidents to involve small retail sales, with the real payoff coming from multiple iterations.

Perpetrators arrested in a market-based offence will therefore have a strong vested interest in hiding the extent of operations – unless they turn informant, in which case they will tend to exaggerate the size and importance of other people's activities. The impact of asset-seizure laws accentuates both effects – the arrested person tries to hide his or her assets, while the informant is sometimes rewarded on the basis of how much of other people's assets are seized.

Nor is the situation better with information that originates in police stings. Police are subject to legal and resource constraints that will predetermine what form their sting operations take. Since stings are exceptional and apply to only a narrow part of highly segmented markets, the best they can yield is a view of what might be going on in that particular segment – information that might have little relevance to anything else. Furthermore, by participating in the market in a particular way, they can affect the structure of the parts of the market with which they deal. Police action can function to mould the marketplace into directions that it would not 'naturally' take. Once the police sting operation ceases to affect the structure and operation of that marketplace, it might revert to its former self, leaving the police with a view that reflects little more than their own preconceptions.

Probably the biggest single problem in working with incident-derived data is that, even if it were not distorted by informant fabrications, by deceit on the part of malefactors in order to evade asset forfeitures, or by the peculiar effects of police stings, the results may still be meaningless from the point of view of the marketplace as a whole. Simply put, there is no 'market' for illegal goods and services. There are just a series of more or less interconnected regional submarkets. For a genuine market to exist, there must be a legally enforceable free flow of information, commodities, and money within it. Within legal markets, the role of the regulators is to guarantee that free flow. Within illegal markets, the role of the regulator is to do the opposite. Hence, data derived from one case likely reflect conditions in one regional submarket (which might be no bigger than a city street), and little more. Consequently, it is impossible to extrapolate from individual cases to the 'market' as a whole, or to use prices and quantities from any one case to compute overall numbers for the size of trafficking in a particular good or service.

Assuming all data problems were satisfactorily solved, there is still a fundamental failing in the entire exercise – it is not at all clear what the numbers prove. With predatory offences, a successful law enforcement strategy, by definition, means that, relative to some appropriate base of comparison, the number of offences should diminish. Predicting what will happen to the value of goods taken in each incident is more problematic. From the point of view of the victim, there is no a priori reason for the sums involved per offence to change. But from the point of view of the perpetrators, there is. To the extent that law enforcement also targets the fencers of stolen goods, they will start discounting the risk by offering lower prices to the thieves. None the less, whether returns to the thieves per incident stay the same or fall (they certainly will not rise in response to a law enforcement blitz), the net effect of successful law enforcement is that the number of offences, and possibly the number of perpetrators, will decrease; and so too will the *total* value of transfers of illegal property.

However, with market-based offences, the opposite is true. As enforcement becomes more effective, the number of participants might well rise. Here there is an important distinction between a legal and an illegal enterprise. In a legal one, there is an incentive to maximize profit by minimizing costs. If the enterprise produces a good or service but leaves it to others to sell it, then some of its potential profit is taken by those intermediaries. The more the enterprise can dispense with intermediaries, the more it can internalize their share of the profit. But in an illegal enterprise, there is the opposite tendency. Criminal entrepreneurs respond to the threat from law enforcement by increasing the number of defensive layers of intermediation between themselves and their customers. In effect, to reduce risks, they are forced to reduce their profits, diffusing earnings among a large number of other operators, simultaneously reducing the danger of being caught with large accumulations of criminal capital. At the same time, the physical quantities involved in each transaction should fall – more participants each handling smaller quantities. Yet prices should *rise* in response to greater risk. Since, presumably, the demand for criminal goods and services is somewhat 'inelastic,' the value of goods and services traded actually *increases* in the face of successful law enforcement. Since the profits are distributed across more participants, there is no way of determining a priori if the net income of each participant should rise or fall.

Hence, unlike with predatory crime, where large and growing numbers of incidents and/or values of involved property are a sign of a law enforcement crisis, with market-based offences they are more likely a sign of success. Therefore, it is absurd for law enforcement to use large numbers representing the apparent value of illegal economic transactions as an indicator of the need for *more* resources and/or greater arbitrary power to deal with the problem. The opposite conclusion could as easily be drawn.

Thus, there is no real proof that a proceeds-of-crime approach really succeeds in accomplishing three of its major declared objectives. It cannot be proven to deter; it likely has little or no impact in preventing the corruption of legal markets; and there is no evidence that it has been able to cripple any criminal 'organizations' by depriving them of capital. Still, there is a fourth rationalization offered for targeting proceeds of crime. It states simply that criminals should not be allowed to profit from their crimes. It is a moral principle with which few would disagree and which requires no empirical verification. However, on the subsidiary issue of how much 'collateral damage' society should be willing to sustain to implement that principle, the amount of disagreement could be considerable.

Taken to the Cleaners?

Although police in other jurisdictions continuously agitate, with increasing success, for improved forfeiture powers, no country yet matches the record in the United States, where the zeal for chasing the money manifests itself in several particularly nasty ways.

The first is the very creation of an offence called money laundering. Unlike the underlying crimes that generate the money, be they trafficking in endangered species or illegal dumping of toxic waste, contract killing or telemarketing fraud, money laundering consists of acts that are innocent in and of themselves. For that reason it has proven very difficult to explain to the general public (or, for that matter, to some experts) just what harm is done by it. Money launderers do not pull guns or con widows and orphans of their savings. Rather, they make deposits, draw cheques, purchase ordinary bank instruments, and wire payments from place to place. Because money laundering involves standard transactions through the legitimate financial system to disguise the origins and destination of illicitly derived money, laws that forbid handling the 'proceeds of crime' have had to criminalize everything from making a series of deposits, each small enough to circumvent a reporting requirement, to rushing to board an international flight with a bearer bond tucked away, undeclared, in the traveller's attaché case. Setting up a shell company, sending a money order, or buying a cashier's cheque can all attract serious penalties. In the United States, even auto dealers, jewellers and real-estate agents who do nothing more than sell to someone later convicted of a criminal offence can be charged with the crime of helping to 'launder' the proceeds (Intriago, 1991: 55).

Indeed, with an anti–money-laundering law, there is no need to make the charge, much less the punishment, fit the crime! Commercial frauds, currency counterfeiting, smuggling of aliens, and many other offences have been prosecuted on the basis of violations of the money-laundering statutes. In that way, the focus shifts from the underlying acts (which genuinely invoke public opprobrium) to the (rather mundane) methods used by the perpetrators to make off with the loot.[25] Such use of the law both trivializes the real offence and casts a chill over the entire criminal justice system by announcing that laws are there not to address crimes but to cater to the convenience of the prosecution.

Not least, the hysteria over money laundering has permitted penalties to become grossly disproportionate. In the United States today, 'money-laundering' charges usually carry much heavier consequences than the underlying offence. Someone convicted of fraud, for example, typically does less time than someone who helped launder the resulting money (Levine and Brandt, 1998).[26]

The second effect has been indiscriminately to burden the U.S. financial system, and, increasingly, the global system as well, with reporting requirements that are at best useless, at worst pernicious.[27]

The main role for financial institutions is to provide information on which the law enforcement apparatus can act. But this raises serious questions – about the efficacy of the reporting apparatus, about the competence of banking personnel to make the required judgments, and about the extent to which rights to privacy are necessarily violated on a routine basis to little or no apparent gain. The problem inheres not just in the information requirements and the way they have progressively escalated, but also in the very nature of the information and the bankers' role in providing it.

These requirements were established first in the United States, and then elsewhere, with the Currency Transaction Report (CTR), a form that has to be filled out by financial institutions in the event of a large cash deposit (or withdrawal). This report details information about the depositor and the origins of the money. Along with it came the Currency and Monetary Instruments Report (CMIR), which required declaring to U.S. Customs any sum in cash or monetary instruments greater than $5,000 imported to or exported from the United States. To deal with the possibility that a criminal might prefer to use his or her cash proceeds to buy high-value consumer durables, the IRS followed with Form 8300, requiring dealers in luxury commodities such as boats, planes, automobiles, jewellery, furs, and so on to demand information similar to that on a CTR from any customer attempting to pay cash of more than $10,000.

As a second line of defence, banks, not just in the United States but increasingly around the world, are required to file Suspicious Transaction Reports should a transaction exhibit certain characteristics. It can be filed on top of a CTR. It can also be filed in cases where the CTR requirement does not apply, but the bank officer feels the transaction fits the 'suspicious' bill.

Finally, a third layer, popular in the European Union and now, after an initial blockage, again on the agenda in the United States, is Know-Your-Client rules.[28] These involve not exogenously required forms but exogenously determined vetting procedures, which, in turn, could yield additional information to be passed on to law enforcement.

Although one type of information requirement seems to flow logically into the next, in fact each level represents a qualitative change in the relations between 'banker' and client, and between financial institutions and the law enforcement apparatus.

A CTR is the least problematic in this regard. If a certain threshold for a deposit (or withdrawal) is reached, then the financial institution is required by a clear, externally imposed rule to gather specified information and ensure it is passed on to the authorities. The financial institution's role is passive – it acts as a conduit for the flow of given types of data between the client and a government agency. The types of data are the same for all clients. And the client acts as a fully informed, conscious participant in the process. This is also true with respect to CMIRs and Form 8300s.

However, even CTRs are not without their problems. U.S. Treasury agents, for years, complained of being overwhelmed by paper; and Congress, for years, debated reducing the number by raising the reporting threshold and encouraging financial institutions to make more liberal use of their right to grant exemptions from the reporting requirements to certain categories of customers.[29] In effect, the efficacy of the system seemed, and still seems, threatened by the sheer volume of information it generates, precisely the reason many countries have refused to follow the U.S. lead.

Furthermore, the efficacy is further thrown into question by a cottage industry committed to circumventing the CTR rule. People carry money out of the country in large-denomination U.S. notes. They entrust money to various 'underground banking systems' that can make funds appear anywhere in the world in the twinkling of an eye without the nuisance of physical transportation. They do deals with cheques and other bank instruments – more often than the police have been prepared to believe – that permit them to make deposits in banks with no reporting legally required. They bribe bankers to avoid filing the forms. If they own businesses, they connive to get those businesses on the bank's exemption list. Alternatively, they ensure that their firm has a business profile that seems to account legally for all of the cash they seek to deposit, and therefore fill out the forms without much fear of detection. And some just file under false names, sure that, by the time the Treasury analysts get around to looking at the records (if they ever do), they and their money will be long gone to the nether regions of the world. An equally impressive catalogue of tricks exists for evading or faking the other required reports such as the Form 8300.

But more importantly, even if the reports are filed correctly, it remains questionable just what they accomplish. Every major money-laundering case seems to start with exogenous information, usually informants' tips, to point the police in the direction of an individual, and the police then pull any forms that person has filed. Far from being a source of breakthrough intelligence to initiate investigations, in the great majority of cases, the data merely reproduce information that could be obtained elsewhere.

If the role of a financial institution in a CTR regime is passive, it is reactive with a Suspicious Transaction Report. The client and/or the client's transaction exhibit certain characteristics that trigger a response. The bank acts not as an automatic conduit but as a police informant. Despite efforts to draw up lists of objective characteristics of 'suspicious' transactions, the bank's decision is really based on subjective hunches. They may be rooted in stereotypes: in Britain, for example, it has been found that a disproportionate share of STRs are filed about transactions made by visible minorities, even though, in the final analysis, they show a lower 'hit rate' than those filed on Anglo-Saxons.[30] They may also be the result of mass-media hyperbole. In the meantime, the client is not informed. On the contrary. The financial institution and/or its staff can themselves face criminal penalties for telling a client that an STR is being filed.

With Know-Your-Client rules, the financial institution expands its role still further. It is no longer passive or even reactive, but proactive. It has, in effect, become deputized by the law enforcement apparatus as a private detective agency. Nor is it clear where its responsibilities for investigating stop. For to really 'know' a client's business, it is necessary to know the client's clients, and perhaps the client's client's clients. Indeed, to protect itself – ironically, from the police rather than from the client – the institution may go overboard. Fear can degenerate into paranoia that can impede efficiency, clutter operations, and compromise the bank's responsibilities to the client. And while all of this is happening, the client is left totally in the dark.

None of this is meant to suggest that banks should not be alert to spot signs of illicit activity. Rather, the question is just how far they are expected to dig into their clients' affairs, and just how much of the job of police or revenue officers, trained for years as specialists in the detection of illicit transactions, the banks can reasonably be expected to do (Villa, 1988: 502). This is particularly the case given that the banks' role as conscripts on the front lines of the 'war on money laundering' presents them with a clear conflict of interest between their role as profit-seeking institutions (which encourages them to roll out the welcome mat to depositors, and maybe throw in a box of cigars for those whose position is exceptionally liquid) and their new (if involuntarily acquired) law enforcement obligations.

Furthermore, these rules fly squarely in the face of modern banking trends – where more and more transactions are initiated and conducted by the client, where tabulation of deposit records is centralized, and where as much business as possible is being impersonalized. Once again, the profit-seeking (cost-reducing) interests of the financial institution put it at loggerheads with efforts to draft the financial sector into the front lines of the 'war' on crime.

This problem of detection will be further exacerbated by the spread of cyber-banking, by the advent of electronic purses with peer-to-peer transfer capacity, and by the propensity for people to enter and leave countries not with cash or travellers' cheques but with debit cards. All this threatens soon to make largely irrelevant the reporting apparatus now being carefully put in place. Yet in response to these trends the police instinct will undoubtedly be to demand still more regulations and more reports.

The third of the problems comes from the muddling of civil and criminal procedures and the accompanying deterioration of the citizen's defences against arbitrary acts by the state or its agents.

In strict theory, civil actions are supposed to involve (a) actions by one private citizen against another; (b) the pursuit of damages that correspond to actual events; (c) the use of procedures that require only a slim margin of proof (balance of probabilities). On the other hand, in strict theory, criminal actions are supposed to involve (a) actions by the state or its agencies against a private citizen; (b) the pursuit of punishment that can involve loss of life and liberty; (c) the use of procedures that, because of the gross imbalance of resources and heavy consequences, require a high standard of proof (beyond reasonable doubt).

The logic of the distinction suggests that there is something fundamentally at variance with natural justice when the state or its agencies can proceed against a private citizen in actions with *punitive* effects while being required to meet only a civil standard of proof. Yet that is the main thrust of *in rem* asset-forfeiture practice, based on the legal fiction of guilty property. Property has no civil rights, no right to counsel, no defence against double jeopardy, and no protection against a reversal of the burden of proof. Once accused, in a process in which hearsay evidence is acceptable, property is assumed guilty unless its owner can find the financial and legal resources to prove otherwise. The use of paid informants in such cases is particularly offensive in logic and justice. It requires relying on the worst motives of the worst people to make cases on the weakest possible legal grounds.

Yet repeatedly the U.S. Supreme Court has upheld the validity of *in rem* forfeitures on the rationale that their purpose is remedial rather than punitive. That is, quite frankly, absurd. It is impossible for seizure of property to be anything but punitive. It is impossible to declare a car or house or bank account to be the proceeds of cocaine sales, for example, without simultaneously smearing its owner with the accusation of drug trafficking. But with no need for a criminal conviction prior to asset seizure, there is also no need for the state to enter into court proceedings a shred of evidence to substantiate the implicit accusation against the owner. Furthermore, in those cases where a criminal process is implemented, and the person charged is found innocent, the U.S. government can relitigate the same facts against that person's property using civil criteria with the onus reversed.[31] Not only does punishment in the form of property forfeiture then occur, but the owner has been to all intents and purposes found guilty – in the eyes not just of the state but also of all of his or her fellow citizens – of the very offence of which he or she was previously acquitted.

A fourth problem is that the proceeds approach has warped law enforcement priorities. The logical targets for police action against economically motivated crime should be, first, predatory offences, since they usually involve force or its threat; second, those crimes associated with particularly blatant forms of commercial fraud; and only third, market-based crimes involving willing participants in a free market dealing in goods and services for personal consumption. Today, thanks to the lethal combination of moral absolutism and asset seizure, those priorities have been reversed.

Pushed by the U.S. Justice Department, which repeatedly urges that more effort should be put into forfeitures, the law enforcement apparatus has shifted attention from violent criminals who would be a genuine threat to society towards wealthy ones. Police in the past used to get performance bonuses and salary hikes based on how many arrests they made – now such rewards are more likely based on how much money they can grab and have forfeited. As a result, they prioritize actions according to the amount and type of assets seizable. They conduct pre-raid planning sessions to determine what should be taken. Cash, jewels, cars, boats, and easily liquifiable commercial real estate have long been the favourites. Generally, though not always, the police avoid seizing entire businesses, since they are hard to resell, especially if there are other partners who might not be subject to charges. Furthermore, between the time of seizure and the time of the court-ordered forfeiture, the police have to operate a seized business. Police forces have found themselves in the intriguing position of running, at various points, a porno cinema, a gambling den, and a Nevada brothel (Bureau of Justice Assistance, 1988: 3; Royal Canadian Mounted Police, 1988–9: 110).

Simultaneously, there has been a reduction in the number of charges filed under laws that might lead to the imposition of fines – which are paid to the public treasury – in favour of charges under laws where assets can be seized and shared among police and prosecutors.

The result of all this is that some police forces and prosecutor's offices run at a profit, with budgets well in excess of what they were formerly voted when they were subject to civic control. Furthermore, the benefit from seizures can depend on an accident of geography – a well-heeled dealer nabbed driving through town – rather than on actual need. There are small-town forces so flush with drug cash that they now boast fully armed, state-of-the-art SWAT teams, though their previous experience with serious crime was an occasional Saturday night brawl in the local saloon.[32]

The chase for money also skews the choice of who gets prison time and who takes a walk, albeit somewhat lightened of cash and property. Wealthy persons can plea-bargain their way out by offering the police part of their property, while the poor get hard time. The wealthier the accused, the greater the chance that this will happen. This is a curious result indeed for a policy rationalized in public as the best way to make sure the kingpins of crime get their just deserts (Levy, 1996: 128–9).

Fifth among the serious results is corruption of law enforcement, an inevitable result of the current fad in the United States of having police budgets (including salaries and bonuses) depend on asset seizures. Deputies have been caught planting drugs and falsifying police reports to establish probable cause for seizure. In airports, customs officers and police use drug courier 'profiles' to target people and shake them down for their money, with ethnic minorities getting the overwhelming share of attention. This tactic is supplemented by the use of drug-sniffing dogs to pick up traces of cocaine on currency, thereby establishing probable cause – even though various tests have shown that the vast majority of U.S. currency carries enough drug residue (a miniscule amount) for dogs to pick up. Indeed, some dogs have become so well trained that they now react to the smell of the money rather than drug residue – producing the intriguing possibility that simply having cash in a wallet constitutes probable cause for it to be seized.[33]

Thus, a law enforcement strategy supposedly required to prevent huge sums of criminal liquidity from corrupting legal markets, undermining financial institutions, compromising the judicial system, threatening general prosperity, and subverting national security has itself become the threat – to innocent property owners, financial efficiency, civil rights, and the very integrity of law enforcement.[34] Perhaps all this 'collateral damage' would be tolerable if there were no real alternative. But there is an alternative – one with a long and proven history – that can easily serve to solve the fundamental objective of taking away from criminals the proceeds of their crimes without the enormous threats to civil rights entailed by asset-forfeiture provisions – even though that alternative will be fought bitterly by a law enforcement apparatus desperate to keep control of the 'drug' cash to which it has become addicted.[35]

Caesar's Due

Tax codes provide for fines and forfeitures, interest and penalties, and, interestingly enough, the means to seize wealth using a reversed burden of proof. This reverse onus has been, legitimately, part of tax enforcement for centuries. In the days when most state revenues came from customs duties, it was normal and natural to require merchants to prove that their cargoes had met all payments rightly due. Today, in the same spirit, a citizen with otherwise unaccounted-for income should be required to demonstrate that all outstanding tax obligations have been met. The origin of the income is irrelevant – what counts is the requirement that all citizens meet their fair share of the overall burden.

Although criminal law provides the final line of offence, most tax procedures are civil, and most tax codes permit the revenue authorities to freeze and seize assets. With tax charges, there is no need to trace particular assets and impute them to any specific crime. All that is necessary is to demonstrate that someone's expenditures exceeded their reported income. When arrears, interest, and penalties are combined, the undeclared portion of the person's income will largely – and quite possibly completely – vanish. Such tax procedures can go ahead with no need for individuals to incriminate themselves with respect to the origins of the money. Unlike *in rem* forfeitures when used as a means of crime control, tax actions do not attach to the person the stigma of a specific crime while denying that person the right to a trial to ascertain the truth or falsehood of the charges. Yet if the underlying theory of targeting the proceeds of crime is correct, the motive and the capital for further offences will vanish.

The counter-case is sometimes made that using the tax code cannot strip criminals of all their ill-gotten gains, for it can only be applied against their illegal income at the marginal tax rate. Furthermore, if tax 'aw is used, criminals would be permitted to deduct expenses to deter-
ne the net amount due, leaving most of the proceeds still in their
ᒣ. But there are several obvious rebuttals.
ᒣgument that a criminal will likely be left with much of the

profit intact could be advanced only by someone who has never tangled with revenue authorities intent on using their full powers. Once fines for failure to file or for filing false returns are added to interest charges on overdue balances, it is unlikely that any of the net income accruing to an enterprise crime will be left for the criminal to enjoy or reinvest. Such a procedure might bite deeply into legally earned net income as well. If it does not, that suggests merely that the general tax rate structure is insufficiently progressive. Furthermore, even if all that disappears is actual profits or net income, that is sufficient, if the theory underlying the proceeds approach is correct, to remove the economic motive from crime. To the extent that money is the overwhelming factor in determining their behaviour, criminals do not enjoy, or get motivated by, 'proceeds' – they enjoy and get motivated by profits. No one looks forward to laying out money to cover the costs of running a business.

By contrast with proceeds-of-crime forfeitures, for fiscal purposes it is perfectly reasonable to start the process on the premise that net profits and proceeds are the same thing, unless and until the individual proves that costs were incurred. While no one will countenance allowing a burglar to deduct the purchase price of his ladder, there is nothing morally objectionable about permitting a market-based criminal to write off costs, since the method used to commit the crime – a market transaction – is inherently legal. Proper use of the penalty provisions of the tax code would then remove most, if not all, of the net income. And there are actual practical advantages. Allowing a convicted market-based criminal to charge off costs actually enhances rather than limits crime control. In order to claim deductions, the criminal must provide details of his/her intermediate suppliers and employees, not only permitting police to roll up entire networks instead of merely isolated individuals, but also giving police intelligence officers and independent researchers the hard data with which to map out networks and understand (for the first time) how criminal markets really operate.

It is also objected that using tax law legitimates criminal business by treating it just like all other economic activity. This, too, is false. If the objective is really to attack the motives and the capital of crime groups, it makes absolutely no difference if the money is taken away using selective asset forfeiture or tax code means. Nor, for that matter, should it matter if the ultimate beneficiary is the state treasury, legitimate creditors of the criminal, family members in need, or even defence attorneys – the only persons or institutions that should be excluded from a division of the loot are the criminal and the law enforcement apparatus. And if the state chooses to go the criminal rather than the civil route in pursuing tax charges, it is difficult to imagine why a criminal should feel better about being jailed for five years for tax evasion than about being jailed for the same term for dealing cocaine. The fact of a jail sentence, a criminal record, and the loss of financial assets constitutes the punishment and, at least to some degree, the deterrent, no matter what the particular charge. Furthermore, attacking criminal profits through the tax code sends out an important message – everyone must pay taxes, and if people fail to do so voluntarily, the state has tough means at its disposal to collect what is due.

Not least of the advantages of using the tax law route is removal of the need for an artificial offence called money laundering. There is no need to criminalize a set of actions that are inherently legal and harmless. Even if those who handle the money for certain serious crimes are just as guilty as those who commit the underlying offence, that is an argument for simply redefining or clarifying the law with respect to the underlying offence to include the money managers firmly in its ambit. Since a market-based crime such as drug trafficking requires – in addition to producers, exporters, importers, distributors, and retailers – skilled personnel to handle the resulting money flows, laws can easily be rewritten (if they actually need to be) to ensure that these people are added to the list of parties guilty of the predicate offence.

Washout?

Everyone agrees with the fundamental principle that criminals should not profit from their crimes. However, beyond that basic conviction, there is no real consensus on how large the problem of criminal money flows really is; on why society is actually worse off when criminals, rather than legitimate business people, consume, save, or invest; or on just what level of 'collateral damage' society should be called upon to accept in the name of a war on criminal profits.

To be sure, it is possible to find the occasional criminal who is, in all senses, filthy rich. The big question – rarely posed and never answered – is how representative is that occasional underworld magnate in relation to the criminal economy as a whole? Is it really sensible to start rewriting laws on the basis of one or a few spectacular incidents, particularly when those laws potentially involve so much 'collateral damage'? Is it not true that laws should be written to deal with a general anti-social trend rather than the occasional aberration? Such questions are particularly serious given how many of the spectacular proceeds-of-crime busts have been the result of stings, therefore making it impossible to determine a priori how much money would actually have been involved had not law enforcement agencies been egging on the process.

To celebrate its hundred and twenty-fifth birthday, the RCMP held in Montreal a major money-laundering conference, boldly announcing in its statement of purpose that 'Crime is a phenomenon that affects every sphere of society. Money laundering in particular poses a direct threat to our institutions' (GRC-RCMP, 1998). Perhaps, as RCMP experts contend, criminal money does pose a serious threat to the integrity of legitimate economic institutions. But perhaps it does not. Perhaps serious crime groups are adversely affected by current legislation and practices designed to take away from them the proceeds of their crimes. But perhaps they are not. The bald fact remains that, after fifteen years of progressive escalation of its use, no one has been able to determine with any remote degree of confidence whether or not the proceeds-of-crime approach to crime control has had any discernible impact on the operation of illegal markets or on the amount, distribution, and behaviour of illegal income and wealth. The entire exercise rests on a series of inaccurate, or at least unprovable, assumptions and involves the commission of a series of sins against common decency and common sense. Yet police forces around the world are being turned loose to find, freeze, and forfeit the presumed proceeds of crime on the basis of little more than a vague assurance that this is the most resource-effective way to deal with economically motivated crime.

Notes

This paper is a précis of two earlier works: 'The Proceeds-of-Crime Approach to Crime Control Policy: A Critical Appraisal,' done for the Nathanson Centre for the Study of Organized Crime and Corruption of York University, Toronto; and 'Washout: A Critique of Follow-the-Money Methods in Crime Control Policy' (Naylor, 1999b). Another version appears as chapter 6 of the author's *Wages of Crime* (2002b). The author would like to thank Margaret Beare, Alan Block, Francisco Thoumi, and Mike Levi for comments and criticisms.

1 See, for example, United Nations, Commission on Narcotic Drugs (1997).

2 Although that result is particularly evident in the United States, in Canada the federal government established Integrated Proceeds of Crime units financed by a Treasury Board loan that the units are expected to repay from the proceeds of their seizures; and, in the province of British Columbia, police can apply to the provincial attorney general to use seized assets for 'special projects.'

3 For the Canadian statute, see 35-36-37 Elizabeth II, Chapter 51, Section 420.17

4 There is a growing critical literature on the use of asset-forfeiture laws in the United States. See especially Fried (1988); Kessler (1994); and Levy (1996).

5 This practice is commonly traced back to the biblical injunction (Ex 21:28) that, 'If an ox gore a man or a woman that they die, then the ox shall surely be stoned and its flesh shall not be eaten. But the owner of the ox shall be quit.'

6 For some of these abuses, see Blumenson and Nilsen (1998). There is an excellent summary of this article entitled 'The Drug War's Hidden Economic Agenda' in *The Nation* (9 March 1998).

7 On the political impact of the criminal violence see Stille (1995).

8 On the genesis and objectives of the Italian law, see the opinions of its intellectual author, Pino Arlacchi (1984).

9 See especially, Arlacchi (1986: 17). There is also a hysterical account of the rise of the new Mafia in Claire Sterling's *Octopus: How the Long Reach of the Sicilian Mafia Controls the Global Narcotics Trade* (1990).

10 See Chubb (1989) for an examination of the various interpretations of the Mafia phenomenon.

11 The most searching recent criticism of the 'model' underlying the Pio La Torre law is in Gambetta (1993).

12 There is a huge literature on the bizarre vagaries of Italian politics in the 1970s and 1980s. See, for example, Willan (1991).

13 That opinion was concurred in by no less prestigious a body than the President's Commission on Organized Crime (1984: 1n): 'Without the ability to freely utilize its ill-gotten gains, the underworld will have been delivered a crippling blow.'

14 'We can strip the entrepreneurs of their illegal profits', not just current but past, claimed the chairman of the House of Representatives Foreign Affairs Committee in 1990 (6). In Italy, too, the minister of the interior declared two years later, 'We must hit them where it hurts most – in the pocket' (*Financial Times*, 1 December 1992).

15 For an interesting dissection of how the drug trade numbers are concocted and manipulated, see Reuter (1996).

16 See, for example, the performance of Ramon Milian-Rodriguez, a former money-launderer for Colombian narcos, who wowed the U.S. Senate with tales of running sums of $200 million a month in and out of the United States and of managing a drug-money-based investment portfolio of up to $10 billion (U.S. Senate, Committee on Governmental Affairs, Permanent Subcommittee on Investigation, 1988).

17 *Washington Post* (18 September 1989). For a dissection of the myth of the 'Medellín Cartel,' see Lee, III (1989) and Thoumi (1995).

18 This numbers game has a long and dishonourable history. See Max Singer's 'The Vitality of Mythical Numbers' (1971).

19 This is the main theme of Naylor, 1994.

20 Testimony of Jeffrey Harris, deputy associate attorney general, 'Drug Enforcement Administration Oversight and Authorization,' U.S. Senate, Judiciary Committee, Subcommittee on Security and Terrorism, 1982. Cited in Fried (1988: 363n).

21 *Federal Reserve Bulletin* (March 1987); *Globe and Mail* (22 August 1988); *Wall Street Journal* (5 February 1987, 4 October 1990); *Financial Times* (12 April 1995); Sprenkle (1993).

22 See, for example, U.S. General Accounting Office (1994).

23 See the analyses of Anderson (1979) and Reuter (1985).

24 For a survey of some of the worst excesses, see Hyde (1995).

25 *Money Laundering Alert* (January 1999; July 1999).

26 Yet the response of the U.S. Department of Justice to revelations of the gap between the sentence guidelines for fraud and those for money laundering was to call for increased penalties for fraud to bring them up to the level of those for money laundering!

27 See especially Hernandez (1993) and Levi (1991).

28 On the imbroglio over KYC rules, see *Money Laundering Alert* (March and April 1999).

29 *Money Laundering Alert* (May 1994, November 1994).

30 The recent report of the National Criminal Intelligence Service stated that British whites make up by far the majority of 'organized crime' groups operating in Britain (see *The Independent* [3 August 2000]).

31 Apart from the works by Levy and Kessler cited above, see chapter 2 of Bovard (1995).

32 See *Sunday Times* (2 August 1992) for how the police force of Little Hampton, Rhode Island, became the richest per capita in America, with all the

latest gadgetry and fancy buildings, even though the village was effectively without crime.

33 *Globe and Mail* (15 November 1994).

34 Many of these outrages were documented by the Pittsburgh press in a series of articles on forfeiture in 1991, and have continued to be documented by an organization called FEAR (Forfeiture Endangers American Rights). See their website, *www.fear.org*.

35 When some states began using taxes on controlled substance to add further charges against drug traffickers, law enforcement fought against the principle, seeing in it the first step to the state's resurrection of its prior claim to illegal profits. The Boston police superintendent, for example, insisted that 'We would fight all the way any attempt by the state to take a cut of that money' (Bulletin of Justice Assistance, 1989: 4).

Bibliography

Abadinsky, H. (1990) *Organized Crime*. (3rd ed.). Chicago: Nelson Hall.

Adamoli, S., Di Nicola, A., Savona, E.U., and Zoffi, P. (1998) *Organized Crime around the World*. Helsinki: European Institute for Crime Prevention and Control.

Adams, J.R. (1990) *The Big Fix: Inside the S and L Scandal*. New York: John Wiley and Sons.

Ades, A., and Di Tella, R. (1996) 'The Causes and Consequences of Corruption: A Review of Recent Empirical Contributions.' *IDS Bulletin* 27(2): 6–11.

Adler, P.A. (1985, 1993) *Wheeling and Dealing: An Ethnography of an Upper-Level Drug Dealing and Smuggling Community*. New York: Columbia University Press.

Adler, P.A., and Adler, P. (1982) 'Criminal Commitment among Drug Dealers.' *Deviant Behavior* 3: 117–35.

Adler, P.A., and Adler, P. (1983) 'Shifts and Oscillations in Deviant Careers: The Case of Upper-Level Drug Dealers and Smugglers.' *Social Problems* 31: 195–207.

Adler, P.A., and Adler, P. (1992) 'Relationships between Dealers: The Social Organization of Illicit Drug Transactions.' *Sociology and Social Research* 67: 261–77.

Alaton, S. (1993) 'Up in Smoke: Does the Tobacco Economy Make Any Sense?' *Globe and Mail*, 6 March: D3.

Albanese, J. (1999) 'The Causes of Organized Crime.' Paper presented at the International Conference on Organized Crime, University of Lausanne, 6–8 October.

Albrecht, H.-J. (1991) 'Ethnic Minorities, Crime and Criminal Justice in Europe.' In F. Heidensohn and M. Farrell, eds, *Crime in Europe* (pp 84–102). London: Routledge.

Albrecht, H.-J. (2000) 'Foreigners, Migration, Immigration and the Development of Criminal Justice in Europe.' In P. Green and A. Rutherford, eds, *Criminal Policy in Transition* (pp 131–50). Oxford: Hart Publishing.

Albrecht, P.-A. (1997) 'Organisierte Kriminalität: Das Kriminaljustizsystem und seine konstruirten Realitäten.' *KritV* 229–47.

Albrecht, P.-A. (1999) *Kriminologie*. Munich: Verlag C.H. Beck.

Albrecht, P.-A., Dencker, F., Kanther, M., Rauchs, G., Schaefer, H.-Ch., Steen-Sundberg, Ch., Waltos, S., and Yenisey, F. (1998) *Organisierte Kriminalität und Verfassungsstaat*. Heidelberg: C.F. Muller Verlag.

Alexander, B.K. (1990) *Peaceful Measures: Canada's Way out of the 'War on Drugs.'* Toronto: University of Toronto Press.

Almond, M.A., and Syfert, S.D. (1997) 'Beyond Compliance: Corruption, Corporate Responsibility and Ethical Standards in the New Global Economy.' *North Carolina Journal of International Law and Commercial Regulation* 22: 389–447.

Altschuler, D.M., and Broustein, P.J. (1991) 'Patterns of Drug Trafficking, and Other Delinquency among Inner-City Adolescent Males in Washington, DC.' *Criminology* 29: 589–621.

Anderson, A. (1979) *The Business of Organized Crime*. Stanford: Hoover Institute Press.

Anderson, B. (1993) *Britain's Secret Slaves*. London: Anti-Slavery International.

Anderson, M. (1993) 'The United Kingdom and Organised Crime – The International Dimension.' *The European Journal of Crime, Criminal Law and Criminal Justice* 1(4): 292–308.

Anderson, M., and den Boer, M., eds. (1994) *Policing across National Boundaries*. London: Pinter.

Anderson, M., den Boer, M., Cullen, P., Gilmore, W., Raab, C., and Walker, N. (1995) *Policing the European Union*. Oxford: Clarendon.

Andreas, P. (1995) 'Free Market Reform and Drug Market Prohibition: U.S. Policies at Cross-Purposes in Latin America.' *Third World Quarterly* 16 (March): 75–87.

Andreas, P., and Snyder, T. (2000) *The Wall around the West: State Borders and Immigration Controls in North America and Europe*. Lanham: Rowman and Littlefield.

Andrieux, J.P. (1983) *Prohibition and St. Pierre*. Lincoln, ON: W.F. Rannie.

Aquino, B. (1987) *The Politics of Plunder*. Quezon City, Philippines: Great Books Trading.

Arlacchi, P. (1984) 'Effects of the New Anti-Mafia Law on the Proceeds of Crime and on the Italian Economy.' *Bulletin on Narcotics* 34(4): 91–100.

Arlacchi, P. (1986) *Mafia Business: The Mafia Ethic and the Spirit of Capitalism.* Oxford: Oxford University Press.

Arlacchi, P. (1993) 'Corruption, Organised Crime and Money Laundering World Wide.' In M. Punch, ed., *Coping with Corruption in a Borderless World* (pp 25–38). The Hague: Kluwer.

Arlacchi, P. (2001) *International Conference on Strategies of the EU and the US in Combating Transnational Organized Crime.* 24 January. Available from United Nations Office for Drug Control and Drug Prevention website: *http://www.odccp.org:80/speech_2001-01-24_1.html.*

Ashworth, A. (1999) *Principles of Criminal Law.* Oxford: Oxford University Press.

Bacon, K.H. (1998) 'DoD News Briefing, (WWW Life News).' Retrieved 5 August 1999 from Office of the Assistant Secretary of Defense (Public Affairs) website: *http://www.defenselink.mil/news/May1998/t05261998_t0526asd.html.*

Bagley, B.M. (1992) 'After San Antonio.' *Journal of Interamerican Studies and World Affairs* 34(3): 1–12.

Bagley, B.M. (1996) 'The Drug War in Colombia, 1989.' In W.O. Walker, III, ed., *Drugs in the Western Hemisphere: An Odyssey of Cultures in Conflict* (pp 201–15). Wilmington, DE: Scholarly Resource.

Bajak, F. (1998) 'US Role in Colombia Is Anti-Drug.' *Washington Post,* 9 September. Retrieved 17 September 1998 from: *http://www.washingtonpost.com.*

Baldwin-Edwards, M., and Hebenton, B. (1994) 'Will SIS be Europe's "Big Brother"?' In M. Anderson and M. den Boer, eds, *Policing across National Boundaries* (pp 137–57). London: Pinter.

Bales, K. (1999) *Disposable People: New Slavery in the Global Economy.* Berkeley: University of California Press.

Banca d'Italia. (1999) *Il riciclaggio nel contesto dei rapporti tra economia criminale ed economia legale.* Rome: Banca d'Italia/Ufficio Italiano Cambi/Osservatorio Antiriciclaggio.

Baratta, A. (1991) 'Les Fonctions instrumentales et les fonctions symboliques du droit pénal.' *Déviance et Société* 15(1): 1–25.

Barfield, T., ed. (1997) *The Dictionary of Anthropology.* Oxford: Blackwell.

Barnes, H.E. (1967) 'The Racket as Ideal.' In G. Tyler, ed., *Organized Crime in America: A Book of Readings* (pp 178–81). Detroit: Ann Arbor.

Bauman, Z. (1998) *Globalization: The Human Consequences.* Cambridge: Polity.

Bean, P., and Billingsley, R. (2001) 'Drugs, Crime and Informers.' In R. Billingsley, T. Nemitz, and P. Beans, eds, *Informers: Policing, Policy, Practice* (pp 25–37). Devon: Willan Publishing.

Beare, M.E. (1996) *Criminal Conspiracies: Organized Crime in Canada.* Toronto: Nelson Canada.

Beare, M.E. (2002) 'Searching for Wayward Dollars: Money Laundering or Tax Evasion – Which Dollars Are We Really After?' *Journal of Financial Crime* 9(3): 259–67.

Beare, M.E., and Martens, F. (1998) 'Policing Organized Crime: The Comparative Structures, Traditions and Policies within the United States and Canada.' *Journal of Contemporary Criminal Justice* 14(4): 398–427.

Beare, M.E., and Naylor, R.T. (1999). *Major Issues Relating to Organized Crime within the Context of Economic Relationships.* Toronto: Nathanson Centre for the Study of Organized Crime.

Beck, U. (2000) 'The Cosmopolitan Perspective: Sociology of the Second Age of Modernity.' *British Journal of Sociology* 51(1): 79–106.

Beelman, M., Campbell, D., Ronderos, M.T., and Schelzig, E. (2000) 'Major Tobacco Multinational Implicated in Cigarette Smuggling, Tax Evasion, Documents Show.' *Report of the Center for Public Integrity.* Available at: *http://www.public-i.org/story_01_013100.htm.*

'Belgium: A Beneficial Crisis – How Brussels Hopes to Do Rather Well from the War.' (2001) *The Times*, 1 November: 21.

Bertram, E., Blachman, M., Sharpe, K., and Andreas, P. (1996) *Drug War Politics: The Price of Denial.* Berkeley: University of California Press.

Bewley-Taylor, D.R. (1999) *The United States and International Drug Control, 1909–1997.* London: Pinter.

Bigo, D. (2000) 'Liaison Officers in Europe: New Officers in the European Security Field.' In J. Sheptycki, ed., *Issues in Transnational Policing* (pp 67–99).

Björgo, T., and Witte, R. (1993) *Racist Violence in Europe.* New York: St Martin's Press.

Block, A. (1991) *The Business of Crime.* Boulder, CO: Westview Press.

Block, A. (1994) *Space, Time and Organised Crime.* New Brunswick, NJ: Transaction.

Block, A., and Chambliss, W.J. (1981) *Organizing Crime.* New York: Elsevier.

Block, A., and Scarpitti, F. (1985) *Poisoning for Profit: The Mafia and the Toxic Waste Business.* New York: William Morrow.

Blok, A. (1974) *The Mafia of a Sicilian Village, 1869–1960.* Oxford: Blackwell.

Blumenson, E., and Nilsen, E. (1998) 'Policing for Profit: The Drug War's Hidden Economic Agenda.' *University of Chicago Law Review* 65 (Winter): 143–9.

Bonner, R. (1997) 'Racketeer Cases Shed Light on Cigarette Smuggling in Italy.' *New York Times*, 2 September: n.p.

Bovard, J. (1995) *Lost Rights: The Destruction of American Freedom.* New York: St Martin's Press.

Bowling, B. (1998) *Violent Racism: Victimization, Policing and Social Context.* Oxford: Clarendon.

Braithwaite, J. (1984) *Corporate Crime in the Pharmaceutical Industry*. London: Routledge and Kegan Paul.

Braithwaite, J. (1993) 'Following the Money Trail to What Destination.' *Alabama Law Review* 44 (Spring): 657–68.

Brake, M., and Hale, C. (1992) *Public Order and Private Lives*. London: Routledge.

Bray, J. (1998) 'Bribe Wars: International Agencies Are Ready to Escalate the Fight against Corruption.' *Accountability* (March): 30–1.

Brewton, P. (1992) *The Mafia, CIA and George Bush: The Untold Story of America's Greatest Financial Debacle*. New York: Shapolsky Publishers.

Brodeur, J.-P. (2000) 'Transnational Policing and Human Rights: A Case Study.' In Sheptycki, ed., *Issues in Transnational Policing* (pp 43–66).

Bulletin of Justice Assistance. (1989) *Asset Forfeiture Bulletin* (December): 4.

Bullington, B. (1993) 'All about Eve: The Many Faces of United States Drug Policy.' In F. Pearce and M. Woodiwiss, eds, *Global Crime Connections* (pp 32–71). London: Macmillan.

Bullington, B., and Block, A. (1990) 'A Trojan Horse: Anti-Communism and the War on Drugs.' *Contemporary Crises* 14(1): 39–55.

Bundeskriminalamt (1999) *Lagebild Organisierte Kriminalitat Bundesrepublik Deutschland 1999*. Available from: *http://www.bundeskriminalamt.de*.

Bureau for International Narcotics and Law Enforcement Affairs. (1999) 'International Narcotics Control Strategy Report 1998.' U.S. Department of State. Retrieved March 1999 from *http://www.state.gov/www/global/ narcotics_law/1998_narc_report/policy98.html*.

Bureau of Justice Assistance (1988) *The Management and Disposition of Seized Assets* (November). Washington, DC: U.S. Department of Justice, Bureau of Justice Assistance.

Bustos, A.F. (1999) 'Piedra en el Zapato son Cifras Sobre Narcocultivos: Dura Pelea entre Policia y CIA.' *El Tiempo*, 8 March. Retrieved 8 March 1999 from: *http://www.eltiempo.com*.

Caballero, M.C. (1998) 'Halcones vs. Palomas.' *Cambio 16*, 1 June: 259.

Calavita, K., and Pontell, H. (1991) '"Other People's Money" Revisited: Collective Embezzlement in the Savings and Loan and Insurance Industries.' *Social Problems* 38(1): 94–112.

Calavita, K., and Pontell, H. (1993) 'Savings-and-Loan Fraud as Organized Crime: Towards a Conceptual Typology of Corporate Illegality.' *Criminology* 31(4): 519–48.

Calavita, K., Pontell, H., and Tillman, R. (1997) *Big Money Crime: Fraud and Politics in the Savings and Loan Crisis*. Berkeley: University of California Press.

Calder, J.D. (1993) *The Origins and Development of Federal Crime Control Policy: Herbert Hoover's Initiatives.* Westport, CT: Praeger.

California Board of Corrections. (1948) *First Interim Report of the Special Crime Study Commission on Organized Crime* (1 March). Sacramento, CA: California Board of Corrections.

Cambio 16. (8 March 1999) 'Pena de Muerte a los Narcos.' 298. Retrieved 8 March 1999 from: *http:www.cambio16.com/1999.*

Cambio 16. (8 May 1999) 'Descuadre Via Satelite.' 307. Retrieved 8 May 1999 from: *http://www.cambio16.com/1999/mar8/portada2.htm.*

Campbell, C. (1999) 'Two Steps Backwards: The Criminal Justice (Terrorism and Conspiracy) Act 1998.' *Criminal Law Review* 941–59.

Campbell, D. (1997) *Writing Security: United States Foreign Policy and the Politics of Identity.* Minneapolis: University of Minnesota Press.

Canadian Association of Chiefs of Police. (1993) *Organized Crime Committee Report* (August). Ottawa: Author.

Caraccioli, I. (1998) *Manuale di Diritto Penale. Parte Generale.* Padua: Cedam.

Carter, T. (1999) 'Ascent of the Corporate Model in Environmental-Organized Crime.' *Crime, Law and Social Change* 31(1): 1–30.

Castells, M. (1989) *The Informational City.* Oxford: Blackwell.

Castells, M. (1998) *The Information Age: Economy, Society and Culture.* Vol. 3. *The End of the Millennium.* Oxford: Blackwell.

Castells, M. (2000) 'Materials for an Exploratory Theory of the Network Society.' *British Journal of Sociology* 51(1): 5–24.

Center for International Policy. (2000) *The Contents of the Colombian Aid Package.* Retrieved 18 July 2000 from Center for International Policy website: *http://www.ciponline.org/colombia/.*

Center for Investigative Reporting. (1990) *Global Dumping Ground: The International Trade in Hazardous Waste.* Washington, DC: Seven Locks Press.

Cepeda, M.J. (1998) 'Democracy, State and Society in the 1991 Constitution: The Role of the Constitutional Court.' In E. Posada-Carbó, ed., *Colombia: The Politics of Reforming the State* (pp 71–108). London: Macmillan.

Cesoni, M.L. (1999) 'Mafia-Type Organizations: The Restoration of Rights as a Preventive Policy.' In E.C. Viano, ed., *Global Organized Crime and International Security* (pp 157–71). Aldershot: Ashgate.

Chamberlin, H.B. (1931–2) 'Some Observations Concerning Organized Crime.' *Journal of Criminal Law and Criminology* 22.

Chambliss, W. (1978) *On the Take: From Petty Crooks to Presidents.* Bloomington: Indiana University Press.

Char, E., and Arcieri, V. (1998) 'Revisión de E.U. a Justicia Penal Militar.'

Bibliography 297

El Tiempo. Retrived 2 December 1998 from *El Tiempo* website: *http:// www.eltiempo.com/hoy/ppg_n001tn0.html.*

Chepesiuk, R. (1999) *Hard Target: The United States War against International Drug Trafficking, 1982–1997.* Jefferson, NC: McFarland and Company.

Chomsky, N. (1992) *Manufacturing Consent: Noam Chomsky and the Media* [Videorecording]. Montreal: Necessary Illusions.

Chomsky, N. (2000) 'The Colombian Plan: April 2000. Through the 1990s, Colombia Was the Leading Recipient of U.S. Military Aid in Latin America.' *Z Magazine* 13(6): 26–34. Retrieved June 2000 from *http://zena.secureforum. com/znet/zmag/zmag.cfm.*

Christie, N. (1981) *Limits to Pain.* Oslo: Universitetsforlaget.

Chubb, J. (1989) *The Mafia and Politics: The Italian State under Siege.* Ithaca, NY: Cornell University Press.

'Cigarette Smuggling at Akwesasne' [Television news broadcast]. (1991) CBC Newsworld, 23 July: time 19:30.

Clark, E., and Horrock, N. (1973) *Contrabandista.* New York: Praeger.

Clark, N.H. (1976) *Deliver Us from Evil: An Interpretation of American Prohibition.* New York: W.W. Norton.

Clarke, M. (1990) *Business Crime. Its Nature and Control.* Cambridge: Polity.

Clarke, R.S. (1995) *The United Nations Crime Prevention and Criminal Justice Program.* University Park, PA: Pennsylvania State University Press.

Clarke, R.V.G., and Hough, M. (1984) *The Effectiveness of Policing.* Farnborough, Hants: Gower.

Clarkson, C.M.V., and Keating, H.M. (1998) *Criminal Law: Text and Materials.* 4th ed. London: Sweet and Maxwell.

Clavell, J., ed. (1983) *The Art of War.* New York: Dell.

Clinard, M.B. (1952) *The Black Market.* New York: Rinehart.

Clinard, M., and Yeager, P. (1980) *Corporate Crime.* New York: Free Press.

Clinton, W. (1995) *Executive Order 12978 of October 21, 1995: Blocking Assets and Prohibiting Transactions with Significant Narcotics Traffickers* (Vol. 60, p. 24579). Washington, DC: Federal Register: National Archives and Records Administration.

Clinton, W.J. (1997) *Presidential Determination No 97–18 Certification for Major Narcotics Producing and Transit Countries* (Vol. 62, p. 11587). Washington, DC: Federal Register: National Archives and Records Administration.

Clinton, W. (1998) *Presidential Determination No 98–15 of February 26 1998. Certification for Major Illicit Drug Producing and Drug Transit Countries* (Vol. 63, p. 12937). Washington, DC: Federal Register: National Archives and Records Administration.

Cloward, R.A., and Ohlin, L.E. (1960) *Delinquency and Opportunity*. New York: Free Press.

Coffin, P. (n.d.) 'Drug Prohibition and the U.S. Prison System.' Retrieved March 1999 from Lindesmith Centre website: *http://www.lindesmith.org/cities_sources/brief13.html*.

Cohen, S. (1985) *Against Criminology*. New Brunswick, NJ: Transaction Books.

Collins, J.M. (1991) *America's Small Wars: Lessons for the Future*. New York: Brassey's.

Collins, L. (1999) 'Holland's Half-Baked Drug Experiment.' *Foreign Affairs* 78 (July): 82–98.

Colombian Human Rights Network. (1999) *Briefing on Developments in US/Colombia Policy Advocacy*. Retrieved from: *http://www.igc.org/colhrnet/newsletter/y1999/wi...art/coletta.htm* (last modified: 23 April 1999).

Comisión Ciudadana de Seguimiento. (1996) *Poder, Justicia e Indignidad: El Juicio al Presidente de la República Ernesto Samper Pizano*. Santafé de Bogotá: Utopica Ediciones.

Connolly, W.E. (1983) *The Terms of Political Discourse*. London: Martin Robertson.

Conteras, J. (2001) 'Bordering on Chaos: Colombia's Drug-Fuelled Civil War Is Infecting the Region.' *Newsweek*, 5 March: 46–7.

Courtenay, A. (1996) 'Washed and Brushed Up.' *Banker* 146 (October): 71–2.

Crawshaw, R., Devlin, B., and Williamson, T. (1998) *Human Rights and Policing: Standards for Good Behaviour*. The Hague: Kluwer.

Crespi, A., Stella, F., and Zuccala, G. (1992) *Commentario breve al Codice Penale*. Padua: Cedam.

Cressey, D. (1969) *Theft of the Nation*. New York: Harper and Row.

Cressey, D. (1971) *Organized Crime and Criminal Organizations*. Churchill College Overseas Fellowship Lecture No. 7. Cambridge: W. Heffer and Sons.

Cullen, P. (1997) 'Crime and Policing in Germany in the 1990s.' *Discussion Paper in German Studies, No. IGS97/13*. Birmingham: University of Birmingham.

del Olmo, R. (1994) *Drogas y Conflictos de Baja Intensidad en America Latina*. Santafé de Bogotá: Forum Pacis.

del Olmo, R. (1998a) *Drogas: Inquietudes e Interrogantes*. Vol. 4. 1st ed. Caracas: Fundación José Félix Ribas.

del Olmo, R. (1998b) 'The Ecological Impact of Illicit Drug Cultivation and Crop Eradication Programs in Latin America.' *Theoretical Criminology* 2(2): 269–78.

Delors, J. (1991) 'European Integration and Security.' *Survival* 33: 99–110.

Demarest, G. (1996, 1999) 'Expeditionary Police Service.' Retrieved from United States Army, Foreign Military Studies Office website: *http://leav-www.army.mil/fmso/lic/pubs/exped.htm.*

den Boer, M., ed. (1997) *Undercover Policing and Accountability from an International Perspective.* Maastricht: European Institute of Public Administration.

den Boer, M., and Doelle, P. (2000) *Controlling Organised Crime: Organisational Changes in the Law Enforcement and Prosecution Services of the EU Member States.* Maastricht: European Institute of Public Administration.

Dennis, I.H. (1977) 'The Rationale of Criminal Conspiracy.' *Law Quarterly Review* 93: 39–64.

Desroches, F. (1999) *Drug Trafficking and Organized Crime in Canada: A Study of High Level Drug Networks.* Toronto: Nathanson Centre for the Study of Organized Crime and Corruption.

Diebel, L. (1998) 'Drug Politics in Colombia a Trap for U.S..' *Toronto Star,* 30 March: A14.

Dietrich, H. (1999) 'Traffico di esseri umani.' Paper presented at Globalization and Migrants Conference, University of Rome, 26 July.

Doig, A. (1998) 'Dealing with Corruption: The Next Steps.' *Crime, Law, and Social Change* 29: 99–112.

Dorn, N., Murji, K., and South, N. (1992) *Traffickers, Drug Markets and Law Enforcement.* London and New York: Routledge.

Dorn, N., and South, N. (1990) 'Drug Markets and Law Enforcement.' *British Journal of Criminology* 30: 171–88.

Dorn, N., and South, N. (1993) 'After Mr. Bennett and Mr. Bush: U.S. Foreign Policy and the Prospects for Drug Control.' In F. Pearce and M. Woodiwiss, eds, *Global Crime Connections* (pp 72–90). London: Macmillan.

Douglas, M., and Ney, S. (1998) *Missing Persons: A Critique of Personhood in the Social Sciences.* Berkeley: University of California Press.

Drucker, P.F. (1997) 'The Global Economy and the Nation-State.' *Foreign Affairs* 76(5): 159–71.

Drug Reform Coordination Network (DRCNet). (1999) 'Fuel to the Fire: Drug Czar Proposes Billion More for Andean Drug War, Mostly Colombia.' Retrieved 6 August 1999 from DRCNet website: *http://www.drcnet.org/wol/100.html#fuelfire.*

Dubro, J. (1985) *Mob Rule: Inside the Canadian Mafia.* Toronto: Totem Books.

Dunn, T.J. (1996) *The Militarization of the U.S.–Mexico Border 1978–1992: Low-Intensity Conflict Doctrine Comes Home.* Austin: University of Texas Press.

The Economist. (2001a) 'The World's Displaced People: A Special Report.' 3 March: 23–7.

The Economist. (2001b) 'Talk of Peace Acts of War.' 31 March–6 April: 29.

The Economist. (2001c) 'Survey: Colombia: Drugs, War and Democracy,' 21 April: 14 pp.

Efe-Reuters. (1998) '"Marines" de E.U. en la Frontera con Perú.' *El Tiempo*. Retrieved 23 April 1998 from: *http://www.eltiempo.com/diario/noticias/int04.htm*.

Elliott, K.A. (1997a) 'Corruption as an International Policy Problem: Overview and Recommendations.' In Elliott, ed., *Corruption and the Global Economy* (pp 175–233).

Elliott, K.A., ed. (1997b) *Corruption and the Global Economy*. Washington, DC: Institute for International Economics.

El Tiempo. (13 April 1998) 'No Aceptamos Ayuda Contra la Guerrilla.' Retrieved 13 April 1998 from: *http://www.eltiempo.com/diario/noticias/ppg01.htm*.

El Tiempo. (10 August 1998) 'Para Lograr la Certificacion en 1999 E.U. Pone Condiciones a Colombia.' Retrieved 10 August 1998 from: *http://www.eureka.com.co/noticias/eltiempo/hoy/ppg_n005tn0.html*.

El Tiempo. (25 July 1999) 'Lo de la Invasión es una Tergiversación.' Retrieved 26 July 1999 from: *http://www.eltiempo.com/domingo/ppg_n002tn0.html*.

Emsley, C. (1997) 'The History of Crime and Crime Control Institutions.' M. Maguire, R. Morgan, and R. Reiner, eds, *The Oxford Handbook of Criminology*. Oxford: Clarendon.

Escohotado, A. (1999) *A Brief History of Drugs: From the Stone Age to the Stoned Age*. Rochester, VT: Park Street Press.

Falco, M. (1996) 'U.S. Drug Policy: Addicted to Failure.' *Foreign Policy*. 102 (Spring): 120–33.

Farah, D. (1998a) 'Colombian Rebels Seen Winning War.' *Washington Post*, 10 April: A17.

Farah, D. (1998b) 'Pentagon Helps Peru Fight Drugs.' *Washington Post*, 22 April: A01.

Farah, D. (1998c) 'A Tutor to Every Army in Latin America.' *Washington Post*, 13 July: A01.

Farer, T., ed. (1999) *Transnational Crime in the Americas*. New York: Routledge.

Feir, N. de (1992) 'Asset Forfeiture: How Far Can U.S. Courts Go?' *International Financial Law Review* 11(3) (March): 26.

Felson, M., and Clarke, R.V. (1997) 'The Ethics of Situational Crime Prevention.' In G. Newman, R.V. Clarke, and S.G. Shoham, eds, *Rational Choice and Situational Crime Prevention: Theoretical Foundations* (pp 197–218). Aldershot: Ashgate.

Fijnaut, C. (2000) 'Transnational Crime and the Role of the United Nations in Its Containment through International Cooperation: A Challenge for the

21st Century.' *European Journal of Crime, Criminal Law and Criminal Justice* 8(2): 119–27.

Fijnaut, C., Bovenkerk, F., Bruinsma, G., and van de Bunt, H. (1998) *Organized Crime in the Netherlands*. The Hague: Kluwer Law International.

Findlay, M. (1999) *The Globalisation of Crime*. Cambridge: Cambridge University Press.

Flannery, R. (1998) 'The State in Africa: Implications for Democratic Reform.' *Crime, Law, and Social Change* 29(2–3): 179–96.

Flick, G.M. (1988) 'L'Associazione a Delinquere di Tipo Mafioso. Interrogativi Riflessioni sui Problemi Proposti dall'Art. 416 BIS C.P.' *Rivista Italiana di Diritto e Procedura Penale* anno 31, fasc. 3: 849–66.

Flynn, S.E. (1994) 'World Wide Drug Scourge: The Expanding Trade in Illicit Drugs.' In S.J. Spiegel and D.J. Pervin, eds, *At Issue: Politics in the World Arena* (pp 443–57). New York: St Martin's Press.

Foss, D., and Hakes, D. (1978) *Psycholinguistics*. Englewood Cliffs, NJ: Prentice-Hall.

Foucault, M. (1977) 'Truth and Power.' In *Power/Knowledge*, ed. C. Gordon (pp 109–33). New York: Random House.

Foucault, M. (1984a) 'Complete and Austere Institutions.' In *The Foucault Reader*, ed. P. Rabinow (pp 51–75). New York: Pantheon Books.

Foucault, M. (1984b) 'Panopticism.' In *The Foucault Reader*, ed. P. Rabinow (pp 206–13). New York: Pantheon Books.

Foucault, M. (1990) *The History of Sexuality: An Introduction, Volume 1*. New York: Random House.

Fox, S. (1989) *Blood and Power: Organized Crime in Twentieth-Century America*. New York: William Morrow.

Francis, D. (1999) 'The Most Dangerous Nation on Earth.' *National Post*, 28 May: A14.

Freedman, S.G. (1998) 'Is the Drug War Racist?' *Rolling Stone*, 14 May: 35–7.

Fried, D. (1988) 'Rationalizing Criminal Forfeiture.' *Journal of Criminal Law and Criminology* 79(2): 328–436.

Friedman, L.M. (1993) *Crime and Punishment in American History*. New York: Basic Books.

Friedrichs, D. (1992) 'White Collar Crime and the Definitional Quagmire: A Provisional Solution.' *Journal of Human Justice* 3(2): 5–21.

Froot, S. (1998) 'U.S. Anti-Corruption Philosophy Gains Ground.' *The China Business Review* (Jan.–Feb.): 26–7.

Galbraith, J.K. (1992) *The Culture of Contentment*. Harmondsworth: Penguin.

Gambetta, D. (1993) *The Sicilian Mafia: The Business of Private Protection*. Cambridge, MA: Harvard University Press.

Garcia Marquez, G. (1990) 'The Future of Colombia.' *Granta* 31: 86–9.

García-Sayán, D., ed. (1990) *Coca, Cocaina y Narcotráfico: Laberinto en los Andes.* Lima: Comisión Andina de Juristas.

Gardiner, J.A. (1970) *The Politics of Corruption: Organized Crime in an American City.* New York: Russell Sage.

Gardiner, J.A. (1993) 'Defining Corruption.' *Corruption and Reform* 7: 111–24.

Garland, D. (1997) 'Of Crimes and Criminals: The Development of Criminology.' In M. Maguire, R. Morgan, and R. Reiner, eds, *The Oxford Handbook of Criminology* (pp 11–56). Oxford: Clarendon.

Gibbons, K.M. (1989) 'Toward an Attitudinal Definition of Corruption.' In Heidenheimer, Johnston, and LeVine, *Political Corruption: A Handbook* (pp 165–72).

Gibson, R.O. (1877) *The Chinese in America.* Cincinnati: Hitchcock and Walden.

Gilfoyle, T. (1992) *City of Eros: New York City, Prostitution and the Commercialization of Vice.* New York: W.W. Norton.

Gilmore, W.C. (1995) *Dirty Money: The Evolution of Money Laundering Counter Measures.* Strasbourg: Council of Europe.

Glasbeek, H. (2002) *Wealth by Stealth: Corporate Crime, Corporate Law, and the Perversion of Democracy.* Toronto: Between the Lines Press.

Glynn, P., Kobrin, S.J., and Naim, M. (1997) 'The Globalization of Corruption.' In Elliott, ed., *Corruption and the Global Economy* (pp 7–27).

Goldstein, P.J. (1985) 'The Drugs/Violence Nexus: A Tripartite Conceptual Framework.' *Journal of Drug Issues* 15: 493–506.

Goldstein, P.J. (1989) 'Drugs and Violent Crime.' In N.A. Weiner and M.E. Wolfgang, eds, *Pathways to Criminal Violence* (pp 16–48). Newbury Park: Sage Publications.

Gomez, S. (1998a) 'E.V. Entrega 20 Millones de Dolares al Ejercito.' *El Tiempo,* 1 October. Retrieved 1 October 1998 from: *http://www.eltiempo.com/hoy/jud_a000tn0.html.*

Gomez, S. (1998b) 'N.Y. Times Advierte riesgos de Ayuda Militar.' *El Tiempo,* 2 December. Retrieved 2 December 1998 from: *http://www.eltiempo.com/hoy/jud_n002tn0.html.*

Gomez, S. (1998c) 'Debate Sobre los Alcances de la Cooperacion en Lucha Antidorogas: viraje de E.U. frente a Colomibia.' *El Tiempo,* 7 December. Retrieved 7 December 1998 from: *http://www.eltiempo.com.*

Gomez, S. (1999) 'Despejado el Camino de la Certificacion Plena "Colombia Cumplio": McCaffrey.' *El Tiempo,* 8 February. Retrieved 8 February 1999 from: *http://www.eltiempo.com.*

Gomez Maseri, S. (2002) 'Espaldorazo de la Camara de E.U. a ayuda militar para Colombia.' *El Tiempo*, 7 March. Retrieved 7 March 2002 from: *http:// eltiempo.terra.com.co/07-03-2002/inte_pf_0.html*.

Goode, J. (1988) *Wiretap: Listening in on the American Mafia*. New York: Simon and Schuster.

Goudie, A.W., and Stasavage, D. (1998) 'A Framework for the Analysis of Corruption.' *Crime, Law, and Social Change* 29: 113–59.

Gramegna, M. (1999) 'Trafficking in Human Beings in Sub-Saharan Africa: The Case of Nigeria.' Paper presented at conference on 'New Frontiers of Crime: Trafficking in Human Beings and New Forms of Slavery.' United Nations, Verona, 22–3 October.

Gray, C.W., and Kaufmann, D. (1998) 'Corruption and Development.' *Finance and Development* 35(1): 7–10.

GRC-RCMP (Gendarmerie royale du Canada – Royal Canadian Mounted Police) (1998) 'Press Release.' International Money Laundering Conference, 17 July.

Green, T. (1969) *The Smugglers*. London: Michael Joseph.

Gregorie, R.D. (1991) 'Extraterritorial Jurisdiction: Its Use, Its Roots and Its Viability.' *Nova Law Review* 15: 625–60.

Gregory, F. (1998) 'Debate: There Is a Global Crime Problem.' *International Journal of Risk, Security and Crime Prevention* 3(2): 133–7.

Gregory, F. (2000) 'Private Criminality as a Matter of International Concern.' In Sheptycki, ed., *Issues in Transnational Policing* (pp 100–34).

Griffin, R. (2000) 'BAT Accused of Criminality.' *The Guardian*, 22 September: 28.

Griffiths, I.L. (1993) 'From Cold War Geopolitics to Post-Cold War Geonarcotics.' *International Journal of the Canadian Institute of International Affairs* 49(1): 1–36.

Gropp, W., Schubert, L., and Wörner, M. (2000) 'Deutschland.' In W. Gropp and B. Huber, eds, *Rechtliche Initiativen gegen organisierte Kriminalität*. Freiburg: ed. iuscrim.

Gugliotta, G., and Leen, J. (1990) *Kings of Cocaine*. New York: Harper and Row.

Guillermoprieto, A. (2000a) 'Our New War in Colombia.' *New York Review of Books* 47(6): 34–40.

Guillermoprieto, A. (2000b) 'Colombia: Violence without End?' *New York Review of Books* 47(7): 31–40.

Guillermoprieto, A. (2000c) 'The Children's War.' *New York Review of Books* 47(8): 37–41.

Hafley, S.R., and Tewksbury, R. (1995) 'The Rural Kentucky Marijuana Industry: Organization and Community Involvement.' *Deviant Behavior: An Interdisciplinary Journal* 16: 201–21.

Hagen, F., and Benekos, P. (1992) 'What Charles Keating and "Murph the Surf" Have in Common: A Symbiosis of Professional and Occupational and Corporate Crime.' *Criminal Organizations (International Association for the Study of Organized Crime)* 7(1): 3–27.

Haller, M. (1971) 'Organized Crime in Urban Society.' *The Journal of Social History* 5: 210–34.

Hampton, M. (1996a) *The Offshore Interface. Tax Haven in the Global Economy* London: Macmillan.

Hampton, M.P. (1996b) 'Where Currents Meet: The Offshore Interface between Corruption, Offshore Finance Centres, and Economic Development.' *IDS Bulletin* 27(2): 78–87.

Handelman, S. (2000) 'Confronting Cross-Border Crime.' *Time Europe*, 24 April, 155 (16).

Hannerz, U. (1996) *Transnational Connections*. London: Routledge.

Hariss-White, B., and White, G. (1996) 'Corruption, Liberalization and Democracy: Editorial Introduction.' *IDS Bulletin* 27(2): 1–5.

Harper, T. (1999) 'Lawsuit Links Sales to Top Brass.' *Toronto Star*, 22 December: A7.

Hartung, F.E. (1950) 'White-Collar Offenses in the Wholesale Meat Industry in Detroit.' *American Journal of Sociology* 56: 25–32.

Harvey, D. (1996) *Justice, Nature and the Geography of Difference*. Cambridge: Blackwell.

Hassemer, W. (1997) 'Rechtstaatliche Grenzen bei der Bekämpfung der Organisierten Kriminalität.' In U. Sieber, ed., *Internationale organisierte Kriminalität* (pp 213–19). Cologne: Carl Heymans Verlag KG.

Hassig, R. (1988) *Aztec Warfare: Imperial Expansion and Political Control*. Norman: University of Oklahoma Press.

Hawkins, E.R., and Waller, W. (1936) 'Critical Notes on the Cost of Crime.' *Journal of Criminal Law and Criminology* 26: 679–94.

Hawkins, G. (1969) 'God and the Mafia.' *The Public Interest* 14: 24–51.

Heidenheimer, A.J. (1989) 'Perspectives on the Perception of Corruption.' In Heidenheimer, Johnston, and LeVine, *Political Corruption: A Handbook* (pp 149–64).

Heidenheimer, A.J., Johnston, M., and LeVine, V.T., eds. (1989) *Political Corruption: A Handbook*. London: Transactor Publishers.

Herbert, R. (1993) 'In America: Tobacco Dollars.' *New York Times*, 28 November: section 4: 11.

Hernandez, B.E. (1993) 'RIP to IRP: Money Laundering and Drug Trafficking Score a Knockout Victory over Bank Secrecy.' *North Carolina Journal of International Law and Commercial Regulation* 18: 235–304.

Hicks, D. (1998) 'Thinking about Organized Crime Prevention.' *Journal of Contemporary Criminal Justice* 14(4): 325–50.

Hobbs, D. (1995) *Bad Business: Professional Crime in Modern Britain*. Oxford: Clarendon Press.

Hobbs, D. (1997) 'Criminal Collaboration: Youth Gangs, Subcultures, Professional Criminals, and Organized Crime.' In M. Maguire, R. Morgan, and R. Reiner, eds, *The Oxford Handbook of Criminology*, 2nd ed. (pp 801–40). Oxford: Clarendon Press.

Hobbs, D. (1998) 'Going Down the Glocal: The Local Context of Organized Crime.' *The Howard Journal* 37(4): 407–22.

Hobbs, D., and Dunnighan, C. (1999) 'Serious Crime Networks: the Police Response to a Local Problem.' In P. Carlen and R. Morgan, eds, *Crime Unlimited? Questions for the 21st Century* (pp 57–75). London: Macmillan.

Holroyd, J. (2000) 'The Reform of Jurisdiction over International Conspiracy.' *Journal of Criminal Law* 64(3): 323–31.

Holsti, O.R., and Rosenau, J.N. (1996) 'Liberals, Populists, Libertarians, and Conservatives: The Link between Domestic and International Affairs.' *International Political Science Review* 17(1): 94–125.

Hood, C. (1996) 'Control over Bureaucracy: Cultural Theory and Institutional Variety.' *Journal of Public Policy* 15(3): 207–30.

House of Commons, Home Affairs Committee. (1992) *First Report on the Accountability of the Security Service* (12 December). Cm 265. London: HMSO.

House of Commons, Home Affairs Committee. (1994–5) *Organised Crime*, no. 18–I/II. London: Stationery Office.

House of Commons, Intelligence and Security Committee. (1995) *Report on Security Service Work against Organised Crime* (December). Cm 3065. London: HMSO.

House of Commons, Intelligence and Security Committee. (1998) *Annual Report for 1997–98* (October). Cm 4073. London: HMSO.

House of Lords, Select Committee on the European Communities (1997–8) *Correspondence with Ministries, 11th Report*. HL paper 60. London: Stationery Office.

House of Representatives, Foreign Affairs Committee. (1990) *International Drug Money Laundering: Issues and Options for Congress*. Washington, DC: U.S. Government Printing Office.

Hufbauer, G. (1998) 'The Snake Oil of Diplomacy: When Tensions Rise, the U.S. Peddles Sanctions.' *Washington Post*, 12 July: C01.

Human Rights Watch. (1996) *Colombia's Killer Networks*. New York: Human Rights Watch.

Hutton, W. (2001) 'Titanic Greed of the Telecom Giants.' *The Observer*, 22 April. Available at: *http://www.observer.co.uk/comment/story/O,6903,476506,00.html*.

Huxley, A. (1959). *The Doors of Perception and Heaven and Hell*. London: Penguin.

Hyde, H. (1995) *Forfeiting Our Property Rights: Is Your Property Safe from Seizure?* Washington, DC: Cato Institute.

Ibbitson, J. (2002) 'Pentagon's False-News Plan Sets off Alarm Bells.' *Globe and Mail*, 20 February: A1, A15.

IELR. (2000a) 'US Congress Votes Approves $1.3 billion for Counterdrug Effort in Colombia.' *International Enforcement Law Reporter* 16(8) (August): 855–87.

IELR. (2000b) 'Europeans and Latin Americans Show Caution on "Plan Colombia."' *International Enforcement Law Reporter* 16(12) (December): 1041–2.

Il Corriere della Sera (1999) 'Quelle ville da sogno vendute con lo slogan: La barca sooto casa.' 14 October: 11.

IMF (International Monetary Fund). (1997) *World Economic Outlook*. Washington, DC: Author.

IMF (International Monetary Fund). (1998) *Annual Report*. Washington, DC: Author.

Ingham, J. (1984) 'Human Sacrifice at Tenochtitlan.' *Comparative Studies in Society and History* 26: 379–400.

International Consortium of Investigative Journalists. (2001) 'Part 2: Tobacco Companies Linked to Criminal Organizations in Lucrative Cigarette Smuggling.' *An Investigative Report of the Center for Public Integrity*. Available online at: *http://www.public-i.org/story_01_030301.htm*.

Intriago, C. (1991) *International Money Laundering*. London: Eurostudy Publishing.

James, W. (1958) *The Varieties of Religious Experience*. New York: Mentor.

Jamieson, A. (1990) *Global Drug Trafficking*. London: Research Institute for the Study of Conflict and Terrorism.

Jamieson, A. (2000) *The Antimafia. Italy's Fight against Organised Crime*. Basingstoke, London, New York: Macmillan and St Martin's Press.

Jaramillo, A.M. (1998) 'Bitácora de un Polémico Instrumento.' *El Tiempo*, 19 April. Retrieved from: *http://www.eltiempo.com/diario/domingo/int02.htm*.

Jenkins, P., and Potter, G. (1987) 'The Politics and Mythology of Organized Crime: A Philadelphia Case-Study.' *Journal of Criminal Justice* 15: 473–84.

Jennings, P. (1998) 'Special Report: Pot of Gold' [Television news broadcast]. ABC: Aired 18 April.

Johnson, T. (1998) 'Medellin Back as Drug Hub, Led by New Breed of Bosses: Discreet Dealers Take over for Flashy Cartel.' *Miami Herald*, 19 April: A1. Retrieved 3 July 2002 from: *http://www.miami.com/mld/miamiherald*.

Johnston, L. (2000) 'Transnational Private Policing: The Impact of Global Commercial Security.' In Sheptycki, ed., *Issues in Transnational Policing* (pp 21–42).

Johnston, M. (1996) 'The Search for Definitions: The Vitality of Politics and the Issue of Corruption.' *International Social Science Journal* 48(3): 321–35.

Jomo, K.S. (1998) 'Introduction: Financial Governance, Liberalization, and Crises in East Asia.' In K.S. Jomo, ed., *Tigers in Trouble: Financial Governance, Liberalization, and Crises in East Asia* (pp 1–32). New York: Zed Books.

Kaufmann, D. (1997) 'Corruption: The Facts.' *Foreign Policy* 107: 114–30.

Kennedy, R.F. (1960) *The Enemy Within.* London: Popular Library.

Keohane, R.O. (1989) *International Institutions and State Power.* Boulder, CO: Westview Press.

Kerry, J. (1997) *The New War: The Web of Crime That Threatens America's Security.* New York: Simon and Schuster.

Kessler, S. (1994) *Civil and Criminal Forfeiture: Federal and State Practice.* New York: Clark, Boardman, and Callaghan.

King, A.D., ed. (1991) *Culture, Globalization and the World-System.* Basingstoke: Macmillan.

King, M. (1994) 'Policing Refugees and Asylum Seekers in "Greater Europe": Towards a Reconceptualisation of Control.' In M. Anderson and M. den Boer, eds, *Policing across National Boundaries* (pp 69–84). London: Pinter.

Klepak, H.P. (1993–4) 'The Impact of the International Narcotics Trade on Canada's Foreign and Security Policy.' *International Journal* 49(1): 66–92.

Klich, A. (1996) 'Bribery in Economies in Transition: The Foreign Corrupt Practices Act.' *Stanford Journal of International Law* 32: 121–47.

Klitgaard, R. (1988) *Controlling Corruption.* Berkeley: University of California Press.

Knox, P.L., and Taylor, P.J., eds (1995) *World Cities in a World System.* Cambridge: Cambridge University Press.

Kong, T.Y. (1996) 'Corruption and Its Institutional Foundations: The Experience of South Korea.' *IDS Bulletin* 27(2): 48–55.

Kopits, G., and Craig, J. (1998) *Transparency in Government Operations.* International Monetary Fund Occasional Paper No. 158. Washington, DC: International Monetary Fund.

Kotler, J. (1998) 'U.S. Colombia Sign Military Pact.' *Washington Post*, 1 December. Retrieved 2 December 1998 from: *http://www.Washingtonpost.com.*

Krasna, J.S. (1999) 'Testing the Salience of Transnational Issues for International Security: The Case of Narcotics Production and Trafficking.' *Contemporary Security Policy* 20(1): 42–55.

Kuhn, T. (1970) *The Structure of Scientific Revolutions.* 2nd ed. Chicago: University of Chicago Press.

Kushner, R.A., Fleener, A., Hughes, R., Padilla, A., and Mendelsohn, A. (1999) *Drug Control: Narcotics Threat from Colombia Continues to Grow* (June). Washington, DC: United States General Accounting Office.

Lacey, R. (1986) *Ford: The Man and the Machine*. Toronto: McClelland and Stewart.

Lackner, K. (1995) *Strafgesetzbuch*. Munich: Verlag C.H. Beck.

Langer, J. (1977) 'Drug Entrepreneurs and the Dealing Culture.' *Social Problems* 24: 377–86.

Laurie, P. (1967) *Drugs: Medical, Psychological and Social Facts*. Harmondsworth: Penguin.

Lavigne, Y. (1999) *Hells Angels at War*. Toronto: HarperCollins.

Leach, P. (1996) 'The Security Service Bill.' *New Law Journal* 146 (Pt 1) (16 February): 224.

Lee, III, R. (1989) *The White Labyrinth: Cocaine and Political Power*. New Brunswick, NJ: Transaction Publishers.

Lee, III, R.W. (1999) 'Transnational Crime: An Overview.' In Farer, ed., *Transnational Crime in the Americas* (pp 1–38).

Leiken, R.S. (1997) 'Controlling the Global Corruption Epidemic.' *Foreign Policy* (Winter): 55–73.

Lessard, D., and Williamson, J. (1987) *Capital Flight and Third World Debt*. Washington: Institute for International Economics.

Lessmann, R. (1997) 'El Narcotráfico y las Relaciones Internacionales.' In R. del Olmo, ed., *Drogas: El Conflicto de Fin de Siglo vol. 1. Second Semester* (pp 53–72). Caracas: Editorial Nueva Sociedad.

Letkemann, P. (1973) *Crime as Work*. Englewood Cliffs, NJ: Prentice-Hall.

Levi, M. (1991) 'Regulating Money Laundering: The Death of Bank Secrecy in the U.K.' *British Journal of Criminology* 31(2): 109–25.

Levi, M. (1998a) 'Credit Card Fraud.' *Journal of Contemporary Criminal Justice* 14 (4) (November): 368–83.

Levi, M. (1998b) 'Perspectives on "Organised Crime": An Overview.' *The Howard Journal* 37(4): 335–45.

Levine, A., and Brandt, C. (1998) 'Dirty Money.' *Criminal Justice* 12(4) (Winter): 18–23.

Levine, H.G. (1979) 'The Discovery of Addiction: Changing Conceptions of Habitual Drunkenness in America.' *Journal of Studies on Alcohol* 15: 493–506.

LeVine, V.T. (1989) 'Transnational Aspects of Political Corruption.' In Heidenheimer, Johnston, and LeVine, *Political Corruption: A Handbook* (pp 685–700).

Levy, L. (1996) *A License to Steal: The Forfeiture of Property*. Chapel Hill: University of North Carolina Press.

Lillie, H. (1998) 'Allemagne/Germany. Specific Offences of Organized Crime and German Criminal Law.' *International Review of Penal Law* 69: 139–54.

Linquist Avey Macdonald Baskerville. (1992) *Contraband Tobacco Estimate – June 30 1992.* Released 29 October. Author.

Lippmann, W. (1967) 'The Underworld as Servant.' In G. Tyler, ed., *Organized Crime in America* (pp 59–69). Detroit: Ann Arbor.

Lisken, H. (1994) '"Sicherheit" durch "Kriminalitätsbekämpfung?"' *Zeitschrift fur Rechtspolitik* 49–88.

Loven, Jennifer. (2002) 'Study: Fewer Facts in Media Coverage.' *Project for Excellence in Journalism.* Associated Press, 28 January. Available online at: *http://www.journalism.org.*

Maas, P. (1967) *The Valachi Papers.* New York: Bantam Books.

Macalister, T. (2000) 'Premier Oil Admits Abuses in Burma.' *The Guardian* 16 May: 21.

MacDonald, G. (2001) 'Media Fear Censorship as Bush Requests Caution.' *Globe and Mail,* 11 October: A9.

MacIntyre, D. (1975) *The Privateers.* London: Elek.

Maguire, K. (2000) 'Clarke Admits BAT Link to Smuggling.' *The Guardian,* 3 February: 2.

Maguire, K., and Campbell D. (2000) 'Tobacco Giant Implicated in Global Smuggling Schemes.' *The Guardian,* 31 January: 1.

Mahaney, M.C. (1981) 'The Foreign Corrupt Practices Act: Curse or Cure?' *American Business Law Journal* 19: 73–86.

Maingot, A.P. (1999) 'The Decentralization Imperative and Caribbean Criminal Enterprises.' In Farer, ed., *Transnational Crime in the Americas* (pp 142–70).

Marbry, D.J. (1994) 'The Role of the Military.' In R.F. Perl, ed., *Drugs and Foreign Policy: A Critical View.* Boulder, CO: Westview.

Martin, J.M., and Romano, A.T. (1992) *Multinational Crime.* London: Sage.

Martin's Annual Criminal Code. (1993) Aurora, ON: Canada Law Book Inc.

Marx, G. (1988) *Undercover: Police Surveillance in America.* Berkeley: University of California Press.

Mastrogiacomo, D. (2000) 'Il grande imbroglio di Tirana.' *La Republica,* 3 March: 5.

Mativat, F., and Tremblay, P. (1997) 'Counterfeiting Credit Cards.' *British Journal of Criminology* 37: 165–83.

Mauro, P. (1997) *Why Worry about Corruption?* Washington, DC: International Monetary Fund.

Mauro, P. (1998) 'Corruption: Causes, Consequences, and Agenda for Further Research.' *Finance and Development* 35(1): 11–14.

Mayer, M. (1990) *The Greatest Ever Bank Robbery.* New York: Scribner.

McBarnet, D. (1992) 'Legitimate Rackets: Tax Evasion, Tax Avoidance and the Boundaries of Legality.' *Journal of Human Justice* 3(2): 56–74.

McCahill, M. (1998) 'Beyond Foucault: Towards a Contemporary Theory of Surveillance.' In C. Norris, G. Armstrong, and J. Moran, eds, *Surveillance, Closed Circuit Television and Social Control* (pp 41–65). Aldershot: Ashgate.

McCoy, A.W. (1991) *The Politics of Heroin: CIA Complicity in the Global Drug Trade.* Brooklyn: Lawrence Hill.

McDermott, J. (2001a) 'US Crews Involved in Colombian Battle.' *The Scotsman.* 23 February: 14.

McDermott, J. (2001b) 'America Sees New Growth in Colombia's Cocaine Crop.' *The Scotsman.* 3 March: 13.

McGlothlin, W.H. (1967) *Longlasting Effects of LSD on Normals.* Los Angeles: University of Southern California.

McInnes, C. (1994) 'Retailers' Group Links Protestors, Tobacco Firms.' *Globe and Mail*, 28 January: A4

McIntosh, M. (1975) *The Organisation of Crime.* London: Macmillan.

McLaughlin, E. (1992) 'The Democratic Deficit: European Union and the Accountability of the British Police.' *British Journal of Criminology* 34(4): 473–88.

McRae, P.B. (1995) *Impact of the Illegal Narcotics Trade on Economic and Legal Institutions in Colombia.* Available from: *http://historicaltextarchive.com/mcrae.*

Mendel, W.W. (1992) 'Counterdrug Strategy – Illusive Victory: From Blast Furnace to Green Sweep.' *Military Review* 74.

Meny, Y. (1996) '"Fin de Siècle" Corruption: Change, Crisis, and Shifting Values.' *International Social Science Journal* 48: 309–20.

Merton R.K. (1949) 'Social Structure and Anomie.' In *Social Theory and Social Structure: Toward a Codification of Theory and Research* (pp 131–61). Illinois: Free Press of Glencoe.

Meyer, J. (1997) 'Organised Crime: Recent German Legislation and the Prospects for a Co-ordinated Approach.' *Columbia Journal of European Law* 3(2): 243–55.

Mieczkowski, T. (1988) 'Studying Heroin Retailers: A Research Note.' *Criminal Justice Review* 13: 39–44.

Mieczkowski, T. (1990) 'Drugs, Crime, and the Failure of American Organized Crime Models.' *International Journal of Comparative and Applied Criminal Justice* 14(1): 97–106.

Mieczkowski, T. (1994) 'The Experiences of Women Who Sell Crack: Some Descriptive Data from the Detroit Crack Ethnography Project.' *Journal of Drug Issues* 24: 227–48.

Miller, R.L. (1994) *The Case for Legalizing Drugs.* New York: Praeger.

Ministerio de Defensa Nacional Comando General Fuerzas Armadas Colombia y E.U. (1998) *Fortalecen Lucha Antinarcoticos.* Available from: *http://www.cgfm.mil.co/foluan.htm* (last modified: 3 August 1999).

Mitsilegas, V. (2001) 'Defining Organised Crime in the European Union: The Limits of European Criminal Law in an Area of Freedom, Security and Justice.' *European Law Review* 26: 565–81.

Moccia, S. (1997) 'Aspects Régressifs du Système Pénal Italien.' *Déviance et Société* 21(2): 137–64.

Mokhiber, R. (1988) *Corporate Crime and Violence.* San Francisco: Sierra Club.

Moley, R. (1926) 'Politics and Crime.' *The Annals of the American Academy of Political and Social Science* 25 (May): 78–84.

Moley, R. (1930) 'Behind the Menacing Racket.' *New York Times,* 23 November: section 5: 2.

Monaco, G. (1998) 'Le Problematiche Costituzionali del "Concorso Esterno" nel Reato Associativo.' *JUS: Rivista di Scienze Giuridiche* anno 45: 133–53.

Moncayo, V.M. (1998) 'Cooperacion Judicial y Presos en los Estados Unidos.' In J.G. Tokatlian, ed., *Colombia y Estados Unidos: Problemas y Perspectivas* (pp 224–38). Santafé de Bogotá: Tercer Mundo.

Moon, P. (1993) 'Smuggling of Cigarettes Grows into Big Business.' *Globe and Mail,* 29 May: A1–A2.

Moore, W. (1974) *The Kefauver Committee and the Politics of Crime.* Columbia: University of Missouri Press.

Morales, E. (1989) *Cocaine: White Gold Rush in Peru.* Tucson: University of Arizona Press.

Morales, F. (2000) *The Little Book of Heroin.* Berkeley, CA: Ronin Publishing.

Morin, Charles H. (Chair, Commission on the Review of the National Policy toward Gambling). (1976) *Gambling in America.* Washington, DC: Commission on the Review of the National Policy toward Gambling.

Muffler, S. (1995) 'Proposing a Treaty on the Prevention of International Corrupt Payments: Closing the Foreign Corrupt Practices Act Is Not the Answer.' *ILSA Journal of International and Comparative Law* 1 (Spring): 3–39.

Muir, W.K. (1977) *Police: Street Corner Politicians.* Chicago: University of Chicago Press.

Murphy, M.J. (1995) 'International Bribery: An Example of an Unfair Trade Practice?' *Brooklyn Journal of International Law* 21(2): 385–424.

Murphy, S., Waldorf, D., and Reinerman, C. (1995) 'Drifting into Dealing: Becoming a Cocaine Seller.' In N.J. Herman, ed., *Deviance: A Symbolic Interactionist Approach* (pp 471–86). New York: General Hall.

Myers, S.L. (1998) 'U.S. Pledges Military Cooperation to Colombia Drug War.' *New York Times,* 1 December: A14.

Nadelmann, E.A. (1988) 'U.S. Drug Policy: A Bad Export.' *Foreign Policy* 70 (Spring): 83–108.

Nadelmann, E.A. (1993) *Cops across Borders: The Internationalization of U.S. Criminal Law Enforcement.* University Park, PA: Pennsylvania State University Press.

National Center for Tobacco Free Kids. (2000) 'The Big Cigarette Companies and Cigarette Smuggling.' 2 March. Retrieved from *http://www.tobaccofreekids.org.*

National Crime Squad. (1999) *Combating Serious and Organised Crime.* Available online at: *http://www.nationalcrimesquad.police.uk/.*

National Crime Squad Authority (1999–2000) *National Crime Squad Service Plan.* London: Author.

Naylor, R.T. (1994) *Hot Money and the Politics of Debt.* Montreal: Black Rose Books. (1st ed. New York: Simon and Schuster, 1985.)

Naylor, R.T. (1995) 'From Cold War to Crime War.' *Transnational Organized Crime* 1(4): 38.

Naylor, R.T. (1996) 'From Underworld to Underground: Enterprise Crime, "Informal Sector" Business and the Public Policy Response.' *Crime, Law and Social Change* 24: 79–150.

Naylor, R.T. (1997) 'Mafias, Myths and Markets: On the Theory and Practice of Enterprise Crime.' *Transnational Organized Crime* 3(3).

Naylor, R.T. (1999a) *Patriots and Profiteers: On Economic Warfare, Embargo Busting and State-Sponsored Crime.* Toronto: McClelland and Stewart.

Naylor, R.T. (1999b) 'Washout: A Critique of Follow-the-Money Methods in Crime Control Policy.' *Crime, Law and Social Change* 32: 1–57.

Naylor, R.T. (2001) *Economic Warfare: Sanctions, Embargoes and Their Human Cost.* Boston: Northeastern University Press.

Naylor, R.T. (2002a) *Criminal Finance and the Financing of Crime.* Ithaca, NY: Cornell University Press.

Naylor, R.T. (2002b) *The Wages of Crime.* Ithaca, NY: Cornell University Press.

Naylor, R.T. (2003, forthcoming) 'Towards a General Theory of Profit Driven Crime.' *British Journal of Criminology.*

NCIS (National Criminal Intelligence Service). (1999) *Annual Report 1998–1999.* Available online at: *http://www.ncis.co.uk.*

NCIS (National Criminal Intelligence Service). (2000) *Annual Assessment of the Organised Crime Threat.* Available online at: *http://www.ncis.co.uk.*

Nelson, D. (1999) 'Slave Oil Rig Workers to be Sacked.' *The Observer*, 21 February: 1.

New York Society for the Prevention of Crime. (1896) 'Annual Report, 1896.' In P.W. Rishell and A.E. Roraback, eds, *A History of the Society for the Preven-*

tion of Crime (p. 29). Unpublished and undated document held in Box 9, SPC Collection, Rare Books and Manuscript Library, Columbia University, New York.

Noonan, J.T. (1984) *Bribes*. New York: Macmillan.

Norton-Taylor, R. (1999) 'Security Spending Runs out of Control.' *The Guardian*, 26 November: 15.

OECD (Organization for Economic Co-operation and Development). (1996) *OECD Working Papers: OECD Symposium on Corruption and Good Governance*, vol. IV, no. 78. Paris: Author.

OECD (Organization for Economic Co-operation and Development). (1997) *Towards a New Global Age: Challenges and Opportunities*. Paris: Author.

OECD (Organization for Economic Co-operation and Development). (1999) *Draft Principles of Corporate Governance*. Paris: Author.

Oldfield, D. (2001) 'Progress Report on a "Systematic Approach to Organised Crime Reduction."' Paper presented at Towards a Knowledge Based Strategy to Prevent Organised Crime: A European Union Conference. Sundsvall, Sweden, 21–3 February (unpublished).

O'Malley, P. (1996) 'Risk and Responsibility.' In A. Barry, T. Osborne, and N. Rose, eds, *Foucault and Political Reason* (pp 189–208). Chicago: University of Chicago Press.

O'Malley, P., and Mugford, S. (1991) 'The Demand for Intoxicating Commodities: Implications for the War on Drugs.' *Social Problems* 18(4): 49–75.

O'Shea, J. (1991) *The Daisy Chain: How Borrowed Billions Sank a Texas S and L*. New York: Pocket Books.

Palazzo, F. (1995) 'La Législation Italienne contre la Criminalité Organisée.' *Revue des Sciences Criminelles* 711–22.

Paoli, L. (1998) 'The Pentiti's Contribution to the Conceptualization of the Mafia Phenomenon.' In V. Ruggiero, N. South, and I. Taylor, eds, *The New European Criminology: Crime and Social Order in Europe* (pp 264–86). London: Routledge.

Papa, M. (1993) 'La Nouvelle Législation Italienne en matière de Criminalité Organisée.' *Revue des Sciences Criminelles* 725–38.

Parascandola, J. (1995) 'The Drug Habit: The Association of the Word "Drug" with Abuse in American History.' In R. Porter and M. Teich, eds, *Drugs and Narcotics in History* (pp 156–67). Cambridge: Cambridge University Press.

Pastrana, A. (1998) 'Palabras del Señor Presidente de la República en la Instalación de la Tercera Conferencia de Ministros de Defensa de las Américas.' Paper presented at the Tercera Conferencia de Ministros de Defensa de las Américas, Presidenca de la República. 29 November–

3 December. Available online at: *http://www.oas.org/CSH/spanish/ docministdsc.htm*.

Pearce, F. (1976) *Crimes of the Powerful*. London: Pluto Press.

Pearce, F., ed. (1992) 'Crimes of the Powerful, Special Issue.' *Journal of Human Justice* 3(2) (Spring).

Pearce, F., and Tombs, S. (1990) 'Ideology, Hegemony and Empiricism.' *British Journal of Criminology* 30(4): 423–43.

Pearce, F., and Woodiwiss, M., eds. (1993) *Global Crime Connections*. Toronto: University of Toronto Press.

Pease, K. (1997) 'Crime Prevention.' In M. Maguire, R. Morgan, and R. Reiner, eds, *The Oxford Handbook of Criminology* (pp 963–95). Oxford: Clarendon.

Pécaut, D. (1996) 'Pasado, Presente, Futuro de la Violencia.' *Colombia-Thema*. Retrieved 23 April 1998 from *http://colombia-thema.org/nov/97/articulo1b.htm*.

Pennsylvania Crime Commission. (1991) *Organized Crime in Pennsylvania: A Decade of Change, 1990 Report*. Conshohocken, PA: Pennsylvania Crime Commission.

Perl, R.F., ed. (1994) *Drugs and Foreign Policy: A Critical Review*. Boulder, CO: Westview Press.

Phythian, M. (1998) *Arming Iraq*. Boston: Northeastern University Press.

Pisa, P. (1997) *Giurisprudenza commentata di Diritto Penale, Vol. 2*. Padua: Cedam.

Pitschas, R. (1993) 'Innere Sicherheit und internationale Verbrechensbekämpfung als Verantworung des demokratischen Verfassungsstaates.' *Juristenzeitung* 48(18): 857–66.

Pizarro, E. (1998) 'Colombia: en el Ojo del Huracán.' *Colombia-Thema* (January). Available online at: *http://colombia-thema.org/cuadro2.htm*.

Pizzigati, S. (1976) 'The Perverted Grand Juries.' *The Nation*, 222 (24) (19 June): 743–46.

Pizzo, S., Fricker, M., and Muolo, P. (1989) *Inside Job: The Looting of America's Savings and Loans*. New York: McGraw-Hill.

Ploscowe, M., ed. (1952) *Organized Crime and Law Enforcement*. Vol. 1. New York: Grosby Press.

Pocock, J.G.A. (1973) *Politics, Language and Time*. New York: Atheneum.

Porteous, S. (1998) *Organized Crime Impact Study: Highlights*. Ottawa: Ministry of the Solicitor General.

Potter, G.W. (1994) *Criminal Organizations: Vice, Racketeering, and Politics in an American City*. Prospect Heights, IL: Waveland Press.

President's Commission on Law Enforcement and the Administration of Justice. (1967) *The Challenge of Crime in a Free Society*. Washington, DC: Government Printing Office.

President's Commission on Organized Crime. (1983) *Hearing 1, Organized Crime: Federal Law Enforcement Perspective.* 29 November. Washington, DC: Government Printing Office.

President's Commission on Organized Crime. (1984) *The Cash Connection: Organized Crime, Financial Institutions and Money Laundering.* Washington, DC: Government Printing Office.

Price, K. (1999) 'Verdict of Canadian Tribunal about Human Rights Abuses in Colombia.' *Colombia Human Rights Network.* Retrieved 5 August from *http:// www.igc.org/colhrnet/newscont/499verdict.htm#top.*

Priest, D. (1998a) 'U.S. May Boost Military Aid to Colombia's Anti-Drug Effort.' *Washington Post,* 28 March: A19.

Priest, D. (1998b) 'Free of Oversight, U.S. Military Trains Foreign Troops.' *Washington Post,* 12 July: A01.

Priest, D., and Farah, D. (25 May 1998) 'U.S. Force Training Troops in Colombia.' *Washington Post,* 25 May: A01.

Punch, M. (1996) *Dirty Business.* London: Sage.

Raine, L.P., and Cilluffo, F.J. (1994) *Global Organized Crime: The New Empire of Evil.* Washington, DC: Center for Strategic and International Studies.

Randall, L.H. (1997) 'Multilateralization of the Foreign Corrupt Practices Act.' *Minnesota Journal of Global Trade* 6: 657–84.

Rawlinson, P. (1998) 'Russian Organized Crime: Moving beyond Ideology.' In V. Ruggiero, N. South, and I. Taylor, eds, *The New European Criminology: Crime and Social Order in Europe* (pp 242–63). London: Routledge.

Rebovich, D. (1992) *Dangerous Ground: The World of Hazardous Waste Crime.* New Brunswick, NJ: Transaction Publishers.

Redlinger, L. (1975) 'Marketing and Distributing Heroin.' *Journal of Psychedelic Drugs* 7: 331–53.

Reiner, R. (2000) *The Politics of the Police.* Oxford: Oxford University Press.

Renborg, B. (1943) *International Drug Control. A Study of International Administrations by and through the League of Nations.* Washington, DC: Carnegie Endowment for International Peace.

La Republica (1999) 'Usa, 3 ordini d'arresto per il Russiagate.' 30 October: 10.

Reuter, P. (1976) 'An Analysis of the Characteristics of Arrested Gamblers in the State of New Jersey.' In Morin, Commission on the Review of the National Policy toward Gambling, *Gambling in America,* n.p. Washington, DC: Commission on the Review of the National Policy toward Gambling.

Reuter, P. (1983) *Disorganized Crime.* Cambridge, MA: MIT Press.

Reuter, P. (1984) *Disorganized Crime: Illegal Markets and the Mafia.* Cambridge, MA: MIT Press.

Reuter, P. (1985) *The Organization of Illegal Markets*. Washington, DC: National Institute of Justice.

Reuter, P. (1990) *Money from Crime: The Economics of Drug Dealing*. Santa Monica, CA: Rand Corporation.

Reuter, P. (1996) 'The Mismeasurement of Illegal Drug Markets: The Implications of Its Irrelevance.' In S. Pozo, ed., *Exploring the Underground Economy* (pp 63–80). Kalamazoo, MI: W.E. Upjohn Institute.

Reuter, P., and Haaga, J. (1989) *The Organization of High-Level Drug Markets: An Exploratory Study*. Santa Monica, CA: Rand Corporation.

Reuter, P., and Petrie, C., eds (1999) *Transnational Organized Crime*. Washington. DC: National Academy Press.

Richards, L.G., Joffe, M.H., and Spratto, G. (1969) *LSD-25: A Factual Account*. Washington, DC: U.S. Department of Justice, Bureau of Narcotics and Dangerous Drugs.

Rid, M. (1989) 'Una Región Amenazada por el Narcotráfico.' In D. García-Sayán, ed., *Coca, Cocaína y Narcotráfico: Laberinto en los Andes* (n.p.). Lima: Comisión Andina de Juristas.

Rishell, P.W., and Roraback, A.E. (n.d.) 'A History of the Society for the Prevention of Crime.' Unpublished and undated document held in Box 9, SPC Collection, Rare Books and Manuscript Library, Columbia University, New York.

'RJR Affiliate Pleaded Guilty to Cigarette Smuggling' [Television news-broadcast]. (1998) CNN, 23 December.

Roberts, J.L. (1989) 'Revision of the Foreign Corrupt Practices Act by the 1988 Omnibus Trade Bill: Will It Reduce the Compliance Burdens and Anti-competitive Impact?' *Brigham Young University Law Review* 2: 491–506.

Rodrick, D., and Rauch, J.E. (1997) 'Comments.' In Elliott, ed., *Corruption and the Global Economy* (pp 109–16).

Rodrigues, L.J. (1993) *Expanded Military Surveillance Not Justified by Measureable Goals or Results*. Washington, DC: U.S. General Accounting Office. Retrieved March 1999 from: *http://mir.drugtext.org/druglibrary/schaffer/GovPubs/gao/gao1.htm*.

Rohter, L. (1999) 'U.S. to Consider $1 Billion More for Colombia Drug War.' *New York Times*, 17 July: A7.

Romano, M. (1985) 'Legislazione Penale e Consenso Sociale.' *JUS: Rivista di Scienze Giuridiche* anno 32: 413–29.

Rose, N., and Miller, P. (1992) 'Political Power beyond the State: Problematics of Government.' *British Journal of Sociology* 43(2): 173–205.

Rose-Ackerman, S. (1997) 'The Political Economy of Corruption.' In Elliott, ed., *Corruption and the Global Economy* (pp 31–55).

Rosenberger, L.R. (1996) *America's Drug War Debacle*. Brookfield, VT: Avebury.

Rosenthal, M. (1989) 'An American Attempt to Control International Corruption.' In Heidenheimer, Johnston, and LeVine, eds, *Political Corruption: A Handbook* (pp 701–18).

Royal Canadian Mounted Police (RCMP). (1988–9). *National Drug Intelligence Estimate*. Ottawa: Author.

Ruggiero, V. (1996) *Organized and Corporate Crime in Europe: Offers That Can't Be Refused*. Aldershot: Dartmouth.

Ruggiero, V. (1997) 'Trafficking in Human Beings: Slaves in Contemporary Europe.' *International Journal of Sociology of Law* 25(3): 231–44.

Ruggiero, V. (1999) 'Trafficking, Immigration and Invisibility.' Paper presented at United Nations conference New Frontiers of Crime: Trafficking in Human Beings and New Forms of Slavery. Verona, 22–3 October.

Ruggiero, V. (2000a) *Crime and Markets: Crime in the Street, Crimes of the Elite*. Oxford: Oxford University Press.

Ruggiero, V. (2000b) *Crimes and Markets: Essays in Anti-Criminology*. New York: Oxford University Press.

Ruggiero, V., and South, N. (1995) *Eurodrugs: Drug Use, Markets and Trafficking in Europe*. London: UCL Press.

Sabetti, F. (2000) *The Search for Good Government*. Montreal: McGill-Queen's University Press.

Sanchez, M. (2000) *Clinton Prende las Alarmas: las cuatro versiones del plan Colombia*. Retrieved 2 January 2000 from: *http://boozers.fortunecity.com/laurel/66/jan2/990126_plan_col-4.htm*.

Saunders, D. (2000) 'How Fierce War on L.A. Gangs Spawned Police Reign of Terror: Hundreds of Cops May Be Implicated in Probe of Massive Corruption.' *Globe and Mail*, 28 February: A1.

Schaffer, C.A. (1999) 'Basic Facts about the War on Drugs.' Retrieved March 1999 from: *http://mir.drugtext.org/druglibrary/schaffer/library/basicfax.htm*.

Schemo, D.J. (1996) 'Under Fire, Colombia's Leader Fans Anti-U.S. Feelings.' *Latino Link*. Retrieved 15 December 1998 from *http://www.latino.com/news/0305col.html*.

Schemo, D.J. (1998) 'Congress Steps up Aid for Colombians to Combat Drugs.' *New York Times*, 1 December: A14.

Schiraldi, V., Kuyper, S., and Hewitt, S. (1996) 'Young African Americans and the Criminal Justice System in California: Five Years Later.' Center on Juvenile and Criminal Justice. Retrieved March 1999 from: *http://www.lindesmith.org/library/cjcj/schiraldi2.html*.

Schlosser, E. (1994) 'Reefer Madness.' *Atlantic Monthly* (August).

Schneider, S., Beare, M., and Hill, J. (2000) *Alternative Approaches to Combating Transnational Crime, Final Report.* 31 March. Ottawa: Solicitor General Canada.

Scott, P.D., and Marshall, J. (1998) *Cocaine Politics: Drugs, Armies, and the CIA in Central America.* Berkeley and Los Angeles: University of California Press.

Seagrave, S. (1988) *The Marcos Dynasty.* New York: Harper and Row.

Semana. (1998) 'Candidato Anunciado.' 26 January: 821.

Semana. (1998) 'Entrevista: Rand Beers: Vamos a Extraditar tan Pronto Como Podamos.' 2 March: 829. Available online at: *http://www.semana.com.co/users/ semana/semana98/mar2/ entrevista.htm.*

Senior, C.M. (1976) *A Nation of Pirates.* London: Newton Abbot.

The Sentencing Project. (1999) Retrieved June 1999 from: *http://www.sentencing project.org/.*

Sesser, S. (1993) 'Opium Wars Redux: Pushing American Cigarettes in Asia.' *New Yorker*, 13 September: 78–9.

Shapiro, M.J. (1997) *Violent Cartographies: Mapping Cultures of War.* Minneapolis: University of Minneapolis Press.

Shelley, L.I. (1995) 'Transnational Organized Crime: An Imminent Threat to the Nation-State?' *Journal of International Affairs* 48(2): 463–89.

Shelley, L. (1997) 'Post-Soviet Organized Crime: A New Form of Authoritarianism.' In P. Williams, ed., *Russian Organized Crime: The New Threat?* (pp 122–38). London: Frank Cass.

Shelley, L. (1998) 'Transnational Crime in the United States: The Scope of the Problem.' Paper presented at the Workshop on Transnational Organised Crime. Washington, DC: National Research Council, 17–18 June.

Shepherd, P. (1986) 'Transnational Corporations and the Denationalization of the Latin American Cigarette Industry.' In A. Teichova, ed., *Historical Studies in International Corporate Business* (pp 201–28). Cambridge: Cambridge University Press.

Shepherd, P. (1989) 'Transnational Corporations and the International Cigarette Industry.' In R. Newfarmer, ed., *Profits, Progress and Poverty* (pp 63–112). Notre Dame: University of Notre Dame Press.

Sheptycki, J.W.E. (1995) 'Transnational Policing and the Makings of a Postmodern State.' *British Journal of Criminology.* 35(4): 613–35.

Sheptycki, J.W.E. (1996) 'Law Enforcement, Justice and Democracy in the Transnational Arena: Reflections on the War on Drugs.' *International Journal of the Sociology of Law* 24: 61–75.

Sheptycki, J.W.E. (1997a) 'Insecurity, Risk Suppression and Segregation: Some Reflections on Policing in the Transnational Age.' *Theoretical Criminology* 1(3): 303–15.

Sheptycki, J.W.E. (1997b) 'Transnationalism, Crime Control and the European State System: A Review of the Literature.' *International Criminal Justice Review* 7: 130–40.

Sheptycki, J.W.E. (2000a) 'The "Drug War": Learning from the Paradigm Example of Transnational Policing.' In Sheptycki, ed., *Issues in Transnational Policing* (pp 201–28).

Sheptycki, J.W.E., ed. (2000b) *Issues in Transnational Policing.* London: Routledge.

Sheptycki, J.W.E. (2000c) 'Policing and Human Rights: An Introduction.' *Policing and Society* 10(1): 1–10.

Sheptycki, J.W.E. (2000d) 'Policing the Virtual Launderette: Money Laundering and Global Governance.' In J. Sheptycki, ed., *Issues in Transnational Policing* (pp 135–76).

Sieber, U. (1995) 'Logistik der Organisierten Kriminalität in der Bundesrepublik Deutschland.' *Juristenzeitung* 15/16: 758–68.

Silbey, S.S. (1997) '"Let Them Eat Cake": Globalization, Postmodern Colonialism, and the Possibilities of Justice.' *Law and Society Review* 31(2): 207–35.

Simmel, G. (1971) *On Individuality and Social Forms.* Chicago: University of Chicago Press.

Simpson, J.A., and Weiner, E.S.C. (1989) *The Oxford English Dictionary.* Vol. 1. 2nd ed. Oxford: Clarendon.

Sinclair, A. (1962) *Prohibition: The Era of Excess.* London: Faber and Faber.

Singer, M. (1971) 'The Vitality of Mythical Numbers.' *Public Interest* 23: 3–9.

Slapper, G., and Tombs, S. (1999) *Corporate Crime.* Harlow: Longman.

Small, P. (1993) 'Task Force Targets Tobacco Smugglers.' *Toronto Star*, 15 October: A10.

Smith, D.C. (1991) 'Wickersham to Sutherland to Katzenbach: Evolving an "Official" Definition for Organized Crime.' *Crime, Law and Social Change* 16(2): 138–42.

Smith, D.J. (1997) 'Ethnic Origins, Crime and Criminal Justice.' In M. Maguire, R. Morgan, and R. Reiner, eds, *The Oxford Handbook of Criminology* (pp 703–60). Oxford: Clarendon.

Smith, J., and Hogan, B. (1999) *Criminal Law.* 9th ed. London, Edinburgh, Dublin: Butterworths.

Smith, P.H. (1999) 'Semiorganized International Crime: Drug Trafficking in Mexico.' In Farer, ed., *Transnational Crime in the Americas* (pp 193–216).

Snider, L. (1992) *Bad Business: Corporate Crime in Canada.* Toronto: Nelson Canada.

Sorfleet, P. (1976) 'Dealing Hashish: Sociological Notes on Trafficking and Use.' *Canadian Journal of Criminology* 18: 123–51.

Sprenkle, C.M. (1993) 'The Case of the Missing Currency.' *Journal of Economic Perspectives* 7(4): 175–84.

Stares, P.B. (1996) *Global Habit: The Drug Problem in a Borderless World*. Washington, DC: Brookings Institution.

Stephens, M. (1996) 'Global Organized Crime.' Paper presented at Woodrow Wilson School Policy Conference 401A, Intelligence Reform in the Post-Cold War Era. 6 January.

Sterling, C. (1990) *Octopus: How the Long Reach of the Sicilian Mafia Controls the Global Narcotics Trade*. New York: Simon and Schuster.

Sterling, C. (1994) *Crime without Frontiers: The Worldwide Expansion of Organised Crime and the Pax Mafiosa*. London: Little, Brown.

Stewart, O.C. (1991) 'Peyote and the Law.' In C. Vecsey, ed., *Handbook of American Indian Religious Freedom* (pp 44–62). New York: Crossroad.

Stille, A. (1995) *Excellent Cadavers: The Mafia and the Death of the First Italian Republic*. New York: Pantheon Books.

Stone, C. (1975) *Where the Law Ends: The Social Control of Corporate Behavior*. New York: Harper and Row.

Storbeck, J. (1999) *Organised Crime in the European Union – The Role of Europol in International Law Enforcement Co-Operation*. The 1999 Police Foundation Lecture. London: Police Foundation.

Strathern, M. (1995) *Shifting Contexts: Transformations in Anthropological Knowledge*. London: Routledge.

Strolberg, B. (1940) 'Thomas E. Dewey: Self-Made Myth.' *American Mercury* June: 140–7.

Strong, J. (1963 [1885]) *Our Country: Its Possible Future and Its Present Crisis*. Cambridge, MA: Harvard University Press.

Sutherland, E. (1937) *The Professional Thief*. Chicago: University of Chicago Press.

Sutherland, E. (1949) *White Collar Crime*. New York: Holt, Rinehart and Winston.

Sutherland, E. (1983) *White Collar Crime: The Uncut Version*. New Haven: Yale University Press.

Sutton, R.H. (1997) 'Controlling Corruption through Collective Means: Advocating the Inter-American Convention against Corruption.' *Fordham International Law Journal* 20: 1427–78.

Swartz, B. (2001) 'Helping the World Combat International Crime.' *Global Issues: Arresting Transnational Crime, An Electronic Journal of the U.S Department of State* 6(2) (August). Available at: *http://usinfo.state.gov/journals/itgic/0801/ijge/gj03.htm*.

Szasz, A. (1986) 'Corporations, Organized Crime, and the Disposal of Hazardous Waste: An Examination of the Making of a Criminogenic Regulatory Structure.' *Criminology* 24(1): 1–27.

Szasz, T. (1975) *Ceremonial Chemistry: The Ritual Persecution of Drugs, Addicts and Pushers.* London: Routledge and Kegan Paul.

Tannenbaum, F. (1936) *Crime and the Community.* New York: Ginn and Company.

Tarkowski, J. (1989) 'Old and New Patterns of Corruption in Poland and the USSR.' *Telos* 80: 51–62.

Teson, F.R. (1994) 'International Abductions, Low-Intensity Conflicts and State Sovereignty: A Moral Inquiry.' *Columbia Journal of Transnational Law* 31(3): 551–86.

Third World Network (1989) *Toxic Terror: The Dumping of Hazardous Wastes in the Third World.* Penang: Author.

Thomas, W.I., and Znaniecki, F. (1960) 'Three Types of Personality.' In C. Wright Mills, ed., *Images of Man* (pp 405–36). New York: George Braziller.

Thoumi, F. (1995) *Political Economy and Illegal Drugs in Colombia.* Boulder, CO: Lynne Reinner.

Thrasher, F.M. (1960 [1927]) *The Gang: A Study of 1,313 Gang in Chicago.* Chicago: University of Chicago Press.

Tilly, C. (1985) 'War Making and State Making as Organized Crime.' In P. Evans, D. Rueschemeyer, and T. Skocpol, eds, *Bringing the State Back In* (pp 169–91). Cambridge: Cambridge University Press.

Tirado Mejía, A. (1998) 'Violence and the State in Colombia.' In E. Posada-Carbó, ed., *Colombia: The Politics of Reforming the State* (pp 111–24). London: Macmillan.

Tita, A. (1998) 'Globalization: A New Political and Economic Space Requiring Supranational Governance.' *Journal of World Trade* 32(3): 47–56.

Tokatlian, J.G. (1997) 'Política Pública Internacional Contra las Drogas de la Administración Gaviria y de las Relaciones entre Colombia y los Estados Unidos.' In F. Thoumi, ed., *Drogas Ilícitas n Colombia: Su impacto económico, político y social* (pp 461–533). Santafé de Bogotá: Ariel, Programa de las Naciones Unidas Para el Desarrollo, Ministerio de Justicia y del Derecho.

Tokatlian, J.G. (1998) 'Crimen Organizado y Drogas Psicoactivas: El Caso de Colombia.' Paper presented at conference Transnational Organized Crime in the Americas. Nathanson Centre for the Study of Organized Crime and Corruption, Osgoode Hall Law School (unpublished).

Tran, M. (1998) 'Drug War Just an Exercise in Futility.' *The Guardian*, 11 June: 19.

Transparency International. (1997) *Transparency International Canada Newsletter* 2(2): 1–4.

Tremblay, P., Cusson, M., and Morselli, C. (1998) 'Market Offenses and Limits to Growth.' *Crime, Law and Social Change* 29(4): 311–30.

Tully, A. (1958) *Treasury Agent*. New York: Simon and Schuster.

Tyler, G. (1967) *Organized Crime in America: A Book of Readings*. Detroit: Ann Arbor.

United Nations. (1994a) *Background Release* (17 November). World Ministerial Conference on Organized Transnational Crime. Naples, Italy, 21–3 November.

United Nations. (1994b) *Background Release, Proposed Formulation of Global Convention against Organized Crime* (22 November). World Ministerial Conference on Organized Transnational Crime. Naples, Italy, 21–3 November.

United Nations. (2000) *United Nations Convention against Transnational Organized Crime. The Convention: A Brief Historical Background*. Available online at: *http://www.odccp.org/palermo*.

United Nations, Commission on Narcotic Drugs. (1997) *Countering Money Laundering* (15 August). Vienna: Author.

United Nations Economic and Social Council. (1994) *Appropriate Modalities and Guidelines for the Prevention and Control of Organised Transnational Crime at the Regional and International Levels, Background Document* (19 September). E/CONF.88/5. Naples: Author.

United Nations, General Assembly, Ad Hoc Committee on the Elaboration of a Convention against Transnational Organized Crime. (1999) *Revised Draft United Nations Convention against Transnational Organized Crime* (19 July). A/AC.254/4/Rev4. Vienna: Author.

Uprimi, R. (1994) 'Narcotráfico, Régimen Político, Violencias y Derechos Humanos en Colombia.' In R. Vargas, ed., *Drogas, Poder y Región en Colombia, Vol. 1* (pp 59–146). Bogota: Cinep.

U.S. Congress, Senate Special Committee to Investigate Crime in Interstate Commerce [Kefauver Committee] 82nd Congress. (1951) *Third Interim Report*. Washington, DC: Government Printing Office.

U.S. Department of Justice. (1998) *Sourcebook of Criminal Justice Statistics*. Retrieved March 1999 from: *http://www.albany.edu/sourcebook/index.html*.

U.S. General Accounting Office. (1994) *Money Laundering: U.S. Efforts to Fight It Are Threatened by Current Smuggling* (March). Washington, DC: Government Printing Office.

U.S. General Accounting Office. (1997) 'Drug Control: Long Standing Problems Hinder U.S. International Efforts.' Retrieved March 1999 from *http://mir.drugtext.org/druglibrary/schaffer/GovPubs/gao/gao8.htm*.

U.S. Senate. (1996) *A Staff Report to the Committee on Foreign Relations: Corruption and Drugs in Colombia Democracy at Risk* (February). Washington, DC: Government Printing Office.

U.S. Senate, Committee on Banking, Housing and Urban Affairs, Subcommittee on Consumer and Regulatory Affairs. (1990) *Drug Money Laundering Control Efforts*. Washington, DC: Government Printing Office.

U.S. Senate, Committee on Governmental Affairs, Permanent Subcommittee on Investigation. (1988) *Drugs and Money Laundering in Panama* (28 January). Washington, DC: Government Printing Office.

U.S. Senate, Select Committee on Intelligence. (1998) *Statement of Lieutenant General Patrick M. Hughes, Director of Defense Intelligence Agency: 'Global Threats and Challenges: The Decades Ahead'* (28 January). Retrieved April 1998 from *http://www.dia.mil/dr_ssciu.html*.

Vallette, J. (1989) *The International Trade in Wastes: A Greenpeace Inventory*. Greenpeace International. 30 January–3 February.

van Duyne, P. (1996) 'The Phantom and Threat of Organised Crime.' *Crime, Law and Social Change* 24(4): 341–77.

van Duyne, P. (2000) 'Introduction.' In P. Van Duyne and V. Ruggiero, eds, *Cross-Border Crime in a Changing Europe* (pp 1–16). Prague: University of Prague Press.

Varese, F. (2001) 'Why the Mafia Must Have Home Cooking.' *Times Literary Supplement*, 23 February: 3–4.

Vargas, R., and Barragán, J. (1996) *Drugs-Linked Crops and Rural Development in Colombia: An Alternative Action Plan*. London: Catholic Institute for International Relations (CIIR).

Veloz, J.J. (1998) 'In the Clinton Era, Overturning Alvarez-Machain and Extraterritorial Abduction: How a Unified Western Hemisphere, through the OAS, Can Win the War on Drugs and Do It Legally.' *Temple International and Comparative Law Journal* 12: 241–69.

Viano, E., ed. (1999) *Global Organized Crime and International Security*. Aldershot: Ashgate.

Villa, J.K. (1988) 'A Critical View of Bank Secrecy Act Enforcement and the Money Laundering Statutes.' *Catholic University Law Review* 7.

Vlassis, D. (2001) 'Drafting the United Nations Convention against Transnational Organized Crime.' In P. Williams and D. Vlassis, eds, *Combating Transnational Crime: Concepts, Activities and Responses* (pp 356–62). London, and Portland, OR: Frank Cass.

Vollmer, A. (1936) *The Police and Modern Society*. Berkeley: University of California Press.

von Lampe, K. (n.d.) *The Concept of Organised Crime in Historical Perspective*. Available online at: *http://members.aol.com/Kvlampe/*.

Walker, C. (1999) 'The Bombs in Omagh and Their Aftermath: The Criminal Justice (Terrorism and Conspiracy) Act 1998.' *Modern Law Review* 62(6): 879–97.

Walker, W. (2001) 'Hollywood Goes to War.' *Toronto Star*, 9 December: B1.

Walker, W.O. (1993–4) 'The Foreign Narcotics Policy of the United States since 1980: An End to the War on Drugs?' *International Journal* 49(1): 37–65.

Walker, III, W.O. (1994) 'U.S. Narcotics Foreign Policy in the Twentieth Century: An Analytical Overview.' In R.F. Perl, ed., *Drugs and Foreign Policy: A Critical Review* (n.p.) Boulder, CO: Westview.

Walter, I. (1989) *Secret Money*. London: George Allen and Unwin.

Watson, A. (1993) *Legal Transplants: An Approach to Comparative Law*. 2nd ed. Athens, GA: University of Georgia.

Wazir, B. (2000) 'How I Paid £350 Bribe to Be Smuggled into Britain.' *The Observer*, 23 April: 15–16.

Weisheit, R.A. (1990) 'Domestic Marijuana Growers: Mainstreaming Deviance.' *Deviant Behavior* 11: 107–29.

Whig Standard (1993) 'Cornwall Mayor Rejoins Battle.' 25 September: 1

White, G. (1996) 'Corruption and Market Reform in China.' *IDS Bulletin* 27(2): 40–7.

Whitebread, C. (1995) 'The History of the Non-Medical Use of Drugs in the United States.' Paper presented to the California Judges Association Conference. Retreived March 1999 from: *http:mir.drugtext.org/druglibrary/schaffer/history/whiteb1.htm*.

Wiebe, R. (1967) *The Search for Order, 1877–1920*. New York: Hill and Wang.

Willan, P. (1991) *Puppet Masters: The Political Uses of Terrorism in Italy*. London: Constable.

Williams, E.H. (1914) 'Negro Cocaine "Fiends" New Southern Menace.' *New York Times*, 8 February: 12.

Williams, P. (1998) *Organizing Transnational Crime: Networks, Markets and Hierarchies*. Washington, DC: Ridgeway University Center, of Pittsburgh.

Williams, P., and Savona, E.U. (1995) 'The United Nations and Transnational Organized Crime.' Special issue of *Transnational Organized Crime* 1(2).

Williams, P., and Savona, E.U. (1996) *The United Nations and Transnational Organized Crime*. London: Frank Cass.

Williamson, K. (2001) 'Traffic Busts the Drug Gridlock.' *The Scotsman*, 31 March: S2 Weekend: 2–5.

Woodiwiss, M. (1988) *Crime, Crusades and Corruption: Prohibitions in the U.S.A.* London: Pinter Press.

World Bank. (1997a) *Helping Countries Combat Corruption: The Role of the World Bank.* Available online at: *http://www.worldbank.org.*

World Bank. (1997b) 'Reducing Corruption.' *World Bank Policy and Research Bulletin.* 8(3): 1–4. Available online at: *http://www.worldbank.org.*

World Bank. (1997c) *World Bank, IMF Escalate War against Corruption: Latest Ranking by Transparency International.* Available online at: *www.worldbank.org.*

World Bank. (1997d) *Private Capital Flows to Developing Countries: The Road to Financial Integration.* London: Oxford University Press.

World Development Movement. (2000) *Premier Oil: Pull Out of Burma.* Press Release, 15 May.

Yeager, M.G. (1975) 'The Gangster as White Collar Criminal: Organized Crime and Stolen Securities.' *Issues in Criminology* 8(1): 49–73.

Young, J. (1971) *The Drug Takers.* London: Paladin.

Zarckinson, J.L., and Bradley, E. (1997) 'Colombia Sovereignty under Siege.' *Strategic Forum* 112.

Zedalis, R.J. (1998) 'How Does the New OECD Convention on Bribery Stack Up against the Foreign Corrupt Practices Act?' *Journal of World Trade* 32(3): 167–84.

Zeid, M. (1998) 'Specific Incrimination of Organized Crime.' *International Review of Penal Law* 69: 515–39.

Zelizer, V. (1994) *The Social Meaning of Money.* New York: Basic Books.

Contributors

Margaret E. Beare is the director of the Nathanson Centre for the Study of Organized Crime and Corruption and is an associate professor in sociology and law at York University, Toronto. Her publications on organized crime, money laundering, and policing issues include *Criminal Conspiracies: Organized Crime in Canada* (1996), and she is completing a second volume, on money laundering. Prior to joining the university, she served as the director of the Police Policy and Research Division of the Department of the Solicitor General, Canada.

Frederick J. Desroches is the director of the Legal Studies and Criminology Program at the University of Waterloo. His publications include: *Force and Fear: Robbery in Canada* (1995), *Behind the Bars: Experiences in Crime* (1996), and a series of articles on high- and mid-level drug traffickers in Canada.

Kyle Grayson is a doctoral candidate in the Department of Political Science at York University. He is a research fellow at the Nathanson Centre for the Study of Organized Crime and Corruption at Osgoode Hall as well as a researcher at the York Centre for International and Security Studies. His current research is examining the interplay of theory and discourse with respect to Canadian responses to the international drug trade.

Valsamis Mitsilegas is a research associate at the Centre for European Politics and Institutions at the University of Leicester. He has a doctorate in law from the University of Edinburgh, where his research focused on money laundering counter-measures in the European Union.

Some of his recent and forthcoming publications include *Money Laundering Counter-Measures in the EU: A New Paradigm of Security Governance versus Fundamental Legal Principles* (forthcoming) and 'Defining Organised Crime in the European Union: The Limits of European Criminal Law in an Area of Freedom, Security and Justice' (in *European Law Review* 26 [2001]).

R.T. Naylor is professor of economics at McGill University. His main fields of research are smuggling, black markets, and international financial crime. He is the author of seven books, including *Hot Money and the Politics of Debt* (1994), *Patriots and Profiteers: On Economic Warfare, Embargo-Busting and State Sponsored Crime* (1999), and *The Wages of Crime: Underworld Entrepreneurs, Illegal Markets and the Proceeds of Crime* (2002). He was a co-author of the United Nations Office for Drug Control and Crime Prevention report *Financial Havens, Banking Secrecy and Money-Laundering*. This publication launched the U.N.-sponsored Global Campaign against Money Laundering.

Juan G. Ronderos holds a Master of Laws from Osgoode Hall Law School, a law degree from the Universidad de los Andes in Bogota, Colombia, and a taxation specialization degree from the same university. Mr Ronderos spent several years working in law enforcement with the Colombian government in different agencies and was in charge of an interagency task force on money laundering. He is currently pursuing a doctorate in jurisprudence at Osgoode Hall Law School and is a senior manager in the firm KPMG Forensic, based in Toronto, Canada.

Vincenzo Ruggiero is professor of sociology at Middlesex University in London, England. He is also co-editor of the journal *Forum on Crime and Society*, published by the United Nations. His latest books include *Organized and Corporate Crime in Europe* (1996), *The New European Criminology* (as co-editor) (1998), *Crime and Markets: Essays in Anti-Criminology* (2000), and *Movements in the City: Conflict in the European Metropolis* (2001).

James Sheptycki teaches criminology and the sociology of law at Durham University, England. Between 1994 and 1998 he was a research fellow in the School of Law at Edinburgh University, where he undertook research on transnational policing in the English Channel region. He has published widely on criminological topics, such as domestic violence, serial killers, money laundering, and transnational policing, in various journals including *The British Journal of Criminology*, *The International Journal of the Sociology of Law*, *The European Journal of Crime*, and *Criminal Law and Criminal Justice*. He has produced an edited collection titled *Issues in Transnational Policing* (Routledge, 2000) and a research monograph titled *In Search of Transnational Policing* (Ashgate, 2002). He is also editor of *Policing and Society*.

James W. Williams received his doctorate in sociology from York University in Toronto during 2002. He is the author of various articles on police decision-making and interrogation practices and is currently involved in an extensive research project on the role of the private sector in the policing of economic crime and its implications for juridical standards around transparency and due process.

Michael Woodiwiss is a senior lecturer in the School of History, University of the West of England. He has written on the subject of organized crime in *Crime, Crusades and Corruption – Prohibitions in the United States, 1900-1987* (1988), and is co-editor of *Global Crime Connections: Dynamics and Control* (1993). His most recent work is *Organized Crime and American Power – A History* (2001), published by University of Toronto Press.

Index

Cocaine Negroes, 150

Cohen, Stanley, 121

Cold War, 18, 140–1, 144n4, 148. *See also* post–Cold War era

Colombia: and cooperation with U.S. military, 227–9; corrupt public officials, 253; court case against tobacco companies, 197–8; and demand for illegal drugs, 30; and extradition policies, 152, 219, 222; and guerrilla conflict, 218–19, 223–6, 229–30, 236n16; and history of conflict, 136, 144n2, 217–19; human rights record, 227–8; political reform, 219–20; rhetoric of war on drugs, xxv, 232; Thousand Days War, 217; and tobacco smuggling, 195–6; and U.S. interference in domestic affairs, 158, 213, 215, 217, 222, 232–4; and U.S. military aid, 211, 223, 225–6, 230–1; and U.S. war on drugs, 135–8; *la Violencia,* 217

Colombian National Police, 228–9

commercial crimes: and the corporate criminal, 41, 53n10; definition of, 36, 44–5, 51; in German definition of organized crime, 64; punishment of, 42; seriousness of, 53n6

Commission on Law Enforcement and the Administration of Justice, 21

commodification of organized crime, xvii

Communism, 18, 26, 148; Sicilian Communist Party, 259

confidentiality. *See* secrecy

Congress International Relations Commission (U.S.), 227–8

Connolly, William, 122–3

conspiracy offence, 86n5; and EU Joint Action, 81–2; and extradition, 71–2, 84; in Germany, 64; in U.K., 66–9

conspiracy theory: and constitutional guarantees (U.S.), 22–3; Mafia in U.S., 20

contraband cigarettes, 187

Convention against Transnational Organized Crime. *See* United Nations Convention against Transnational Organized Crime

Corallo, 'Tony Ducks,' 23

Cornwall, Ontario, 183, 189; and tension with Aboriginal reserve, 201–2n1

corporate criminal, 41; difficulties in tracing, 199–200; outside organized crime, 200; and tobacco smuggling, 191. *See also* commercial crimes

corporate *mens rea,* 42, 53n10

corruption: and additional cost of investing, 108–10, 118n5; of Canadian customs officers, 184; causes of, 96; crisis of, 90; discourse on, 89, 94, 98–9, 106, 110, 113–14; and drug couriers, 252–3; as a form of economic risk, 90–1, 108–9, 113; as global political issue, 88–9, 116–17; history of, 117n1; increase in, 91–2, 118nn6–7; and integration of world economies, 100–1; and international economic governance, 102–3; legislation against, 111–13; of legitimate business with criminal assets, 270; motives for fight against, 112; and organized crime investigations, 24; police, 17, 31;

and corruption, 89, 94–9, 114–15; intrusive campaigns of, 99–100; and prison populations, 166n12; supported by U.N. anti-organized crime conventions, 79; threat to, 27, 235n1

Democratic party (U.S.), 5

deodand, 258–9

Department of Defense (U.S.), 210

Department of Foreign Affairs and International Trade (Canada), xxixn14

depoliticization of drug prohibition, 159–60

deregulation. *See* regulation/deregulation

designer drugs, 240

Detroit: wholesale meat industry, 18

deviance, 154, 159, 167n25, 182; and criminal drug traffickers, 248–9; and outlaw motorcycle gangs, 251; and transnational crime, 177

discourse of crime, 129–31, 139, 147–8, 154–6

Dispositions against the Mafia (Law 575), 56

distribution of wealth, 51–2

dominant paradigms, 131

Dominican Republic: local criminals, 30

Dorn, N., Murji, K., and South, N., 245, 247–8, 253

Dorr, Goldthwaite H., 12–15

Douglas, Michael, 137

Drug Enforcement Administration (U.S.), 137, 152, 162–3, 167n16, 169n42; and abduction of foreign citizens, 209

drug traffickers: the business of, 240, 254; criminal and non-criminal,

248–51; division of labour, 246–7; fee-for-service, 244, 247; friendship and kinship networks, 241–3; good businessmen, 241; high-risk tasks to employees, 247; prior business experience, 240–1; in small organizations, 243–5, 253–4; as specialists, 239; terminology of, 239–40

drug trafficking: and American idealists, 26; as a business, 243; demand side of, 174; dominated by Mafia, 22–3, 237; and federal enforcement against, 20; and global drug prohibition, 28–9; and guerrillas in Colombia, 218, 227; hierarchical system, 239; independent drug wholesalers, 244; international economic consequences of, 49–50, 164–5; and interrelation between guerrilla groups and coca growers, 224–5; local criminal context, xxvi; military threat of, 145–6, 210; not a monopoly, 243, 247; price discounts, 247; and producing countries, 11, 174, 211, 213–14; profits from, 262–3; requirements of, 238; rivalry among syndicates, 29; as a threat to nation-state, 208; and tobacco smuggling, 200; and U.S. foreign policy, 130, 208

Drug Trafficking Offences Act (U.K.), 65

drugs, illegal: accepted facts about, 155; depoliticization of prohibition of, 159–60; discourse in U.S., 147–8, 154–6, 168n28; and foreign investment, 160; harm-reduction discourse, 133; history of the drug

for, 244; penalties for in U.S., 277, 289n26; process of legitimization, 269; and profits of drug trafficking, 25–6; Russian politicians' and New York bankers' partnership, 174–5; and tobacco companies, 196, 199–200; use of tax code to deter, 285–6, 290n35; war on terrorism, xiv

monopoly in drug trafficking, 243, 247, 251–2

Montreal: fraudster networks, xxvi

moral campaigns: anti–money-laundering rules, 267; ethical race to the bottom, 182; political currents supporting, 39–40, 53n8; Puritan roots, 169n45; and temperance movement, 39–40; and tobacco smuggling, 190; and unenforceable laws, 6–7, 10; use of stereotypes, 5; and war on drugs, 148–9, 167–8n27, 233

Moretti, Willie, 19

Morris, Stan, xiv–xv

motorcycle gangs. *See* outlaw motorcycle gangs

muckraking journalism: early-twentieth-century, 7

Muir, William Ker, 131

Murji, K. *See* Dorn, N., Murji, K., and South, N.

Murphy, M.J., 100

Nabisco, 199

Naim, M. *See* Glynn, P., Kobrin, S.J., and Naim, M.

Naples Declaration and Global Action Plan against Organized Transnational Crime, 76–7. *See also* World Ministerial Conference on

Organized Transnational Crime (Naples)

narcoguerrilla, 225, 230

narco-terrorism, 130–1, 141, 219, 231–2, 236n18

National Commission on Law Observance and Enforcement (U.S.), 12–15

National Constitutional Assembly (Colombia), 219

National Council for Civil Liberties (U.K.), 140

National Crime Squad (U.K.), 65–6, 141

National Criminal Intelligence Service (U.K.), 65–6, 68–9, 141, 289n30

National Defense Authorization Act (U.S.), 211

national development, 107, 114

National Liberation army (Colombia), 218

National Outlaw Motorcycle Gang Seminar, xvi

National Police Corps (Brazil), 210

National Strategy to Combat Outlaw Motorcycle Gangs, xvii

National Tobacco Administration, 193

Native American Church, 157

Native Americans. *See* Aboriginal communities

NATO: missiles in Sicily, 261

Navigation Acts, 258

Navy SEALs, 226

Netherlands, 159, 168n36

New Deal, 32

New Kanawha Power Company, 14

New York: garment district, 44–5; history of organized crime, 4–5